Colonialism and Gramm

Publications of the Philological Society, 41

Colonialism and Grammatical Representation

John Gilchrist and the Analysis of the 'Hindustani' Language in the Late Eighteenth and Early Nineteenth Centuries

Richard Steadman-Jones

Publications of the Philological Society, 41

Oxford UK & Boston USA

Blackwell Publishing Ltd
9600 Garsington Road, Oxford, OX4 2DQ, UK

and
350 Main Street,
Malden, MA 02148, USA

Library of Congress Cataloging-in-Publication Data

Steadman-Jones, Richard.
  Colonialism and grammatical representation: John Gilchrist and the analysis of the "Hindustani" language in the late eighteenth and early nineteenth centuries/Richard Steadman-Jones.
    p. cm. – (Publications of the Philological Society ; 41)
  Includes bibliographical references and index.
  ISBN 978-1-4051-6132-9 (alk. paper)
  1. Hindustani language – Study and teaching – History. 2. Hindustani language – Study and teaching – Political aspects – History. 3. Gilchrist, John Borthwick, 1759-1841.
  I. Title.

PK1981.S84 2007
491'.4315–dc22

2007004736

A catalogue record for this publication is available from the British Library.

Set in Times by SPS (P) Ltd., Chennai, India
Printed and bound in Singapore by
Seng Lee Press Pte Ltd

The publisher's policy is to use permanent paper from mills that operate a sustainable forestry policy, and which has been manufactured from pulp processed using acid-free and elementary chlorine-free practices. Furthermore, the publisher ensures that the text paper and cover board used have met acceptable environmental accreditation standards.

For further information on Blackwell Publishing, visit our website:
http://www.blackwellpublishing.com

This book is dedicated to my parents, Marilyn and Frederick Steadman-Jones, who themselves have a passionate interest in language and history.

CONTENTS

CONTENTS

PREFACE

I would like to thank everyone who offered me support and guidance during the writing of this book: the friends who discussed my work with me when I was a doctoral student at the University of Cambridge, the senior members of that university, who were so generous with their time and expertise, my colleagues past and present at the University of Sheffield, and the members of the other intellectual communities to which I belong, especially my friends in the Henry Sweet Society for the History of Linguistic Thought.

A number of people advised me while I was preparing the biographical part of the study: the Headmaster of George Heriot's School, the Treasurer of George Heriot's Trust, Dr Brian Lockhart (the historian of Heriot's), Mrs R. A. Everidge of the Gilchrist Educational Trust, and Canon John Wilson, himself a descendant of John Gilchrist. I am grateful to them all for sharing their knowledge and insight with me.

In particular, I want to express my gratitude to Dr Vivien Law, who supervised the dissertation on which this work is based. Vivien died in February 2002. She was a remarkable person and it is a source of sadness to me that I cannot thank her face to face.

School of English
November 2006 *University of Sheffield*

INTRODUCTION

In 1782 a young Scot named John Gilchrist arrived in India looking for employment in the service of the East India Company. After leaving school at the age of 14, Gilchrist had been apprenticed to a surgeon in Falkirk and for some years he had served as a surgeon's mate in the Royal Navy. On the basis of this experience, he was now appointed to the position of 'Assistant Surgeon on the Bengal Establishment' and took up a post with a regiment stationed in western India. Some 40 years later, long after Gilchrist had returned from India and at a time when his relations with the Honourable Company had somewhat soured, a biographical work appeared under the title *A Succinct Narrative of Dr. Gilchrist's Services from 1782 to 1821*. Despite the fact that it is written in the third person, the defensive tone of the work makes it clear that the man himself had at least a hand in its composition, and the entire text constitutes a self-justificatory account of his actions over the previous four decades. At the beginning of the narrative we are presented with two anecdotes relating to Gilchrist's early experiences in the army; in the first of them we find him assuming responsibility for a party of 'sepoys', Indian soldiers serving in the Company's forces:

> Before he had been *two months* in the Country, he was forced for self-preservation to assume the command of a small party of native troops, who, while escorting a valuable convoy of ammunition and grain, were suddenly attacked, in the casual absence of the European Officer, by a large body of Pindarees; but which was soon dispersed under the arrangements and orders of DR. GILCHRIST, communicated to the Sipahees through his groom, who fortunately understood a little English, and happened to be on the spot when the skirmish began. (Gilchrist 1821: 3)

At one level, this passage serves to cast Gilchrist as the hero of his own narrative. It invites us to admire a young man's exemplary conduct under fire and his cool resolve in the face of danger. However, the anecdote also betrays anxiety about the difficulties of communication in an institution where those in authority do not have a language in common with their subordinates. Happily, Gilchrist's groom 'understood a little English', but the implication is clearly that, if this had not been the case, the incident might have ended in disaster, a possibility that is actually realised in the second story, which follows hard on the heels of the first:

> Not long after this occurrence, he was sent *alone* as Assistant Surgeon, with a considerable detachment, which had orders to storm a Marhutta camp in the neighbourhood, where a few lives were lost, and several people badly wounded; to all of whom it was impossible in the heat of action, to do justice, when no interpreter was at hand to compensate for his total ignorance of the Hindoostanee, at that *early period* of his medical career with the army. (Gilchrist 1821: 3)

This time the difficulties of communication are not resolved by the chance presence of a multilingual groom, and the wounded are left to suffer because Gilchrist cannot speak to them in a language they understand. The hero of the first anecdote is now faced with failure because of his lack of linguistic knowledge, and the typographical emphasis placed on the fact that he was sent '*alone*' and at an '*early period*' of his career also implies that he has been compromised by his superiors, who have carelessly placed him in an impossible position.

The function of these anecdotes is clearly to establish Gilchrist's motivation as he embarked on the activities that form the main theme of the 'succinct narrative'. At some point in the early 1780s, Gilchrist took the decision to learn 'Hindoostanee',[1] the Indian language widely used as a lingua franca both in the army and beyond, and, finding few resources to help in the study of the language, he sought leave of absence to travel among the cities of northern India and collect material for a dictionary and grammar. The process of compiling the texts was long and arduous, but the dictionary was published in instalments between 1786 and 1790, while the grammar finally became available in 1796. By this stage Gilchrist had transformed himself into an acknowledged expert on the language, at least in the British community, and in 1800 he became the first professor of 'Hindustani' at Fort William College, Calcutta, a new institution founded by the governor-general, Marquis Wellesley, to train recruits to the Company's service who had recently arrived in India. Thus, when he took the decision to learn 'Hindustani', Gilchrist was embarking on an enterprise that had significant ramifications both for himself and for the British empire in India. On the one hand, the project transformed him from a lowly surgeon – not a highly regarded profession in the late eighteenth century – into a well-known orientalist scholar; on the other, it resulted in the institutionalisation of 'Hindustani' as an important administrative language within the colonial state. The two incidents described in the 'succinct

---

[1] The term 'Hindoostanee' is somewhat problematic and the implications of using it will be discussed more fully later in the introduction. In the meantime, I shall simply echo the eighteenth-century usage, modernising the spelling, but enclosing the term in inverted commas to emphasise that it is Gilchrist's own.

narrative' serve to explain Gilchrist's decision and to define its meaning. As we imagine Gilchrist travelling across northern India to collect the material for the three volumes of his dictionary and grammar, we are invited to understand his actions in terms of a particular set of values: the military commander's devotion to his men, the surgeon's compassion for his suffering patients and the young man's assumption of personal responsibility in the face of official incompetence. In short, the decision is constructed as a surrender to duty – the duty that derives from military service, from the practice of medicine and, by implication, from common humanity.

When I first encountered Gilchrist's work – his dictionary and grammar with the long and rambling preface that he wrote retrospectively to introduce them both, the numerous pedagogical works that he produced to interpret the material in a more 'conciliating' form, and the eccentric collection of texts that he produced later in life, defending his work and his reputation, as his standing with the Company collapsed – it was the political dimensions of the material that interested me most. The late eighteenth and early nineteenth centuries saw a considerable increase in the attention paid to Indian languages by the British in South Asia. To a large extent this change occurred because after the military victory at Plassey the East India Company had effectively become a territorial power in Bengal, and was faced with the need to collect the revenues of the province, to administer the legal system, to engage in diplomacy with other Indian polities and generally to consolidate its authority over the new territory. The servants of the Company therefore needed to be able to understand historical documents relating to land tenure, to interpret legal texts, to engage in official correspondence with the rulers of other states and in general to grasp the province of Bengal, in the sense both of understanding and of controlling it. All of these activities required that they master Indian languages, and for this reason the learning of languages was often connected with the need to exercise authority in the various departments of the colonial state.

Gilchrist's work clearly has to be understood in the context of these developments. It is significant, for example, that he was motivated to learn 'Hindustani' as a result of his experiences in the army. The practice of recruiting Indian soldiers and training them in western methods of warfare was a central factor in the Company's ability to assert and maintain political authority in India. As such, the capacity of British officers to lead Indian troops effectively was crucial to the stability of the British state in Bengal. The anecdotes about failures of communication in the military context can therefore be read as warnings. The mastery of an Indian language is essential to the functioning of the army, and that in turn is fundamental to the maintenance of colonial authority. However, it is important to note that the 'succinct narrative' does not make this argument explicit. Instead we have dramatic glimpses of our young hero struggling to discharge his duties and, in one tragic case, failing to 'do justice' to the wounded. In this sense, the anecdotes of the 'succinct narrative' serve to naturalise the exercise of colonial power in terms of a moral rather than a political discourse – they do not dwell on the politics of the conflict between the British and the Mahrattas or on the need to cement the colony's bulwark against hostile Indian states, for example, but on the surgeon's duty to tend to the men in his care and do what is right by them in moments of crisis. And this is often the case in Gilchrist's writing. It is not only in military contexts that Gilchrist sees the mastery of 'Hindustani' as a crucial resource, but whichever context he is discussing, the study of Indian languages is presented as important largely because it guarantees the welfare of Indians themselves. Gilchrist's programmatic statements are complex, however, and it would not be true to say that he is merely covering up the political implications of his project by emphasising the supposed benevolence of the British regime. In fact, as we shall see later, he is sometimes astoundingly frank in his insistence that the British need to learn 'Hindustani' in order to suppress the resistance that colonial rule inevitably elicits from the subject population, and this alternation between performances of idealism and pragmatism is a striking feature of his work.

It was issues of this kind, the politics of using Indian languages in the colonial administration and the construction, or naturalisation, of that appropriation in contemporary colonial discourse, that first led me to look closely at Gilchrist's linguistic texts. However, as the past tenses indicate, I have since become interested in another set of problems relating to Gilchrist's work. That is not to say that the considerations outlined here are not vitally important: in the first chapter of this study I shall be examining what a number of contemporary scholars have had to say about them, notably the anthropologist Bernard S. Cohn and the historian David Lelyveld. However, as I have worked on Gilchrist's descriptions of 'Hindustani', I have become increasingly interested in the technical difficulties that faced writers such as Gilchrist as they attempted to describe Indian languages using the resources that western approaches to language made available to them. I am aware that I run the risk of presenting this change of focus as a move away from the political into a depoliticised study of purely technical issues. However, this would be entirely misleading. The central concern of this book is to show that technical linguistic problems are inextricably linked with political ones, certainly in eighteenth-century linguistic work and – although this broader claim lies beyond the scope of the book – over a broader timescale as well. Nevertheless, it is true that the foregrounding of details of linguistic description has to be seen as a movement away from the kind of scholarship undertaken by commentators like Cohn and Lelyveld; and before discussing the relationship between the political and technical more explicitly, it is important to say something about the way in which I am using the latter term.

This study is concerned with the properties that distinguish the languages of northern India, foremost among them 'Hindustani', from the European languages with which British commentators such as Gilchrist were familiar. It will examine the ways in which British grammarians understood these differences and interpreted them for their readers. In particular, it will explore the difficulties that writers like Gilchrist experienced in using the tools supplied by western language study to analyse, describe, explain and interpret the distinctive properties of languages like 'Hindustani'. The languages of northern India mostly belong to the Indo-European family, and as such they are not as different from the languages of Europe as some of those encountered by the British in other areas of colonial expansion – North America, for example, or South-East Asia. Nevertheless, they certainly display some features that seemed surprising, if not downright baffling, to Europeans when they encountered them for the first time, and, at this point it might be helpful to give an example. Later in the book, I shall be looking in detail at the morphosyntactic characteristics of some of the languages of northern India and the ways in which they presented problems for early European grammarians. A particular issue that I shall be discussing is the fact that some of these languages display ergative case-marking. I shall not give a detailed description of the phenomenon here. It is enough to note that in 'Hindustani', the language that Gilchrist was analysing, the subject of a verb that is aspectually perfect will appear in a different form depending upon whether the verb is transitive or not. By way of example, let us look at the following sentence:

(1)   laṛkā   āyā
       boy.DIRECT   *come*.PERF.MASC.SING.
       'the boy came'

Here the verb is intransitive and its subject, *laṛkā*, appears in its citation form, the uninflected form that would appear in the dictionary. The verb also agrees with the subject in number and gender. Compare this with the following sentence:

(2)   laṛke-ne   kitāb   likhī
       boy.OBLIQUE.AGENT   *book*.DIRECT   *write*.PERF.FEM.SING[2]
       'the boy wrote a book'

Here the noun that seems to be the subject of the verb appears in an inflected form, *laṛke*, rather than in its citation form, *laṛkā*, and it is followed by the particle *ne*. What is more, the verb, *likhī*, has taken a

---

[2] The examples are adapted from McGregor (1972).

feminine singular inflection to agree with *kitāb*, which appears to be its object, rather than with its subject, *laṛke-ne*.

It is difficult to exaggerate how vexing this pattern was to Europeans encountering the language for the first time. It seemed to resist interpretation within the framework of contemporary linguistic scholarship. It is not that there was no metalanguage to describe the structure – it is perfectly possible to give a formal description of it using terms that were available to eighteenth-century grammarians, and indeed, Gilchrist's own account is relatively successful at this level. The point is more that applying these terms to the description of this pattern produced assertions that seemed bizarre, if not self-contradictory. If one were to translate the two sentences cited here into Latin, the word for 'boy' would appear in the same form in each. To be specific, it would appear in the form known to grammarians as the nominative. In eighteenth-century philosophical approaches to grammar, sentence structure is often analysed with reference to the organisation of the logical proposition as it was defined within contemporary syllogistic logic. The proposition is understood as consisting of a subject – the entity that is picked out for comment – and a predicate – the comment that is then made about the subject. And the sentence is seen as expressing a proposition of this kind, the nominative being characterised as the form that marks the logical subject, or picks out a particular entity for comment.[3] In an eighteenth-century logical analysis, the propositions expressed by both the sentences presented here would be seen as having 'boy' as their logical subject. Thus, the fact that Latin would use the same form in both sentences is understood not as a contingent fact about that particular language but as deriving from the universal structure of logical propositions. The word has the same logical function in both cases, so it appears in the same form. The apparent strangeness of the 'Hindustani' sentences lay in the fact that they seemed to ignore these logical principles. If the boy is the logical subject in both cases, then why does the word *laṛkā* appear in such different forms in each?

This is exactly the kind of issue with which the following study will be concerned. Writers such as Gilchrist approached the newly encountered languages of the colonies armed with a particular understanding of the nature of human language, an understanding that derived from a variety of sources – the terms and categories supplied by the western grammatical tradition, the philosophical approaches to language that were such a feature of eighteenth-century linguistic enquiry, and the aesthetic discussions taking place within contemporary rhetoric, to name a few. The forms and structures of the languages they encountered sometimes seemed to defy assimilation into this complex and at times self-contradictory framework of

---

[3] In Chapter 4, this argument will be developed through a discussion of James Harris's influential discussion of general grammar, *Hermes* (1751).

understanding. The sentence pattern described above, for example, conflicted with what Europeans believed themselves to know about language on the basis of the conceptualisation of noun case developed within the field of general grammar. And these problematic issues can be seen as constituting flashpoints within grammatical texts – moments of danger that provoked authors to engage in explicit discussion of what they saw as the strange properties of the languages they were describing. Gilchrist is a good example of such a writer. Even in the more popular texts that he produced for readers who might have been put off by the scale and complexity of his original grammar, he cannot resist lingering upon the features of the language that mark it out as distinct from the languages of Europe, exploring the nature of these differences and speculating on what they might mean.

To a certain extent his discussion of such issues operates at a technical level, by which I mean that the process of fitting data to theory constitutes an autonomous field of enquiry, with distinctive principles and practices of its own. Gilchrist himself provides an explanation of the structure described above, and although his account of it will be discussed at some length in Chapter 4, it will be useful to provide a very brief summary here. Gilchrist claims that the use of the particle *ne* in sentences like *larke ne kitāb likhī* is intended to clear up potential ambiguities that may occur in sentences where the verb is transitive but that do not occur in ones where the verb is intransitive. In short, he uses an argument built on the desirability of transparency in grammatical structure. His contemporaries did not find this explanation convincing, and an alternative argument emerged to the effect that *larke ne kitāb likhī* is actually passive and means 'the book was written by the boy'. This makes *kitāb* the subject, which explains why the verb has been inflected to agree with it in gender and number, while also allowing for the possibility that *ne* is a particle expressing agency and is thus equivalent to 'by' in the English version of the sentence. However strange this debate might seem today, it is important to take notice of the way in which it functions, and particularly of what counts as a valid contribution to the discussion. The essential point is that both Gilchrist and his adversaries attempt to resolve the perceived problem of the ergative with reference to concepts derived from within the existing framework of western linguistic thought. As we shall see, the notion that grammatical facts might be explained with reference to a supposed risk of ambiguity has precedents in the eighteenth-century grammatical literature. And, similarly, the argument that *larke ne kitāb likhī* is passive attempts to account for the pattern by identifying it with a structure that is fully documented in the same body of scholarship. In many ways, therefore the discussion of difficult structures constitutes a kind of game, the rules of which are to be inferred from the practice of previous participants within the western scholarly literature.

However, it is important to understand that the discussion of these issues is not *merely* technical. Although Gilchrist's explanation of difficult structures took place within what I have described as 'an autonomous field of enquiry', this does not mean that the problems explored within that field had no connection with ordinary experience. The apparent strangeness of structures like the 'Hindustani' ergative was not solely the product of a technical field of enquiry. The fact is that English-speaking learners of Hindi and Urdu still find the ergative puzzling, and struggle to use the structure in conversation. They express frustration at its difficulty, and feel thwarted when they realise that they are still not producing it where a native speaker would. They sense the disappointment of their teachers and feel embarrassment at not meeting their expectations. And anyone who has studied a foreign language will recognise this kind of experience. The practice of the native speaker constitutes a kind of ideal before which one is constantly falling short, and this experience can be productive of all kinds of responses – frustration, shame, embarrassment and anger, all perhaps underpinned by a lurking sense of anxiety. At the same time, however, it can also be productive of feelings of pride and pleasure when, occasionally, one manages to get it right. The point is that the apparent strangeness of foreign languages is not constituted solely within a technical field of discussion. It derives from the practical difficulty of producing language that seems acceptable to native speakers and the sense of risk in the attempt. Thus, rather than *producing* an experience of difference out of nowhere, grammatical texts can be seen as *mediating* an experience of difference that is often potential in cross-linguistic interaction, whether or not the participants have any technical linguistic awareness. This is true even if one studies a grammar before meeting any native speakers, since the text can be understood as mediating a future encounter by preparing readers for what may happen when they finally have to engage in interactions using the medium of the foreign language.[4]

Of course, technical texts can mediate the experience of difference in very different ways. It is easy to see how the difficulties that arise in the context of cross-linguistic interaction might give rise to negative claims about the foreign language itself. I used to teach English to speakers of Italian, who often found the English vowel system vexing. Standard Italian has seven pure vowels, while the variety of English that I speak has twelve, and the two systems do not map onto each other in any straightforward way. The result is that some of the English vowels are difficult for Italian learners to

---

[4] It is true that some of Gilchrist's readers were armchair philologists who did not have any direct experience of interaction with speakers of South Asian languages. But, at the same time, his assumption was always that the bulk of his readership would consist of Company servants whose interest in the text derived from a practical need to communicate, and who would come face to face with native speakers at some point, even if they had not done so already.

perceive, especially in the early stages of their encounter with English. The frustration of trying to distinguish *feel* from *fill* from *fell* would sometimes lead learners to describe the English vowel system as ridiculous or mad. Why on earth would anyone need so many vowels, they would ask, especially given that so many of them are such ugly sounds? Comments of this kind were always uttered in a humorous tone and provided an effective means of venting frustration before we returned to the rather starchy textbook, which did not, of course, confirm these views of the English language. However, learners who harboured similar opinions in the eighteenth century could easily have found support in contemporary linguistic scholarship, and it is not unusual to find texts from the period depicting foreign languages in highly pejorative terms. This is especially true of works about non-European languages, which often mediated the experience of difference by confirming stereotypes of the languages as chaotic and lawless. Some texts merely asserted this interpretation, but others supported it with reference to features of the languages that were inexplicable within the parameters of western linguistic thought, features like those discussed earlier.

It might be possible to read such texts in the style developed by Edward Said in his famous discussion of colonial culture, *Orientalism*. The pejorative depiction of non-European languages could be interpreted as a way of relegating the colonial other to an inferior status and, in this way, enabling the exercise of colonial power. However, to understand the phenomenon in these terms is to sideline its psychological dimensions, and it is with the intention of foregrounding these aspects of representation that I have made the comparison with the experience of contemporary learners, who sometimes engage in this kind of stereotyping, even though they receive no official support in doing so. In both cases, the stereotype of the language as ridiculous or mad can be understood as dealing with the anxiety of communicating in a foreign language by figuring the problem as a failing in the language itself. In his essay 'The Other Question', which appears in the collection *The Location of Culture*, first published in 1994, Homi K. Bhabha discusses the way in which stereotyping deals with the anxiety associated with difference by producing a reassuring fixity, an idea that is relevant here. The bewildering difference of the foreign language is reduced to a knowable fact, namely that the language itself is ridiculous or mad. And the resulting stereotype *contains* the idea of unpredictability, in the sense that it figures the feeling that the language is strange and impossible to grasp as a deficiency in the language and not in the learner's understanding of it. This strategy allows the learner to *accept* the existence of difference but also to *reject* it by retreating to the reassuring fixity of the stereotype, which is thus 'as anxious as it is assertive'. The difference between the two contexts I have outlined is that, for contemporary learners, stereotyping is not officially sanctioned, whereas eighteenth-century learners might well have found the strategy they employed at an unofficial level replicated in the official context of the scholarly text. Today the humorous jibe at the language being studied represents little more than light relief. In the early years of the colonial encounter, the representation of the language as ridiculous or mad was not infrequently sanctioned from above.

It is important to understand that, although many colonial texts work in this way, Gilchrist's do not, and his account of ergativity is a case in point. Far from playing upon the structure as a sign of the perverse or chaotic nature of the language, Gilchrist's efforts to explain it can be read as an attempt to dispel the sense that there is anything different about it at all. Here, as at other points in the grammar, Gilchrist anticipates the possible reactions of European readers to some notable evidence of the language's difference, and attempts to minimise that sense of difference by insisting that the organisation of the language is perfectly comprehensible in western terms. Earlier I described structures like the ergative as flashpoints, and by now I hope that the relevance of this image will be clearer. The flashpoint is the lowest temperature at which a volatile substance produces sufficient vapour to ignite in the presence of heat. When a substance reaches this point, one can either let the vapour catch light and watch the pyrotechnics or one can attempt to lower the temperature and prevent the explosion. Pejorative representations of non-European languages take the former course, reacting to signs of difference with an explosion of stereotypical vilification. Gilchrist's texts generally follow the latter route, almost always attempting to avert the possibility that they will generate this kind of response. As such, they mediate the encounter by showing that the technical resources of contemporary language study can accommodate phenomena that, on the face of it, might seem ridiculous or mad to the European reader. In this way, they work to reconcile such readers to these problematic phenomena. In some ways, this practice might seem similar to that which is usual in the contemporary academy, where the stereotyping I described earlier is bracketed off as a kind of humorous relief and the idea that all languages are ordered and lawful in their own terms is a basic axiom of enquiry, at least within the discipline of linguistics. However, this is not Gilchrist's position at all. He is perfectly prepared to accept that some language varieties are, to use his own terms, 'vile' and 'barbarous'. The point is that, for him, 'Hindustani' is not among these varieties, and it is important to consider why he goes to such lengths to insist upon this view.

It is at this point that we need to reconnect these issues of technical representation with the political issues that I touched upon earlier. British interest in Indian languages increased in the late eighteenth century, when the East India Company emerged as a territorial power in Bengal. The need to administer the colonial state in an effective fashion led to the appropriation of Indian languages as part of the apparatus of colonial rule. But this process of appropriation required that the languages be perceived in particular ways by the agents of colonialism – not as irremediably chaotic and lawless, but as sophisticated media of communication with which it was necessary to engage seriously. In the argument that follows, I shall suggest that, in order to render the 'Hindustani' language available for use in this way, it was necessary to reorder British perceptions of the language, and I shall argue that Gilchrist's technical representations of 'Hindustani' can be understood as contributing to this process of reordering. As I have suggested, the stereotyping of non-European languages in both official and unofficial contexts provided a means of retreating from the anxious experience of difference to the safety of fixity. It did this by shifting the problem of communication from the learner to the language. Gilchrist's insistence that there *was* no problem with the language threw responsibility back onto the learner, challenging the colonial agent to take control and get it right. In their systematic attempts to deny difference and assert the possibility of grasping the language, even at those moments when it seemed most strange, Gilchrist's texts challenged the lack of engagement associated with stereotyping and demanded that his readers look again. Of course, the idea that the learner could ever really take control could be viewed as a species of colonial fantasy, a view that would very much accord with the work of theorists such as Bhabha, for whom colonial culture is by definition hybrid and unstable. However, the fantasy of control can be seen as fulfilling an important function in the sense that it reopens the possibility of engagement, a possibility closed down by the practice of stereotyping languages as ridiculous, mad, chaotic, lawless, vile or barbarous.

In this book I shall be examining the way in which Gilchrist assimilated the forms and structures of the language he calls 'Hindoostanee' into the framework of western linguistic knowledge, focusing particularly on the meanings that this process had for contemporary readers. On the one hand I want to acknowledge that the process of assimilation took place within an autonomous field of enquiry with principles and practices of its own, a fact that discussions of late eighteenth- and early nineteenth-century language study have not always taken seriously. In her influential account of the politics of language in the late eighteenth and early nineteenth centuries, for example, Olivia Smith (1984) characterises the linguistic thought of the period as *reductively* political, suggesting that movements such as general grammar were intrinsically conservative in their insistence that all languages instantiated the same underlying categories. A similar approach emerges in Janet Sorensen's account of the linguistic relationship between England and Scotland in the later eighteenth century. This work, published in 2000, is stimulating and provocative in its treatment of English and Scots but tends towards a similarly reductive analysis in its treatment of the description of Gaelic in the same period. I shall discuss the work of both Smith and Sorensen at greater length in Chapter 3. The important point here is to underline the fact that, although scholarly characterisations of language can almost always be understood as having a political character, they also have an internal logic of their own, which sometimes renders problematic the political roles into which they are pressed. At the same time, I want to acknowledge that the political aspects of language study represent more than a regrettable distraction from more serious technical questions, a view that is also quite commonly expressed within the scholarly literature. In his thorough and thoughtful account of the Hindi grammatical tradition, for example, Tej K. Bhatia (1987) develops a narrative of progress, in which the work of earlier writers is characterised in terms of the extent to which it moved the study of Hindi onwards towards a distinctively modern understanding of the language. But, given that Gilchrist often betrayed an acute awareness of the political readings to which his analyses were susceptible and worked to influence them in the way he organised his texts, it seems inappropriate to treat them as failed, or limited, attempts to produce the kind of apolitical analyses sanctioned within contemporary linguistics. They were written in order to produce in readers a certain response to the language, and this must be acknowledged if we are really to understand them.

The technical and the political interact at the level of Gilchrist's assault on the stereotype of the chaotic and lawless language. As I have suggested, the widespread nature of such stereotypes can be understood in relation to questions of anxiety about the dynamics of cross-linguistic encounter, an issue that is particularly pronounced in the colonial context. The stereotype serves to mask the difference that is the source of anxiety, but in doing so it precludes any more sophisticated engagement with the colonial other. The pressure to deny the difference of the Indian language leads Gilchrist to ransack the resources of western language study for ways of normalising its forms and structures for western readers. Can the ergative be understood as a means of disambiguation, for example? Would it be better represented as a passive? Curiously, this procedure leads Gilchrist into a kind of unofficial empiricism, despite the fact that the reconceptualisation of language study as an empirical discipline was still some way off at the time he was writing. Instead of dismissing the language as chaotic because it will not fit the usual theoretical model, he constantly looks for ways in which the theoretical model can be manipulated to accommodate the data.[5] At any rate, his work can be seen as a struggle to find ways, within the parameters of contemporary language study, to move beyond the fixated representation of the stereotype and re-engage with difference. At times, as we might expect, this re-engagement can itself be productive of anxiety. The sheer

---

[5] Given that the emergence of an empirical approach to language study is often understood in top-down terms with ideas originating in the work of the major figures of the comparativist movement, it is interesting to contemplate the idea that the political will to appropriate non-European languages like 'Hindustani' might have been a factor in the process.

difficulty of finding a convincing explanation of the ergative produces an account in which Gilchrist's discomfort is palpable, and his frequent claims to have analysed the structure successfully seem almost to become fixated in turn. At times, however, the re-engagement with difference actually seems productive of pleasure, as if the self is seen anew in relation to difference, something that emerges particularly in those passages where Gilchrist rethinks some aspect of his theoretical model in response to what he has found in his 'Hindustani' data; and this rethinking of self at the level of language has echoes in the self-transformation Gilchrist achieved over the course of his career from surgeon's mate to orientalist scholar.

The focus of this book is thus on the forms of representation that were available to eighteenth-century writers as they described non-European languages, and on the ways in which those forms of representation mediated the experience of difference in the context of the colonial encounter. The book is divided into two parts, the first of which examines the contexts in which Gilchrist's scholarship was produced – the political context in Chapter 1, the personal context in Chapter 2, and the technical, or intellectual, context in Chapter 3. Chapter 1 discusses contemporary approaches to the politics of colonial language study, focusing particularly on the work of Bernard S. Cohn and David Lelyveld. It argues that, while their characterisation of linguistic scholarship as an APPROPRIATION is very compelling, it is necessary to acknowledge another side to the experience of language learning – the extent to which it was an ambivalent and anxious affair. To a large extent, Gilchrist's work can be seen as fuelled by anxiety over the dangers of speaking Indian languages badly. However, the stereotyping of colonial languages can itself be understood as a response to the same anxiety, and Chapter 1 will also examine the framework of categories through which this process of stereotyping was realised, focusing particularly on the distinctions between CLASSICAL and VERNACULAR, JARGONIC and POLITE languages. In this way, the chapter will set out the problems of representation that Gilchrist faced as he began his work on 'Hindustani'.

Chapter 2 examines the ways in which Gilchrist's personal circumstances shaped his linguistic work. It takes the form of a selective biography, focusing particularly on the lack of scholarly credentials with which Gilchrist came to India and on his commercial and intellectual rivalry with George Hadley, his only major competitor in the market for 'Hindustani' grammars. Had Gilchrist had a more prestigious educational history and had he not been locked in rivalry with a producer of popular grammatical texts, his work might have developed in a very different fashion. An account of the particular conditions under which he was working will therefore help to explain how the political project examined in Chapter 1 came to take the specific forms that it did. Chapter 3 will move from the political aspects of representation to the technical ones and explain how the two are connected. It will focus on the prevalence of evaluative approaches to language in late eighteenth-century thought, focusing first on the epistemology of such approaches and second on five specific forms of linguistic enquiry, each of which presented Gilchrist with both problems and resources as he set about naturalising the language and averting negative evaluations of it.

Once these various aspects of context have been covered, it will be possible to move on and look in detail at four particular issues relating to Gilchrist's representation of 'Hindustani' grammar. Chapter 4 focuses on his treatment of nominal morphology, and particularly on the issue of case-marking, both what Masica (1991: 231) has called its 'layered' quality – the combined use of terminations and postpositions to mark the semantic and syntactic roles played by nouns – and the occurrence of ergative case-marking in certain types of 'Hindustani' sentences. Both phenomena seemed strange, given the interpretive resources available within the western tradition, and Gilchrist's attempts to normalise them will form the central theme of the chapter. Chapter 5 turns from nominal to verbal morphology, an area of the grammar in which western evaluative approaches tended to suggest that 'Hindustani' was particularly well organised. However, Gilchrist's rival, Captain George Hadley, had analysed the verbal system in a way that effectively obscured its orderly character, leaving Gilchrist with the task of dismantling his predecessor's analysis and replacing it with one which brought out the uniformity and regularity of the system. How he negotiated this task and the resources he employed in doing so will be at the centre of the discussion. Chapter 6 will examine an obstacle of a different kind that confronted Gilchrist – the popularity of dialogues as a medium for language learning in the late eighteenth and early nineteenth centuries, and the pressure placed upon him to include such materials in his own work. As far as Gilchrist was concerned, the problem with dialogues was that they distracted attention from the description of grammatical structure and so provided few opportunities for the kind of normalising project examined in Chapters 4 and 5. As we shall see, he bowed to commercial pressure and supplied his readers with what they wanted, but at the same time littered his collections of dialogues with warnings about the dangers of not engaging with structural issues–warnings that make use of flashpoints in the grammar, the ergative, for example, in order to highlight the importance of such an engagement.

Chapter 7, the last of the case studies, brings together the issues of grammatical description discussed in Chapters 4 and 5 with a discussion of methods of language learning related to the questions explored in Chapter 6. Like other writers of the period, Gilchrist was strongly influenced by the contemporary vogue for etymological analysis, and he frequently produces speculative etymologies of both lexical and morphological items in 'Hindustani'. At one level, this kind of material serves to uncover new layers of orderliness in the grammar of the language and thus to contribute to the representation of 'Hindustani' as a highly ordered system of communication. At another, it provides the basis for a pedagogy that is focused on the study of grammar in contrast with methods involving the memorisation of dialogues or phrases. However, etymological analysis proved to be a dangerous area for Gilchrist. To study the etymology of words is to study their history, and to study the history of 'Hindustani' requires some engagement with Sanskrit. Gilchrist's knowledge of Sanskrit was minimal, and at some point in the early nineteenth century he withdrew from the field of historical discussion, the implication being that the limitations of his expertise in this area were becoming increasingly obvious. At this point, the indigenous scholarship of South Asia, and in particular the Sanskrit grammatical tradition and the archive of Indo-Persian lexicography, become particularly important. Gilchrist's impulse was always to characterise these areas of scholarship as mere 'pedantry', an attitude that became less and less tenable as other western thinkers became more and more immersed in them.

Through this combination of contextual description and close textual analysis, I hope that a particular picture of Gilchrist's grammatical work will emerge for the reader – one in which technical analytical problems interact with issues of political representation in a fashion that privileges neither dimension of the work to the exclusion of the other. To underline the way in which these two aspects of Gilchrist's thought interpenetrate throughout his published writing, the book will end with a discussion of an extended metaphor from the preface to his dictionary and grammar (1798b). In this passage, Gilchrist compares the reader's progress through his grammar to a journey through an Indian landscape. The image alludes to contemporary aesthetic categories, particularly that of the picturesque, in a way that emphasises the role of human interpretation in the perception of the natural world. As such, it figures grammatical analysis in terms of the grammarian's capacity to see the virtues in a language, just as the theory of the picturesque locates the qualities of a view in the mind of the viewer as much as in the landscape itself. In this way, the metaphor of the journey emphasises the importance of *viewing* in the encounter with Indian languages, the stigmatisation of those languages through stereotypes of disorder and chaos constituting a failure of imagination and not a problem that is located in the languages themselves.

Before moving on to look at the political context of Gilchrist's work in more detail, there is one final area of introductory discussion that needs tackling – the nature of the term 'Hindustani' itself, its reference and its connotations. Both the term itself and the history of the language to which it refers are controversial, and since this is a book about the way in which grammar functions as a descriptive discipline and not a history of Indian languages, I shall not be developing a highly specified position with regard to that controversy. The following discussion is intended to provide a clear sense of the meaning of the term 'Hindustani' in a way that is helpful to readers who are not immersed in the field. It is not intended to form a substitute for more specialised texts on 'Hindustani', Hindi and Urdu that are specifically concerned with the history of those languages.

Modern Hindi and Urdu both developed from a New Indo-Aryan variety that was current in the area of Delhi in the late twelfth century, when the city was captured by Mohammad of Ghor, a Muslim leader from the western regions of the Ghaznavid empire. As Delhi became an increasingly important centre in the new political landscape, the eponymous centre of the Delhi Sultanate, it began to attract a diverse population of settlers, including Muslim speakers of Persian and Arabic. As a result, the local variety of Indo-Aryan, often known as *kharī bolī*, 'upright speech', absorbed a considerable body of lexis from those languages and, in this form, was subsequently used as a lingua franca throughout the Indo-Muslim empires. Texts by Muslim writers usually referred to it as *hindī* or *hinduī*, terms which, as Shackle and Snell (1990: 4) point out, mean respectively 'Indian language' and 'Hindu language'. The emergence of this variety as a literary language first took place in the Deccan, where, as McGregor (1992: ix) notes: 'Contact with the world of Persian culture was much less close [...] than in Delhi and use of Hinduī could serve a valuable cultural purpose for settlers from the north and their descendants.' The use of the language as a vehicle for literature was subsequently brought to the courts of northern India in the early eighteenth century, reputedly by the poet Valī. There the language received extensive patronage, particularly in Lucknow, to which many poets moved with the decline of Mughal authority in Delhi. Indeed, the years when Gilchrist was travelling in the cities of northern India represent a period of considerable creativity in the literary history of the language, and Gilchrist cites the work of poets such as Sauda and Miskin as models of good usage.

Gilchrist rejected the terms *hindī* and *hinduī* as names for this variety and coined one of his own, 'Hindustani'. As we shall see in Chapter 1, this is largely to do with his wish to construct this variety as the national language of the area known to the British as 'Hindustan'. It seemed appropriate to him that the language of 'Hindustan' should be known as 'Hindustani', just as the language of England was known as 'English'. It also seems clear that he saw 'Hindustani' as a distinctively Muslim language, in comparison with other New Indo-Aryan dialects like Braj, which he saw as the property of Hindus. The evidence does not seem to bear out this polarised view of the situation. The language of a distinctively Indo-Muslim culture was, right up into the eighteenth century, Persian, *hindī* having a more diverse population of speakers. And Muslim writers were working in supposedly Hindu varieties such as Avadhi and Braj long before they cultivated *hindī* as a literary medium. At any rate, having detached the term *hinduī* from *kharī bolī*, Gilchrist reassigned it to Braj and other related varieties, presumably on the grounds that he saw them as distinctively Hindu. This reification of 'Hindustani' as both national and Muslim was clearly problematic, and will be discussed further in Chapter 1.

In this context, it is important to understand that, by the end of the nineteenth century, a split had developed between two competing varieties, both with origins in what Christopher King (1994) refers to as 'the khari boli continuum', one known as Urdu and one as Hindi.[6] The causes of this split are extremely controversial. It involved the emergence of the two varieties as markers respectively of Muslim and Hindu identities, and the assignment of blame for the division has been an integral part of much of the discussion surrounding it. In a well-known discussion of the issue, Amrit Rai (1984) interpreted the polarisation of the two varieties as the product of Muslims' attempts to mark off a distinctive language of their own during the eighteenth century. And in an alternative view of the problem, Christopher King (1994) foregrounds attempts to develop a Sanskritised style of 'the khari boli continuum' in the context of late nineteenth-century Hindu nationalism. The role of British colonialism in the process is particularly problematic. The view that Gilchrist contributed to the reification of Urdu as a separate language by prioritising a Persianised variety in his publications may be to attribute too much influence to the decisions taken at Fort William College. And, in an article discussed at greater length in Chapter 1, David Lelyveld (1993) suggests that it was not so much the nature of the variety enshrined in Gilchrist's grammar that was influential as the very concept of languages as markers of national and communal identities, which, he suggests, was not a feature of the Indian intellectual landscape prior to the arrival of the British. In the context of these debates, some commentators have tried to reclaim the term 'Hindustani' as a label for that which is common to both Hindi and Urdu, a famous proponent of this idea being no less a figure than Gandhi. This strategy is also controversial however, and has not been adopted as the basis of modern language policy.

To unravel these controversies is not the function of this book; indeed, Hasnain and Rajyashree (2004: 261) recently expressed the pessimistic view that '[a]ny discussion with regard to the matter of Hindi and Urdu is futile'. The focus of the following discussion is the way in which features of South Asian languages that seemed strange to British observers were assimilated into the framework of western grammatical analysis – the way in which western grammar functioned as a medium of representation for languages that were unknown to the pioneers of that tradition. This being the case, I have decided throughout the book to refer to the language described in

---

[6] The term *Urdu* originated in the expression *zabān-e urdū-e muallā*, which means 'the language of Delhi' and which until the late eighteenth century had actually referred to Persian. The formulation *urdū-e muallā* literally means 'the exalted camp', but was used as a conventional term for the city of Delhi.

Gilchrist's work with the term that the author himself used, 'Hindustani'. I do this largely in recognition of the fact that the texts constitute an attempt to *represent* the variety to the reader in a certain way. They embody a certain vision of the language as an ordered, 'national' 'vernacular', and the term 'Hindustani' serves to draw attention to the nature of that vision. This being the case, the term should perhaps appear in inverted commas throughout the book, but since this device rapidly becomes tiresome for the reader, I have chosen not to use it. I want to emphasise, however, that I am not endorsing the use of the term in contemporary contexts – I am simply using Gilchrist's own term as a way of referring to the object of his enquiry as he himself saw it.

I want to close this introduction by reiterating the point that this is a book about the politics of grammatical representation. Like everyone trained in modern linguistics and like many language-conscious liberals, I adhere strongly to the axiom that no languages are defective or faulty. And, for this reason, it concerns me that we, as linguists, have not been successful in persuading the broader population – and I mean here the educated population – of the validity of this viewpoint or of the extent to which language study can be pursued scientifically. The more I have investigated the intellectual landscape in which Gilchrist was operating, the less I feel that we can win the argument by simply telling people they are wrong. Earlier in this section I discussed the fact that, for eighteenth-century westerners, the ergative structure seemed particularly strange because of the expectation that morphology and syntax should reflect the structure of the logical proposition as it was understood at that time. It is common to dismiss such evaluative approaches to language study on the grounds that it is misguided to discriminate between structures that are logical and ones that are not. But this does not really constitute an *explanation* of our position. Linguists themselves do not, in fact, believe that language and logic are unconnected, and syntacticians working in the generativist paradigm routinely use a concept of argument structure that derives directly from the logical analysis of predication. The point is, of course, that since the eighteenth century logic itself has abstracted away from the structure of western languages, and so we are now able to approach these questions with a more abstract set of concepts and hence a more mediated understanding of the relationship between language and thought. The eighteenth century is an exciting period to study because, in certain important senses, we are still living there. The ideas of that period are still in circulation in one form or another – not in the linguistics departments of universities but in the wider world. They no longer serve to shore up colonial ideologies but they *are* mobilised in support of a range of positions in the field of education, all of which have political implications. To engage with eighteenth-century thinkers at a technical level is to develop a sense of our own distinctiveness as professional students of language, and in particular with how we have become reconciled to linguistic diversity. And it is important that we do develop such an informed understanding of our place in history if we are to speak in a persuasive fashion with those beyond our own community who are as yet unconvinced by our arguments.

PART I

CONTEXTS

1

THE POLITICAL CONTEXT

1.1 INTRODUCTION

The aim of this book is to examine the relationship between the political and the technical dimensions of the grammatical work of John Gilchrist.[1] A grammar is, after all, a *representation* of a language. And processes of *representation* take place in the political and technical realms simultaneously. They are political in the sense that they influence the way in which audiences view phenomena in the world around them. And they are technical in the sense that they exploit media and genres that have their own characteristics and qualities. A photographic image can influence the way in which viewers perceive a particular place, person or event. But photography is also a technical process that depends in important ways on the light conditions obtaining when the image is made, and on the nature of the available equipment. Like photographs, grammars can be seen as influencing the ways in which readers perceive particular entities – languages and their speakers. But, like photographers, grammarians also work within the parameters of a particular medium, and the representations they produce are shaped by a number of factors, including the highly conventional structure of the grammatical text, the particular modes of visual display associated with it and the range of metalanguage that is recognised at the time of writing. The political and technical dimensions of photography interact in important – even startling – ways. To photograph a council estate in gloomy black and white is to imply something quite specific about contemporary housing policy. And the argument of this book is that similar technical choices influence the ways in which languages are envisioned within grammatical works such as Gilchrist's. Photographs and grammars tend not to foreground their status as media of representation in the way that specimens of some genres do. Nevertheless, both are selective in their depiction of real-world phenomena, and both are heavily dependent upon the technical state of the medium at the time when the image or text was made.

Before interpreting a photographer's images of a council estate, we would need to examine the political debates surrounding the issue of social housing at the time when the images were made. In just the same way, any interpretation of early accounts of Hindustani must make reference to the

---

[1] See the Introduction for a full discussion of these terms.

political context in which they were produced. Gilchrist's analyses of
Hindustani have often been incorporated into a narrative that envisions
colonial language study as a process of APPROPRIATION. By learning Indian
languages, codifying them, specifying which were to be used in particular
administrative contexts and setting in place institutions for their study, the
British in India are said to have taken control of those languages and, in
the process, turned them into instruments through which colonial power
could be exercised. This view of colonial language study has been set out in
two important and influential articles: 'The Command of Language and
the Language of Command' by Bernard S. Cohn, originally published in
1985 and revised in 1996, and 'Colonial Knowledge and the Fate of
Hindustani' by David Lelyveld, which appeared in 1993. It will be useful to
examine the narrative developed by Cohn and Lelyveld, both of whom
present a compelling picture of the way in which British intervention in
Indian languages can be understood as a dimension of colonial power.
However, much of the argument of this book requires that another aspect
of colonial language study be acknowledged, one that is barely touched
upon by either commentator. While it certainly makes sense to see the
appropriation of Indian languages as a mode of political control, it is also
necessary to understand that the use of those languages opened up a space
for Indians to *resist*, or at least *subvert*, colonial authority. It is true that
Gilchrist and his contemporaries often argue for the study of Indian
languages on the basis of their utility to the colonial state. But the same
writers simultaneously acknowledge the dangers of speaking Indian
languages badly, and the damaging impact this can have upon the ability
of colonial agents to represent themselves authoritatively before the
colonised population.

In looking at the relationship between the political and the technical in
works of grammatical analysis, this aspect of language study – the
vulnerability to which it can expose the foreign learner – is of particular
importance. The danger, after all, is in the detail. Distinctions that feel
subtle, if not downright trivial, to the non-native learner are loaded with
significance for the native speaker. And we must not lose sight of the fact
that, however great the power exercised by coloniser over colonised, it was
the colonised who had the authority of being native speakers in the
contexts examined within this book. Colonial texts sometimes minimise this
fact, an interesting case in point being Nathaniel Halhed's grammar of
Bengali, first published in 1778, where the entire text is constructed as an
attempt to save the language from the alleged ignorance of the Bengalis
themselves. But there is evidence that, in face-to-face interaction, the agents
of British colonialism did not always find it so easy to maintain their
authority in front of native speakers. And this is important because the
technical details of grammatical analysis to a large extent serve to
externalise what native speakers already know and thus allow learners to

avoid producing utterances that native speakers perceive as wrong. In this sense, engaging with the grammar of a language at a technical level can be understood as an acknowledgement of how important the perceptions of native speakers truly are and how much scope they provide for localised resistance and subversion.

For Cohn and Lelyveld, western understandings of what a language actually is – a bounded entity, separable from other such entities, interpretable as a marker of nationality, susceptible to classifications such as CLASSICAL and VERNACULAR, POLITE and JARGONIC – when translated into the Indian context, also constituted a means by which Asian reality was reshaped and mastered. But while there is something to be said for this viewpoint, the framework of linguistic understanding that the British brought with them to India could also be understood as an obstacle to an effective engagement with the languages of the subcontinent. The valorisation of European classical languages at the expense of modern 'vernaculars' such as French, German and, indeed, English is a notorious theme in British educational history, and the English gentleman with perfect Greek and appalling French was once a familiar figure in the British cultural landscape. But the gentleman traveller, bellowing in broken French as he negotiated the familiar circuits of the grand tour, would have been in a far less vulnerable position than the Company servant who was unable to communicate well in a modern Indian 'vernacular' because he had devoted so much time to learning a 'classical' language such as Persian or Sanskrit. The former might be ridiculous but the latter – at least, according to contemporary writers such as Gilchrist – might well be in real danger. And what is more, his very ridiculousness might in itself be a threat to the armature of colonial authority.[2]

Simply to assert this point was not enough for grammarians such as Gilchrist. In the late eighteenth and early nineteenth centuries, 'classical' languages were often seen as qualitatively different from 'vernaculars' in the details of both their vocabulary and grammar. To elevate the status of a 'vernacular' – to persuade others to take it seriously – required the grammarian to demonstrate its virtues and show that it too was a 'polite' language and not a 'jargon'. And this could best be achieved through a detailed engagement with its structure. Indeed, the first problem facing a grammarian of a 'vernacular' was to show that the language actually had a structure, or, in the terminology of the day, could be 'reduced to rules'. If native speakers' knowledge of Indian languages constituted a minefield for

---

[2] Many of the gentlemen who embarked on the grand tour would have been accompanied by servants who were native speakers of English and who would, to some extent, have provided insulation against contact with native speakers. The colonial agent, in contrast, would have employed servants who were themselves native speakers of Indian languages, and so the master/servant relationship was itself a space in which exchanges with the 'natives' were transacted.

Company servants, then the practice of using such languages while simultaneously denying that they were rule-governed can only be likened to an attempt to cross a minefield while at the same time refusing to acknowledge that it is there. If the danger was in the detail, then to insist that there was no detail to master was to expose oneself to a heightened level of danger. In this sense too, then, Gilchrist's technical engagement with a modern Indian language can be understood as an attempt to undo the stigmatisation of the language, a stigmatisation that he consistently argued was detrimental to British authority.

Before moving on to examine these issues in more detail, it might be useful to comment briefly on the theoretical underpinnings of the discussion. In their work on colonial linguistics, both Cohn and Lelyveld acknowledge a debt to Michel Foucault,[3] pointing to Foucault's theorisation of power/knowledge as a means of understanding the role of language study in the context of the colonial project. Of course, Foucault's conception of power is complex, and develops throughout his published work. However, two themes in his analysis of power have proved particularly influential. The first is the notion that knowledge and power are fused – that wherever there are relations of knowledge, there are also relations of power, hence the need for the formulation power/knowledge to reflect the intimate relationship that exists between the two entities. The second is that power is not a sort of commodity that one carries around with one but something that is dispersed throughout a network of relations and exercised by virtue of one's position within that network. Power can be exercised from many points, including ones that may not (on the face of it) seem like centres of power in any conventional sense. This conception of power as dispersed, localised and reversible may seem problematic in the sense that it risks underplaying the crushing inequalities that have characterised many societies, past and present. But Foucault argued that large inequalities can be understood in terms of the aggregation of localised flows of power:

> [T]he manifold relationships of force that take shape and come into play in the machinery of production, in families, limited groups, and institutions, are the basis for wide-ranging effects of cleavage that run through the social body as a whole. (Foucault 1990: 94)

In the colonial context, for example, one might argue that the imbalance of power between coloniser and colonised was unmistakable and real, but that within the network of relations that constituted colonial society, power could also be seen flowing back from colonised to coloniser in specific moments of resistance, subversion and refusal. To focus on these moments

---

[3] Cohn (1996: 22) and Lelyveld (1993: 670 n. 14).

is not to deny the larger asymmetry of power but to examine the factors that produced and defined its specific characteristics.[4]

The following section will look at the account of colonial language study developed by Cohn and Lelyveld, focusing particularly on the place of Gilchrist's writing within the narrative. In developing this account, both commentators are clearly influenced by Foucault in their subtle treatment of the interpenetration of knowledge and power within the British colonial state. But, having said that, the narrative that they offer has to be understood as partial, downplaying as it does the nature of the native speaker's knowledge as a space for resistance and subversion. This being the case, it is a shame that neither writer makes use of Foucault's notion of power as dispersed, localised and reversible. This is no doubt because the model of power that they allude to is one developed in Foucault's earlier work. However, using a framework of analysis that alludes to Foucault's later writing would actually make it possible to incorporate an account of language as a site of resistance into the historical narrative, something that would be desirable, given the anxiety that colonial agents often seem to have felt about using Indian languages. Section 1.3 will attempt to redress the balance by dealing with the idea of language learning as an inherently risky activity, and providing a detailed reading of a section of Gilchrist's grammar where this idea is explicitly discussed. Once this fuller picture of colonial language study has been developed, it will be important to conclude the discussion by examining the role of classificatory schemata such as the distinction between the 'classical' and the 'vernacular' or the 'polite' and the 'jargonic' in articulating the field. The use of these western linguistic categories in defining an area of enquiry gave rise to a network of relations in which power flowed not in a single direction, from coloniser to colonised, but back and forth in a complex exchange of authority and resistance. It is in these classificatory terms that power and knowledge – the political and the technical – are most closely fused, and a closer look at these terms will set the scene for a detailed examination of Gilchrist's grammatical writing later in the book.

---

[4] The ideas presented here are most fully developed in Foucault's later work and particularly in *Discipline and Punish: The Birth of the Prison* and the first part of *The History of Sexuality*. They are also explored in the collection of interviews and essays, *Power/Knowledge: Selected Interviews and Other Writings, 1972–1977*. The most compact statement appears in *The History of Sexuality*, vol. 1, where Foucault (1990: 94) asserts: 'Relations of power are not in a position of exteriority with respect to other types of relationships [...] but are immanent in the latter.' Among these 'other types of relationships' are 'knowledge relationships'. He goes on to suggest that 'there is no binary and all-encompassing opposition between rulers and ruled at the root of power relations, and serving as a general matrix'. Dreyfus & Rabinow (1982: 184–204) provide a useful discussion of Foucault's understanding of the relationship between power and knowledge.

Bernard S. Cohn characterises colonial language learning as political in a number of different senses. An important part of his argument is that British work on Indian languages was motivated to a large extent by the needs of the emergent empire, and fulfilled a practical function in the government of the colonial state. But, on top of this relatively uncontroversial claim, Cohn develops the more obviously Foucauldian argument that, by reshaping fields of knowledge that had previously been the sole property of Indians, the British also restructured the networks of relations through which power was exercised within the colony. As Cohn (1996: 53) puts it himself: '[T]hey had not only invaded and conquered a territory but, through their scholarship, had invaded an epistemological space as well.' Indian scholars were absorbed into colonial institutions in subordinate roles as informants, assistants and teachers under the supervision of British scholars; the demarcation and classification of Indian languages resulted in the 'creation and reification of social groups' each with its own 'varied interests'; and the languages themselves, both written and spoken, were 'transformed' by their assimilation into the framework of western linguistic scholarship. In the following discussion, the view of language as a practical instrument of government will be treated first. This will help to set Gilchrist's work in the broader context of contemporary colonial language study and point out the ways in which his writing both resembles and diverges from other scholarship that was emerging at the same time. Once these issues have been examined, it will then be possible to comment on the more nuanced arguments developed by both Cohn and Levyveld concerning the reordering of Indian fields of knowledge as a result of the colonial encounter.

As Cohn successfully shows, British interest in Indian languages escalated in the last quarter of the eighteenth century as a direct result of the foundation of the colonial state in Bengal. The East India Company had been trading with India since the early seventeenth century, and since that time Company servants had often remarked on the utility of Persian, the administrative language of the Mughal empire, as a medium for political and commercial negotiation. Indeed, when the orientalist scholar William Jones published his famous grammar of Persian in 1771, he noted that it was with the protection of the 'princes of the country' that the agents of the Company had 'gained their first settlement in India', and that this client relationship had stimulated an interest in Persian among the British:

> [T]he servants of the company received letters which they could not read, and were ambitious of gaining titles of which they could not comprehend the meaning; it was found highly dangerous to employ the natives as interpreters, upon whose fidelity they could not

depend; and it was at last discovered that they must apply themselves to the study of the Persian language, in which all the letters
from the Indian princes were written. (Jones 1771: xii)[5]

As Cohn (1996: 19–20) states, however, relatively few Company servants
seem to have developed any real competence in Persian, despite this general
sense of the language's usefulness. It is true that some individuals applied
themselves to its study and some clearly had a practical knowledge of
Hindustani as well. But few in number, located mainly in the 'cosmopolitan
port cities' of India, interacting mainly with other Europeans at a social
level and attended by servants who spoke at least some English or
Portuguese, the servants of the Company were faced with too many
obstacles for a serious engagement with Indian languages to become a
priority.

It was the transformation of the East India Company from an almost
exclusively commercial organisation into a colonial power that ultimately
brought about change. As Cohn (1996: 20) puts it: 'The British success at
Plassey and the subsequent appropriation of the revenues of Bengal were to
provide the impetus for more and more British civilians and military
officers to learn one or more of the Indian languages.' This fact arose from
the very nature of the colonial state itself. When the British assumed control
in Bengal in the second half of the eighteenth century, it was not possible
for them simply to sweep away the existing political and administrative
structures. Their administration was not an entirely new creation,
independent of all existing social practices. On the contrary, it depended
upon indigenous systems of administration, communication and exchange,
systems embedded in the existing social structure and regulated through the
medium of Indian languages. As such, the servants of the East India
Company had to engage with indigenous administrative systems, and hence
indigenous languages, in order to carry out their work. Always recognised
as important, Persian, the language used by the Mughals for legal and
administrative purposes, now came to be seen as a vital acquisition for an
'ambitious cadet or junior writer' in the service of the Company (Cohn
1996: 24). And at the same time Sanskrit became an object of attention for
legal scholars in search of an appropriate law code for the Hindu subjects of
the colonial state. The Sanskrit *dharma* literature was appropriated for this
purpose and, already an important focus of attention for Indian scholars,
now became an object of scrutiny for westerners too.[6]

---

[5] Also quoted by Cohn (1996: 23).
[6] Flood (1996: 11) defines *dharma* as 'that power which upholds or supports society and the
cosmos; that power which constrains things into their particularity, which makes things what
they are'. Human beings are subject to the constraints of *dharma* and consequently the word
is connotative of 'religion' and 'duty' as well as 'law'.

In his discussion of these developments, Cohn recognises the importance of the western distinction between 'classical' and 'vernacular' languages. Both Persian and Sanskrit came to be identified in the European consciousness with the western languages of learning, Latin and Greek. The eastern and western 'classical' tongues were comparable in a number of senses – in their social prestige, in their association with formal, public functions and in their status as languages accessible mainly to the educated. Like Latin and Greek, Sanskrit was also an ancient language, codified and passed on through a sophisticated grammatical tradition of its own, and, while Persian was not an ancient language in the sense that it still had large numbers of native speakers, the fact that in India it was a language of learning and not a language of the bazaar qualified it for inclusion in the same category. Just as Latin and Greek dominated western education, particularly the education of young men, so Persian and Sanskrit became the focus of attention for servants of the Company – the former almost instantly and the latter gradually, as its uses became more apparent. But texts also appeared arguing for the systematic study of modern Indian 'vernaculars' – initially Bengali, the language of the region in which British colonial power was first established, and subsequently Hindustani on the grounds that it was widely spoken across the areas of northern India into which British authority was beginning to expand. The first important grammar of Bengali was published by Nathaniel Halhed[7] in 1778, while Gilchrist's work occupies a similar position in the history of Hindustani scholarship. Writers like Halhed and Gilchrist, whose work focused on modern Indian 'vernaculars', often had to *argue* for the importance of their objects of study in a way that was less important for writers whose work dealt with the 'classical' languages. And the arguments they presented were also connected with the nature of power under the new regime.

To a certain extent, the advocates of the 'vernaculars' pointed to practical considerations: the utility of Bengali in the commercial life of the colony and the prevalence of Hindustani as a lingua franca in the Indian army. At the same time, however, they often resorted to a more ideological argument, one that involved constructing the British regime as a liberating force charged with the responsibility of rescuing the people of India from the tyranny of Mughal authority. Persian and Sanskrit were required so that colonial agents could engage with legal documents in an unmediated fashion, but Bengali and Hindustani were needed so that Company Servants could communicate directly with the *people* without relying on what they saw as corrupt interpreters as intermediaries. In his grammar of Bengali, for example, Nathaniel Halhed (1778: ii) argues that a 'general medium of intercourse' is required between 'the Natives of Europe who are

---

[7] See Rocher (1983) for an account of the life and work of Halhed, and Qayyum (1982) for a discussion of his approach to the Bengali language.

to rule' and 'the Inhabitants of India who are to obey'. Such a 'medium of intercourse' will enable the British to 'explain the benevolent principles of that legislation whose decrees they inforce' and 'be at once the dispensers of Laws and of Science to an extensive nation'. The country is still 'fluctuating between the relics of former despotic dominion, and the liberal spirit of its present legislature', and, since instability creates a breeding ground for corruption, it is imperative that the British appoint 'gentlemen of mature experience in the manners and customs of the natives' to protect villagers from 'the exactions of an imperious Landlord or grasping Collector'. The 'gentlemen' who take on this onerous responsibility will need to speak Bengali:

> [T]his important commission will be more immediately and more extensively beneficial, in proportion as it is conferred on those only whom a competent knowledge of the Bengalese has previously qualified for a personal investigation of every unwarrantable exaction, and scrutiny into every complicated account. (Halhed 1778: xvi–xvii)

As one of the early champions of Hindustani, Gilchrist develops a similar argument in favour of that language. In a preface to his dictionary and grammar, written and published retrospectively in 1798, he expresses concern that ignorance of Indian languages is compromising the administration of justice within the colony. It is as if magistrates in British courts spoke only French. Native officers have to be entrusted with translating pleas from Indian languages into Persian and they are allowed to take the transcript away in order to do this, a procedure that is hardly secure. For this reason, court proceedings are more like the 'spells of a conjurer' or the 'sibyle leaves' than a proper judicial hearing (Gilchrist 1798b: xxviii). What is more, by using Persian in the judicial process the British are encouraging, 'along with benevolent British laws and regulations, the acquisition of a foreign perfectly odious badge of slavery, and subjection' (Gilchrist 1798b: xxvii). Persian is the language of the regime from which the British are liberating Indians, and as such should be used as little as possible in dealings with the mass of the population.

Gilchrist (1798b: xxvii) even suggests that the native elite, the 'cormorant crew of *Deewans, Mootusuddees, Surkars, Nazirs, Pundits, Moonshees*, and a tremendous role of harpies, who encompass power here', might try to prevent British officials from acquiring the 'means of immediate communication with *the great mass of the people*, whom these *locusts of the land* conceive their lawful hereditary prey'. Thus Gilchrist presents the study of Hindustani as a way of foiling the corrupt schemes of the Indian elite and making the promise of benevolent administration a reality. And benevolent administration was not merely an ethical responsibility. In a much-quoted letter of 1784, Warren Hastings, then governor-general of British India, famously stated that 'every accumulation of knowledge' was useful to the state.[8] Knowledge of Indians and their society would inspire the British with a 'sense of obligation and benevolence', which in turn would lessen 'the weight of the chain' by which Indians were 'held in subjection', thus heading off discontent and contributing to the security of the regime (Wilkins 1785: 13). Under this analysis, learning the Indian 'vernaculars' would enable colonial agents to govern impartially and efficiently, and in this way secure the consent of Indians in their own subjection. Thus the study of modern Indian languages constituted a means of shoring up colonial power by minimising the resentment Indians felt towards the new regime.

So far the discussion has focused on the fact that early colonial language study was to a large extent motivated by political and administrative considerations – the need to collect revenue, administer justice, communicate with soldiers and so on. However, Cohn (1996: 21–2) argues that, in the field of language learning, the relationship between knowledge and power extended far beyond the instrumental value of languages as a means of getting things done. He points to the fact that, in the last quarter of the eighteenth century, linguistic scholarship ceased to be a private matter, undertaken by individual servants of the Company using whatever resources they could find. Instead, as he points out, an official 'apparatus' of language study emerged in the form of a barrage of texts – 'grammars, dictionaries, treatises, class books, and translations'. The production and publication of this material – a wholesale textualisation of Indian reality – resulted in the refashioning of 'Indian forms of knowledge' into what Cohn calls 'European objects'. To reorganise a field of knowledge according to other modes of understanding and other textual conventions is effectively to transform it. And because these transformed fields of knowledge, these 'European objects', were legitimised and even sponsored by the colonial regime, they can be seen as having brought into existence a new order of things. As Cohn sees it, they did not constitute mere approximations to an underlying reality that endured unchanged, but acquired a force and validity of their own.

As he explores these issues, Cohn works with a fairly broad definition of language study. A fair proportion of his discussion is taken up with what happens when a text is translated from one language to another rather than with the conceptualisation of language itself. In his discussion of Hindustani, however, he engages more closely with the ways in which western writers defined, labelled and delimited the languages of India, and in this context he discusses a number of important passages in which Gilchrist tries to explain the status of Hindustani to his readers – its history, its relationship with other languages and its patterns of use. Having pointed

---

[8] Cited e.g. by Cohn (1996), Kopf (1969: 18) and MacKenzie (1995: 3).

out the importance of such processes of delimitation, Cohn does not go on
to provide a particularly developed interpretation of how they functioned
as vehicles of power. At this point David Lelyveld's article becomes
important, presenting as it does a challenging account of the way in which
the colonial study of Hindustani 'intruded' into Indian political and
cultural life from the publication of Gilchrist's dictionary onwards.
Lelyveld does not overstate the extent to which Indian languages
themselves were transformed by the British. Indeed, he emphasises the
agency of Indians in these processes, stressing that it was they who
'formulated the particular usages and boundaries of their own languages'.
Colonial language study, he argues, affected the linguistic situation in India
in a rather more subtle way – 'by setting down methods of inquiry and their
political implications and by framing the institutional forms and ideological
constellations now taken for granted among most Indians with regard to
language' (Lelyveld 1993: 682). In particular, the idea that it is possible –
and indeed desirable – to delimit a particular form of speech as a 'national'
language is one of the dubious legacies of European scholarship and one
that Gilchrist himself bequeathed to India in his own publications. The
following discussion will present the argument initiated by Cohn and
developed by Lelyveld, but will also provide more detailed readings of
relevant passages of Gilchrist's work than either of them was able to offer,
given the quantity of material each was discussing.

A wide range of what a modern linguist would call related language
varieties were spoken across the central regions of northern India at the
time when Gilchrist began his linguistic work. These varieties are often
known, rather confusingly, as dialects of Hindi.[9] Most of them had a certain
regional extension – thus, by way of example, it is possible to specify the
geographical areas in which Avadhi or Braj were dominant. By contrast,
Hindustani, understood as the descendant of the *kharī bolī* spoken around
Delhi in the twelfth century and including a large admixture of Persian and
Arabic lexis, was spoken as a first language by a population that was, as
Shackle and Snell (1990: 41–2) put it, 'not geographically concentrated'.
And it was also widely used as a lingua franca across northern India and,
indeed, beyond. This being the case, it is easy to see why Gilchrist saw it as
having a particular utility. If Company servants were going to study one
Indian language, it was a good idea to choose one that was spoken across a
wide expanse of territory. However, Gilchrist does not construct
Hindustani merely as a lingua franca, describing it instead as a 'national'

---

[9] To refer to these varieties as dialects of Hindi is to run the risk of implying that they are non-
standard variants and are to be seen in opposition to Modern Standard Hindi. This is
misleading for two reasons. First, several of the so-called dialects of Hindi themselves have
literary, if not exactly standard, forms. And second, both the modern standards, Hindi and
Urdu, derive from one of these varieties, the *kharī bolī* spoken around Delhi in the medieval
period.

language. This is significant, because languages that were used for purposes of communication by traders were not highly regarded in the eighteenth century. Indeed, in the preface to his dictionary, Samuel Johnson suggests that a language is in some way damaged when it is used as a medium of communication by people from different communities. Moreover, the pejorative term 'jargon', which had often been applied to Hindustani by the British, was very often used of such varieties. Thus, to describe Hindustani as a 'national' language served the purpose of emphasising how widely spoken it was, while also defending it from the charge of being a mere lingua franca or 'jargon'.[10] What, then, did Gilchrist mean by a 'national' language? And how does he argue for the applicability of the term to Hindustani?

In developing his argument, Gilchrist uses two overlapping modes of argumentation. One characterises Indian languages by means of a historical comparison and one draws on the rhetorical tradition.[11] To look at the historical argument first, Gilchrist states that Hindustani has its origins in the 'irruptions' and 'subsequent settlement' of Muslims in northern India. Before this, he claims, a language called 'Hinduwee' was spoken in that area, and the 'irruptions' of Muslims from the north led to the emergence of a new language formed through the transfer of large numbers of Persian and Arabic words into this earlier variety. Gilchrist says that the Muslims labelled the new language 'Oorduwee', 'Rekhtu' or 'Hindee', but that he prefers to use a label alluding to the geographical distribution of the variety – 'Hindoostanee', the language of 'Hindoostan'. In developing this account of the relationship between 'Hinduwee' and 'Hindoostanee', he compares the former to Anglo-Saxon and the latter to modern English:

> This ancient tongue, under various modifications is to Hindoostan, exactly what the Saxon was to England, before the Norman conquest, while the *Hindoostanee* is in fact, nothing more than *Hinduwee* deluged, after repeated successful invasions by the M*oo*sulmans, with Arabic and Persian, bearing the very same relation in almost every respect to its original basis, that the English which sprung from the parent Saxon, obscured by an influx of French and other continental tongues, now does to its own source also. (Gilchrist 1798b: xx)

In interpreting this comparison, it is vital to understand that Gilchrist identifies the modern 'Hindi dialects' of northern India with the 'ancient' language, 'Hinduwee'. In particular he draws an equivalence between 'Hinduwee' and Braj, apparently seeing the other northern varieties as

---

[10] See Majeed (1995) for a discussion of the term 'jargon' as it was used in the context of imperialism in South Asia.

[11] Cohn (1996: 36–8) discusses both modes of argument, although without tracing the origins of the second of them in the western rhetorical tradition.

variants of the latter.[12] And this makes the comparison between 'Hinduwee' and 'Saxon' highly problematic. In Gilchrist's usage, the term 'Hinduwee' denotes a variety – or, better, a group of varieties – that was alive and flourishing at the time he was writing, whereas Anglo-Saxon and Modern English never coexisted at all. In fact, Gilchrist (1798b: xx n.) acknowledges this fact himself: 'the Hinduwee is certainly more a living distinct speech here, than the Saxon is in England.' But this brief acknowledgement merely modifies the comparison and does not sweep it away. Varieties such as Avadhi and Braj may not be dead, but for Gilchrist they still constitute remnants of an 'ancient tongue', while Hindustani is not merely one among a group of living varieties but the real modern language of northern India – the obvious choice for foreign learners in the same way that English is for visitors to England.[13]

This historical narrative is intimately related to arguments that Gilchrist draws from the western rhetorical tradition. Having painted a picture of Hindustani as the distinctively modern language of northern India, he goes on to emphasise how widely it is spoken and how important it is in holding the 'people' together:

> If general diffusion and utility can constitute sufficient claims to the title of language, I fancy few will be found with higher pretensions in those essentials, than the Hindoostanee has to that paramount discriminative. Nay if we behold it, as the indissoluble cementing link of people whose laws, and religion, constantly clash with each other, we may almost recognise a living irresistible principle in this speech without one parallel in the History of mankind, as no country perhaps in the world ever exhibited for a length of time, the conquerors and conquered as far as concerns language, and religious tenets in the exact situation of the Hindoos, and Moosulmans respectively here. (Gilchrist 1798b: xxi)

To underline this point he quotes the Scottish rhetorician George Campbell on the subject of 'national' language. The quotation is drawn from a section

---

[12] He puts it like this: 'Before the irruptions and subsequent settlement of the Moosulmans, the Hinduwee or *Hindoo,ee* [...] was to India, what the *Hindoostanee* is now to Hindoostan, varying more or less in its territorial excursions from the pure speech, called by way of pre-eminence the Brij *B,hasha* or *the language* of the Indian Arcadia' (Gilchrist 1798b: xx).

[13] Faruqi (2001: 29–31) is highly critical of Gilchrist's narrative, castigating him for the arrogant way in which he suggests that the name 'Hindoostanee' is preferable to those actually used by native speakers and pointing out that *hindvī*, Gilchrist's 'Hinduwee', was actually 'an early name for the language for which [Gilchrist] was now prescribing the name "Hindoostanee"' and not a language separate from it. Faruqi also draws attention to an error in the terminology that Gilchrist employs. The term 'Oorduwee' is Gilchrist's rendering of the form *urdū-e*, which is an oddly truncated version of the expression *urdū-e mu'allā*, 'the language of the *urdū*', the latter term meaning 'royal city' and hence referring to Delhi. As Faruqi puts it: 'Gilchrist doesn't know that [*urdū-e mu'allā*] is a compound, and its first part standing alone is meaningless, so that no one ever wrote, or spoke, "*urdū-e*".'

of Campbell's *Philosophy of Rhetoric*, in which we are presented with a number of criteria for deciding what constitutes 'correct' usage. One of these criteria is historical – writers and speakers should follow 'present' usage: 'To me,' says Campbell, 'it is [...] evident, either that the present use must be the standard of the present language, or that the language admits of no standard whatsoever' (Campbell 1776 I: 361). This is important because Gilchrist's discussion of the origins of Hindustani clearly has the effect of constructing that variety as 'present usage' in contrast with the other dialects of Hindi, which are the remnants of an ancient language. Thus, the historical comparison effectively valorises Hindustani with reference to Campbell's doctrine of 'present usage'. And the discussion of Hindustani as a 'cementing link' builds on this argument with reference to another of Campbell's evaluative criteria, namely the idea that 'correct' usage is 'national' in contrast to 'provincial', 'professional' and 'foreign' usage. This point is developed in the quotation presented by Gilchrist:

> In every province there are peculiarities of dialect, which affect not only the pronunciation and the accent, but even the inflection and the combination of words, whereby their idiom is distinguished from that of the nation, and from that of every other province. The narrowness of the circle to which the currency of the words and phrases of such dialects is confined, sufficiently discriminates them from that which is properly styled the language, and which commands a circulation incomparably wider. (Gilchrist 1798b: xxi)

Thus, when Gilchrist states that Hindustani can claim that 'paramount discriminative', the title 'language', on the grounds of its 'general diffusion and utility', he is echoing Campbell's distinction between a 'language', which is nationally recognisable, and a 'dialect', which has limited application outside the province where it is spoken. Gilchrist goes on to quote the following uncompromising argument from Campbell:

> [T]he language properly so called is found current, especially in the upper and middle ranks, over the whole British empire. Thus, though in every province, they ridicule the idiom of every other province, they all vail to the English idiom, and scruple not to acknowledge its superiority over their own. For example; in some parts of Wales (if we may credit Shakespeare in his character of Fluellin in Henry V.) the common people say *goot* for good; in the south of Scotland they say *gude* and in the north they say *gueed*. Whenever one of these pronunciations prevails, you will never hear from a native either of the [other] two; but the word good is to be heard every where from natives as well as from strangers; nor do the people ever dream that there is any thing laughable in it, however much they are disposed to laugh at the country accents and idioms

which they discern in one another. Nay more: though the people of distant provinces do not understand one another, they mostly all understand *one who speaks properly*. (Gilchrist 1798b: xxi)

This quotation provides Gilchrist with a way of constructing Hindustani's status as a lingua franca, not as a problem in the way that Johnson's remarks about the corrupt nature of trade languages might suggest, but as a guarantee that it is a 'language' and not a 'dialect'. The fact that Hindustani is less easily tied to a particular region than varieties like Avadhi or Braj is interpreted as evidence of its 'national' status – its equivalence with the English spoken 'over the whole British empire' rather than the 'country accents and idioms' of the British Isles. By drawing upon Campbell's formulation of 'correct usage', Gilchrist characterises Hindustani as a language that has already brought a high measure of unity to India – the 'cementing link' that unites Hindus and Muslims in a fashion 'without one parallel in the History of mankind'.

This characterisation of Hindustani sits uneasily with claims made elsewhere in the same text. As Cohn (1996: 36) notes, Gilchrist (1798b: xli) identifies three 'styles' of Hindustani – the 'high court or *Persian* style', the 'middle or genuine *Hindoostanee* style', and the 'vulgar or *Hinduwee*'. And once again the metalanguage is drawn from western rhetoric, recalling the 'grand', 'plain' and 'middle' styles discussed by rhetoricians from Cicero onwards. Gilchrist goes on to give examples of texts in each 'style'. For the 'high' style he mentions the 'elevated poems' of Sauda, Vali and Mir Dard and for the 'vulgar' style he cites 'the greatest part of the Hindoostanee compositions written in the Naguree [as opposed to the Perso-Arabic] character', 'the dialect of the lower order of servants and Hindoos', the speech of 'the peasantry of Hindoostan', and – oddly – the 'Regulations of Government' as translated by an Englishman, 'Mr. Forster'. For the 'middle' style, to which he gives 'preference', he cites the elegies of Miskin, the satires of Sauda, the articles of war, translated by another Englishman, Colonel William Scott, and 'the speech of well-bred Hindoostanee *Moonshees* and *servants*'. He compares the 'middle style' to the 'true centre point' of a circle, an image which suggests that the 'high' and 'vulgar' styles are somehow at the periphery of acceptable usage. And indeed, a little further on in the same passage, he associates those styles, or at least the 'high' one, with 'pedantry', which, 'so far from being decried' in India, 'is esteemed the touchstone of learning'. The same division into styles is presented in *The Oriental Linguist*, where Gilchrist underlines his assertion that Hindus and Muslims will regard the language varieties used in northern India rather differently:

> [T]he Hindoos will naturally lean most to the *Hinduwee*, while the Moosulmans will of course be more partial to Arabic and Persian; whence two styles arise, namely the court or high style; and the

country or pristine style, leaving the middle or familiar current style between them, which I have recommended as the best, and described it also at full length along with the rest. (Gilchrist 1798a: iv)

We now have three ways of conceptualising linguistic varieties mapped onto each other in an uneasy pattern of equivalence. One is built on a distinction between 'ancient' and 'modern' languages; one contrasts the 'national language' with 'provincial dialects'; and one understands language varieties in terms of 'high', 'vulgar' and 'middle' styles. What is more, there is a sense that the 'national' language is associated with the 'middle' style and, as such, exists as a point of equilibrium between a 'high' style associated with Muslims and a 'vulgar' style that is associated with Hindus.

Faruqi (2001: 28–30) is highly critical of this tendency to associate Hindustani with Muslims and 'Hinduwee' with Hindus, asserting that it is simply not an accurate depiction of eighteenth-century patterns of language use. As an interpretation of the Indian linguistic context, it is clearly influenced by the situation that Gilchrist had left behind him in Scotland, and the fact that he chooses to quote from George Campbell's work, *The Philosophy of Rhetoric*, is evidence of this. This text is very much a contribution to the eighteenth-century debate about the formation of a distinctively British national identity after the union of England and Scotland in 1707. The insistence that one particular version of English is found 'over the whole British empire', and that English pronunciations are 'national' in contrast to 'provincial' Scottish ones, contributes to a very particular envisioning of how a distinctively British identity is to be understood and, in particular, how it is to be instantiated culturally. As Bayly (1996: 292) says, '[Gilchrist] wrote as a lowland Scot who had seen Gaelic and Catholic Scotland dissolve in his own lifetime.' And, by citing Campbell, Gilchrist communicates an acute sense that the emergence of a 'national' language often involves the subjugation of other communal identities.

At any rate, for a number of commentators, foremost among them David Lelyveld, the sense that a language can be 'national' and the idea that languages are unified markers of socio-religious identities were the real instruments of transformation that colonial linguists brought to bear on Indian reality. It was within this conceptual framework, they argue, that the language debates still raging in South Asia – particularly those over the relative statuses of modern Hindi and Urdu – first emerged. As Lelyveld (1993: 668–9) puts it, many Indian languages had distinctively Muslim varieties, written in Perso-Arabic script, employing words borrowed from Arabic and Persian and using 'poetic metres and literary genres shared with the wider Islamic world'. But, in spite of this, only the 'Musalmānī' variety of Hindustani emerged as a standard – Urdu – during the period of British colonial rule. And this in itself became a problem:

> Whether it was by definition Musalmāni [i.e. simply a Muslim variety of a common language] or the confluence of all Indian history [i.e. the language most effectively reflecting the nature of modern Indian society], whether it was Urdu or Hindustani, came to have much bearing on the definition of India as a national community and the place of Muslims within it. (Lelyveld 1996: 669)

Gilchrist had effectively laid the ground for this kind of debate by characterising the language he was describing not as a 'Musalmāni' variety but as a 'national' language deriving, to use Lelyveld's exceptionally elegant phrase, from 'the confluence of all Indian history' – a contentious claim, given that he also associated the variety with Muslim identities. David Washbrook (1991: 190) makes a similar point when he suggests that what has sometimes been seen as the modernisation of Indian languages in the context of British colonial rule 'manifested itself particularly in the way that the new concepts of language began to inform questions of social and political identity and to provide symbols of self-conscious ethnicity'. Languages ceased to be shared, variable and fluid and became particular, invariant and carefully policed, a process that inevitably led to dissent and confrontation.

Of course, it is important that Gilchrist's vision of Hindustani was disseminated not merely in publications like the dictionary and grammar but in an institutional context as well. In 1800, when a training college for Company servants was established in Calcutta, Gilchrist was appointed to the position of Professor of Hindustani. In fact, in 1798 he had been selected by the governor-general, Marquis Wellesley, to run a pilot project in order to provide evidence that such a scheme could work. In his role at Fort William College, Gilchrist not only taught Hindustani to a succession of new arrivals and wrote textbooks for them, but also set up a printing press, gathered a team of 'learned natives' to assist him in his work, supervised them as they translated a range of material into Hindustani and published their translations.[14] At one time, it was common to view this work as a crucial factor in the emergence of a modern Urdu literary culture, and Gilchrist himself made it clear that the translations emerging from the 'Hindoostanee Press' were intended not simply as reading matter for British learners but as a stimulus to the development of Hindustani literature. In his influential account of the relationship between British orientalist scholarship and the 'Bengal Renaissance', for example, David Kopf (1969: 83) quotes a letter of 1803, in which Gilchrist states his continuing plans in the following terms:

---

[14] Kopf (1969: 83) notes that in August 1803 the Hindustani department produced an inventory of works so far translated and 44 texts were included, most of them versions of Persian and Arabic originals. Das (1978: 17–18) provides useful information about the Indian scholars employed in the Hindustani department.

I shall engage soon to form such a body of useful and entertaining literature in that language as will ultimately raise it to that estimation among the natives which it would many years ago have attained among an enlightened and energetic people. [...] May not we then reason thus from analogy, that the Hindoostanee will ascend as high on the Indian scale [...] as the English has done in a similar predicament in our own country [...].

But more recent histories of Indian literature play down the influence that these publications had on the emergence of modern Urdu prose. Zaidi (1993: 209–10), for example, devotes just 16 lines of a 459-page volume to the influence of Fort William College, noting simply: 'The college publications helped in the evolution of simple purposeful prose.' Shackle and Snell (1990: 85) state that most of these texts have 'the lifeless quality to be expected in a series of officially-sponsored translations', pointing out just one that 'stands as an exception to this general rule', Mir Amman's *Bāgh o bahār*, a translation of the Persian *Tale of the Four Dervishes*. But, even here, Zaidi (1993: 123), while commenting positively on Mir Amman's work, downplays its stylistic originality with the following comment:

The change of style noticed in *Bagh-o-Bahar* is often traced to the new concepts percolating through contacts with the British. The historian has, however, to remind himself that it was Mir Insha in Lucknow who first attempted early in the 19ᵗʰ century *Rani Ketki ki Kahani*, in simple language, eschewing even the commonly used Persian and Arabic words and phrases.[15]

The idea that Gilchrist's work was directly responsible for the modernisation of Hindustani has in recent years receded before arguments of the kind developed by Cohn and Lelyveld. The work of colonial linguists such as Gilchrist has come to be seen as transformative in the sense that it disseminated the concept of languages as fixed entities directly linked with categories such as 'Hindu' and 'Muslim' or 'provincial' and 'national'. In particular, the intersection of this pair of binaries – the uneasy mapping of 'national' onto 'Muslim' – generated a political problem that has renewed itself endlessly over the last two centuries and, to a large extent, explains the heat with which linguistic issues are still discussed today, even in the most academic contexts. Cohn has sometimes been charged with overstating the role of colonial scholarship in shaping the modern intellectual landscape of South Asia. As Bayly (1996: 287 n.) says, 'this seminal article attributes too great a capacity on the part of the British to "construct" Indian society independently of the agency of its social formations and knowledge communities'. Indeed, to a certain extent, the strength of Lelyveld's

---

[15] Mir Insha (1752–1817) did not work in the context of British institutions but spent much of his career at the court in Lucknow. See Zaidi (1993: 135–8) for more details.

argument is the fact that it identifies the origins of contemporary political problems in the conceptualisations of language imported from eighteenth-century Europe while never denying the agency of India's indigenous 'social formations' and 'knowledge communities'. However, the argument developed in the coming chapters requires that we recognise a dimension of colonial language study that is barely touched upon in Lelyveld's account, namely the anxiety associated with the process of communicating in a language that is not one's own. At the fine level of grammatical analysis, Gilchrist's texts are shaped by an urgent belief in the importance of detail, an attitude that is not merely the product of some kind of individual perfectionism but is intimately connected with the sense that failure to use the language in a way that native speakers perceive as correct may result in a disastrous loss of face. To appropriate a language is not quite as straightforward a process as is sometimes suggested, and to represent oneself through the medium of a language that one does not speak well can be a very dangerous activity indeed.

1.3 LANGUAGE AND ANXIETY

Towards the end of Gilchrist's grammar there is an interesting discussion of the Hindustani pronouns, in which he characterises this part of the grammar as fraught with danger for the British learner:

> The proper colloquial use of the personal pronouns, is rather difficult to explain, from the great variety that exists in this particular only, and from the confusion of singular and plural numbers, that has been the natural consequence of such diversity of address to superiours, equals, inferiours, friends, &c. distinctions which are not less troublesome than odious at the best, both in conversation and conduct to those we meet with. Any particular mode in this respect may subject us alternately to the reproach of being unpolite, arrogant or servile, as the medium is indeed not easily observed in our intercourse with the multifarious inhabitants of this widely extended country. (Gilchrist 1796: 298–9)

Thus Gilchrist argues that if colonial agents attempt to speak Hindustani and do not take the trouble to select the right pronouns, they risk accusations of impoliteness, arrogance or servility. His concerns about how the servants of the Company will be perceived by Indians arise from the nature of colonial government itself. In the contemporary imagination, there is a popular stereotype of the colonial official simply issuing orders to all and sundry and never engaging in interactions of a more sophisticated kind. However, this is a gross oversimplification. In the last section the point was made that the British administration in India was not an entirely new creation, independent of all existing social practices, but depended upon indigenous systems of administration and exchange. While communication with servants no doubt consisted largely of a string of commands, the transaction of more complex business required that colonial agents negotiate a position within indigenous systems of communication, a process that required a more nuanced awareness of the status of other participants. Since Indian languages encode relative status within their pronominal systems, it was impossible to make use of them without expressing one's own position in relation to others. And to make a mistake might result in one's insulting a person of rank or abasing oneself before a social inferior. In the passage quoted above Gilchrist expresses some contempt for the stratified nature of Indian society, which he sees as 'odious' at a moral level and 'troublesome' at a practical one. But it is important to understand that this sense of disdain is intimately bound up with anxiety about the difficulty of administering the colony through indigenous structures and, in particular, through the medium of Indian languages. The array of distinctions encoded in the pronominal system forced British learners to express the way in which they perceived their relationships with others, and for Gilchrist this was as disquieting as it was oppressive and burdensome.

He continues his discussion of the Hindustani pronouns by remarking on first-person usage and outlining the distinction, familiar to speakers of modern Hindi and Urdu, between the intimate (or contemptuous) second-person form *tū* and the more distant forms, *tum* and *āp*:[16]

> At the courts, and in the capital cities of the Moosulman Princes in India, the singular *myn* I, and its cases, are mostly in use among polite people when talking of themselves, while they invariably address others *toom*, &c. in the plural, or rather *ap*, &c. in the third person, reserving the singular *too*, thou, for objects of adoration, familiarity, affection, inferiority and contempt, which will account for their *hum* we, being often rendered by our *I*. (Gilchrist 1796: 299)

Thus, although a first-person singular form, *myn* ('I'), is in regular use, it is sometimes replaced by the plural form *hum* ('we') to answer to the second-person plural forms *toom* and *ap* ('you'). In conversation with 'polite people', Gilchrist sees this usage as raising few problems. The real difficulties arise in interactions with less exalted people:

---

[16] Gilchrist does not make any distinction between *tum* and *āp*. McGregor (1972: 12–13) expresses the distinction as instantiated in Modern Standard Hindi in terms of adherence to and varying degrees of divergence from 'high honorific reference'. Thus, *āp* expresses 'high honorific reference'; *tum* expresses 'moderate divergence from high honorific reference'; and *tū* expresses 'extreme divergence in different directions from high honorific reference'.

When a native of rank applies *myn* to himself, *toom* and *ap*, to the hearer, it would be only common civility and politeness to treat him in the same manner; but to hear an inferiour or even equal, introduce himself under the royal style of *hum*, we, *humara*, our, and in that event to persist in the humble strain of *myn*, *mera*, *mooj,he*, is really a species of self degradation, that I trust the manly spirit of a Briton will never submit to, except in cases where ignorance or inadvertency may lead him astray; because even small points like this, after all may be found of more consequence in our daily transactions with the Hindoostanees, than we have hitherto been aware of. (Gilchrist 1796: 299)

A much more acute sense of anxiety is in evidence here. Gilchrist sees the use of the first-person plural, *hum*, as comparable with the 'royal *we*' in English, and, as such, a mark of extreme insubordination when used by 'inferiours' and even 'equals' in interactions with British interlocutors. For a colonial agent to continue using the singular form, *myn*, in this situation would produce considerable loss of face and, as the dark hint at the end of the passage suggests, Gilchrist sees this loss of face as a potential catastrophe for the maintenance of British authority in India. He develops this point by talking about the importance of the 'thread of opinion' in colonial government. The point of this image is to suggest the potential frailty of colonial authority. The colonial state is not an all-powerful entity, immovable and unchallengeable. It hangs by a thread, and that thread is the 'opinion' of the state's Indian subjects or the extent to which they *perceive* the regime as unquestionably authoritative. The loss of face arising from the inappropriate use of personal pronouns may seem trivial, but according to Gilchrist it constitutes another broken fibre in the thread from which the state depends, and, as such, forms part of a more general trend which is currently undermining the colonial project in India:

I may venture to affirm, that the most evident thing to weaken this thread is the fashionable debasement of our own countrymen in India, which has prevailed to such an alarming degree of late years, that the natives themselves mark it with astonishment, and time may yet discover, whether the sentimental, equalizing and depressing notions of the modern systems in Europe, have originally been dictated by finished hypocrisy, or sound policy; and whether they be at all applicable to British subjects in a distant empire, which the sword alone can permanently secure to Great Britain; let her laws and rule of conduct to the natives be humane even to impotency, in a quarter of the Globe, too, where on the one hand, mercy and forebearance will be construed generally into fear, and on the other, multiplied forms of Justice into the worst specimens of tyranny. (Gilchrist 1796: 299)

In the 1780s and 1790s, the activities of the East India Company had come under increasing scrutiny in the metropolis and action had been taken to regulate them. A landmark event in this process was the trial of Warren Hastings, the former governor-general, on charges of corruption. While these interventions were motivated to a large degree by political and economic considerations, they were frequently discussed with reference to the need for humane and equitable government in the colonies, and it is to this kind of discourse that Gilchrist is alluding here. He is constructing the loss of face in immediate encounters with Indians as the thin end of a very long wedge that ends in the systematic interference of the government in London with the effective administration of the colony. And his warning now assumes an apocalyptic tone:

> No relaxation of the reins of Government, no milky mildness of conduct, no delusive preference of the natives to our own country-men, will ever conciliate them so far as to prevent their taking complete advantage of any sinister event that may befal [sic] us as a People, whom they will always *consider as Aliens* in this country; let Philanthropists or sycophants think or say what they please to the contrary; And if an opportunity fatal to us do offer, these very harmless Indians will embrace it and expel us accordingly, perhaps the sooner in consequence of that same lenity and great indulgence, which your outragiously honest men swear must have a different effect. (Gilchrist 1796: 299–300)

So when Gilchrist warns his readers that, if they do not pay enough attention to linguistic detail, they risk being reproached as 'unpolite, arrogant, or servile', he is not calling for 'milky mildness of conduct' in relations with the colonised population. On the contrary, he is constructing colonial power as fragile and easily destroyed. Relatively subtle details may seriously undermine the authority of the colonial state, and the agents of that state should be in no doubt about how serious the consequences are likely to be. Gilchrist ends his prophetic warning by returning explicitly to questions of language and suggesting that the very fluency, the linguistic facility, of Indians makes the problems he has outlined all the more difficult:

> If action be the essence of oratory, we must admit that the people here are all orators from the plough tail, to the foot of the throne, as few nations can be more animated in that respect than they seem to be; and I have frequently noticed with admiration, the uncommon facility and fluency with which the lowest Indian expatiates upon any topick he is interested about; nor is he apt to be confused or embarrassed when detected in the commission of a crime. His answers even then are in general so pertinent and plausible,

accompanied with such vehement protestations of innocence, or fervent imprecations on actual guilt, that a man is often at a loss what to think of a transaction which bears on the face of it every mark of iniquity, and which a clown of our's would at once acknowledge, by awkwardly stretching his head, while conscience claps her padlock on his tongue. (Gilchrist 1796: 300)

Thus, the need to master Indian languages is represented as particularly urgent because of the linguistic facility of Indians, who, Gilchrist suggests, will use language as a mode of obfuscation and resistance at any possible opportunity.

I have discussed this passage from the grammar in some detail because it illustrates a point that is often overlooked in accounts of colonial language study, namely that language learning involves an inherent element of risk. In a sense this is something that we already know, at least those of us who have ever tried to learn a foreign language. To attempt to communicate in a language other than one's own is to open oneself to a multitude of potential indignities. One may utter absurdities; one may find oneself deceived as result of not fully understanding what is happening; one may suspect that others are being satirical or even abusive but not be sure enough to challenge them; or one may simply grind to a humiliating stop in the middle of a conversation because one cannot find the words to continue. But if I experience these anxieties when I try out my German in the streets of Berlin, how much more dangerous must they seem in contexts where power is contested at a fundamental level, in the context of the colonial encounter, for example? In a situation where a powerful group is already exercising considerable vigilance over possible outbreaks of resistance or insubordination, the anxiety inherent in the use of a foreign language must surely become charged with a significance that is simultaneously powerful and disturbing. Gilchrist's text, and others like it, confirm that a sense of danger and disquiet really were central to colonial language learning, and in looking more closely at the nature of Gilchrist's work, it will be important to keep this fact firmly in mind.

This dynamic is acknowledged by both Cohn and Bayly. Cohn (1996: 43–4) cites the comments of the administrator F. J. Shore, who in the 1830s compared the poor Hindustani of many British officials to 'the broken English of Frenchmen or Italians who are made objects of fun or contempt on the stage', and argued that their lack of linguistic ability 'encouraged Indians to be equally slovenly or mannerless' in return. And Bayly (1996: 289) notes that anxiety about using Indian languages incorrectly often led British officials to avoid using them entirely:

In India, the expatriate press constantly ridiculed the misuse of Indian languages by the British and poor English among Indians. It is surprising how sensitive Britons who probably knew virtually no

Indian literature were to linguistic sloppiness in Persian or Urdu. Incorrect usage would debase them in the eyes of Indian notables. It was better to speak no Indian languages at all.

In discussing these issues, Cohn (1996: 44) talks about the way in which those British officials who could speak Indian languages well were able to use this knowledge to 'manage their official persona', a formulation that aptly captures the goal of Gilchrist's linguistic research. His close engagement with the forms and structures of Hindustani can be read as an acknowledgement of the fact that, for native speakers, the details of the language had an enormous significance – that to ride roughshod over them was to invite ridicule, whereas to master them could contribute to the construction of a more robust official persona. In this context, it is significant that Gilchrist resorted to rhetorical concepts in presenting the nature of the language to his readers. Rhetoric, after all, is concerned with the construction of authority, and ideas such as 'present' and 'national' usage or the 'high', 'low' and 'middle' styles constitute elements in a theory of self-representation. The application of these concepts to the Indian context constituted an attempt to ascertain the most effective means by which colonial agents could present themselves before the colonised population, and to find an Indian equivalent for the styles of English that carried such weight at home.

Throughout his published work, Gilchrist argues for the importance of Hindustani to the colonial project. But, as well as emphasising what can be achieved through a mastery of the language, he also stresses the dangers of operating without such a knowledge. Impending disaster is never far away in Gilchrist's discussions of colonial language learning, and a sense of anxiety permeates the prefaces of his books. But, in communicating this perspective to his compatriots, Gilchrist faced certain obstacles. First, the prioritisation of the 'classical' languages – Sanskrit and Persian – made it necessary to argue actively for the importance of a 'vernacular' like Hindustani. This might not have been so difficult had it been sufficient simply to point out the utility of the 'vernacular'. But a second problem made the situation more complex. The 'vernacular' languages were often seen as intrinsically disordered and irregular. And if a language is disordered – if it has no grammatical structure – then how is it possible to engage with it? In the face of this objection, it was not enough to argue for a 'vernacular' from a purely instrumental perspective. It was also necessary to show that it was ordered and regular, or, to use the eighteenth-century terminology, that it was not a 'jargon' but a 'polite' or 'polished' mode of speech that could be 'reduced to rules'. Thus, the very act of analysing the grammar of a 'vernacular' constituted an assertion that the language was rule-governed and, as such, had to be negotiated with caution and care. The process of analysis was itself hazardous, and forms and structures that resisted assimilation into the framework of the western grammar were likely to be condemned as evidence that the language really was a 'jargon' after all. These issues will be discussed at length in Chapter 3. In the final section of this chapter, however, it will be appropriate to consider the terms introduced here in more detail – 'classical' and 'vernacular', 'jargonic' and 'polite'. It is important to realise that these terms were defined in formal as well as functional terms. A 'classical' language was not simply one that was used in certain contexts and for certain purposes. A 'classical' language was seen as qualitatively different from a 'vernacular' in both its grammar and lexicon. And this is why the technical and political are so closely fused in the work of writers like Gilchrist. To convince the servants of the Company that they needed to engage closely with the grammar of Hindustani, it was necessary for Gilchrist to show them that it actually had a grammar in the first place.

1.4 CLASSIFYING LANGUAGES IN THE LATER EIGHTEENTH CENTURY

In the later eighteenth century, the terms 'classical' and 'vernacular' had an important functional dimension. When the orientalist scholars of the period described Sanskrit, Persian and Arabic as the 'classical' languages of Asia, what they were saying, in part, was that these languages fulfilled similar functions in Asian societies to those that in the west were fulfilled by Latin and Greek – they were languages of learning; they were well-established objects of scholarship; they had long and distinguished literary histories; they were the property of an educated elite; they could all, in slightly different senses, claim the status of 'ancient tongues'. Conversely, when Bengali and Hindustani were described as 'vernaculars', a comparison was implied with the modern languages of Europe, which, despite having gained considerable ground in the early modern period, were still emergent both in terms of their status and with respect to the range of domains in which they were used. As we saw earlier in the chapter, there were good practical reasons for colonial scholars to engage with the 'classical' languages. But, in 1784, when William Jones founded the Asiatic Society of Bengal in order to promote the study of Asian cultures by the British, he prioritised the study of the 'classical' languages because he also saw them as the key to understanding the histories and hence the essential qualities of the 'nations of the East'.[17] Between 1786 and 1790, Jones delivered five lectures to the assembled members of the Asiatic Society, exploring in turn the civilizations of the Hindus, Arabs, Persians, Tartars and Chinese. Collectively these five

[17] See Cannon (1990) for an account of the life and work of William Jones. Robins (1987) also provides a useful discussion of his linguistic work, and Kejariwal (1988) explores the early history of the Asiatic Society of Bengal.

lectures constitute an overview of what Jones regarded as the 'principal nations' of the East, and formed a kind of manifesto for British intellectuals in late eighteenth century Bengal. Jones's declared intention was to establish whether the various 'nations' could be traced to a single origin or whether each was descended from a different 'primitive stock'. His method was to compare different aspects of each civilization, among them their languages and literatures, considering, as he did so, whether sufficient affinities could be identified to postulate a common origin. In a project of this kind, earlier states of language and literature are clearly more important than recent ones, being nearer to the point of 'origin' that forms the goal of the enquiry. Thus, Jones's emphasis on the search for origins and his essentialist understanding of what a 'nation' is both reinforced the classicism of British colonial scholarship in Bengal.[18]

But the terms 'classical' and 'vernacular' also had formal dimensions. According to the *Oxford English Dictionary*, both terms originate in the early modern period. The first citation in which the term 'vernacular' is used in a linguistic context dates from 1601. Prior to this, the term 'vulgar' was used in much the same way, the first citation in which it has a linguistic application appearing in 1483. Conversely, the first citation in which the term 'classical' is used with reference to the cultures of Greece and Rome dates from 1607. And it is no accident that a vocabulary for the discussion of ancient and modern languages emerged at this point. Between the fifteenth and seventeenth centuries, the status of the modern languages of Europe was transformed as they began to supplant the traditional languages of learning in a range of functional contexts and were assimilated into the grammatical tradition as objects of analysis and study. But this latter process, the production of 'vernacular' grammars, was one fraught with controversy and dissent. Some critics expressed scepticism about the idea that 'vulgar' or 'vernacular' languages *could* be reduced to rules. The 'classical' languages were eternal and unchanging – the grammatical tradition had ensured that. But surely the modern languages were by nature disordered and changeable? Would it really be possible to bring them under control in the same way that the grammarians of late antiquity had fixed the structure of Latin? In a sense, the traditions of 'vernacular' grammar that emerged in early modern Europe can be seen as responding to these fundamental questions. The only way to show that English, French, Spanish and German could be reduced to rules was through the production of grammars. And the only way to demonstrate that these languages could have the kind of longevity enjoyed by Greek and Latin was to vest authority in those grammars and disseminate them as guides to polite usage. In a sense, Gilchrist's advocacy of Hindustani, and his conviction that it could be assimilated effectively into the framework of western grammar, parallel the intellectual projects of the

---

[18] For a discussion of Jones's anthropology, see Trautmann (1997).

early grammarians of the western vernaculars. And just as critics valorised the structures of Greek and Latin while claiming that the modern languages of Europe were disordered and changeable, a similar characterisation can be found in eighteenth-century accounts of the languages of Asia. When Jones addressed the gentlemen of the Asiatic Society and discussed the languages of the Hindus, Arabs and Persians, he did not restrict his comments to the richness of their literatures or to the antiquity of their earliest texts. He commented extensively on their formal characteristics, a feature of his work which is worth looking at in more detail.[19]

One passage of Jones's discourse 'On the Hindoos' is particularly well known – the section in which he points out the resemblance that Sanskrit bears to Latin and Greek. The extent to which this passage was influential in the subsequent development of comparative philology is a subject of perennial discussion. What is less often remarked upon is the normative nature of the language Jones uses in expressing his point: 'The Sanscrit language [...]', he states, 'is of a wonderful structure; more perfect that the *Greek*, more copious than the *Latin*, and more exquisitely refined than either [...]' (Jones 1993: 34). Throughout the eighteenth century, the terms 'perfect' and 'copious' are consistently used to express the extent to which particular languages are constructed in accordance with metaphysics and logic. A language is 'perfect' if its morphology is rich enough to instantiate all the categories demanded by philosophy – nuanced temporal distinctions should be marked on the verb, for example, and concepts of causation must somehow be marked on the noun. Conversely, a language is 'copious' if it has a large vocabulary, a feature that shows its speakers to have a sophisticated awareness of the world around them. By using these terms and reinforcing them with the expression 'exquisitely refined', Jones does not merely draw attention to parallels in the structure of Greek and Latin, but makes the evaluative point that Sanskrit is every bit as effective a tool for the expression of thought, if not more so.

Jones is certainly not unique in characterising Sanskrit in this way. Throughout the eighteenth century, the Society of Jesus published numerous volumes of letters written by Jesuit missionaries and felt to be worthy of dissemination. The volume published in 1743 includes a letter from a missionary in India, Jean-François Pons, in which Pons (1743: 221–4) asserts that all the arts and sciences that were cultivated by the Greeks and Romans have also flourished among the Brahmins.[20] To prove his point, he surveys the state of the various disciplines represented in Sanskrit texts, beginning his discussion with grammar. He observes that the Sanskrit language is 'admirable for its harmony, abundance and energy',

---

[19] See Hüllen (1996) for a wide-ranging discussion of evaluative approaches to languages in the early modern period.
[20] Translations from Pons's text are my own.

stating that it was once a living language but that, as it became corrupted through popular usage, it was fixed by philosophers, who produced grammars of the language to preserve it through time. These grammarians, he says, used analysis 'to reduce the richest language in the world to a small number of primitive elements', and then supplied a barrage of grammatical rules through which the words used in discourse could be derived from them in a systematic and predictable fashion:

> Thus, provided he knows the grammar, a simple scholar can perform operations on a root or primitive element according to the rules and so derive from it several thousand words that are truly *Samskret*. It is this art that has given the language its name, since Samskret means synthetic or composite. (Pons 1743: 225–6)

In this passage, Pons is clearly talking about the Paṇinian grammatical tradition, which originated in the need to guarantee the comprehensibility of the Vedas as the languages of India evolved and changed around them. But Pons does not see the achievements of the Sanskrit tradition as purely descriptive. For him, the Sanskrit grammarians have rendered the language perfect by laying down an authoritative statement of the rules that govern it, a characterisation that clearly echoes early modern representations of Greek and Latin as languages rendered eternal through the achievements of their early grammarians. Rosanne Rocher (1995: 188) comments on the influential nature of Pons's interpretation and the fact that, through his description, Sanskrit achieved an iconic status among western thinkers as the archetype of a rule-governed language – fixed, unchanging and regular. Thus, Jones's comments fit into a larger tradition in which Sanskrit is assimilated to Latin and Greek, not only on functional grounds but because of the supposed perfection of its form.

In his discussion of Arabic, Jones (1993: 52–3) also praises the language for its copiousness: 'it yields to none ever spoken by mortals in the number of its words and the precision of its phrases.' To emphasise the point he tells a story about the 'great author of the *Kámùs*', an allusion to the fourteenth-century Arabic lexicographer al-Firuzabadi. The title of al-Firuzabadi's work derives from the Greek word *ōkeanos* ('world ocean'), which was borrowed by Arab geographers from Ptolemy, and the function of the image is to draw attention to the vastness of the Arab lexicon, which rivals the oceans of the world in scale (Gibb et al. 1960–97 II: 926–7). While compiling the dictionary, al-Firuzabadi is said to have had difficulty discovering the meanings of three particular words and to have 'sought [them] in vain from grammarians, and from books, of the highest reputation' (Jones 1993: 55). Eventually, Jones tells us, he learned them 'by accident from the mouth of a child, in a village of Arabia'. Thus, we are to understand, even the wisest and most learned cannot encompass the full richness of the Arabic language, which is so copious that it rivals Sanskrit with its 'ocean of words' (Jones

1993: 54). Speculating on how the early Arabs, despite their illiteracy, were able to cultivate their language so effectively, Jones (1993: 67) states:

> [They made] the improvement of their idiom a national concern, [organised] solemn assemblies for the purpose of displaying their poetical talents, and [held] it a duty to exercise their children in getting by heart their most approved compositions.

Again, Jones's comments fit into a larger tradition. In his *Dissertation on the Languages, Literature, and Manners of the Eastern Nations*, published in 1777, the British scholar of Arabic John Richardson states that 'the richness of the *Arabic* has been long proverbial; and many circumstances have concurred to render it [...] the most copious of any known tongue' (Richardson 1777: 4). The 'general language of Arabia', he says, derives from the dialect of the '*Koreish*', who were the guardians of Mecca 'before the era of Muhammad'. The fact that so many pilgrims gathered in Mecca led to the enrichment of the dialect with material from other varieties of Arabic, and, '[b]y this singular idiomatic union, like the confluence of many streams into one large river', the language 'acquired an uncommon fullness' (Richardson 1777: 5–7). Richardson refers us to the work of Edward Pococke, the first Professor of Arabic at the University of Oxford, and also to George Sale's translation of the Qur'ān, which was first published in 1734. Pococke (1661: *4ᵛ)[21] states that the enumeration of the different Arabic words for one single entity has often supplied the matter for a whole book, while Sale (1734: 26) praises the language on the grounds that it is 'very harmonious and expressive, and withal so copious, that they say, no man, without inspiration, can be perfect master of it, in its utmost extent'. Both Richardson (1777: 6–7) and Sale (1734: 27–8) also comment on the early cultivation of Arabic through the medium of poetic competitions. Once again, the valorisation of classical Arabic by western scholars has formal as well as functional dimensions. It is not merely that Arabic has an extensive and distinguished literature. The point is that the language is capable of serving as the *medium* of such a literature because of its formal properties and, in particular, its extensive vocabulary.

To turn to the third of the classical languages of South Asia, we find Jones, who was himself a scholar of Persian, dwelling upon the beauty of the language in a succession of different texts. It is, he says, 'rich, melodious, and elegant' (Jones 1771: i). It is 'the softest, as it is one of the richest [languages], in the world' (Jones 1772: 190). Its excellence is evident from the fact 'that it remained uncorrupted', despite the invasion of Persia by the Tartars (Jones 1773: 181). The earlier history of Persian was less well known than that of Sanskrit or Arabic. During this period, however, a

---

[21] The relevant portion of Pococke's text is not conventionally paginated but the page can be distinguished by the mark provided to guide the binder, a single asterisk.

young French scholar, Abraham Anquetil-Duperron, had opened up the history of Persian for discussion by claiming that the scriptures preserved by the Parsis of Gujarat were to be identified with the *Zend-Avesta*, the sacred texts of Zoroastrianism, previously believed to be lost. Angrily rejecting these claims, Jones (1773: 157–8) states:

> [We] may reasonably conclude that the gibberish of those swarthy vagabonds, whom we often see brooding over a miserable fire under the hedges, may as well be taken for *old Egyptian*, and the beggars themselves for the *priests of Isis*, as as the jugglers on the coast of *India* for the disciples of *Zoroaster*, and their barbarous dialect for the ancient language of *Persia*. (Jones 1773: 157–8)

And Richardson (1777: 11), echoing this denunciation, argues that both Zend, the language of the texts that Anquetil had located in India, and the script in which it was written were 'barbarous corruptions or inventions'. The language's 'harsh texture', he says, 'seems opposite to the genius of Persian pronunciation', which, like Jones, he sees as soft and melodious. And the verbal morphology of Persian, he states, is extremely regular, while that of Zend is 'irregular to the last degree' (Richardson 1777: 200 n.). Thus, Persian is valorised not only for its literature but for its sound as a spoken language and for the regularity of its morphology. While the classicism of early British orientalism derived in large part from the sense that Sanskrit, Arabic and Persian provided a key to understanding the cultures of South Asia at both a practical and a philosophical level, the formal properties of the languages were frequently represented either as a factor in the literary achievements of the language's speakers or as a product of their insight and taste.

Conversely, the 'vernacular' languages of India were often stigmatised, as the 'vernaculars' of Europe had been previously, on the grounds that they were formally incoherent and not susceptible to grammatical analysis. A term often used in this process of stigmatisation is one that we saw Jones using in his denunciation of the scholarship of Anquetil-Duperron – 'jargon'. To a certain extent, 'jargon' was simply a term of abuse, and any language that was stigmatised for social or political reasons was likely to be referred to in this way. In his introduction to a collection of essays dealing with the notion of 'jargon', Peter Burke notes that in the eighteenth century the term was used to denote 'the various kinds of lingua franca which enabled different language groups to communicate with one another', and he cites a number of texts in illustration. Daniel Defoe, for example, refers to the trade language of the Mediterranean, the original 'lingua franca', as 'the Levant jargon which we call lingua Frank'.[22] And in the preface to his

---

[22] See Cifoletti (1989) for an account of the Mediterranean lingua franca and a range of texts that mention it.

dictionary, Samuel Johnson mentions 'the jargon which serves the traffickers on the Mediterranean and Indian coasts'.[23] Burke also draws attention to the use of the term in describing the private languages of particular social groups, especially the Romany and members of the criminal underworld, the specialist vocabulary attached to the various trades and professions, and 'mixed' language, English spoken with a heavy larding of French words, for example. He notes that Diderot uses the term in an article in the *Encyclopédie*, where he says that 'jargon' denotes the 'corrupt' language spoken in the provinces (Burke & Porter 1995: 3–4). And the same term was also used of the language of 'savage' peoples. In all these different contexts, 'jargon' has both functional implications – these are the languages of stigmatised groups – and formal ones – they are 'mixed', irregular and hopelessly disordered.

When Nathaniel Halhed published his grammar of Bengali in 1778, he specified that he was attempting to produce a description of the 'pure Bengal dialect' and not of 'the modern jargon of the kingdom'. What he meant by the 'pure Bengal dialect' was 'the Bengal language meerly [*sic*] as it is derived from its parent the Shanscrit'. In the preface he states that the 'modern jargon of the kingdom' has diverged from that ideal as a result of the 'many political revolutions' that the region has undergone, and also as a result of 'long communication with men of different Religions, countries and manners', which has 'rendered foreign words in some degree familiar to a Bengal ear'. However, he also states that changes in the language have come about as a result of failings of the Bengalis themselves. In the chapter on the 'elements' of the language, its speech sounds and the characters used to represent them, he states that in Sanskrit there are three characters and three sounds roughly corresponding to *sh* in English – one 'is ranked under the cerebrals', the second 'belongs to the palate' and the third is 'a dental'. Halhed tells us that the three characters are still used in modern Bengali but that:

> The modern Bengalese, equally careless and ignorant of all arts but those of gain, indiscriminately give the sound of *sh* to each of the three characters, and apply them indifferently, as chance or caprice directs; so that there is no possible difference to be observed in their pronunciation. (Halhed 1778: 15)

Thus, the modern 'jargon' has been formally impoverished because of the failings of its speakers. Similarly, Halhed laments the loss of *sandhi*, the morphophonological processes that are such an important feature of Sanskrit grammar:

---

[23] When he writers of a 'jargon' used on the coasts of India, Johnson probably means the pidgin varieties of Portuguese spoken throughout Asia in the eighteenth century. See Yule & Burnell (1985: xxv) for a brief account of 'Indo-Portuguese Patois'.

[A]lmost any two or three consonants may be blended together, to provide for the omission of the intervening vowels. In the Shanscrit language their several forms easily unite and run together, to make one compound letter; like two drops of quicksilver upon approximation. The rules for the proper formation of these mixed characters, which shew how to remove occasionally such as are not compatible, and to supply their places with others that admit an union, occupy a considerable part of the Shanscrit grammar; but are never attended to by the illiterate and careless race of modern Bengalese: by whom propriety of diction and orthography is not even considered as an accomplishment. (Halhed 1778: 23)

By way of a final example, we might note the comments that Halhed (1778: 32) makes about the Bengali letter 'wo', which 'has entirely lost its proper use and power, in modern Bengalese', so that 'even where it occurs in words of Shanscrit origin, [it] is now universally pronounced like [...] bo'. Thus, 'wochon a word, is always bochon, with the Bengalese'. This has 'reduced them to the necessity of inserting the vowel [...] o, or [...] oo wherever the sound of W is to be preserved'. Thus 'for [...] khawaa freight, they substitute [...] kya-oyaa'. In doing this, says Halhed, they 'confuse all derivation and orthography'. This comment is significant: the implication is not merely that the practice is 'careless' but that it has obscured the etymology of terms in which it has happened. The relationship between form and meaning is no longer transparent, and as far as Halhed is concerned this is a distinctly retrograde step.

Halhed's grammar effectively constitutes an attempt to provide a description of the 'pure Bengal dialect' by means of a systematic comparison between Bengali forms and Sanskrit ones. But if this comparative study of a modern and an ancient language seems astonishingly forward-looking in terms of its methodological framework, it is very much of its time in its insistence that the Bengalis have neglected their language and allowed it to slide into the status of a 'jargon'. Like the 'jargons' mentioned by Defoe and Johnson, Bengali has absorbed a range of material from other languages as a result of commercial contact. For Halhed, this is not intrinsically disastrous, since the framework of the 'pure' language can be located underneath. But the neglect of phonetic distinctions, the loss of *sandhi* and the anomalies produced by sound change all strike him as evidence of an overall trajectory of decline. The modern Bengalis, he suggests, have shown so little interest in the cultivation of their language that it has lost many of the excellent qualities instantiated in its 'classical' parent. Thus, the distinction between a 'classical' language and a 'vernacular' is mapped onto that between a proper 'language' – a 'polite' or 'polished' tongue, to use terms that were also in circulation at the time – and a 'jargon'. Sanskrit represents the 'classical' ideal and Bengali its 'vernacular' offspring.[24] But the 'vernacular' is degenerating into a 'jargon', and it is Halhed's task, as self-appointed protector of the language, to establish its 'pure' form or, as he puts it, the language 'meerly as derived from its parent the Shanscrit'. He will not, he indicates, be able to undo all the damage, but he can at least provide an authoritative account of the language as it is.

Gilchrist's work on Hindustani both resembles and differs from Halhed's account of Bengali. The two bodies of work are similar in that both attempt to assert the claims of a 'vernacular' language and, in the process, show that it should not be dismissed as a 'jargon'. But, whereas Halhed freely accepts that the everyday speech of the Bengalis is 'jargonic' and constructs his own work as the instrument by which the 'pure' speech can be established, Gilchrist systematically refuses to apply the term 'jargon' to any variety of Hindustani that is actually spoken by Indians. The reason for this difference arises from the way in which Hindustani had been represented prior to Gilchrist's own intervention. There is evidence that, in the middle of the eighteenth century, Hindustani was seen by many British observers as merely a corrupt variety of Persian. For example, in the introduction to his Persian grammar, William Jones states that his knowledge of Persian enables him to read 'the jargon of Indostan' without difficulty. Moreover, until Gilchrist's grammar became available, most British students of Hindustani made use of a set of 'grammatical remarks' by an army officer named George Hadley, which were originally published in 1772. In the preface to this work, Hadley goes to some lengths to show his readers that Hindustani 'has nothing to do with Persian', setting out a range of equivalent forms from the two languages in order to show how different they are, and stating that the use of Persian words in Hindustani does not constitute evidence that the latter is 'derived' from the former any more than the word 'philanthropy' shows that English is derived from Greek.

But even Hadley persists in using the term 'jargon' to label the language and refers to it throughout the text as 'Moors', a term that resembles the form 'petit mauresque', which was an alternative name for lingua franca, the 'jargon of the Mediterranean'. This pejorative labelling of the language seems to have had both functional and formal reflexes. The status of Hindustani as a lingua franca across northern India and beyond suggested to European commentators that it belonged in the same linguistic category as the trade jargons discussed by Defoe and Johnson. And in this sense it contrasted with Bengali, which, whatever its demerits as far as Halhed was concerned, could at least be understood as the language of a particular territory or 'nation'. Given this functional status and the prevalent

---

[24] Halhed's account of Sanskrit is rather less breathless than that of Pons, and he takes the earlier author to task for his 'fabulous account of the wonderful structure of this dialect', by which he has 'misled many subsequent writers' (Halhed 1778: vi–vii).

association of trade languages with irregularity and disorder, it is not surprising that Hindustani was also viewed as largely ungoverned by rules. Indeed, in the form that British officials used it in communicating with their servants – and that is the version of the language represented in Hadley's grammar – it has a number of the formal features associated with contact languages, including the marking of plurality through grammaticalised particles rather than through 'terminations' on the noun. However, as we shall see in Chapters 4 and 5 (and this is a crucial point in the argument of this book), some of the features found in the most formal styles of the language – ergative morphology, for example, or the marking of certain verbal forms – were also disconcerting to western learners and suggestive of a kind of lawlessness or irrationality. It is significant that Hadley himself was unable to provide a systematic and economical account of either ergativity or the relevant features of verbal morphology, and to learners who encountered these particular phenomena in the course of using the language, they must have seemed inexplicable. I suggested in the Introduction that features such as these constituted flashpoints in Gilchrist's texts – moments when the apparent strangeness of the material under examination threatened to spark an explosive reaction from the reader. To treat such difficulties as evidence of the disordered state of the language is easier and more reassuring than to engage with them and try to understand how they work. This was a central problem facing Gilchrist as he set about the work of analysing Hindustani.

In order to understand Gilchrist's response to this situation, we need to think back to sections 1.2 and 1.3 above. On the one hand, as commentators in the tradition initiated by Cohn have pointed out, Hindustani constituted a powerful instrument of government for the British in India. On the other hand, as will be evident from my own account of the anxieties surrounding the learning of Indian languages, to speak such a language badly was to undermine the construction of colonial authority in a fairly fundamental sense. Throughout his published work, Gilchrist argues against the characterisation of Hindustani as a 'jargon' on the grounds that, to benefit from the potential of the language as a medium of government, it was vital to accept that it was indeed ordered and regular, and that to speak it without reference to its own standards of correctness was to court humiliation in the eyes of Indians. In short, Gilchrist was faced with the kind of problem that 'vernacular' grammarians have encountered in a wide variety of contexts. The colonial establishment had so far prioritised the 'classical' languages of India, which already had long traditions of cultivation, commentary and analysis. The 'vernacular' languages were treated with much less respect, on the grounds that they were thought to be corrupt and irregular 'jargons'. Gilchrist's task was to raise the status of the 'vernacular' by showing that it was not indeed a 'jargon' but a proper 'language', with standards of correctness that needed to be taken seriously.

It was the representation of Hindustani as a 'jargon' that Gilchrist was resisting when he resorted to the arguments found in Campbell's rhetorical writings and sought to represent it as the 'national' language of 'Hindoostan'. The fact that it was used as a medium of communication between people of different linguistic groups conferred on it the dubious status of a lingua franca. But as Gilchrist's quotation from Campbell suggests, a 'national' language is also recognised by people whose local varieties may actually be very different from one another. Thus, by replacing the former characterisation with the latter, Gilchrist was able to account for the distribution of Hindustani in a way that was likely to be more impressive to his contemporary readership. Similarly, by including extensive quotations from poetry to illustrate the analyses presented in his grammar, Gilchrist was able to show that Hindustani was the medium of a literary culture in much the same way that Johnson had deployed quotations from English literature in the development of his dictionary. But these functional arguments were not in themselves sufficient. Gilchrist also needed to argue for the status of Hindustani at a formal level. He needed to show that it was not an irregular and disordered 'jargon' but a rule-governed 'vernacular'. In doing this he faced certain challenges. Because of the intellectual climate in which he was working (and this context will be discussed at length in Chapter 3), Gilchrist was faced with the task of justifying forms and structures that seemed not merely strange to western learners but irrational or unphilosophical – evidence that Hindustani was not merely different but out of kilter with reason. How he did this is the overall theme of this book.

In large part, his formal arguments mirror his functional ones. Just as he attempted to represent the widespread use of Hindustani as evidence of its status as a 'national' language rather than as a lingua franca, so he often tried to replace one analysis of a problematic form or structure with another that would naturalise the phenomenon – render it less susceptible to interpretation as a defect or anomaly. As I put it in the Introduction, whenever he came to a flashpoint in the structure of Hindustani, he attempted to lower the temperature and pre-empt any explosive condemnation of the language as inherently disordered and irregular. Thus, in the technical details of his grammatical analysis he works through a politics of representation whereby the status of Hindustani as an organised system with its own rules of correctness and propriety is endlessly reiterated to his readers. Hindustani can be a powerful medium of government in the colonial state; but to treat it as a 'jargon', disordered and irregular, is to weaken the armature of colonial authority; and so the experience of learning it must be organised in such a way that British learners come to appreciate that it is a polished 'vernacular' and not a 'jargon' at all.

1.5 CONCLUSION

The colonial language study that took place in British India has often been characterised as a process of appropriation. As Cohn argues, the study of Indian languages became a priority for the British when, after years of commercial contact, the East India Company emerged in the mid-eighteenth century as a territorial power with responsibilities for the collection of revenue and the administration of justice. Furthermore, the process of studying those languages – and here Cohn includes the making of translations, the formation of scholarly institutions and the analysis of the languages themselves – resulted in the reorganisation of Indian reality as aspects of South Asian culture were reinterpreted and hence transformed with reference to European concepts. Recent scholarship has downplayed the extent to which British attempts to modernise Indian languages and literatures really had a significant impact on the communicative practices of Indian communities. More emphasis is now placed on the way in which particular conceptualisations of language infiltrated the Indian intellectual scene and transformed the ways in which both individuals and communities understood the nature of language as a marker of religious, communal and national identities. In developing an analysis of exactly this kind, David Lelyveld has pointed to the work of John Gilchrist as a significant factor in the emergence of contemporary debates over the relative status of Hindi and Urdu. These more sophisticated analyses are persuasive in a way that earlier claims about the role of British scholarship in the recent development of Indian languages were not, and they must be taken seriously by any student of South Asian linguistic history.

At the same time, however, there is another side to the experience of colonial language study. The process of engaging with Indian languages exposed individual servants of the Company to the usual risks that face people who attempt to communicate in a foreign language. To use a language other than one's own is to expose oneself to judgement by native speakers – or, indeed, by more experienced learners – to whom the most subtle details of pronunciation and grammar signal the extent to which a speaker is fluent, confident and at home in the language. Unsurprisingly, then, a sense of anxiety surrounded the use of Indian languages by British learners, something that emerges both in Gilchrist's texts and those of other contemporary writers. For F. J. Shore in 1837, the poor Hindustani of some British officials made them look like the comic Frenchmen served up for ridicule on the English stage. And Gilchrist himself warns that a considerable weight hangs on the details of linguistic performance. The colonial state, he asserts, is dependent on the 'thread of opinion'; relatively minor errors may contribute to the severing of that thread and ultimately to the loss of the Indian empire. To emphasise the anxiety that surrounded colonial language learning is emphatically not to suggest that the relationship between coloniser and colonised was one of equality or that colonial appropriations were completely counterbalanced by anti-colonial resistance. Rather, it is to identify a micro-politics underlying the larger processes commented upon by writers such as Lelyveld. The anxieties of writers like Gilchrist constituted a kind of ground against which their political interventions took place, and as such are vital for an understanding of their work.

As Gilchrist refashioned himself as an expert on the Hindustani language, he had to find a means of resisting the classicism of the colonial establishment. To argue for the importance of a 'vernacular' language was in many ways an uphill task, given the current lie of the land in the area of colonial scholarship. And the task was made more difficult by the sense, familiar from debates that had taken place in Europe during the early modern period, that 'vernaculars' were inherently inferior to 'classical' languages, not having undergone the same processes of cultivation and hence being exposed to the corrosive influence of popular use. Hindustani, in particular, partly because of its status as a lingua franca and partly because its lexicon included so many loanwords from Persian, was often perceived as a 'jargon' – a mere trade language, perhaps a corrupt variety of Persian, uncultivated by anyone and unencumbered by rules or principles of correctness. In texts such as Hadley's 'grammatical remarks', the learner is presented with constant assertions of the allegedly irregular state of the language and the limitations inherent in any attempt to formalise its grammar. And the concept of anxiety is important here because Gilchrist's careful engagement with the forms and structures of Hindustani is closely connected with his sense of the dangers to which colonial agents were exposing themselves when they neglected the subtleties of the language. To persuade them of the need to master these subtleties, he needed first to convince them that the language was not a 'jargon' but a polished 'vernacular', comparable with the 'classical' languages in the extent of its orderliness.

Gilchrist's grammatical work attempts to achieve this reinterpretation by highly technical means. At points in the grammar where the language might seem strange and hence irrational to eighteenth-century learners, he attempts to find ways of naturalising the forms and structures to be learned and assimilating them into the framework of the western grammar in a way that will minimise the feeling of strangeness and avoid disrupting the western reader's sense of the language's normality. It is in these practices that the political and technical aspects of the work come together. Writers like Lelyveld have examined the politics of representation with regard to the *functional* aspects of Indian languages, emphasising the role of notions such as 'national language' in shaping the ways in which language and languages have been perceived in South Asia over the last two and a half centuries. In this book I shall be looking at the politics of representation as it is played out in relation to the *formal* aspects of an Indian language, in particular the ways in which the technical assimilation of Hindustani into the framework of the western grammar was under-pinned by political imperatives, particularly the need to induce learners to engage with it properly by minimising the sense that it was strange, particularly when it came to those flashpoints where there was a real risk that learners would simply withdraw from the language and condemn it as inherently and irremediably flawed.

2

THE PERSONAL CONTEXT

2.1 Introduction

At the beginning of *Orientalism*, Edward Said's well-known study of 'western conceptions of the Orient', stands an epigraph from Benjamin Disraeli's novel *Tancred* – 'The East is a career'. For John Gilchrist this maxim was certainly true. The colony provided Gilchrist with a means of personal advancement more productive and more powerful than any of the opportunities that would have been open to him had he stayed in Britain. By travelling to India and reinventing himself as an expert on one of its languages, Gilchrist was able to transform himself from a relatively unregarded sawbones into a person of considerable status within the colonial community. And he saw his project not only as a means of acquiring prestige but also as a source of financial advancement. The assimilation of the Hindustani language into the framework of western thought and the publication of the results in the form of grammars, dictionaries and textbooks effectively constituted a process of commodification – the creation of a viable commercial product that would meet the demands of a new and potentially profitable market.

It is important to understand this dimension of Gilchrist's project because the political elements of his work, which I discussed at some length in the last chapter, were focused through the lens of personal ambition in ways that gave the finished texts a highly individual character. In many of his publications, for example, Gilchrist engages in vitriolic detail with the work of his predecessor and rival, Captain George Hadley. As we shall see in Chapter 5, for instance, he goes to considerable lengths to dismantle Hadley's analysis of the Hindustani verbal system and point out the superiority of his own. Gilchrist's re-analysis of the Hindustani verb had a certain political function, in that it constituted a part of his technical defence of the language against the charge that it was a 'jargon'. But the way in which that defence unfolds at a textual level is strongly influenced by Gilchrist's commercial rivalry with Hadley. In effect, the political struggle over the nature of the language maps directly onto a commercial struggle over who was to corner the market in Hindustani textbooks and thus benefit at a personal level from the remaking of the language as a commodity.

Some commentators have suggested that Gilchrist's publications are entirely analysable in terms of a commercial venture and, in the words of

David Lelyveld (1993: 673), were not a part of the 'project of the colonial state'. Lelyveld does not deny that Gilchrist's work had political consequences, but suggests that these were largely unforeseen and the result not of planning but of the dissemination of western ideas within the Indian intellectual context. In support of this viewpoint, he stresses, first, that Gilchrist was a political radical and, second, that, while he was writing his descriptions of Hindustani, the linguistic ideas of John Horne Tooke were in the ascendancy, ideas that were intended to 'undercut the mystification of philosophers and demonstrate that the language of the common people was valid and legitimate for exercising power'. Lelyveld himself provides a counter-argument to his first assertion, pointing to scholarship that explores the ways in which 'radicalism in Britain became authoritarianism in India'. However, he does not give this point any serious consideration, which is unfortunate because this is demonstrably what happened in Gilchrist's case. As we saw in Chapter 1, Gilchrist, like other writers of the period, constructs British rule in India as liberating ordinary people from the supposed tyranny of the Mughal empire. The emphasis he places on 'vernacular' languages, while certainly bearing some resemblance to Paine's and Cobbett's valorisation of English as a medium of political struggle, is connected with his sense that power should be taken away from what he saw as corrupt Indian elites and vested in the agents of the colonial state, who were to become the protectors of ordinary people. In Gilchrist's thought, the colonial regime in India is comparable not with the oppressive monolith of the conservative aristocracy but with the radical intelligentsia who favoured reform.

The same problem arises in relation to the assertion about John Horne Tooke. Even if Lelyveld is right to follow Olivia Smith in her insistence that Horne Tooke's work constitutes a plea for the vernacular,[1] Gilchrist's advocacy of 'vernacular' language study, while presented in characteristically adversarial terms, was not distinct from the colonial project but constituted an alternative perspective within it, and did, after all, win him a position on the faculty of Fort William College. The appropriation of an Indian vernacular did not constitute a subversive movement against the colonial establishment but a bid for recognition from that establishment. And Gilchrist's frequent conflicts with the colonial authorities arose not from some wish to undermine them but from his abiding sense that he deserved more from them than they were prepared to offer. In short, the

---

[1] Actually, the idea that Horne Tooke's work serves to cut through the 'mystification of philosophers' seems strange, given that it is itself a contribution to an epistemological debate about the role of sensation in the formation of knowledge. It is true that Horne Tooke attacks contemporary figures like James Harris, whose language study is often understood as having a conservative orientation. As I shall show in Chapter 3, however, the view that the ideas of Harris are intrinsically conservative is not well founded. And, in fact, Gilchrist cites thinkers who wrote from a range of political perspectives and not only radicals.

political and the commercial are closely intertwined in Gilchrist's published work. When Gilchrist says that it is necessary to learn the vernaculars well because small details 'may be found of more consequence in our daily transactions with the Hindoostanees, than we have hitherto been aware of', he is making a political point about the need for colonial agents to 'manage their official persona' more effectively before the colonised population (Cohn 1996: 44). And in making this point, he is simultaneously presenting an advertisement for his work on the basis that it will allow Company servants to achieve the goal of effective self-representation more success-fully than Hadley's publications.

The aim of the present chapter is to develop this account of the focusing of the political through the commercial by presenting a selective account of Gilchrist's life. The earlier part of his biography will be examined in more detail than the later part because it is of more significance for the interpretation of the grammatical material that forms the subject of the book. Gilchrist was certainly involved in interesting projects later in his life, including the movement for the reform of Parliament and the foundation of Birkbeck College, London. However, these events took place after his most influential texts had already been published, and while it is tempting to read the radicalism of his later years back into the work he produced in his late 30s and early 40s, there are risks in doing so, as Lelyveld's comments demonstrate. First, there is the point made above that radicalism was often transformed into authoritarianism in the colonial context. Second, there is the fact that the East India Company of the 1790s and 1800s was not an environment in which oppositional ideas could be openly expressed. Indeed, the foundation of Fort William College was, to a certain extent, a measure to counteract the dissemination of 'seditious' ideas among the servants of the Company. Thus, while it is certainly true that aspects of Gilchrist's work can be read in the light of the ideas that were circulating in the radical circles with which he was connected later in his life, the relationship is often quite a subtle one, a point that will be developed in the discussion of education at the end of Chapter 6.

The following discussion will characterise Gilchrist's life very much in terms of the opportunities that 'the East' presented for the forging of a career. It will focus on the ways in which Gilchrist exploited the opportunities that the colony offered as a means of self-transformation, building and then capitalising on a base of expertise, fighting off competitors, and ultimately attempting to establish a fiefdom for himself within the walls of Fort William College. Gilchrist was always an obstreperous character, quick to take offence and constantly in conflict with someone or other, a trait that ultimately led to the souring of his relationship with the Company. In his later years he appears a rather eccentric figure, still full of ideas but so caught up in a web of anger, jealousy and disappointment that opportunities for the realisation of those ideas became more and more limited as time passed. But his work on Hindustani had a longevity that his own bad temper could not curtail. And in his descriptions of the much-maligned 'vernacular' and his vocal insistence on the absurdity of prevalent views of the language as a 'jargon', we find the young Gilchrist engaged in the intertwined projects of envisioning his own career and developing his own perspective on what the colonial state should be. As he saw it, his career was to support the fortunes of the state by harnessing the 'national' language of 'Hindustan' to the colonial yoke, while the state was to underwrite that career, as the importance of his work became evident to an establishment previously blinded by the prejudices of its classical outlook. This focusing of the political through the medium of personal ambition had important consequences for the nature of Gilchrist's linguistic analyses, and so the material discussed in this chapter constitutes a foundation for the analyses presented in the second half of the book. When Gilchrist writes about the structure of Hindustani sentences or the morphology of Hindustani verbs, he is simultaneously presenting a defence of the language and a statement of his own authority, each informing the other in a process of mutual reinforcement. And this process can only be fully understood with reference to the specific details of his life and career.

2.2 BEGINNINGS

After Gilchrist's death, his will was disputed in Chancery and a range of documents relating to the case were assembled under the title *Appendix to the Case of the Respondents* (henceforth, *ACR*). We know that Gilchrist was born in Edinburgh on 19 June 1759.[2] According to the documentation relating to his will, his father, Walter, was a Merchant Burgess and a Guild Brother of the city and his mother, Henrietta, was the daughter of Charles Farquharson, a Writer to the Signet.[3] Walter and Henrietta married on 8 August 1756, and their daughter, Helen, was born on 18 October 1757. John was their second child. In view of their father's status, Helen and John might reasonably have looked forward to a fair measure of financial security within a well-to-do family of the 'middling sort'. But they were denied this comfortable start in life. In the very year of his son's birth, Walter Gilchrist left Edinburgh, abandoned his family and went to live in the American colonies. His reasons for doing this and the details of his progress thereafter are uncertain. A number of witnesses involved in the dispute over Gilchrist's will made statements about these events but their

---

[2] Three days later his birth was registered under the name John Hay. He later changed his middle name to Borthwick by royal licence. The Borthwicks are a titled family with whom Gilchrist's mother was distantly connected.

[3] Writers to the Signet performed certain clerical functions within the Scottish legal system.

testimony does not agree. Whatever Walter Gilchrist's motives, however, the important point is that, right at the start of his son's life, he effectively abrogated all responsibility for the welfare of his dependants, a fact that constituted a major blow to the family. When John was about 10, his mother left Edinburgh and went to North America in search of her husband. She did not find him, and eventually settled in St John's, Newfoundland, where she is said to have had further children with one John McGrath and to have 'kept a ladies' school' (*ACR* 124–5). Thus, John was not the only one to try to find financial stability in the colonies. Helen followed her mother across the Atlantic, where she too married, her husband being a man named Thomas Whicker. John too would subsequently attempt to contact his father, making 'diligent searches' with a view to finding him (*ACR* 59) and causing 'advertisements for his discovery to be published in various places' (*ACR* 104). However, his searches came to nothing.

The one thing that Walter Gilchrist left to his son was the possibility of an education. At the age of 10, John was admitted to George Heriot's Hospital, a charitable foundation providing board and education for the orphaned or fatherless sons of Edinburgh freemen, a place to which he was entitled because of his father's status.[4] Under the statutes of 1627, the institution had undertaken to teach its 'Foundationers' to 'read and write Scots distinctly, to cipher and cast all manner of accounts, as also to teach them the Latin rudiments but no further' (Steven 1859: 124). By the late eighteenth century, the curriculum was widening. A library was opened in 1756, and in the following year a master was employed to teach music. In 1766, furthermore, the governors gave permission for a pair of globes to be purchased, along with books for the teaching of geography and navigation. Accounts were taught whenever a master was available to teach them. As this summary suggests, the primary object of the curriculum was not to endow the boys with a liberal education but to prepare them for apprenticeships in the city of Edinburgh. It is true that there was provision for able scholars to proceed to Edinburgh High School and ultimately to the University, but in the 1760s the governors of Heriot's were sceptical about the quality of the teaching that the High School offered and few of the boys were sent there. The majority became apprentices, the Foundation paying for their indentures, and this was the path that Gilchrist seems to have followed.

[4] The school records include the following entry for 20 April 1767: 'The children afternamed [...] and John Hay son to Walter Gilchrist merchant burgess and gild [*sic*] brother were admitted and received to be educated and entertained in the Hospital upon this express condition that they be found to be sound of body by the physician and surgeon of the Hospital and that they be certified to be so and not otherwise.' I am grateful to the Headmaster of George Heriot's School, the Treasurer of George Heriot's Trust, and Dr Brian Lockhart, the historian of the school, for their help in researching this part of Gilchrist's life and for drawing my attention to this entry in the records.

Because he was known in later life by the title 'Doctor', it is often assumed that Gilchrist must have qualified as a physician at the University of Edinburgh. This idea appears in Chambers' *Biographical Dictionary of Eminent Scotsmen*, for example, and also in the latest edition of the *Dictionary of National Biography*. However, there are grounds for doubting this assumption. Gilchrist only began to use the title 'Doctor' when the University of Edinburgh conferred an honorary degree on him after his return from India. Furthermore, when his will was disputed, an affidavit was supplied by his friend and sometime business associate, James Inglis:

> [I]n or about the year One thousand seven hundred and seventy-four the said John Borthwick Gilchrist was by the governors and guardians of the said hospital bound apprentice to Mr. Thomas Wood a surgeon of Falkirk in Scotland. (*ACR* 252)

It is certainly possible that Gilchrist attended medical lectures in Edinburgh while he was serving as an apprentice, but there is no record that he actually matriculated at the University. Someone named 'Joann. Gilchrist' is recorded as having graduated in 1774, after submitting a dissertation under the title *De Febre anomala inter Dumfrisienses epidemica anno 1767*. However, if this is the same John Gilchrist that later wrote the Hindustani grammar, he would have been 15 years old at the time of his graduation and that would have been very young, even in the second half of the eighteenth century, making the identification rather dubious. Since study at medical school and an apprenticeship with a surgeon constituted *alternative* routes into the medical profession, the fact that Gilchrist was 'bound apprentice' in about 1774 suggests that he did not attend the University, and that it was a course of practical training that the governors and guardians of Heriot's Hospital chose for Gilchrist rather than the liberal education of a gentleman.

In his affidavit, Inglis goes on to indicate that Gilchrist did not finish his training as a surgeon. 'Some time before the regular expiration of such apprenticeship,' he states, 'the said John Borthwick Gilchrist left the said city of Edinburgh for the West Indies, and remained there some short time pursuing his profession' (*ACR* 252). There are also suggestions that during this period Gilchrist made attempts to determine the whereabouts of his father. By the 1780s, however, he had found employment as a surgeon's mate in the Royal Navy. The succession books indicate that on 24 July 1780 he was serving on a sloop called the *Scout*, and that on 20 August in the same year he took up an appointment on a 30-gun ship called the *Isis*.[5] As Rosner (1991: 20–21) observes, the cost of setting up a private practice in Britain was prohibitive, but there were plenty of opportunities for surgeons and physicians who were prepared to travel. However, an appointment in

---

[5] Public Record Office, Series DJ, ADM 106/2899, 379 and 198.

the Royal Navy was considered the least desirable of all available posts. Rosner (1991: 20–21) quotes a letter by one Alexander Lessassier, who was reluctant to become a navy surgeon owing to the 'little profit to be gained and the poor plight one's character is in when one wishes to settle in the world'. She also refers to the comments of William Cullen Brown, who taught medicine at Edinburgh, to the effect that it was considerably more difficult for a navy surgeon to establish and maintain a reputation as a gentleman than for a surgeon in the army. With these comments in mind, it is unsurprising that in 1782 we find Gilchrist travelling to India in search of an assistant surgeoncy in the East India Company. Crawford (1930: 28) notes that Gilchrist was still an assistant surgeon in the Royal Navy when he went to India, and this is rather unusual. Company servants were usually engaged in Britain and were not encouraged to travel to India speculatively. However, Gilchrist was fortunate: in February 1782 he was appointed assistant surgeon on the Bengal establishment and took up a post with General Goddard's detachment, then stationed in Bombay.

From the details presented so far, a powerful picture emerges of a young man cheated of the prospects that should have been his but determined through his own initiative to overcome the limitations of his circumstances. And it is interesting that, even at this early stage, Gilchrist turned to cultural activities as a means of self-promotion. In the late 1770s and early 1780s he wrote a series of poems, some of which were 'inserted' into the *General Advertiser*, a popular daily newspaper published in London between 1730 and 1798. In these short texts, offered up for public scrutiny in the pages of the metropolitan press, Gilchrist's desire to be – and to be seen to be – more than a surgeon's mate first becomes apparent. His efforts do not seem to have won him much acclaim, and in a poem written in 1778, 'To The Criticks' (Gilchrist 1977: 77), he defends his work on the grounds of his youth:

> Forgive ye Critics whom I cannot please
> Whats crude at first, will mellow by degrees
> The infant babe, before it walks must creep
> And little birds before they sing must cheap [*sic*].

Many of these poems are on sentimental themes, one being written 'on hearing a Young Man complain of being slighted by his Mistress' and another 'on finding a Gold finch shot near the foot of a willow tree'. But one of them, 'wrote on the American War – 1776' (Gilchrist 1977: 101), addresses an explicitly political question. And it is interesting, in view of the supposed importance of Gilchrist's later radicalism, that the poem consists of little more than a plea for peace and an end to 'faction'. The text is fairly even-handed in its treatment of the political controversy and this may in itself suggest a certain sympathy for the American position. However,

Gilchrist certainly does not take up a radical political stance, and the poem ends with a conventional call for harmony:

> Through the Main
> From Shore to Shore
> Th'Atlantick O'er
> May Peace, May Plenty reign.

The decision to master the Hindustani language and become its advocate in the British community in India can to a large extent be seen as a continuation of this early bid for attention. And the obstacles that faced Gilchrist in this project became apparent to him soon after he arrived in India. As we saw in the Introduction, Gilchrist later stated that his initial efforts to learn the language were motivated by a sense that he could not discharge his duties as a surgeon if he did not speak the language of the 'sepoys', the Indian soldiers whose recruitment into the forces of the Company had enabled the establishment of the colonial state back in the 1750s and 1760s. And when he first looked around for materials to assist him with his studies, it was the work of a pair of army officers that first came to his attention. By the early 1780s, two writers had published works in English that purported to be descriptions of 'Moors': Captain George Hadley, whose grammar first appeared in 1772, and Captain John Fergusson, whose work was published a year later in 1773. Gilchrist (1798b: vi) tells us that he 'was of course referred to Hadley for the rudiments', and in this way had his first encounter with an author about whom he was to fulminate in print for the rest of his literary career.[6] Relatively little is known about the life of George Hadley. He tells us himself that he received his commission in 1763 and became a lieutenant in 1764, '[h]aving [...] by Mr. Vansittart's favour, obtained the then great object of military subaltern emulation, an appointment to the Seapoys'. Later he was 'honoured by Lord Clive with the command of a battalion of Seapoys' and was promoted to the rank of captain on 26 July 1766 (Hadley 1772: vi). We also know that he retired from the service in 1771 and died in 1798.

In 1772, Hadley's *Grammatical Remarks on the Practical and Vulgar Dialect of the Indostan Language commonly called Moors* were published in London. Six further editions appeared, and in 1776 Hadley published a similar work on Persian, although this latter text was never reissued. Like Gilchrist, Hadley had professional reasons for learning Hindustani. In the preface to his *Grammatical Remarks* he states that, on joining the

---

[6] In his account of Hindustani Fergusson writes more respectfully of the language than Hadley does. But, like Hadley, Fergusson seems to be describing a kind of pidgin variety, and Gilchrist makes some very critical comments about his work. Since only one edition of Fergusson's grammar ever appeared, whereas Hadley's text went through several editions, most of Gilchrist's invective is reserved for the latter writer. Bhatia (1987: 77–9) provides a useful account of Fergusson's grammar.

Company's army, 'I soon became sensible that it would be impossible to discharge my duty in the manner I could thus wish, without a knowledge of the language spoken by those whom I was to command' (Hadley 1772: vi). He therefore set himself the goal of working out the grammar of the language, or, as he puts it, reducing it to a system. He makes the rather conventional claim that the work was originally intended 'for his own immediate use only' and asserts that, had he not become aware that a pirated edition had been published in London, he would never have considered publication:

> An accident determined me to do what neither the success I met with in the undertaking, the benefit I received therefrom, nor the desire of several of my friends in Bengal, could ever prevail with me to execute, and give it to the public. (Hadley 1772: vii)

The resulting publication is only 30 pages long, and does not describe the formal styles of Hindustani to be found, for example in the poetry of the Indian courts. Chatterji (1972–9 I: 245–7) uses Hadley's text as evidence for 'bazaar Hindustani', the lingua franca used between Indians of different linguistic groups in the context of commercial transactions, and some features of the variety presented are certainly reminiscent of contact languages. At the morphosyntactic level, for example, Hadley claims that 'terminations' are not used to mark nouns for number 'as in Latin, Greek &c.', but that the word 'sub (*all*)' is added to 'impersonals' and 'loag (*people*)' to 'personals' (Hadley 1772: 2). Hindustani does in fact mark plurality by morphological means, while grammaticalisation of this kind is commonly found in contact varieties. However, it is difficult to be certain which features of Hadley's variety arose from its use amongst Indians of different linguistic groups and which derive from its use by the servants of the Company. Some features of Hadley's description clearly demonstrate that the material has been refracted through the understanding of an English speaker. His system of transcription fails to distinguish systematically most of the phonological contrasts that are difficult for English speakers to detect – that between dental and retroflex consonants, for example, and that between oral and nasal vowels. These contrasts, however, would certainly be accessible to speakers of Indo-Aryan languages other than Hindustani.

At any rate, Hadley's critics claimed that the variety had arisen from the attempts of Europeans to communicate with servants and soldiers. Halhed (1778: xiii), for example, notes that 'several elegant poems and tales have been composed' in the 'mixed species of Hindostanic', but that this is not the variety that the British typically learn:

> Europeans on their arrival in India, reduced to a necessary intercourse with Mahometan servants, or Sepoys, habitually acquire

from them this idiom in that imperfect and confined state which is the consequence of the menial condition of their instructors: yet this curious system of study hath produced more than one attempt to a Grammar and Vocabulary. (Halhed 1778: xiii–xiv)

And Gilchrist himself makes a similar point:

[This variety] exists no where, but among the dregs of our servants, in their snip snap dialogues with us only; for even they would not degrade themselves by chattering the gibberish of savages, while conversing with, or addressing each other, in the capacity of human beings. (Gilchrist 1798b: v)

In this brief passage, the anxiety about effective self-representation that informs much of Gilchrist's work is already evident, the emphatic statement that 'Moors' does not actually exist beyond the context of the servant/ master relationship underlining the dangers of using it in encounters with what Bayly calls 'Indian notables'. And two of Gilchrist's successors, Duncan Forbes and Sandford Arnot, reinforce this sense of anxiety with their account of the same phenomenon. Suggesting that Hadley's 'jargon' has arisen from Europeans' learning the language by ear, 'a method by no means the most unerring', and managing to make themselves understood despite faulty pronunciation and grammar, they imply that the variety was consolidated by the mimicry of Indian servants:

Their hearers were [...] too polite to find fault with it and would naturally address them in the same style, in return, not merely as a compliment to the superior taste and judgement of their masters, but thereby having the best chance of making themselves understood. (Arnot & Forbes 1828: 16)

The subversive power of mimicry has been much discussed within contemporary postcolonial studies, the most famous theorist of this issue being Homi K. Bhabha, who suggests that 'to the extent to which discourse is a form of defensive warfare, mimicry marks those moments of civil disobedience within the discipline of civility: signs of spectacular resistance' (Bhabha 1994: 121). The implication is that mimicry is closely associated with mockery, apparently a deferential 'compliment to the superior taste and judgement' of the colonial agent, but in fact a display of satirical and subversive disrespect. Whatever the merits of this argument, it is certainly the case that, by identifying 'Moors' as the product of interaction with servants, Halhed, Gilchrist, Forbes and Arnot all gesture towards its inappropriacy as a medium of self-representation in other contexts.

As stated earlier, we know little about the details of Hadley's life, but there are hints in the sources that his family had a history of service in the East India Company, and if that were the case, it would reinforce an interpretation of his grammar as a late manifestation of the makeshift language learning of the pre-colonial period. In the summer of 1730, one John Hadley, vice-president of the Royal Society, completed work on a new variety of reflecting quadrant for the use of navigators. Such was the success of this instrument that in 1835 the *Nautical Magazine* published an account of the inventor's life and of those of various other members of his family (Anonymous 1835: 650–57). This John Hadley had a nephew, the son of his brother, Henry, and the nephew's name was George (Anonymous 1835: 650–57). The author admits that he cannot provide much information about this part of the family, but states that George Hadley was the second of Henry's three sons and the only one to survive him. He was dead by 1799 and, despite having inherited from his father, seems to have died in poverty, since 'his cousin was in the habit of allowing a little annuity of £10 to his widow Elizabeth who, in 1811, was lodging in a small house (No.36, Church-street, Soho.)'. The couple had at least one child, a daughter named Caroline-John. The author also notes that 'Mr. George Hadley is said, during the later years of his life, to have taught the Oriental languages in London', and asserts that 'this combined with other circumstances make it probable that he was the same individual of that name who died in Gloucester-street, Queen-square, in September 1798'. It seems that this latter gentleman was George Hadley, the author of the grammar from which Gilchrist attempted to learn the rudiments of 'Moors'.[7]

If this is so, then George's father was one Henry Hadley, who was born in London in June 1697 and christened in July at St Ann's, Soho. He went up to Oxford in April 1713 as a member of Oriel College but left in December 1715 to study medicine at Leiden. By December 1719 he had returned to England, where he worked with his brother on the reflecting quadrant. In about 1730 he married for the first time, his wife being a Dutch woman

---

[7] The 'other circumstances' that make this identification likely are fourfold. First, the fact that George Hadley (the author) and Henry Hadley were both employed by the East India Company is telling. As the author of the article says, Henry Hadley's involvement in the China trade might well have 'procured him those friends' through whom he could secure an appointment for his son. Second, Henry Hadley appointed 6 executors to his will but his own son was not amongst them, a possible explanation being that he was 'then at a distance which would interfere with the probability of his being able to fulfil the duties attached to such a trust'. Third, George Hadley (the author) obtained leave to resign and embark for England in November 1771 'between seven and eight months after the death of Henry Hadley, when the interval would have been sufficient for the news to reach the East Indies'. Fourth, the author of the article says that, since he had been able to find no will or papers for the administration of the property of George Hadley (the author) in the Prerogative-office, 'he may be supposed to have been possessed of nothing at the time of his death', a claim which has also been made for George Hadley (husband of Elizabeth) (Anonymous 1835: 654–5). In addition, we know that on 6 March 1772 one George Hadley, a passenger on the *Ponsbourne*, travelling to Britain from Bengal, married a fellow passenger, Elizabeth Carolina Thompson, on the island of St Helena (British Library Oriental and India Office Collections N/6/1/f.3). Since the widow of George Hadley, son of Henry, was also called Elizabeth, this provides further evidence for identifying Henry Hadley's son with the author of the *Grammatical Remarks*.

named Ann, George's mother, whom he probably met while studying in Holland. The author of the article in the *Nautical Magazine* speculates: 'It is probable that he did not succeed in his profession, for in 1732 he appears to have abandoned the very title of it, being mentioned at that time by his brother in the Philosophical Transactions, as plain Mr. Henry Hadley' (Anonymous 1835: 651). He suggests that this is why Henry entered the service of the East India Company and, in 1740, went to China 'as the fourth, in rank, of five super-cargoes on board the ships Godolphin and Northampton'.[8] Henry Hadley pursued this career for at least 10 years and 'accumulated a very considerable property from it' (Anonymous 1835: 651).[9] The Company's records for 'the China Trade' are fragmentary in this period. However, Morse (1926–9 V: 2) notes that in 1744 three ships were dispatched to Canton but were deterred from putting in by three Spanish ships of war. One of the Company's ships went on to Amoy, which had been visited by a British ship only once since 1704. Morse continues:

> Mr. Lascoe Hide and Mr. Henry Hadley, went on shore to obtain the 'Protection of the Port' against the Spanish, and to engage the services of a 'Linguister' to act as interpreter in their conferences with the officials. No proper linguist could be found in Amoy, and the only man obtainable spoke a pidgin English of such a rudimentary character that he was quite unequal to the task of acting as interpreter. (Morse 1926–9 V: 2)

The supercargoes had difficulty setting up a trade agreement and placed much of the blame on the 'linguister'. Indeed, during their visit they kept a journal, the last entry of which states that this unfortunate functionary has been 'severely bambooed' (Morse 1926–9 V: 4). The biographical article also tells us that, after the death of Henry's eldest son, John, his library was sold and that '[i]t contained a considerable number of Chinese books'. He adds that 'it may be doubted whether they had been his own or had been added by his father' (Anonymous 1835: 654). While Henry was working for the Company, China was pursuing a rigidly isolationist policy. The Chinese were forbidden to teach their language to foreigners and Chinese books could not be exported (Hibbert 1984: 4). If Henry did smuggle Chinese books home to Europe, it suggests an active attempt on his part to gather information about Asian languages.

---

[8] The term 'supercargo' denotes an officer on a merchant ship who was responsible for overseeing the handling of the cargo and all commercial activity.
[9] The article indicates that Henry Hadley died at Gray's Inn on 25 June 1771. His eldest son, John, studied at Queens' College, Cambridge, and became a fellow of the College in 1756. He became professor of chemistry later that year but subsequently trained as a doctor, and in 1763 was elected physician at the Charterhouse, where he died in 1764. The author of the article says that 'nothing has been discovered' of Henry's youngest son 'excepting that he was brought up a surgeon, and died before the middle of 1769'.

It is interesting that George Hadley's father was involved in the pre-colonial trade with China, and that the one glimpse we have of his activities reveals him desperately seeking a means of communication with the merchants of Amoy, where the lack of an officially sanctioned mechanism for interaction between Chinese and western merchants made his task extremely difficult. In the pre-colonial period, the Company did not have any real language policy and communication was left largely to the ingenuity of individual employees. Henry Hadley had been expected to exercise such initiative in China and his son, George, went on to do so in India, picking up information about Hindustani from the soldiers he commanded. Thus, George Hadley's work looks back to the experiences of his father in the days when the Company was concerned entirely with trade and not with empire. It constitutes a private solution to the problem of communication, and at this point we might recall the disclaimer in which Hadley characterises his work as originally intended solely for personal use. Gilchrist, by contrast, from very early in his career conceived his work on Hindustani as a contribution to public life. In effect, the ensuing print war between Hadley and Gilchrist represented a struggle between the older way of doing things, the ad hoc problem solving of the early Company servants, and a distinctively colonial approach to the appropriation and use of Indian languages. For Gilchrist, effective self-representation could only be achieved through a systematic understanding of Indian communicative practices, and this was certainly not to be found in the notes that Hadley had prepared for personal use and then transferred from the private to the public domain.

In condemning Hadley's variety, Gilchrist compares it to 'jargons' of other kinds. Not only is it like 'the gibberish of savages', it is comparable with 'a pedlar's speech, or cant'; it is 'viler than English butchered by Negroes in the West [...] Indies' and it is like 'a species of maritime cant'. What it is not, however, is the genuine 'language of Hindoostan'. And here he draws upon the authority of a native speaker, explaining that, after he had worked with the *Grammatical Remarks* for a short period, his teacher or 'moonshee' told him that, if he persevered with Hadley's text, he would eventually be forced to unlearn everything he had acquired (Gilchrist 1798b: vi–vii). At this point he began to collect literary materials in Hindustani, and perceived that the language of these texts was very different from Hadley's 'jargon'. He made some progress in his private studies, and then decided to write and publish a range of materials through which his compatriots could study the variety he had seen exemplified in Hindustani literature.

Thus we have arrived at the moment when Gilchrist first conceived the project outlined in the previous chapter. And the biographical detail presented here shows how that project was actually focused through the concrete situation in which he found himself. The political dimensions of his project were intertwined with his own desire for self-advancement. His work on Hindustani was the means by which he transformed himself into a significant literary figure. But, for his work to have any prestige, it was essential that his object of study be considered worthwhile, and this meant showing that the language was not a lawless 'jargon'. Similarly, the study of Hindustani was intended to transform colonial agents from grotesque spouters of 'gibberish' into dignified figures worthy of respect. And this also involved persuading them that there was more to the language than the bastardised variety that was currently used with servants. What is more, both projects would involve displacing Hadley from his position of authority and showing the inadequacy of his work. In effect, it would require a 'battle of the books' to be fought and won in the marketplace.

2.3 RISE

In the early 1780s Gilchrist's project was at an embryonic stage. To produce a published work on Hindustani he needed time for research and financial support. He found two advocates in Captain John Rattray and Dr Francis Balfour, both servants of the Company. Rattray and Balfour made an application for him to receive leave of absence and this was granted by Sir John MacPherson, who became governor-general of India in 1785, 'with a liberality, and politeness, becoming his high station and worthy the gentleman and scholar' (Gilchrist 1798b: vii). Gilchrist was to use his leave to produce a dictionary and grammar of Hindustani, and the work was to be funded by subscription. In April 1785, therefore, he travelled to the town of Faizabad:

> [T]hat I might at so considerable a distance from all my own countrymen, faithfully dedicate without the possibility of interruption, every moment I could safely snatch from the devouring jaws of Indian slumbers, to my projected work. (Gilchrist 1798b: vii)

He provides a dramatic account of this period of his life, describing his trepidation at the 'herculean task' he had undertaken and portraying himself 'shudder[ing] on the brink of a precipice, from which retrocession was not less dishonourable, than advancement seemed perilous' (Gilchrist 1798b: vii). He comments on the 'keen flashes of reproach' that he felt at his own arrogance:

> [I was] a young man, who had hardly been three years in India, and yet dared to dissent from, and teach those wise heads, who had grown grey in the service, that the Hindoostanee was a language worthy of their acquisition, in every respect, and moreover that such a thing as a jargon being current over mighty civilised empires, was a monstrous conception, that could exist no where but in their own brains. (Gilchrist 1798b: vii)

He determined, nevertheless, that he would begin work on a dictionary, and gathered around him 'several learned Hindostanees'. It seems that early on in the project he asked these informants if a dictionary or grammar were available in the language itself and was told that no such texts existed. In fact, this statement is not entirely true. Texts describing and reflecting upon the language were certainly in existence at the time when Gilchrist began work on his dictionary. As Ali Jawad Zaidi (1993: 66) points out, the *Nawadir-ul-Alfaz* of Khan-e-Arzu, which dates from the 1740s, contains roughly 5,000 words and is not an isolated work but builds upon an existing tradition. Gilchrist's insistence that such works did not exist arises partly from his determination to characterise himself as a pioneer in the field and partly from his failure to appreciate the nature of the material he was offered. He admits that his informants presented him with a copy of the *Khāliq Bārī*, a poetic glossary, the authorship of which has been disputed but which is usually attributed to the medieval poet Amir Khusrau (Zaidi 1993: 23–4). But, not acknowledging that the work was a lexicon of poetic terms and assuming that it represented an attempt at a dictionary in the western style, he dismissed it as a 'Tom Thumb performance' and 'the shrivelled mummy of an old meagre school glossary' (Gilchrist 1798b: vii–viii). The apparent absence of descriptive materials led him to compare the present state of Hindustani with the former state of English, which 'long before it had a grammar *visible to the vulgar*, was nevertheless no more a jargon, than the object of our present enquiries' (Gilchrist 1798b: viii). And this telling remark gestures towards the dynamic outlined in the last chapter, whereby 'vernacular' languages remain perceived as 'jargons' until it is shown that they are, to at least a certain extent, comparable with 'classical' ones, at which point they can have the status of a 'polite' language conferred upon them.

The supposed lack of existing materials created practical difficulties for Gilchrist but he persisted with work on his dictionary and 'in the space of a few months' collected a large body of data.[10] At this point he heard that one 'Captain (now Major) Kirkpatrick, Persian Interpreter and Secretary to the Commander in Chief' had also been working on a dictionary and that part of it had already been published. Gilchrist (1798b: viii) relates his anguished response to this development in terms that will resonate with any contemporary academic. The terrible news, he says, combined with the hard work of the preceding months, induced in him 'an alarming affection of the liver', which led him to leave Faizabad and hurry 'by land across a district flooded with water, in the very height of the rains to Benarus'. The allusion to this strange and elemental journey serves to heighten the sense of drama with which Gilchrist characteristically surrounded his work. In

---

[10] Gilchrist (1798b: viii) states that he systematically presented his informants with possible words and syllables, asking them if they had any meaning in Urdu. Thus he began with '*a, ab, abab, ababa, abach*' and proceeded through the alphabet. He also used literary sources. See Kidwai (1972: 99–107) for a critical discussion of Gilchrist's lexicography.

Benares, he tells us, he was able to recuperate and consider the situation more calmly. He decided to press on with his work despite the competition, his intention being to produce a 'double or reversed Dictionary' on such a scale that its superiority to Kirkpatrick's would be evident to everyone.[11] He also concluded that, of the two components of the work, the English-to-Hindustani section would be 'most acceptable to the reader', and undertook to 'deliver the whole in monthly numbers', setting the price of a subscription at 40 rupees.

As Gilchrist (1798b: viii–xii) tells it, the process of publication was nightmarish. The price he had fixed was too low and the self-imposed deadlines excessively optimistic. He characterises the former problem as the result of his youthful naivety and the latter as the product of his desire to provide his subscribers with constant reassurance that he could be trusted, a strategy that obviously backfired. The distribution of instalments presented huge problems, which ate into the time he could devote to his linguistic work. And he also claims that many of the subscriptions were never paid and that he was defrauded of a great deal of money by his agents, while 'not a little [was] taken up by men in my name, who had no authority to do so, and of which I have never yet received any account to this day'. His 'establishment' of informants was expensive to maintain, and the task of correcting typographical errors while living some 500 miles away from the press presented almost insurmountable difficulties.[12] The result, he states, is that he came close to financial ruin and therefore began to look for some additional means of support.

He took advantage of a scheme that the Company was implementing with the aim of developing the trade in indigo, which was to be opened to private individuals and to Company servants, the Company's ships being made available to transport the product to Britain. The aim of the scheme was to create competition, thus reducing the cost of production, raising the quality of the product and ultimately rendering the trade profitable enough to warrant the Company's involvement (Narain 1959: 97–8). In 1787 Gilchrist received permission to begin cultivating and manufacturing indigo at Ghazipur near Benares and he continued to do this until 1795, venturing also into opium production. As Bayly (1996: 290) notes, Gilchrist's activities as an indigo grower led him into conflict with almost everyone else who was involved in the trade and '[s]everal of his aggressive and litigious letters are preserved in the records of the Judge's Court of Banaras'. Both those contemporary documents and the vitriolic account of these years in the preface of 1798 underline

---

[11] Gilchrist (1798b: viii) states that late in 1785 he met Kirkpatrick in Calcutta and they discussed the possibility of combining their work. They found, however, that the 'scope' and 'intentions' of their work were 'opposite, and incompatible' and abandoned any idea of producing a joint publication.

[12] See Shaw (1981: 23–7) for an excellent account of the problems surrounding the process of publication in eighteenth-century Bengal.

the fact that Gilchrist was not a 'gentleman scholar' of the sort who had the means to develop his work at leisure. Financial considerations were never far from his mind, a fact that is connected with the catastrophe that hit his family in the very year that he was born. And when his dictionary and grammar finally appeared, the former reaching completion in 1790 and the latter in 1796, he clearly hoped that they would bring about a reversal in his fortunes.

Gilchrist's dictionary and grammar proclaim their own significance through their assertive claims to scholarship. As designed objects, both make claims to erudition and importance. Collectively they comprise three quarto volumes; their print quality is high; they include large quantities of Perso-Arabic typeface; and the grammar is crammed with footnotes. In 1798, furthermore, a set consisting of the dictionary, the grammar and Gilchrist's latest publication, *The Oriental Linguist*, would have cost the reader the princely sum of 100 rupees, the sheer expense of the material also functioning as a sign of its importance.[13] Parallel strategies are found in the description of the language. As we shall see in the case studies in Part II of this book, Gilchrist often asserts his status as a scholar by engaging with controversies initiated by well-known authorities, and an example of this strategy confronts the reader at the very start of the grammar.

In discussing his method of romanising Hindustani words, Gilchrist (1796: 1) declares his disappointment at the 'failure' of his 'philological predecessours', a circumstance that has led him, he says, to invent his own system of transcription. Gilchrist's 'predecessours' included a range of illustrious figures including Nathaniel Halhed (the author of the Bengali grammar), Charles Wilkins (the translator of the *Bhagavad Gita*) and William Davy (interpreter to the governor-general in the late 1770s and translator of the *Institutes of Timour*), each of whom had developed an original system for the romanisation of one or other Asian language.[14] By

---

[13] Gilchrist gave these three collected works the title *Hindoostanee Philology*. In a speech that he made in Parliament in 1783 on the subject of Fox's East India Bill, Edmund Burke (1981: 432) discusses transactions in which the exchange rate for the rupee stood at two shillings and one penny. It is clear that he considered this rate disadvantageous to British borrowers, but it gives an idea of the expense of Gilchrist's publications.

[14] Commenting on the work of these three writers in his own essay on romanisation, William Jones (1784: 4–8) is also critical but a little more respectful than Gilchrist. Of Davy, who advocated transcriptions based on the pronunciation and not the orthography of Persian words, Jones (1784: 6–7) says that his system is defective since it does not render the sounds of words as they would be spoken by a Persian, an observation that leads him to comment satirically upon Davy's claims to have acquired a 'refined articulation' of the language. Of Halhed's system, which, like that of Wilkins, is based on orthography rather than pronunciation and which is exemplified in his Bengali grammar, Jones (1784: 7–8) says that he is dissatisfied with the use of double letters to represent long vowels and the 'frequent intermixture of *Italick* with *Roman* letters in the same word'. And of Wilkins's system, which Halhed himself declared to be superior to his own, Jones (1784: 8) states that the major problem lies in the use of diacritics to represent long and short vowels. Since these symbols are usually used to denote long and short syllables in metrical analysis, Jones argues that to employ them for another purpose is unnecessarily confusing.

declaring himself dissatisfied with their solutions to the problem of transcription and by using the term 'failure' in doing so, Gilchrist was clearly asserting his status as a serious orientalist scholar. The one person who escapes his criticism is William Jones himself, whose essay 'On the Orthography of Asiatick Words' had appeared in the first volume of *Asiatic Researches*, the journal of the Asiatic Society of Bengal. Gilchrist (1798b: i) describes Jones's essay as 'the only valuable and scientific dissertation' that he knows of 'on this interesting subject'. But he also states that he did not encounter Jones's discussion until his own dictionary was virtually complete and was therefore not in a position to make use of it. And this too is a powerful rhetorical strategy, since it both underlines the fact that Gilchrist settled upon his system of transcription entirely unaided and implies that Jones was the only scholar who might have taught him something. He goes on to discuss his system at some length, paying attention to difficulties arising from discrepancies between pronunciation and spelling in the original language, the appearance of Arabic and Persian words in Hindustani and the fact that the language is sometimes also written in the devanagari script. Thus, in discussing the process of romanisation, Gilchrist performs his role as scholar with a bravura that at times borders on arrogance, and in much later texts he continued to present his system as one of his major achievements. In the 'succinct narrative' of his life that was published in 1821, for example, the reader is presented with no fewer than five endorsements of his system, including one from the then governor of Bombay, the Honourable Mountstuart Elphinstone (Gilchrist 1821: 14–5).[15]

Gilchrist's self-representation certainly won over an important section of the British community, and when Marquis Wellesley founded Fort William College in 1800, Gilchrist was appointed Professor of Hindustani. Having left Ghazipur in 1795 as a result of ill health, he had come up with the idea of establishing daily classes in both Hindustani and Persian for the junior writers of the Company. At that time, the Company routinely paid for its new recruits to receive lessons in Persian from Indian teachers (or 'munshis'). But the system was often felt to be unsatisfactory because the lack of a common language made it difficult for the teachers to explain the principles of the language to their students. On these grounds, Wellesley supported the new proposal, and in 1798 Gilchrist received a letter from the governor-general inviting him to

---

[15] See Das (1978: 60–63) on the debate over the romanisation of South Asian languages. Raley (2000) presents an interesting argument in which she suggests that Gilchrist's decision to present the Hindustani language in roman characters in publications after his dictionary and grammar constituted a first step towards the introduction of English as a colonising language in India. The argument perhaps places too much emphasis on Gilchrist's eccentric later works, in particular *The Orienti-Occidental Tuitionary Pioneer*, but is stimulating in its account of the politics of 'vernacular' language study.

provide lessons in both languages for the junior writers 'until they shall have made such a proficiency as to enable them to study these languages with a Moonshy'. In return he was told that, for each of the pupils that 'attended' him, he could draw the allowance that would normally have been paid to an Indian teacher (Siddiqi 1963: 73). The committee formed to examine Gilchrist's students commented very favourably on his work and in a report dated the 17 August 1800 they praised him in the highest terms:

> We cannot conclude [...] without expressing our sense of the merits of Mr. Gilchrist. That gentleman has been assiduously employed, for several years, in forming a grammar and dictionary of the Hindoostanee language, the universal colloquial language throughout India, and therefore of the most general utility. From the want of a grammar of this language, and the difficulty of its construction, it has hitherto been spoken very imperfectly by Europeans. The literary labours and talents of Mr. Gilchrist have furnished the means of acquiring a knowledge of this language with facility and correctness.[16] (Siddiqi 1963: 97)

The success of Gilchrist's 'seminary' confirmed Wellesley's sense that it would be desirable to establish an educational institution for the Company's recruits in Calcutta, and the regulation for the foundation of Fort William College was passed in July 1800. The new institution was to teach a range of Indian languages as well as a number of other subjects, including law and political economy. It is also clear that the project was intended to shape the opinions of its young students, and in particular to discourage them from engaging with radical political thought. As Wellesley himself put it in a letter to the Court of Directors:

> [D]uring the convulsions with which the doctrines of the French Revolution have agitated the continent of Europe, erroneous principles of the same dangerous tendencies have reached the minds of some individuals in the civil and military service of the Company in India. [...] The progress of this mischief would at all times be aided by the defective and irregular education of the writers and cadets. An Institution tending to fix and establish sound and correct principles of religion and Government in their minds at an early period of life, is the best security which can be provided for the stability of the British power in India. (Das 1978: 11)

This statement should serve as a warning against reading Gilchrist's later radicalism back into his work on Indian languages. Whatever his private

---

[16] It is worth noting that the inspectors consistently use the style 'Mr.' rather than 'Dr.', again suggesting that Gilchrist had not graduated in medicine from the University of Edinburgh.

views, Gilchrist forged his career in a conservative institution, where radical politics were simply not acceptable. His advocacy of a 'vernacular' language certainly resembles the position taken by radical writers such as William Cobbett, but conservative writers like Robert Lowth also deplored the lack of attention that had been paid to the 'vernacular' in the early modern period; and if Gilchrist's superiors in the East India Company had perceived his existing work as embodying radical principles, it is highly unlikely that he would have been invited to take a leading role in the foundation of Wellesley's 'University of the East'.

As we saw in the last chapter, Gilchrist's activities at the College extended well beyond the provision of teaching and included the founding of a press, the supervision of work by Indian scholars employed within the institution and the publication of a range of resources for the study of Hindustani.[17] The work undertaken at Fort William College has received considerable scholarly attention, and since the details are not directly relevant to the subject of this book – Gilchrist's representation of the grammar of Hindustani – they will not be explored closely here.[18] It will be sufficient to make two points about this period of Gilchrist's life, and both concern his drive to self-advancement. The first concerns his attitude to what Kopf (1969: 81) has called 'the race for patronage benefits'. Not content to rest on his laurels, Gilchrist strove to create a fiefdom for himself within the institution, pushing to ensure that his department received what he saw as a share of funding commensurate with the importance of the language it taught. And he also pressed for financial recognition of his own achievements, informing the College Council that, if they expected him to meet the objectives they had set him, they would need to pay him 'at least an additional 1,000 rupees annually for the laborious work required in philological research' and drawing their attention to the fact that 'the government already owed him 63,000 rupees for previous linguistic research (Kopf 1969: 81). Gilchrist's insistent approach to financial matters quickly led to a souring of his relationship with the authorities, and when he returned to Britain in 1804, it seems that the ostensible reason for his retirement, a breakdown in his health, was actually a cover story for a breakdown in his relations with his superiors. The second important point is that Gilchrist continued to see his publications as an important source of personal income; in order to promote the sale of his work, it was necessary for him to win over readers beyond the elite circles of the government and the College.

---

[17] Among the most important of the publications that he supervised are *The Oriental Fabulist*, a multilingual translation of fables by Aesop and other authors, and a translation of the *Gulistan* from Persian into Hindustani.

[18] See Kopf (1969), particularly ch. 6, Das (1978) and Siddiqi (1963).

In the very year that Gilchrist's grammar was published, a fourth edition of Hadley's *Grammatical Remarks* appeared under a grandiose new title, *A Compendious Grammar of the Current Corrupt Dialect of the Jargon of Hindostan (Commonly Called Moors)*.[19] On the title page the reader is told that the text has been 'corrected and much enlarged', and the improvements include a 'Moors and English' vocabulary to supplement the original one, which was only 'English and Moors', as well as a range of 'notes descriptive of various customs and manners of Bengal' to enhance the dialogues that had been added in the third edition. In the preface, furthermore, it was claimed that the practicality of the book had been endorsed by no less a person than Sir William Jones. He is said, on seeing it, to have exclaimed, 'This book is small change of immediate use: mine [i.e. his own grammar of Persian] is bank notes, with which in his pocket one may starve, and not be able to get what one wants. Where one buys mine you will sell a hundred.' The republication of Hadley's text was clearly an opportunistic attempt to share in the interest created by the publication of Gilchrist's work, and in the preface of 1798 Gilchrist presents the reader with a clear indication of how he viewed the work of Hadley and other rivals. He presents the reader with a survey of recent British scholarship on India, the aim of which is to represent the study of Hindustani as the one area of research that, until the publication of his own works, had been entirely devoid of merit. He draws attention to the wonderful achievements of his compatriots in recent years:

> This era of oriental literature dawned with Mr. Hastings, was illumined with the radiant spirit of Sir William Jones, [...] sparkled with the diverging rays of the Asiatick Society, and finally was cherished with a fostering hand by a sovereign Company of British Merchants, whose trade and possessions in Asia certainly constitute the brightest jewel in the crown of Great Britain. (Gilchrist 1798b: i)

And he goes on to assert that only Hindustani has languished without attention from scholars of the calibre of Halhed and Jones. It is true, he says, that there are some texts by missionaries, David Mills having published a grammar in 1743 and Benjamin Schultz in 1745.[20] However, the first is 'so crude, superficial and incorrect, that the scholar can derive little or no advantage from its perusal', while the second is a 'meagre, lame performance [...] clothed [...] in the toga Romana [i.e. written in Latin], which kindly throws its venerable shade over deformities, that would arrest every eye in the texture of a modern garb' (Gilchrist 1798b: i). Similarly, the grammars of Hadley and Fergusson have, 'in their lowering progress through our eastern sky, made the foregoing darkness still more visible'

---

[19] The earlier editions had appeared in 1772, 1774 and 1784.
[20] See Bhatia (1987: 45–50; 50–56) on Mills and Schultz.

(Gilchrist 1798b: v). By using the phrase with which Milton characterised hell in *Paradise Lost*, Gilchrist presents his readers with a forceful sense of the inadequacy of his predecessors' work. Thankfully, he does not identify himself with any particular character in Milton's narrative, but the implication is clearly that his own work will fill the lamentable gap in contemporary scholarship that the work of Mills, Schultz, Hadley and Fergusson has left wide open.[21]

However, not everyone was persuaded by Gilchrist's damning comments, and he was forced to acknowledge that the size, expense and dense technicality of his work were deterring some of his potential readers. In 1798 he published a new work entitled *The Oriental Linguist*, based on the dictionary and grammar but much abridged. In the preface he states that he has been obliged to put his works in this 'more conciliating [...] form' because of 'pecuniary embarrassments' caused in part by '[t]he sale of Hadley's insignificant catch-penny production', which had interfered considerably with the 'circulation and disposal' of his own publications. He also states that Hadley's grammar was 'intimately connected with the appearance, aim, and scope' of *The Oriental Linguist* (Gilchrist 1798a: i). Thus, despite all Gilchrist's fulminations against Hadley, the new publication was designed specifically to resemble the latter's *Compendious Grammar* and provide readers with a text that appealed to them in the same way. It is easy to understand why ordinary readers might have preferred Hadley's work to Gilchrist's. An officer in the field could hardly carry three quarto volumes around for reference, whereas Hadley's octavo volume was eminently portable. Moreover, Hadley's description of the language is more accessible than Gilchrist's. It is divided into just three sections, dealing with nouns, pronouns and verbs, and it presents the forms and structures of the language with close reference to the accidence of Latin, claiming that, like Latin, Hindustani has six cases, including the vocative, and six tenses. As mentioned earlier, it also includes popular pedagogical material, including dialogues and notes on local customs. In *The Oriental Linguist*, Gilchrist responds to all these points: the text is compressed into a single volume, albeit one of quarto size; the grammatical exposition is confined to the rudiments; more traditional grammatical terminology is used; and dialogues are included. What is more, a copy of *The Oriental Linguist* would have cost the reader just 24 rupees in sheets or 28 rupees bound, a considerable saving when one considers that, for less ambitious readers, it rendered the dictionary and grammar redundant.

But the publication of *The Oriental Linguist* does not represent complete surrender to the prejudices of the general public. Even this new work can be

---

[21] Gilchrist (1798b: ii–iii) notes that a Mr Gulston, the Persian translator to Mr Vansittart, had written a more successful grammar of 'Hindoostanee' but that it had never been published.

read as an attempt to demonstrate that Hindustani is not a 'jargon', and the new elements, incorporated in response to Hadley's text, are carefully integrated so that they do not interfere with this central goal. Thus, after the initial work of learning and analysing Hindustani, Gilchrist faced a new challenge – that of adapting his texts so that they were seen to meet the pedagogical needs of a heterogeneous readership without compromising the representation of Hindustani as a language and not a 'jargon'. Chapter 6 below explores that problem in some detail with reference to Gilchrist's approach to dialogues as a medium for language study. The main point, however, is that, even as he presents the reader with the materials that had won such popularity among learners of the modern European languages, he continually sounds a warning about the dangers of methods that he sees as all too prone to the production of 'jargonick' speech. In a sense, then, the dynamics of Gilchrist's later publications are more complex than those of his earlier ones, and at times seem to lead to self-contradiction – something that is already evident in *The Oriental Linguist*, in which Gilchrist obliges his readers by including a collection of dialogues while simultaneously decrying them as 'productive of indolence and ignorance' (Gilchrist 1798a: iv). In this and other works, Gilchrist is not merely summarising the contents of the dictionary and grammar, or abandoning his earlier principles as a result of commercial pressure, but attempting to produce a representation of Hindustani as a real language within the framework of a more popular kind of text.

In 1800 Gilchrist produced a work that effectively constitutes a revised edition of *The Oriental Linguist* in octavo form, another sign of the influence of Hadley's publication. This text was cheaper again than *The Oriental Linguist*, costing just 16 rupees in boards or 20 rupees bound. And its title, *The Anti-Jargonist*, emphasises that Gilchrist saw it as a direct response to the popularity of Hadley's *Compendious Grammar*. In 1801, however, a fifth edition of Hadley's grammar was published; the fact that Hadley himself had died in 1798 demonstrates the extent to which his text had become detached from its author and acquired a life of its own as a commodity. The following year, Gilchrist responded with two new works, *The Stranger's East Indian Guide to the Hindoostanee* and *The Hindee Directory*. The former is a duodecimo volume designed for immediate use on disembarkation at Calcutta. The contents of the latter are very similar but the text has a larger format. Both include a series of numbered paragraphs, each containing a useful nugget of linguistic information. In 1804, the year that Gilchrist returned to Britain, a sixth edition of Hadley's grammar appeared. Gilchrist responded with a further textbook, *The British Indian Monitor*, the first volume appearing in 1806 and the second in 1808. The two volumes were intended to form part of a large-scale work on Hindustani that Company Servants could study on the voyage out to India. The grammatical exposition is similar to that in the works of 1802, but, as we shall see in Chapter 7, a new and very unusual style of analysis, drawing inspiration from the contemporary vogue for etymological analysis, is also introduced. But despite all these attempts at the production of a suitably 'conciliating' text, a seventh edition of the *Compendious Grammar* was published in 1809, and just four years later John Shakespear, a new and more scholarly rival, published the first edition of his grammar of Hindustani. The struggle to communicate the distinctiveness of his work in the marketplace pursued Gilchrist throughout his productive life.[22]

2.4 FALL

By the time that Gilchrist returned to Britain in 1804 he had transformed himself into something of a literary celebrity. It was at this point that he received his honorary doctorate from the University of Edinburgh, and he was welcomed into society by no less a person than Robert Anderson, the leading light of literary Edinburgh (Nichols & Nichols 1817–58 VII: 136). He also secured his admission as Burgess and Guild Brother of the city, a position that his father had of course occupied in the 1750s, and 'caused his armorial bearings to be matriculated in the Lyon office', another symbol of his social advancement (*ACR* 178). He initially settled in London, where he gave lectures, 'which he called gratuitous', but which required his pupils to purchase copies of his text books (*ACR* 179). He also had the opportunity to take up a professorship at Hertford College, the Company's academy, also known as Haileybury, but he resigned this position after 'a few months trial' (Gilchrist 1821: 6). This understated phrase, taken from a work that was almost certainly written by Gilchrist himself, conceals the fact that, as at Fort William, Gilchrist could not negotiate the benefits that he felt he deserved within the institutional context. In 1806 he moved to Edinburgh, where he opened a bank in partnership with his friend James Inglis. In 1808 he married one Mary Ann Coventry and, according to the documents assembled when his will was disputed, 'bound himself his heirs executors and successors to pay [her] an annuity of Three hundred pounds a year for life' (*ACR* 213). He continued to teach throughout the time he was engaged in this venture, and it was in this period of his life that his radical politics began to emerge in an unambiguous form. He was a friend of the radical Member of Parliament Joseph Hume, and in 1815 he published a political work, *Parliamentary Reform on Constitutional Principles*. In the same year we find him actively supporting John Cartwright's campaign in Scotland.

---

[22] During the course of his dispute with Hadley, Gilchrist accused his rival of plagiarism; I have explored the subsequent conflict in another publication (Steadman-Jones 2003).

Cartwright, who by this stage had been campaigning for parliamentary reform for 30 years, wrote to his wife in September 1815: 'I have been at Paisley and Renfrew with Dr. Gilchrist, of Edinburgh, who is become a radical, and who, as a literary character, active, animated and zealous, will be a great acquisition to our cause' (Cartwright 1826 II: 114).

A combination of factors eventually led Gilchrist to leave Edinburgh. His commercial activities were failing and he claimed that he was the victim of political persecution. Furthermore, he was concerned that profits from the sale of his various books were declining owing to 'ungenerous competition' (Gilchrist 1821: 6). In 1816 he moved to London in order to 'preserve his large stock of literary property in that market from menaced destruction' (Gilchrist 1821: 6). Once again he resumed teaching, initially in his own house and then, from 1818, at the 'Oriental Institution', which he set up Leicester Square with the blessing of the Company. Each year he wrote a report on the achievements of his students and these, together with a range of letters accusing the Company of cheating him, and various pieces of linguistic material including a 'panglossal diorama for a universal language and character' and a 'new theory of Latin verbs', were published in 1826 under the title *The Orienti-Occidental Tuitionary Pioneer*. The 'ungenerous competition' continued and in 1820 Gilchrist published an extended attack on one of his rivals, William Carmichael Smyth, under the title *The Oriental Green Bag!!!* He claimed that Smyth had been attempting to lure away his students and wreck his reputation by playing upon his political radicalism:

> Lest the friends of my students should be falsely alarmed by Mr Smyth's horrific denunciation of me as a NOTORIOUS RADICAL, [...] I shall fairly state to them the whole of my radical propensities that have been brought into action, since the establishment of my Hindoostanee lecture-room, whence religious and political creeds have been carefully excluded, as the most dangerous shoals and quicksands for juvenile minds to meddle with, who should learn at an early period [...] that POLITICS is not an article well calculated to brighten the prospects of any adventurer in British India. (Gilchrist 1820: 67)

He goes on to develop a play on the word 'radical', asserting that, although he has not been propagating political radicalism among his students, he has been using a method of teaching that has brought about a 'radical reform' in the 'republic of letters'. This 'reform' will be discussed in Chapter 7, and the important point here is that it draws upon the etymological work of John Horne Tooke, who was also known as a 'notorious radical'. Gilchrist insists that he warns his students 'to let [Horne Tooke] alone in his political capacity', but that he does so because his doctrines are 'not suitable for *subordinates*, either in the civil or military service of the King or Company'.[23] It is clear from this observation that Gilchrist's political views had by this stage become closely connected with his sense of injustice at the way in which the Company had treated him. Even here, though, Gilchrist's emergent radicalism can be seen as flourishing in the environment of his decaying relationship with the Company, and this should not lead us to assume that his earlier descriptions of Hindustani in some sense embody a radical view of language. In 1798, when his prospects with the Company were still promising, Gilchrist writes of the need to 'fix' the spelling of English and rebukes Samuel Johnson for not being prescriptive enough in his approach to the language. And, alluding to the revolution in France, he goes on to say that, if the French had focused on reforming the spelling of their language rather than on 'disengaging the minds of men from every religious tie', they would have 'acted with more wisdom and more chance of ultimate success' (Gilchrist 1798b: xxxv).

In 1824 Smyth published *The Hindoostanee Interpreter*, in the preface to which he asserts that the grammatical section of the book 'has been selected principally from the second edition [...] of that of the late George Hadley, Esq.' (Smyth 1824: i). He states that, 'after the example of Captain Hadley', he has given all Hindustani words in Roman rather than Perso-Arabic script. This is the method that Gilchrist himself had employed after the publication of the dictionary and grammar, but Smyth provocatively points out that 'the author who has since become so great an advocate for this method' did not publish his first works until long after Hadley's early editions had appeared and can, therefore, be seen as 'in some measure imitating him' (Smyth 1824: 3). Smyth alludes to Gilchrist again when he defends Hadley as having 'considerably more merit than he has (in one quarter at least) been allowed to possess' (Smyth 1824: 3). Gilchrist must have felt as though Hadley had come back to haunt him. Furthermore, his connection with the Oriental Institution ended in 1826. It was said that he had been using his classes as a way of forcing students to buy his books and his teaching was also criticised. Chambers (1875 II: 107) tells us: 'his lectures [...] were extemporaneous and, governed by the fitful impulses of the moment, [...] a singular medley of "orient pearls at random strung".'

---

[23] This explains the title of the work. In 1795, Caroline, the daughter of the duke of Brunswick, had married George, prince of Wales. They had separated in 1796, but when George III died in 1820 and his son became George IV, she returned to England and attempted to take up her position as queen. In July, a Bill of Pains and Penalties was introduced in order to divorce her from the king. The evidence against her was held up before Parliament in a green bag. Ironically, Caroline received support from radicals, who used the affair as an opportunity to goad Lord Liverpool's Tory ministry. Gilchrist's title is apt, therefore. The work represents an answer to defamatory charges. At the same time, however, it does not deny involvement in radical politics but merely asserts that Gilchrist refrains from political pamphleteering in the classroom. See Woodward (1962: 66–9).

Gilchrist handed the school over to Sandford Arnot and Duncan Forbes but then tried to set up a rival class nearby. He was also involved in a range of other educational projects. In 1823 he contributed money to the Mechanics' Institution at the instigation of George Birkbeck and subsequently became a member of the committee. The Institution, which later became Birkbeck College, provided technical education for working men. In the final years of his life Gilchrist travelled extensively in continental Europe; he died in Paris in 1841.

Despite his financial travails, Gilchrist's estate was worth a considerable sum of money, since he owned a plot of land in New South Wales, the value of which had increased with the development of the city of Sydney. He left some of his money in trust for the purpose of promoting education, and the resulting foundation still operates today.[24] The documents assembled when his will was disputed brought to light information that is not evident in more official accounts of his life, including the fact of his father's departure in 1759. Among these documents is a draft of a letter to his mother, dated 5 March 1807, in which he states:

> I have no less than seven children, most of them young and a heavy expense upon me. Little Henrietta, your name daughter, is a fine smart girl but rather browner than my Helen. Tom is going as captain's clerk to India that we may make a purser of him in a voyage or two. Mary Ann is there already and will I trust soon get a good husband. I have Betsy, Violet, and little Richard all at a boarding-school in Hackney. I am looking out for a good wife for myself to live and die now in my native place.[25] (*ACR*: 332)

Given that he was supporting seven illegitimate children, it is little wonder that financial considerations continued to weigh heavily on Gilchrist's shoulders throughout his later life. Elsewhere in the material, we find indications that at least some of these children had Indian mothers, something that is also implied by the comment that 'Little Henrietta' is 'browner' than her sister (*ACR* 123). And there is a certain irony in the fact that, like his own father, Gilchrist was unable to share his success with his children, who, as Anglo-Indians living at a time when racial attitudes were hardening, would hardly have been welcome in the circles to which Gilchrist himself had aspired. He had used his intelligence to lever himself out of the position in which he found himself as a result of his father's departure, but in 1807 he was sending his son to sea in the hope that he might, in time, find a position as a ship's purser. As for himself, there is no doubt that Gilchrist squandered the cultural capital that he had stored up a result of the hard work he had undertaken between 1782 and 1804. His

[24] See Shuttleworth (1930) for information about the Gilchrist Trust.
[25] The original lacks punctuation and I have added full stops and commas.

relentless insistence that he was being cheated of what was rightfully his brought him into irreconcilable conflict with the East India Company itself, and it is hard to detach his self-destructive attitude from the experiences of his youth. Deprived of status by his father's departure, he again and again deprived himself of opportunities because of his constant sense that he was not receiving the recognition that was his due.

2.5 CONCLUSION

The preceding discussion is intended to demonstrate the ways in which Gilchrist's political project was focused through his personal circumstances and three important themes emerge from the narrative. First, Gilchrist used his linguistic work as a means of self-advancement, and, since he was not a gentleman scholar in the mould of William Jones, this often involved a struggle to demonstrate his abilities in an overt and even performative fashion. Whereas Jones's grammar of Persian is a virtually seamless text and presents the reader with few clues as to the process that led to its construction, Gilchrist's works often foreground the process of research, commenting upon the problems facing the eighteenth-century grammarian of Hindustani and describing how they have been overcome. By presenting his material in this way, Gilchrist drew attention to the scale of his own achievement; indeed, in the 'succinct narrative' of his life that appeared in the early 1820s, the author, probably Gilchrist himself, reinforces his claims about the importance of his achievements by quoting the words that one 'Mr. Edmonstone' uttered at 'the College Disputation, Fort William, 27th of July, 1815':

> The nice and intricate rules which govern the construction of the Hindoostanee Language; the peculiarities which distinguish that language; the elegance, the variety, and the power of which it is susceptible, were brought to light by the long and arduous labours of DR. GILCHRIST, who had the merit of exploring, by the mere force of genius and industry, the nature and conformation of that complex and intricate language. (Gilchrist 1821: 16)

It is easy to see why this passage might have been selected for inclusion in what amounts to a hagiographical biography, both acknowledging the virtues of Hindustani as a 'polite' language rather than a 'jargon' and attributing this discovery entirely to the 'genius and industry' of Gilchrist himself. In this sense it gestures towards both the political project outlined in the last chapter – that of reorganising western perceptions of Hindustani so that the language could be appropriated as an instrument of colonial rule – and the personal project described in this chapter – that of demonstrating Gilchrist's own worth as a scholar. Again and again in his published work, Gilchrist dramatises the technical process by which he assimilated

Hindustani into the framework of the western grammar; and this dramatisation serves both to highlight the fact that such an assimilation is possible and to draw attention to the fact that it was Gilchrist who had the scholarly clout to make it happen.

The second theme to emerge from the narrative of Gilchrist's life is his constant preoccupation with money – as Lelyveld (1993: 672) puts it, 'his sheer entrepreneurship'. For the purposes of this book, the most important reflex of Gilchrist's drive to improve his material circumstances is his commercial feud with Hadley. All of Gilchrist's descriptive work on Hindustani can be seen as a direct response to the way in which the language was envisioned in both the *Grammatical Remarks* and the *Compendious Grammar*. Even at the most technical levels of grammatical representation, Gilchrist's presentation of the data of Hindustani engages directly with Hadley's statements about the language and attempts to demonstrate their bankruptcy to his readers. As we shall see in Chapters 5 and 6, this property of Gilchrist's work is most strikingly evident in his treatment of the verbal system and in the statements he makes about the uses and abuses of pedagogical dialogues in language learning. His account of the morphology of Hindustani verbs constitutes an overt attack on Hadley's highly redundant analysis, and indeed this is one of the issues that led to Gilchrist's accusing Hadley of plagiarism, since the later editions of the Captain's work present a new analysis of the Hindustani verb that is closely modelled on Gilchrist's. When it came to the provision of dialogues, Gilchrist took the decision to bow to commercial pressure and provide his readers with what they evidently wanted. Even so, he worked hard to distinguish his dialogues from those that appeared in Hadley's grammar, and used the sections of his texts in which this kind of material appears as a platform to lecture his readers on the dangers of 'jargonic' speech. Once again, Gilchrist's rivalry with Hadley has both political and personal dimensions. For Gilchrist, Hadley was both the arch-advocate of a politically dangerous 'gibberish' and an unworthy commercial rival who had seduced the public into spending their money on his obviously inferior work.

The final theme to emerge in Gilchrist's biography is the development of political radicalism as a central feature of his public persona. Gilchrist's visibility as a radical in the first two decades of the nineteenth century has led some critics to assume that his approach to Hindustani must in some sense be informed by radical principles; and this approach is, once again, aptly exemplified in David Lelyveld's claim that 'his ideas about language were anti-authoritarian in the context of British thought' (Lelyveld 1993: 672). Here, however, we need to be more cautious about Lelyveld's characterisation of Gilchrist, whose early works certainly indicate that he saw the adoption of an Indian 'vernacular' as a liberatory act, but only to the extent that it would allow the 'benevolent' British regime to protect ordinary Indians from the predations of indigenous elites. And if one looks at the sources which Gilchrist used as he prepared his grammar of Hindustani, a line of enquiry that will be central to the case studies in Part II of this book, one finds him drawing indiscriminately upon the ideas of both radical and conservative thinkers. Gilchrist was certainly an admirer of John Horne Tooke and, as we have seen, by the early 1820s this fact was being used against him by critics and rivals such as William Carmichael Smyth. But in the grammar and in the preface of 1798 he also cites the work of Samuel Johnson, James Harris, Robert Lowth and James Burnet (Lord Monboddo), none of whom could be described as radical and some of whom were deeply conservative in their political attitudes. In the Introduction to this book, I asserted the importance of recognising that eighteenth-century language study, although certainly highly politicised, was not *reducible* to politics. Applying the tools of western language analysis to Hindustani raised a range of problems at a technical level, and if the ideas of a conservative thinker made it possible for Gilchrist to overcome those problems, then he was quite happy to make use of them. Gilchrist's defence of Hindustani is not built on a claim that the language use of ordinary people is always valid. His work acknowledges the eighteenth-century principles that some languages are better than others, and works hard to show that Hindustani is one of the better ones.

The political is always enmeshed with the personal at the level of human experience, and the claims that Gilchrist made for the political power of Hindustani as a medium of government have to be read against the background of his own biography. The East India Company offered Gilchrist the promise of a new life, and he showed an extraordinary level of drive and ambition in seizing the opportunities he was offered. In all his early work he emerges as an aspiring figure, asserting his credentials as a serious scholar, fighting off the threat posed by the commercial success of Hadley's work and pushing for recognition from the conservative elite that ran the Company. What he offered that elite was the promise of a more effective medium for the exercise of authority; and if he had received what he saw as adequate recompense for what he offered, perhaps the benefits of a comfortable life in the upper echelons of the Company might have led him to rein in whatever radical sympathies he nurtured during his years in India.

The question 'What if?' can never really be answered, but the fact that Gilchrist's radicalism emerged at the same time that his grievances against the Company were finding more and more vitriolic expression suggests that we should be wary of oversimplifying the relationship between his politics and his linguistic work. It is unrealistic to see the dictionary, the grammar and the 'conciliating' textbooks of the 1790s and 1800s as asserting a radical position, not least because, if they had been seen in that light, his prospects with the Company would have been damaged. Those texts are better understood as dealing with the central technical problem of how

Hindustani could be shown to be an orderly and rule-governed language, not through a radical assertion of the value of all languages but through the conventional channels of grammatical analysis. By bringing to light 'the elegance, the variety, and the power' of the language, Gilchrist felt that he was offering the Company something of real political value, and he hoped that this fact would result in tangible benefits for him at a personal level. In many ways it did, but not to the extent that he expected. And the disappointment that this caused him led him back to the radical intelligentsia – to figures such as Hume and Cartwright – from which position he articulated his anger in the strange mixture of personal and political invective that boils away in *The Oriental Green Bag!!!* and is so eloquently summarised in the title of that very work.

3

THE INTELLECTUAL CONTEXT

3.1 INTRODUCTION

At the centre of John Gilchrist's work lay the conviction that agents of British colonialism needed to engage seriously with the forms and structures of the Hindustani language. But standing in the way of this engagement was the sense that 'vernacular' languages were less worthy of study than 'classical' ones, not least because they were really just 'jargons' rather than 'polite' or 'polished' modes of communication like their 'classical' rivals. At the beginning of Gilchrist's philological career, a number of factors rendered this obstacle particularly problematic: Gilchrist's own lack of scholarly clout, the popularity of George Hadley's 'jargonist' publications and the expectations of the contemporary readership, not all of whom were the kind of gentleman scholars who attended the meetings of the Asiatic Society of Bengal. And yet, in spite of these problems, Gilchrist was in fact very successful in his attempts to represent Hindustani as a 'polite' and 'polished' mode of speech worthy of serious attention. I have argued in the last two chapters that this project was politically motivated, or, at least, that Gilchrist represented it to his readers as such. However, its successful realisation was largely the result of a technical achievement: the fact that Gilchrist was able to assimilate the data of the Hindustani language into the framework of the western grammar in a way that contemporary readers found both convincing and compelling. Before engaging with the particularities of Gilchrist's texts and examining this process of assimilation in detailed and concrete terms, it is necessary to look at one final aspect of the context in which he was writing, namely the ways in which language and languages were conceptualised in the later eighteenth century. As the preceding discussion has suggested, the idea that some languages were *better* than others – more rational, more expressive – was quite uncontroversial in this period. The aim of this chapter will be to examine the grounds on which such judgements were made, and the problems and possibilities that faced grammarians like Gilchrist as they attempted to cast particular languages in a more or less favourable light.

The discussion will fall into two sections. First, it will be important to examine the epistemological foundations of language study in Gilchrist's day, drawing contrasts with our own contemporary understanding of what linguistic work is all about. The central point here is that, whereas contemporary linguistic research normally aspires to the status of empirical science, in the eighteenth and early nineteenth centuries theoretical or philosophical statements about language did not usually derive from the empirical investigation of linguistic data but from principles laid down a priori by philosophers or rhetoricians. As a result, the relationship between theory and data was entirely different from that which we are used to. Today linguists see theory as having a provisional status. A theory is constructed in order to explain certain linguistic data, and if there is a mismatch – a lack of fit – between theory and data, it is the theory that must be rejected, or at least revised. In the eighteenth century the validity of linguistic theory did not depend on its fit with observed data but on the authority of philosophical or aesthetic argument. For example, the morphosyntactic categories of nominative and accusative were not seen as constructs designed to capture patterns of data but as logical categories that natural languages needed to instantiate formally if they were to allow speakers to describe the world in rational terms. The result was that, if there was a mismatch between theory and data, this was not seen as implying that there was anything wrong with the theory. On the contrary, if a particular language did not mark the categories of 'nominative' and 'accusative' systematically – and the ergative case-marking found in many Hindustani sentences was certainly seen as violating this principle – then the language itself was likely to attract criticism. In short, the way in which language study worked at an epistemological level shored up the practice of language evaluation outlined in Chapter 1.

Once this point has been explored, section 3.3 will examine five areas of eighteenth-century language study in more detail, focusing on the problems that each field generated for grammarians such as Gilchrist. The five areas are:

1. general grammar, namely the practice summarised above of correlat-ing logical or metaphysical categories with grammatical ones;
2. the debate over 'analogy' and 'anomaly', which examined the idea that languages operate by making functionally similar items alike at a formal level;
3. the debate over typology, which considered the rhetorical effectiveness of the different ways in which languages mark grammatical categories formally;
4. the discussion of 'harmony', which examined the aesthetic properties of spoken discourse and the potential shown by different languages in this regard; and
5. the study of the history of English, which served to explain the origins of forms in Anglo-Saxon and to justify certain philosophical approaches to language.

In each case we shall see that a priori principles developed by philosophical and rhetorical thinkers could be mobilised to produce a critique of natural languages. This is a point that has already been made by some critics, particularly with respect to the field of general grammar, and in discussing that topic it will be important to look in some detail at the work of Olivia Smith and Janet Sorensen. However, we shall also see that none of these areas constituted a monolithic field of theory with total agreement among all participants, a fact that has important implications for Gilchrist's project. Although scrutiny within any of these fields certainly could result in a language's being dismissed as strange, alien and inferior, it did not *necessarily* have that effect. In some ways the diversity of opinion within each area created a resource for grammarians interested in defending a language from criticism, and it is important to be wary of assuming that an approach such as universalism is necessarily a conservative force in linguistic thought in the way that Smith and Sorensen sometimes do. Indeed, in the last of the five areas covered here, the study of the history of English (see 3.3.5), discussions of Anglo-Saxon often proceed from an impulse to show that the modern language fits perfectly into patterns predicted by philosophy and that, if this is not immediately obvious, it is only because changes in the language have hidden the fact, as paint hides the materials from which a wall is made. The case studies in Part II will provide detailed examples of the ways in which Gilchrist drew upon the resources of contemporary language analysis as he attempted to defend Hindustani against the charge that it was a 'jargon'. In each case, the attempt to mediate between theory and data in such as way as to produce a positive representation of the language is a central feature of Gilchrist's grammatical scholarship. It is in these practices of mediation that the political and technical dimensions of his work interrelate most closely, and the issues examined in this chapter are thus at the heart of this book.

3.2 THE EPISTEMOLOGY OF LANGUAGE STUDY

As soon as first-year students embark upon the study of linguistics they are told that the discipline they are encountering is a science, or, at the very least, that it is scientific. What their teachers usually mean by this is that contemporary linguists understand the process of making knowledge in terms of the formulation and testing of theory in response to empirical evidence. The framework most widely used in conceptualising this process is probably the hypothetico-deductive model of scientific inquiry. The scientist observes data informally and devises hypotheses to account for those data. Deductive reasoning is used to work out the implications of the hypotheses and to make predictions that will be true if the hypotheses are correct. Further data is collected in accordance with more formally articulated protocols, and this data is used to test the predictions. If the predictions hold, the hypotheses can stand, at least for the time being. If not, the hypotheses are modified and retested, or perhaps even discarded. Thus the validity of an explanation is dependent on its success in accounting for observed data. Of course, there are some problems with this model of scientific enquiry. It is not clear that research within such archetypal sciences as physics and chemistry is entirely reducible to this pattern. Nevertheless, the idea that the making of knowledge is a process involving the testing of theory against evidence is very influential within the discipline, if only as an ideal to be aspired to.

In the late eighteenth century, writers also employed the term 'science' to talk about certain forms of language study, but the term was not used in the same way that it is now. Today linguistics is said to be a science because it is like the natural sciences in its concern with testing theory against empirical evidence. But in the eighteenth century, experimental disciplines such as physics and chemistry were known not as sciences but as 'natural philosophy', and when writers of the period called language study a science they were not comparing it to those disciplines. A popular text published in Gilchrist's home city of Edinburgh when he was in his final years at school provides an insight into what it meant to talk about a science of language study in the later eighteenth century. In his article on grammar in the first edition of the *Encyclopaedia Britannica*,[1] William Smellie distinguishes between grammar considered as an 'art' and grammar considered as a 'science', and he begins with a definition of the 'art':

> Grammar considered as an *Art* necessarily supposes the previous existence of language; and as its design is to teach any language to those who are ignorant of it, it must be adapted to the genius of that particular language of which it treats.—A just method of grammar, therefore, supposing a language introduced by custom, without attempting any alterations in it, furnishes certain observations called rules, to which the methods of speaking used in this language may be reduced; this collection of rules is what is called a grammar of any particular language. (Smellie 1769–71 II: 728)

This passage is clearly describing the work of a practical grammarian such as Gilchrist. And already we sense the kind of evaluative attitudes associated with the practices of valorisation and condemnation discussed in Chapter 1. The practical grammarian may well feel that the language under scrutiny is defective in some way, and experience the impulse to alter it rather than merely describe it. But this impulse must be resisted. The language has been formed by use, and the art of grammar must confine itself to providing observations that summarise the 'methods of speaking' used within it. These, it seems, are the limits of the practical grammarian's

---

[1] See Kafker (1994) on the first edition of the *Encyclopaedia Britannica*.

brief, and they stand in stark contrast to those of the practitioner of the 'science' of grammar:

> [G]rammar considered as a *Science*, views language in itself: neglecting particular modifications, or the analogy which *words* bear to *each other*, it examines the analogy and relation between *words* and *things*; distinguishes between those particulars which are *essential* to language, and those which are only *accidental*; and thus furnishes a certain standard by which different languages may be compared, and their several excellencies or defects pointed out. (Smellie 1769–71 II: 728)

For the practitioner of the science of language it is not necessary to stifle the urge to criticise the language under scrutiny. Far from it: the whole point of this type of enquiry is to work out what the essential properties of languages are – what functions they need to fulfil, what concepts they need to express – and to assess how well particular languages meet these various requirements.

What is more, one works out these essential properties not by poring endlessly over the details of individual languages but by turning to philosophy. As Smellie puts it: '[A]s it is by words that we express the various ideas which occur to the mind, it is necessary to examine how ideas themselves are suggested, *before* we can ascertain the various classes into which words may be distributed' (my emphasis). Thus word classes are not postulated a posteriori as a result of observing patterns in particular languages, but a priori ('before the fact') on the basis of philosophical principles. Metaphysics tells us that things in the world are divided into 'substances' and 'attributes'. The first kind of ideas we usually form are those of 'substances', and there is a class of word to denote ideas of this kind, 'substantives'. Next we form ideas of 'attributes', and there is a corresponding class of words called 'attributives'. And thus the argument unfolds. Reality sets the agenda and individual languages mirror reality within their own grammatical structure, some well and others not so well. In investigating these issues we need to use various branches of philosophy, including logic and metaphysics, to find out how the best minds have understood the structure of reality and the universal principles of reasoning. Then we can look at the structures of particular languages to see if they conform to these patterns. This is clearly quite different from the procedures we expect modern linguists to adhere to. Today we justify the claim that categories such as noun and verb are universal by reference to the data of particular languages. In Gilchrist's day, nouns and verbs were said to be universal categories because all languages needed to express the underlying metaphysical categories of 'substance' and 'attribute'.

The rudimentary typology of disciplines sketched out in Smellie's article derives ultimately from the classical tradition and can be traced in the works of Plato and Aristotle. Within this typology, the more a discipline is founded on reasoning and the less on experience, the stronger are its foundations. At the top of the ladder is the *epistēmē*, or 'science', which is built exclusively on deduction, the obvious example being mathematics. Next is the *technē*, or 'art', which is built on experience but systematised explicitly through a system of rational rules. Medicine would be an example of an 'art', since it starts with the experience of patients' symptoms and the effects of certain kinds of treatment but systematises that experience into a body of knowledge articulated according to rules and principles. Lower again comes the *empeiria*, often translated as 'knack', which is acquired entirely through experience without any real reflection on underlying principles. The skills of craftsmen are often seen as belonging to this category, since it is quite plausible that artisans should acquire their skills through extensive practice and experience without necessarily being able to articulate them at an explicit level.[2] Clearly, the emergence of 'natural philosophy', what we now call natural science, disrupted this hierarchy of disciplines in a radical sense. 'Natural philosophy' made claims to be the most powerful way of understanding the natural world, but far from relying entirely on deductive reasoning, it placed experience at the centre of its epistemology. In the later eighteenth century, however, language study is not thought of as 'natural philosophy' and is often discussed in relation to the old typology of 'science', 'art' and 'knack', with the speculative student of language as the practitioner of a science, the practical grammarian – Gilchrist, for example – as the practitioner of an art, and the lowly native speaker, unable to articulate the structure of his or her language in any explicit fashion, as the 'empiric' at the bottom of the heap.

It is difficult to specify the moment when the movement towards identifying language study with natural science begins. Usually, however, it is seen as taking place in the early nineteenth century, a key text being Friedrich Schlegel's essay *Über die Sprache und Weisheit der Indier*, first published in 1808, in which Schlegel calls for the comparative study of grammar on the model of comparative anatomy. This is the first of a series of metaphors in which the German pioneers of comparative-historical linguistics re-imagined language as a natural object akin to a plant, an

---

[2] In the *Gorgias* (465ᵃ), a dialogue concerned principally with criticising the claims of teachers of rhetoric, Plato says of their discipline: '*technēn de autēn ou phēmi einai all'empeirian*', 'I say that it is a knack rather than an art'. In the *Laws* (720), he distinguishes between doctors and doctors' assistants. The former study the art of medicine; the latter learn their skills entirely through experience, '*ex empeirias*'. The English word *empiric*, meaning a doctor whose expertise is based entirely on experience, derives from this passage. To the contemporary reader, it may seem strange that the term 'knack' could have a pejorative force. However, eighteenth-century writers regularly use it to indicate that a person's skills are insubstantial and ungrounded. We even find it used in a Grub-Street attack on the poet Alexander Pope: 'About this time there came to Town [...] one *Pope*, a little diminutive Creature, who had got a sort of Knack in smooth Versification and with it was for setting up for a Wit and Poet [...]' (Dobrée 1963: 38).

animal or a geological formation. And this re-imagining ultimately eroded the practice of language evaluation. One does not, after all, criticise flowers, birds or rock strata; one accepts that they are as they are, while seeking to learn more about their forms and functions. In the older typology of linguistic disciplines presented by Smellie, however, language is not conceptualised as a natural object but as a human practice. If it remains an *empeiria* or 'knack', our language use is simply a kind of habit, learned through imitation and practice. Taken to the level of a *technē* or 'art', our use of language becomes systematised and rendered explicit through a system of rules – a grammar. But when we elevate language study to the status of an *epistēmē*, or 'science', we reflect upon why language is as it is, and whether it could be different, or better. In this realm belong critical responses to style, prescriptive approaches to grammar and more radical projects including the invention of perfect or 'philosophical' languages.

There is a certain irony in the fact that the great re-imagining which took place with the rise of nineteenth-century comparativism had its roots in work undertaken in India at the very time that Gilchrist was living and working there. Schlegel's call for a comparative philology arose from his experience of studying Sanskrit in Paris under the tutelage of Alexander Hamilton, who had arrived in India in the very same year as Gilchrist, was employed in the army of the East India Company, just as Gilchrist was, and soon after his arrival developed a fascination for the languages of the subcontinent, exactly as Gilchrist did. Of course, the early texts of comparativism continue to take a highly evaluative approach to individual languages. Schlegel's division of languages into 'organic' and 'mechanical', the former being definitely superior to the latter, was, as Anna Morpurgo Davies (1998: 74) puts it, 'capable of a divisive and to a certain extent racist interpretation'. Nevertheless, while Gilchrist was struggling to show that Hindustani could be reduced to rules – assimilating the language into the province of 'art' – and, indeed, that the language was extremely effective in fulfilling the functions that languages in general have to fulfil – taking his work into the realm of 'science' – developments were taking place that would ultimately sweep away this kind of thinking entirely.

Yet in some ways Gilchrist's own work seems to gesture towards a new way of thinking about language. The fact that he was motivated to defend Hindustani in the face of criticism led him to sift through the theoretical material available to him for doctrines, metalanguage and patterns of analysis that would fit the language he was describing and allow him to develop an elegant account of it, a procedure that looks very like a kind of unofficial empiricism. The official story of how linguistics became empirical focuses largely on the great thinkers of the comparativist movement – Schlegel, Bopp, Grimm, Rask – and their response to the striking resemblance of Sanskrit to the classical languages of Europe along with the intellectual problems posed by this resemblance. But the perceived

strangeness of languages like Hindustani and the conviction of grammarians like Gilchrist that they had to be assimilated into the theoretical
framework of western language study, if only for political reasons, can also
be seen as motivating a movement away from knee-jerk condemnation
towards a more critical engagement with linguistic theory. We shall see
examples of this kind of unofficial empiricism in the case studies in Part II
of this book, and the final section of this chapter will also examine the role
of scientific metaphor in Gilchrist's self-representation. What is important
here, though, is to acknowledge that Gilchrist was drawn to comment on
the 'science of grammar', in Smellie's sense of the term, precisely because
that 'science' threatened to cast the language he was so keen to valorise in a
potentially damaging light. The next part of the chapter will, therefore, look
more closely at the link between language study and language evaluation in
the later eighteenth century, focusing on five areas of inquiry that had
implications for Gilchrist's work on Hindustani.

3.3 FIVE AREAS OF LANGUAGE STUDY

3.3.1 *General grammar*

Much of William Smellie's discussion of the 'science of grammar' is taken
up with an explanation of why natural languages have grammatical
categories such as 'nouns substantive', 'pronouns', 'nouns attributive',
'verbs' and so on. This explanation depends upon the idea that the structure
of language reflects both the structure of reality and the forms of human
reasoning. The grammatical categories of human languages are said to
correspond to ontological and logical categories that can be uncovered
through philosophical investigation, and the more effectively a language
instantiates these categories, the more powerful it is said to be as a medium
of communication and thought. Smellie is far from unique in seeing these
issues as central to the study of language. The practice of correlating
grammatical and philosophical categories is central to much of the
linguistic scholarship of the period, and this trend is often said to have
been initiated in the famous 'Port-Royal Grammar' of 1660. This text, more
properly known as the *Grammaire générale et raisonnée*, was the result of a
collaboration between a language teacher, Claude Lancelot, and a logician,
Antoine Arnauld, both associated with the Jansenist college at Port-Royal
in France. The stated aim of the work was to investigate the 'causes' of
language, the reasons that human language is as it is, and it followed very
much the procedures outlined here, using examples drawn mainly from
Latin and French to illustrate its claims. However, while it is true that the
'Port-Royal Grammar' was highly influential in Britain for the century and
half after its publication, Gilchrist's excursions into general grammar tend

to make reference to other writers, usually British ones. In particular he alludes to John Wilkins's *Essay towards a Real Character and a Philosophical Language*, first published in 1668, and James Harris's *Hermes*, which appeared in 1751.[3]

Wilkins's *Essay* constitutes a lengthy proposal for a new philosophical language that will avoid the many pitfalls into which existing human languages have fallen, and thus provide a rational and universal means of communication of particular benefit to the growing class of people interested in natural science. Earlier in the century, Francis Bacon had been critical of the role of language in the making of knowledge, pointing out that human languages often characterise the world in a very misleading fashion. Wilkins's project, sponsored by the Royal Society, was intended to overcome these 'idols of the marketplace' by offering a new means of communication that would reflect the nature of reality more accurately than any language currently available to scholars. Wilkins (1668: 19) argued that such a language was necessary because it was impossible to improve existing ones. Various attempts had been made to do so, but 'so invincible is Custom, that still we retain the same errors and incongruities [...] which our Forefathers taught us'. The problem is, he says, that grammar, 'that very Art by which Language should be regulated', is of very much '*later* invention *than Languages themselves*'. The result is that the art is adapted to its existing subject matter and hence is in no position to reform it, a point clearly echoed in Smellie's account of the art and science of grammar, where we are told that the 'art of grammar' must adapt itself to its subject matter, whereas the 'science of grammar' must free itself from the particularities of individual languages and consider how language *should* be.[4] For Wilkins, the only way out of this vicious circle is to develop an entirely new language. The first stage in this process will be the formation of a lexicon built upon a rational and all-encompassing description of reality, and this is the part of Wilkins's project that has attracted most attention from scholars. But Wilkins also suggests that the new language must have a grammar that will perfectly embody all that is essential and necessary to language, the devising of which leads him into the practice of correlating grammatical and philosophical categories that is at the heart of general grammar.[5]

---

[3] See Probyn (1991) for an account of the life and work of James Harris, and Miyawaki (2002) for a discussion of his approach to general grammar.

[4] In the preface to his dictionary and grammar, Gilchrist (1798b: xviii n.) quotes a passage by the Scottish philosopher Dugald Stewart in which a very similar point is made: '[The errors in reasoning to which words give rise] will appear the less surprising, when we consider that all the languages which have hitherto existed in the world, have derived their origin from popular use; and that their application to philosophical purposes was altogether out of the view of those men who first employed them.'

[5] See Salmon (1979: 97–126) on the sources that Wilkins drew upon in devising his 'natural grammar' and Subbiondo (1992) on the context of his work.

Whereas Wilkins's *Essay* has an avowedly practical purpose – the construction of a 'philosophical' language – the preface to James Harris's *Hermes* suggests rather different reasons for studying general grammar. '*There are*', Harris (1751: xiii) states, '*few Sciences more intrinsically valuable than* MATHEMATICS.' And mathematics is valuable both because of its utility and because it is '*the noblest Praxis of* LOGIC, *or* UNIVERSAL REASONING'. His point is that mathematics is a discipline that operates largely by applying the principles of deductive reasoning to '*the Predicament of* Quantity', and as such provides an excellent training in logic, while also providing opportunities for reflection on the mental operations involved in logical reasoning. This valorisation of deductive reasoning is reminiscent of the typology of disciplines in which the *epistēmai* are at the top, distant from experience and deductively grounded, while the *empeiriai* are at the bottom, built entirely on experience with no rational systematisation at all. But Harris (1751: xiv) goes on to say that, despite its undoubted virtues, there is a danger when mathematics is used '*not to exemplify* LOGIC, *but to supply its place*'. When this happens, the universal principles of reasoning are neglected and people imagine that the study of 'Lines and Numbers' constitutes all there is to say on the matter. Thus he implies that even mathematics is too particular to form a real foundation for learning, and that the application of 'universal reasoning' to another issue – the nature of language – will provide a way to draw attention to the fact that logic is more abstract than mathematics and applicable to categories other than 'the predicament of quantity'. Harris's ambivalence over the role of mathematics in contemporary learning may seem strange to contemporary readers, and has a lot to do with the importance of mathematics in natural science. For Harris, what is powerful about mathematics is that it does not depend upon experience for its validity, and so its becoming enmeshed with a form of inquiry that prioritises experience to the extent that natural science does is problematic in that it may distract enquiring minds away from what is truly valuable about mathematical learning.

As this introductory discussion suggests, general grammar played a variety of roles in the intellectual life of the seventeenth and eighteenth centuries – as a necessary preliminary to the creation of a new language of scholarship and as a way of encouraging enquiring young minds to look beyond 'lines and numbers' to the basis of rational thought itself. The reason that this kind of material makes an appearance in Gilchrist's work is that, in investigating what is essential and necessary to language, thinkers like Wilkins and Harris set out requirements for human languages – categories that must be fulfilled if a language is to function effectively as a medium of communication and thought. And if a language that is only now being analysed according to the principles of western grammar does not instantiate those categories, there is a risk that it will seem irrational or unphilosophical. However, lest it be thought that general grammar was an entirely conservative force in eighteenth-century language study, it will be important to consider a claim that is sometimes made about the alleged valorisation of 'classical' languages within the field. In her influential discussion of eighteenth-century language study, *The Politics of Language 1791–1819*, for example, Olivia Smith characterises general grammar as a reductively political practice. Since a classical education was the preserve of a social elite, she argues, the valorisation of classical languages within general grammar served to justify the insistence that 'vernaculars' should aspire to be as much like 'classical' languages as possible, and thus, functioned to exclude the less privileged from serious public discourse. But this is a simplistic account of the field. For Wilkins, Latin and Greek were as open to criticism as any other languages. Indeed, his *Essay* includes an extensive critique of the grammar of Latin, the point of which is to show that, despite having functioned as a lingua franca in learned circles for centuries, it was really not fit for the purpose and was vastly inferior to the new language that Wilkins himself was devising. And even in the work of Harris, who shows much more respect for the traditional languages of western learning, the possibility of criticism is left open.

Commenting on Harris's discussion of the verbal category of tense, Smith (1984: 23) states: 'Harris argues that any language with less than [...] twelve tenses, the number of those in Greek, is necessarily corrupt.' Now it is simply not the case that Greek has 12 tenses; nor is it true that eighteenth-century grammarians thought it did. What Harris actually does in his discussion is to develop a matrix of 12 *possible* tenses. He begins by pointing out that time can be thought of in three different ways – as past, as present, or as future – and then suggests that each subdivision can be broken down further in terms of whether the action is 'inceptive' (about to happen), 'middle' (in process), 'completive' (finished) or 'aorist' (not specified in these terms). In effect he projects a series of imaginable tenses by a process of logical subdivision. It is true that he is working with distinctions that are relevant to the analysis of Greek. The term 'aorist', for example, was and is used of a form of the Greek verb that characterises an action as past without any of the aspectual information associated with the language's other past forms. But Harris pushes these distinctions beyond what is required for the explanation of Greek itself. The Greek aorist is quite definitely a past form, and it is not conventional to claim that the language also has present and future aorists. In order to *find* present and future aorists, Harris has to use periphrastic forms that would not have been described as 'tenses' in any conventional grammar of Greek. These involve the construction of a participle or infinitive with a lexical verb such as *mellō* ('be about to') or *tugchanō* ('be in the midst of'). Furthermore, he also provides a set of English forms that express the very same set of distinctions.

There is thus a certain irony in the fact that Smith has chosen this passage to argue for the reductively political nature of eighteenth-century classicism. Far from supporting this claim, Harris's discussion of tense actually demonstrates the importance of philosophical issues in mediating the evaluation of languages in that period. It was not sufficient simply to assert that Greek was better than other languages. It was necessary to argue for that position on the basis that Greek instantiated the categories required for the adequate description of reality better than its rivals. And in this respect Harris's argument is in fact rather delicate. Having elaborated a schema by using all the temporal and aspectual distinctions he can think of, he has to fill the schema up with dubious periphrastic forms masquerading as 'tenses'. Indeed, the Greek verbal system seems to contain the seeds of its own critique, in the sense that the existence of a past form specified for aspect in a particular fashion seems to imply the possibility of similarly specified present and future forms that do not actually exist and have to be invented. Finally, as Michael (1970: 412) points out, the scheme was subsequently rejected on the philosophical grounds that the inceptive tenses collapse conceptually into the future ones: Harris's English example of an 'inceptive present' is 'am going to write', for example, which seems to belong straightforwardly to the 'future' category.

Similarly, in her account of the eighteenth-century linguistic relationship between England and Scotland, Janet Sorensen (2000: 172–96) discusses the Scots Gaelic grammar of William Shaw, pointing out that Shaw cites Harris's *Hermes* as one of the texts he 'found of the most use' in preparing it. She goes on to point to a number of ways in which Shaw's universalist conception of language created problems for Gaelic, and some of these are indeed very plausible. But in discussing the verbal system, she is so convinced that Shaw is 'forcing Gaelic into an equivalent Latin structure' that she misreads what he has to say about verbal forms:

> While linguistic relativists make much of the significance of the tense structures of a particular language in relation to the particular world view of its speakers, Shaw rejects the possibility of distinct tense structures in different languages, writing, "Some say a language has only as many tenses as are regularly formed without the auxiliary, yet I am of opinion, a verb cannot be better conjugated than by stating it in all its different times of action whatsoever". (Sorensen 2000: 183, citing Shaw 1778: 46)

Sorensen clearly sees Shaw's comment as a rejection of particularism and specificity. Yet his point is that, rather than only counting forms created through the addition of a termination as tenses, periphrastic forms involving an auxiliary should also be included. This decision would have important implications for the way in which a language was viewed. For example, if grammarians of English only included tenses that were 'formed without the auxiliary', they would have just two to point to: a present form, *love*, and a past form, *loved*. However, if periphrastic forms involving auxiliaries were also counted, English could then be shown to have many more: *have loved*, *has loved*, *is loving* and so on. Of course, modern linguists might well argue that, if tense is systematically distinguished from aspect, many of these forms actually contrast in terms of the former not the latter. For an eighteenth-century grammarian, however, this distinction was not clearly articulated, and what was really at stake was how rich the language was in verbal forms rather than precisely how many of them expressed distinctions of time. By suggesting that 'a verb cannot be better conjugated than by stating it in all its different times of action', Shaw is acknowledging that not all languages have tense systems like Latin and Greek, where auxiliary verbs are relatively unimportant, and that in many of the modern languages of Europe it is desirable to include forms with auxiliaries in order to show the full resources of the languages. Again, there is a certain irony that in Shaw's call for forms with auxiliaries to be gathered into the fold as proper tenses, he is echoing Harris, who opens up the Greek verbal system in a very unconventional fashion to include periphrastic forms with *mellō* and *tugchanō*. Even Greek can be made to look better if one follows this strategy.

Similar things can be seen happening in both Wilkins's and Harris's account of noun case. It is by now a commonplace of writing on early vernacular grammars that they frequently apply the category of noun case to modern languages that do not, in fact, have case endings. Indeed, one of Sorensen's criticisms of Shaw is that he insists on citing Gaelic forms under all five headings of the Latin declensional system when the language does not have five forms corresponding to these various functional categories. However, the notion that all languages 'should' have five cases is certainly not propagated by either Wilkins or Harris. Wilkins absolutely denies that cases are an essential and necessary feature of a language, and states that there will be none in his 'philosophical' language. The ideas signified by the nominative and accusative cases are better expressed by positioning the noun before or after the verb. Moreover, the '*Genitive, Dative, Ablative* Case is nothing else but that obliquity in the *sence* [*sic*] of a Substantive, which is caused and signifyed by some Preposition annexed to it' (Wilkins 1668: 352). There is no reason for a language to pick out these 'obliquities' from all others and mark them with case endings, and thus the theory of cases collapses into the theory of the preposition. In the part of the grammar dealing with prepositions, Wilkins (1668: 309) lists all those he believes to be necessary and provides glosses for each in Latin. Interestingly, the glosses include both prepositions (including *ab* 'from', *ex* 'out of' and *cum* 'with' and Latin case names (including 'Cas[us] Gen[itivus]' and 'Ca[sus] Abl[ativus]'), again reinforcing the idea that there is no essential difference between a noun with a case ending and a noun constructed with a preposition.

Although Harris does include some discussion of the category of case, he states at the end of that part of the discussion that, although he could not pass over cases 'from their great importance [...] both in the *Greek* and *Latin* tongues', they cannot be viewed as being 'among the Essentials of Language' and, as such, 'can be hardly said to fall within the limits of our Inquiry' (Harris 1751: 288). He could hardly give a clearer signal that cases are *not* philosophically necessary for a language to function well. He argues that there is some philosophical justification for distinguishing between the nominative and accusative cases, although this can be done through word order, as in English, just as effectively as through a termination. But the argument for marking other cases is far less convincing. The genitive and dative terminations could perfectly well be replaced by prepositions and are only marked by endings because they express the most important 'Relations of Substantives' – 'the Term or Point which something commences FROM' and 'the Term or Point, which something tends TO'. Since the ablative case is found in Latin but not in the language of those founders of philosophy, the Greeks, it is difficult to see how it can really be essential:

> THE ABLATIVE likewise was used by the *Romans* only; a Case they seem to have adopted *to associate with their Prepositions*, as they had deprived their *Genitive* and *Dative* of that privilege; a Case certainly not necessary, because the *Greeks* do as well without it, and because with the *Romans* themselves it is frequently undistinguished. (Harris 1751: 276–7)

In her discussion of Shaw's grammar of Gaelic, Sorensen (2000: 183) particularly castigates the author for referring to 'a Gaelic ablative' when this is 'a Latin case that does not exist in an inflectional form in Gaelic'. Now it is certainly true that Shaw's 'Gaelic ablative' is redundant and could be seen as implying an uncritical reliance on the structure of Latin. But Sorensen goes further and characterises this kind of practice as arising from the inherent conservatism of eighteenth-century universalist thought, at one point describing a 'belief in universality' as a 'neoclassical' position as opposed to the 'emerging [...] ethos of cultural relativism', which is 'Romantic' (Sorensen 2000: 179). The point here is not to defend Shaw against Sorensen's general charges but to point out that, if he had engaged more closely with texts that articulated a 'neoclassical belief in universality' – and one suspects that he had not read Harris as carefully as he says he had – he would have found plenty of authority for jettisoning the 'Gaelic ablative', along with almost all the others, had he wished.

There were other, more practical forces pushing eighteenth-century grammarians into using the Latin case names, whether or not they could find forms that fitted them. Foremost among them was the fact that they had almost no means of describing syntax except with reference to the Latin case names. If they could not find nominatives, accusatives, genitives and datives in the languages they were describing, it became difficult for them to describe how words fitted together into sentences. Another consideration was the fact that their readers were likely to be familiar with these terms and to find them readily comprehensible. Considerations like these were powerful factors in the inertia that is often identified in early modern grammatical writing. But, although linguistic universalism certainly could cause problems for grammarians like Gilchrist in some areas of the grammar, it simultaneously offered a means of escaping from the tyranny of Latin in other areas. Gilchrist's treatment of noun case, which provides an excellent example of universalism functioning in this way, will in fact form the theme of the first case study in Part II of this book. In the meantime, it is sufficient to reinforce the point made in the introduction, that eighteenth-century language study was not reducible to politics. General, or universal, grammar did not inevitably lead to the criticism of 'vernacular' languages, and the ideas of universalist thinkers could certainly be mobilised in their defence.

3.3.2 *The debate over 'analogy' and 'anomaly'*

This second area of discussion has a very long history. In fact, recognition of the phenomenon known as ANALOGY seems a precondition for undertaking grammatical analysis at all, while recognition of the phenomenon known as ANOMALY seems an almost inevitable consequence of the first couple of setbacks in such an analytical project. It is worth briefly summarising the meaning of both as they were used by eighteenth-century grammarians, not least because the current use of the term 'analogy' in historical linguistics is rather different. In eighteenth-century linguistic work, the term is used of the phenomenon whereby functionally similar items are marked in a formally similar fashion. Thus, in English, the past forms of the verbs *jump*, *pass* and *look* are all formed in the same way – with the addition of the tense marker *-ed* or /t/. Noticing this kind of pattern is clearly the first step in uncovering the way in which a language is structured, and it is in this sense that the recognition of analogy seems a precondition of grammatical analysis. But, of course, not all forms are quite so well behaved. The past forms of the verbs *take* and *think* (*took* and *thought*) are not formed in the same way as those of *jump*, *pass* and *look*. Nor is it easy to find other verbs that behave similarly. And forms like these that do not fit into dominant patterns of 'analogy' – what we now usually refer to as irregular forms – are said to be examples of 'anomaly'. Thus, 'analogy' really just referred to morphological patterning and 'anomaly' to examples of forms that did not fit into a regular morphological pattern. To talk about 'analogy' did not imply that a form had *changed* in order to fit a morphological pattern, as it usually would in contemporary historical linguistics, but merely that a pattern was identifiable.

The earliest extant work that deals at length with issues of analogy and anomaly is by the Roman grammarian Marcus Terentius Varro. It dates from the first century BCE, is entitled *De lingua latina*, and summarises a debate, already well advanced by the time Varro was writing, concerning which of these two principles was dominant in human language. Today it seems strange that such a debate should have raged with quite the force that it evidently did. It seems obvious that grammar presupposes patterning (or 'analogy') but that patterns are often disrupted by examples of irregularity (or 'anomaly'), and we understand this tension between patterning and irregularity largely in terms of diachronic processes. However, as Robins (1997: 27) wisely points out, at a time when the contrast between inflectional and derivational morphology had not yet been worked out in a systematic fashion, morphological patterning must have looked considerably less regular than it does to us. As such, the debate over 'analogy' and 'anomaly' constituted an important working through of issues surrounding the kinds of patterning that occur in human language and the most appropriate ways of talking about them.

However, it is important to understand that the debate also had a normative dimension, and this is very much the form it took in eighteenth-century intellectual culture. For some thinkers the issue was not so much whether language *was* organised according to the principle of analogy as whether it *should* be. True, the forms *took* and *thought* are examples of anomaly, but is that just a fact about the English language or is it a regrettable example of a point where the order of a beautiful language has been shattered by irrationality? As the earlier discussion suggested, the epistemological assumptions of eighteenth-century language study tended to militate against accepting that anything was a mere fact about language. And for many writers, 'analogy' was indeed a rational principle that would ideally govern the formal realisation of the essential categories identified within general grammar. For John Wilkins, one of the failings of the Latin language was that its rules were not 'general and constant':

> [T]he exceptions and Anomalisms [...] are so very numerous that there is much more pains required for the remembering [*sic*] of them, than of the Rules themselves: insomuch that many eminent Grammarians have written against Analogy, both in Greek and Latin. (Wilkins 1668: 449)

He offers a brief view of these 'anomalisms', stating that there are so many exceptions in the conjugations of verbs, particularly in the formations of preterites and supines, that it is difficult to list them all. 'Some are wholly without them, others have them without any Analogy; as *Fleo Flevi, Sero Sevi, Fero Tuli.*' These three pairs of present and preterite forms, he says, are instances where '*à Dissimilibus Similia, à Similibus Dissimilia*', 'dissimilar forms are derived from similar ones and similar forms from dissimilar ones', a formulation that echoes Varro (VIII.xviii) directly, emphasising the ongoing relevance of the classical debate to early modern thinkers.

Wilkins's solution, unsurprisingly, was to ensure that the grammar of his newly devised 'philosophical' language conformed entirely to the principle of analogy with no regrettable anomalies. For writers concerned with the nature of existing languages, however, the problem of 'analogy' and 'anomaly' was compounded by its association with questions of *ratio* ('proportion') and *usus* or *consuetudo* ('use'). Analogy was often understood in terms of proportionality, and the formal resemblance of functionally similar items could be expressed using the conventional notation used to express ratios:

jump : *jumped* :: *pass* : *passed*

However, the fact that *ratio* also means 'reason' added a kind of force to the sense that proportionality was the more desirable state of affairs. And the association of anomaly with 'use' – the actual practice of human speakers – contributed further to the characterisation of the pristine language governed by the principle of 'analogy' but constantly threatened by the ignorance and laziness of its speakers. Already in the *De lingua latina*, the association of 'analogy' with *ratio* and 'anomaly' with *usus* had been problematised, with Varro arguing that, since people use both analogous and anomalous forms in discourse, both 'analogy' and 'anomaly' have to be seen as aspects of use. However, the politicised notion of the corrupting effects of use proved powerful in eighteenth-century thought, and it will be helpful to allude briefly to two thinkers who grappled with this idea in their work on the English language: Samuel Johnson in the preface to his dictionary and Noah Webster in his work on the standardisation of American English.

In the preface to his *Dictionary*, Samuel Johnson discusses the idea that the main purpose of such a work must be to 'fix' the language and bring an end to 'flux' or change. He associates flux with illiteracy and states that:

> [W]hile words were unfixed by any visible signs, [they] must have been spoken with great diversity, as we now observe those who cannot read to catch sounds imperfectly, and utter them negligently. When this wild and barbarous jargon was first reduced to an alphabet, every penman endeavoured to express, as he could, the sounds which he was accustomed to pronounce or to receive, and vitiated in writing such words as were already vitiated in speech. (Johnson 1755: 1a1ʳ)

The consequent variation, he states, 'perplexes or destroys analogy and produces anomalous formations, which once being incorporated, can never be afterward dismissed or reformed'. So, for example, the nouns formed from the English adjectives *long* and *broad* are the anomalous forms *length* and *breadth* rather than the analogous forms *longth* and *broadth*.[6] Such features, Johnson states, are 'defects' or 'spots of barbarity'. Thus his terminology is unambiguously normative; he even uses the familiar term 'jargon' to describe 'barbarous' forms of speech. In his *Plan of a Dictionary*, Johnson (1747: 32) had boldly expressed his intention of putting an end to the process of decline and producing a work 'by which the pronunciation of our language may be fixed, and its attainment facilitated; by which its purity may be preserved, its use ascertained, and its duration lengthened'. By the time the dictionary was published in 1755, however, Johnson, famously, had become more cynical and admitted that it was with some justice that a lexicographer could be derided:

> who being able to produce no example of a nation that has preserved their words and phrases from mutability, shall imagine that his dictionary can embalm his language, and secure it from corruption and decay, that it is in his power to change sublunary nature, or clear the world at once from folly, vanity and affectation. (Johnson 1755: 1C2ʳ)

He remarks upon the failure of the French and Italian academies to fix their respective languages, commenting that 'to enchain syllables, and to lash the wind, are equally the undertakings of pride, unwilling to measure its desires by its strength' (Johnson 1755: 1C2ʳ). In the contest between proportionality and use – *ratio* and *usus* – the former is simply no match for the latter, and it is arrogant to think that one can wade in on its behalf.

But Gilchrist himself, in the same passage in which he expresses his enthusiasm for the project of developing a universal language, takes Johnson to task for this defeatist attitude. It makes him furious, he says, when the 'literati themselves' pour scorn on the project of ascertaining and fixing the language: 'it is so very easy to attach ridicule, by talking of lashing the wind, and chaining sounds that people sculk away from the task themselves, without having the courage to try it' (Gilchrist 1798b: xxxiv). He suggests that an automaton might be built which could produce all the sounds of the language, and thus act as a standard on which a 'fixed pronunciation and orthography' could be established. And in a footnote he adds: 'Our coarsest clocks now distinctly articulate *kookoo*', and suggests that it would not be difficult to 'construct similar machines to indicate an alphabet in all its changes'. As a final contribution to this debate, he also remarks that both the French and the Americans have recently been presented with the opportunity of undertaking language reform owing to

---

[6] Johnson (1755: 1a1ʳ) notes that Milton often writes 'highth' rather than 'height' and, in a phrase richly evocative of Puritan naming, suggests that this is a result of his 'zeal for analogy'.

the political dislocations represented by their respective revolutions. Indeed, he suggests that, if the French had focused on reforming their language rather than 'disengaging the minds of men from every religious tie', they would have 'acted with more wisdom and chance of ultimate success' (Gilchrist 1798b: xxxv). With these comments, Gilchrist shows himself immersed in the issues described in this section – the sense that language use is always tending towards decline – and he gestures towards the context in which Noah Webster found himself at the end of the 1780s, although without explicitly mentioning Webster's work.

In 1789, Noah Webster, self-proclaimed pioneer of a distinctively American approach to the study of English, published his *Dissertations on the English Language,* in which he calls for a uniform standard of American English to be adopted across the United States. This standard is to fulfil two functions: first, it will be entirely distinct from British English and constitute a marker of American identity; second, it will be uniform and promote cohesion among the diverse regions of the Union. In the first of his dissertations, Webster (1789: 27) states that the standard should be formed upon two principles: the *'rules of the language itself'*, by which he means 'analogy', and *'the general practice of the nation'*. Ideally the language would be entirely analogous but '[w]hen a deviation from analogy has become the universal practice of a nation, it then takes place of all rules and becomes the standard of propriety'. In other words, *ratio* is always desirable but, where *usus* has destroyed *ratio*, it is generally impossible to undo the damage. In the second dissertation, Webster (1789: 126–7) goes on to make some critical remarks about the English of England, stating that '[i]n the fashionable world, *heard* is pronounced *herd* or *hurd*', a phenomenon that was 'almost unknown in America till the commencement of the late war'. Obviously this is undesirable:

> [F]or centuries, the word has been uniformly spelt *heard*; the verb *hear* is in analogy with *fear*, *sear*, and yet *e* in the past time and participle has been omitted, as *heard*, not *heared*. That *herd* was not formerly the pronunciation is probable from this circumstance; the Americans were strangers to it when they came from England, and the body of the people are so to this day. (Webster 1789: 127)

So the American pronunciation is more appropriate because it preserves 'analogy', and it transpires that this is neither an accident nor an isolated example. '[I]n many instances,' Webster (1789: 129) states, 'the Americans still adhere to the analogies of the language, where the English have infringed them.' And 'considering the force of custom and the caprice of fashion', the practice of the English 'must be as liable to changes as to errors, as the practice of the well educated yeomanry, who are governed by habits and not easily led astray by novelty' (Webster 1789: 129–39). Thus, American English is in a better state than the English of England because the English are flighty and swayed by fashion, whereas the solid and well-educated American yeomanry are steady and considered in their response to change.[7]

The point to be emphasised here is, once again, that it is problematic to assume that the valorisation of analogy always served to shore up the status quo. While the supposed erosion of analogy was associated with popular usage and used to justify authoritarian approaches to language like that envisaged by Johnson, the *preservation* of analogy in American English also provided the basis for Webster's oppositional account of the history of English in the *Dissertations*. While Webster was certainly engaged in a project of standardisation, which can in some ways be seen as comparable with the interventions of writers like Lowth and Johnson, his strategy is frequently to celebrate the good sense Americans have already shown in preserving the integrity of the English language rather than trying to change the way they speak. In the second of the case studies that follow this chapter, we shall see Gilchrist celebrating the prevalence of 'analogy' in Hindustani in a remarkably similar fashion, although without making quite such laudatory comments about the language's speakers. There is something a little eerie about the fact that Webster and Gilchrist independently employ this strategy in a space where colonialism is a key contextual factor. Of course, one might object that, unlike Webster, Gilchrist is writing from the perspective of the coloniser and not the colonised. But here it is worth remembering the point made in Chapter 1 that Gilchrist, like others in the same period, often constructs British rule as liberating the ordinary people of India from the regime of the Mughals and from the authoritarianism of the Brahmins. His espousal of the 'vernacular' as opposed to either of the 'classical' languages, Persian or Sanskrit, is connected with this vision of what British intervention is all about. As such, we should perhaps not be surprised to find him deploying apparently oppositional strategies in works ultimately intended to shore up the colonial system.

3.3.3 *The debate over typology*

The two debates covered so far were concerned first with the grammatical categories that were essential to human language and as such should be universally instantiated, and second with the assertion that it was rational to mark functionally similar forms in formally similar ways. The third

---

[7] Webster is fond of this contrast and restates it in the fourth dissertation, claiming that 'in many instances' the American yeomanry 'retain correct phrases, instead of which the pretended refiners of the language have introduced those which are highly improper and absurd'. And, lest English readers confuse these yeomen with 'the illiterate peasantry of their own country', Webster goes on to describe their means, their education, and their preferred reading, which includes 'the best English sermons and treatises upon religion, ethics, geography, and history; such as the works of Watts, Addison, Atterbury, Salmon, &c.' (Webster 1789: 288–9).

debate, to be covered in this section, relates to the first in that it was made possible by the development of general grammar and to the second in that it is largely concerned with the way in which languages mark grammatical categories at a formal level. Having abstracted away from the form of a particular language, if only partially, and having identified underlying categories believed to be universally required, if not universally instantiated, it became possible for grammarians to look at the various formal means that different languages used to mark those categories. So, for example, general grammar suggested that the structure of a language should make it possible to express the time at which an action took place and perhaps also certain aspectual information as well. But it was evident that some languages did this by adding terminations to the verb, while others did it by constructing part of the verb with an auxiliary. As usual, the question arose as to whether one of these arrangements was better, and the matter was discussed with reference to rhetorical concepts such as 'precision' and 'harmony'.

A key text in the emergence of typological analysis was the introduction to Gabriel Girard's *Les vrais principes de la langue françoise*, which was first published in 1747 and which constituted an attempt to describe the French language with reference to the principles of general grammar.[8] Gilchrist almost never cites sources in French and so it seems inappropriate to look in detail at Girard's work. However, a summary of the ideas presented there appeared in the same popular work to which I referred in the discussion of the 'science of grammar', the first edition of the *Encyclopaedia Britannica*. As well as the article on grammar mentioned earlier, the encyclopaedia also includes a treatise simply entitled 'language'. In this article, Smellie (1769–71 II: 864) – he, in fact, wrote most of the articles in the work – states that he is going to 'make some remarks on the advantages or defects of some of those idioms of language with which we are most acquainted'. The term 'idiom' has a technical meaning here and Smellie glosses it as a language's 'general mode of arranging words into sentences', identifying two idioms that occur frequently among European languages. This typology derives directly from Girard and is based on the way in which different languages express what Girard takes to be the universal structure of logical propositions. As Smellie (1769–71 II: 846) puts it, some 'express their ideas in the natural order in which they occur to the mind; the subject which occasions the action appearing first; then the action [...]; and, last of all, the object to which it has reference'. Such languages are described as ANALOGOUS, a term that is slightly confusing because it is not being employed in the sense that Johnson and Webster use it. The analogy here is not between different linguistic forms but between the structure of a logical proposition and the structure of a sentence.

---

[8] For a discussion of typological work that pre-dates Girard's text, see Van Der Wal (1995).

Other languages 'follow no order in their construction than what the taste or fancy of the composer may suggest' (1769–71 II: 846). These are labelled, less ambiguously, TRANSPOSITIVE. The flexible word order of 'transpositive' languages may lead to confusion. In 'analogous' languages, we know which noun is the subject of a sentence because of its position within that sentence, but in a language where the subject can appear anywhere, how will the subject be distinguished from the object? The answer is that 'transpositive' languages have a rich morphology through which words are 'made to refer to the others with which they ought to be connected, in whatever part of the sentence they occur' (Smellie 1769–71 II: 864–5). In other words, transpositive languages mark the functions of nouns by using case endings. What is particularly interesting about this argument is that, far from regarding the 'classical' languages as the model of how a language should be and seeing 'vernaculars' like English and French as mitigating their lack of case endings through the makeshift expedient of word order, the sentence structure of the 'vernaculars' is characterised as mirroring the structure of the proposition, and the free word order of the 'classical' languages is seen as a deviation from the underlying logical structure of the sentence, a problematic feature that has to be solved through the invention of cases Once again, therefore, the notion that languages should necessarily have cases is called into question.

Having identified these two types of language, Smellie proceeds to evaluate them by considering the expressive possibilities of each. He asserts that the rigid word order of 'analogous' languages 'cramps the harmonious flow of composition' (Smellie 1769–71 II: 870). In Latin, words can be placed in whatever order is most aesthetically pleasing, whereas in English, only one order is possible. In this respect, 'the Transpositive language shines forth in all its glory, and the Analogous must yield the palm without the smallest dispute'. However, that is not the whole story. Looking at a different aspect of the grammar, Smellie notes that analogous languages make use of auxiliary verbs rather than verbal terminations, and that this renders their word order freer than might at first appear. Latin has just one way of expressing the present tense, *scribo* ('I write'), for example. English, on the other hand, has four: 'I write', 'I do write', 'write I do', 'and 'write do I'. Smellie admits that the final example is somewhat bizarre, but notes that 'the sagacious Shakespeare' makes effective use of such forms in delineating characters such as 'ancient Pistol'. These different formulations allow for the expression of different nuances of meaning, and what is more, the use of auxiliaries also allows sentences to be emphasised in different ways. 'I do write' can be pronounced 'I DO write' or 'I do WRITE', permitting 'a greater precision and accuracy in fixing the meaning'.

Smellie's discussion of the two types of language relates closely to the way in which discourse is evaluated within rhetorical theory, and since the application of rhetorical concepts to the evaluation of languages is the theme of the next section, it will be sufficient to comment on it briefly here. According to Smellie, the main virtue of the transpositive languages is that their flexible word order facilitates the 'harmonious flow of composition', whereas the advantage of analogous languages is that the use of auxiliary verbs rather than terminations makes it possible to achieve particular clarity of meaning. Both qualities – the 'harmonious flow of composition' and the precise expression of meaning – are extensively discussed in the rhetorical tradition. In the *Rhetorica ad Herennium*, for example, an influential rhetorical treatise long attributed to Cicero, it is suggested that the speaker aim at 'an arrangement of words which gives uniform finish to the discourse in every part'. This will involve avoiding, amongst other faults, 'the frequent collision of vowels', 'the excessive recurrence of the same letter' and 'a continuous series of words with like case endings'. Flexibility of word order clearly makes it easier to avoid all three of these problems. At the same time, the clear and precise expression of meaning is always presented as a central virtue of style, with Quintilian stating, for example: 'Discourse ought always to be obvious, even to the most careless and negligent hearer.' So, to a large extent, this third area of discussion is constituted in terms of a battle between the 'vernaculars', which are 'analogous', and the 'classical' languages, which are 'transpositive', the crux of the matter being which type of language is more expressive in the terms set out by rhetoricians. The 'classical' languages have something of an advantage in the sense that the rhetorical tradition was founded by native speakers of Greek and developed by native speakers of Latin, so that much of the material traditionally found in texts on style has its origins in the discussion of those two languages. Once again, however, there is a level of abstraction in the debate which allows advocates of the 'vernaculars' to argue effectively for their chosen languages. Harmony and clarity are, after all, open-ended aesthetic categories, and, as Smellie demonstrates, the classical languages do not have the monopoly on either. In the first of the following case studies, issues of typology will be relevant to Gilchrist's discussion of Hindustani, and there we shall see that even the structuring opposition so central to Girard and Smellie's typological work is available for scrutiny and critique.

3.3.4 *The discussion of harmony*

The last section touched upon the issue of the composition of discourse and the best ways of combining words to create a harmonious effect. In fact, however, the rather general comments quoted there constitute the tip of a very large iceberg. The rhetoricians of the later eighteenth century discuss this issue at considerable length, and an excellent example is to be found in the *Lectures on Rhetoric and Belles Lettres*, published in 1783 by Hugh

Blair, professor at the University of Edinburgh.[9] Blair (1783 I: 247–71) devotes an extensive chapter to the 'harmony of sentences'. He argues that sound, although 'a quality much inferior to sense', should not be neglected by rhetoricians:

> For, as long as sounds are the vehicle of conveyance for our ideas, there will be always a very considerable connexion between the idea which is conveyed, and the nature of the sound which conveys it. Pleasing ideas can hardly be transmitted to the mind by means of harsh and disagreeable sounds. The imagination revolts as soon as it hears them uttered. (Blair 1783 I: 247)

In attempting to create a harmonious effect, one can either focus on producing 'an agreeable sound' but 'without any particular expression', or one can order the sounds so that they become 'expressive of the sense'. 'The first', Blair says, 'is the more common; the second, the highest beauty.' Referring to classical sources including Cicero, Quintilian and Dionysius of Halicarnassus, Blair sets out the principles by which both types of effect may be achieved. In choosing the words to be used, one must be aware of the effects that particular sounds have on listeners:

> It may always be assumed as a principle, that whatever sounds are difficult in pronunciation, are, in the same proportion, harsh and painful to the ear. Vowels give softness; consonants, strength to the sound of words. The music of language requires a just proportion of both; and will be hurt, will be rendered either grating or effeminate, by an excess of either. (Blair 1783 I: 258)

The chosen words must then be arranged into sentences with an awareness of the metrical effects that can be achieved in prose – the musicality, as Blair puts it, of which discourse is susceptible. Finally, sound can be made evocative of sense by recalling other sounds, producing an effect of motion, or representing the 'emotions and passions of the mind'. It is relatively easy for a writer to evoke other sounds:

> No very great art is required in a poet when he is describing sweet and soft sounds, to make use of such words as have most liquids and vowels, and glide the softest; or, when he is describing harsh sounds, to throw together a number of harsh syllables which are of difficult pronunciation. (Blair 1783 I: 266)

With respect to movement, a succession of short syllables in a line will produce an effect of rapid motion, while 'long syllables naturally give the impression of slow motion'. Blair accepts that the evocation of emotion or passion through sound is more subjective but suggests that pleasure and joy

---

[9] For a useful discussion of Hugh Blair's approach to rhetoric, see Ferreira-Buckley (1994).

can be voiced with 'smooth, liquid, and flowing numbers', while 'brisk and lively sensations' require 'quicker and more animated numbers', and 'melancholy and gloomy subjects, naturally express themselves in slow measures'.

What is particularly interesting about this discussion is that at several points, both in this chapter and in one dealing specifically with the structure of English, Blair comments on the extent to which particular languages lend themselves to the production of harmonious discourse. He suggests that classical Greek is the language most suited to harmonious composition, while Latin, 'although a very beautiful language', is not as adaptable, having 'more of a fixed character of stateliness and gravity'. Of the modern languages, Italian is foremost in 'the great beauty and harmony of its sounds', while English is often 'taxed with its deficiency in harmony'. This discussion echoes comments that Smellie makes in the second half of his treatise on 'language'. Having used Girard's typological ideas to develop a discussion of 'idiom', Smellie goes on to talk about the 'genius' of particular languages, a term that he uses to refer to the 'particular set of ideas which the words of any language, either from their formation or multiplicity, are most naturally apt to excite in the mind of any one who hears it properly uttered'. English, for Smellie, is 'bold, nervous, and strongly articulated', Italian 'more soothing and harmonious' and Spanish 'more grave, sonorous, and stately'. These ideas are said to arise from what we would call the phonological and morphophonological characteristics of each language, and are, in turn, seen as having a connection with the national characteristics of their speakers. Thus, Italian, Smellie says, is the language of an 'effeminate people', which accounts for the fact that Italian words usually end in vowels:

> The strong consonants which terminated the words, and gave them life and boldness, being thought too harsh for the delicate ears of these sons of sloth, were banished from their language – while sonorous vowels which could be protracted to any length in music were substituted in their stead. (Smellie 1769–71 II: 875)

For these reasons, Smellie argues, Italian is 'destitute of those nerves which constitute the strength and vigour of a language'. However, Italian is not the only language that comes in for criticism. English, despite being 'bold' and 'nervous', has the disadvantage that both the plurals of nouns and the third person singular of verbs are marked by the letter <s>, and this produces a 'general hiss' through the language, 'which must be exceedingly disagreeable to every unprejudiced ear'.

As it happens, Blair (1783 I: 176) takes issue with this particular judgement, arguing that, 'though every native is apt to be partial to the sounds of his own language, and may, therefore, be suspected of not being a fair judge', there are nevertheless grounds on which the harmony of

English could be defended. Here Blair turns for support to Thomas Sheridan, one of a group of eighteenth-century rhetoricians known as the 'elocutionists'.[10] The elocutionists worked with a highly circumscribed definition of rhetoric, focusing entirely on the fifth of the traditional five arts, *pronuntiatio*, or the 'delivery' of spoken discourse. As Ulman (1994: 148–9) notes, the elocutionists are often treated as an embarrassing sideshow in the history of rhetoric, but their preoccupation with delivery has to be understood as reflecting the social context in which they worked. They were active in a period when the relationship between accent and social status was a particular concern of the rising middle class, and the materials they supplied promised to present aspiring provincials with a means of mastering their own self-representation by allowing them to speak in a way that was valued by the social elite. Thomas Sheridan's career as a teacher of speech begins in 1756 with the publication of *British Education*. For our purposes, however, his most important work is *A Rhetorical Grammar of the English Language*, which appeared prefixed to his *General Dictionary* in 1780. This text purports to teach 'propriety of pronunciation' through articulatory descriptions of the various 'letters', and in this sense contributes to the ongoing process of analysing the nature of spoken sounds.[11]

In dealing with the issue of the 'general hiss' created by the realisation of two common grammatical markers with the letter $<s>$, Blair (1783 I: 177) draws upon Sheridan's phonetic analyses:

> Our consonants, [Sheridan] observes, which appear so crowded to the eye on paper, often form combinations, not disagreeable to the ear in pronouncing; and, in particular, the objection which has been made to the frequent recurrence of the hissing consonant *s* in our language, is unjust and ill-founded. For, it has not been attended to, that very commonly, and in the final syllables especially, this letter loses altogether the hissing sound, and is transformed into a *z*, which is one of the sounds on which the ear rests with pleasure; as in *has*, *these*, *those*, *loves*, *hears*, and innumerable more, where, though the letter *s* be retained in writing, it has really the power of *z*, not of the common *s*.

This point seems blindingly obvious to the modern reader. In English, the relationship between sounds and written letters is notoriously problematic and it is obviously fallacious to imagine that the written character $<s>$ always represents the sound [s]. However, both grammar and rhetoric had traditionally used the 'letter' as the primary unit of

---

[10] For a useful discussion of Thomas Sheridan's approach to rhetoric, see Benzie (1994).

[11] See Firth (1946), Abercrombie (1948) and Asher & Henderson (1981) for surveys of the early history of phonetics.

analysis in the study of pronunciation, and even in the later eighteenth century the relationship between the letter as written character and the letter as speech sound had not been fully explored and worked through. The analyses produced by elocutionists such as Sheridan were pioneering in their attempts to clarify the relationship between speech and writing, and, as was the case in the other debates examined earlier, they opened up a field of controversy which threw into doubt certain assumptions about the aesthetic properties of particular languages. Thus, the idea that English does not lend itself to harmonious discourse because of the unfortunate preponderance of the 'hissing s' is challenged not through subjective debate about whether the sound is attractive but at the technical level of articulatory analysis.

There is no doubt that Sheridan and the other elocutionists were pursuing an agenda that was in many ways conservative, reinforcing the notion that one particular accent of English had a propriety that others lacked. (Although, as usual with prescriptive pedagogy, there is also the argument that giving others access to the prestige variety is actually a progressive act.) Once again, however their work is not reducible to politics. It was built on a considerable body of work in the area of articulatory analysis, and this work had an autonomy that allowed it to be mobilised for political purposes other than those intended by its authors. Gilchrist himself refers to Sheridan's discussion of speech sounds at a very technical level, and his reasons for doing this will be explained in the second of the case studies. The important point is that Gilchrist's discussion of Sheridan can be seen as an attempt to secure authoritative support for a positive representation of Hindustani. As in the field of general grammar, the debate over 'analogy' and 'anomaly', and the emergent discussion over typology, the rhetorical idea that harmony is a positive quality of human languages, constituted a resource that could be appropriated for various different ends by practical grammarians such as Gilchrist. And the technical work on speech sounds undertaken by elocutionists like Sheridan and discussed by rhetoricians such as Blair provided a means of contesting the critical approach often taken to the phonology and morphology of particular human languages.

3.3.5 *The study of the history of English*

We have now looked at four areas of controversy in eighteenth-century language study, each of which presented both problems and possibilities for practical grammarians. Each supplied a vision of how human language should be, and thus a means of criticising languages that did not conform to that vision. But, at the same time, each of them also supplied a means of resisting such critical approaches, often by providing alternative accounts of a single phenomenon or suggesting ways in which one requirement might be played off against another. This section will develop the discussion by examining two writers who mobilise information about the history of the language in order to demonstrate how neatly English fits into the patterns that philosophy predicts. The first is Robert Lowth, the famous eighteenth-century grammarian of English, and the second is John Horne Tooke, whose well-known philosophical study, *The Diversions of Purley*, mobilises vast quantities of etymological evidence in support of a particular conception of the relationship between language and mind. Gilchrist alludes to the work of both these writers and produces analyses that are closely modelled on their work. This might seem strange, since Lowth and Horne Tooke held radically opposed opinions about the nature of language. This apparent inconsistency seems in large part explicable as the result of Gilchrist's selective reading of Horne Tooke's argument; indeed, the way in which the two writers mobilise historical evidence is actually rather similar, even if their philosophical views are diametrically opposed.

Robert Lowth's grammar of English was first published in 1762 and it begins with a reference to Jonathan Swift's 'public remonstrance, addressed to the Earl of Oxford', in which he criticised the imperfect state of the English language, claiming that 'in many instances it offended against every part of Grammar' (Swift 1735 I: 186–207). Lowth claims, however, that the deficiencies of English are not intrinsic but are errors of 'practice'. It is not, therefore, necessary to alter the language fundamentally, but rather to demonstrate how English realises the principles uncovered by general grammar and to discourage usage that deviates from this standard. Lowth (1762: xiv) does not discuss general grammar at length himself, but cites *Hermes* as an appropriate source for anyone who wants to find out more about it.[12] The resulting text is sometimes dismissed as a negative project devoted entirely to criticism, and it is true that it contains many warnings against 'corrupt' grammar and holds up numerous examples from famous writers for censure. However, it is crucial to recognise that the work has another, more positive mission. Lowth's grammar sets out to prove that English is not in itself debased and corrupt, but that it really does exemplify the principles of philosophical grammar. If the reader can come to see these universal regularities instantiated in the grammar of English, then careful, accurate usage will naturally flow from this awareness.

When dealing with structures that apparently contradict the principles of general grammar but which are too deeply embedded – too much confirmed by usage – to be censured, Lowth does not condemn the language itself, but instead attempts to 'resolve' the problem. In other words, he tries to find a

---

[12] Although he cites *Hermes* as the best source on general grammar for the curious reader, Lowth also refers to the other general grammar that has been highlighted in this chapter, John Wilkins's *Essay*. In his discussion of modality, for example, Lowth (1762: 59 n.) quotes Wilkins at length, using the term 'elegant' to describe the analysis offered in the *Essay*.

way of analysing the structure that will be sanctioned by philosophy.[13] Practices of this kind influence Gilchrist far more powerfully than the censorious, prescriptive ones. Gilchrist never, to my knowledge, uses general grammar to condemn any Hindustani form or structure. His aim, on the contrary, is to demonstrate that this 'vernacular' tongue is not a 'jargon', and this involves explaining away aspects of the grammar that seem strange to European learners. He finds a model for this kind of explanation in Lowth's discussion of English pronouns. Noting that some English sentences apparently contain two objects, Lowth (1762: 131–2) explains that, with personal pronouns, '[t]he Prepositions *to* and *for* are often understood [i.e. not realised explicitly]; as, "give me the book; get me some paper;" that is, *to me, for me*'. The apparently strange phenomenon of two objects appearing together is thus explained with reference to the principle of ellipsis – these sentences really include a preposition, either *to* or *for*, but the preposition can be elided, leaving just the pronoun.

In a note, however, Lowth provides an alternative and possibly more powerful resolution. He suggests that in phrases of this kind, *me, thee, him* and so on may in fact be dative forms. As we saw earlier, Harris saw the dative as a form that, although not necessary, was used by the Greeks and Romans to mark out one of two particularly important relations, 'tendency to', instead of a construction with a preposition. By claiming that in *give me the book*, *me* is dative, Lowth abandons the idea that a preposition has been omitted and claims that the force of the preposition is contained within the pronominal form itself. This is an elegant reanalysis because it helps Lowth to resolve a number of other problematic phrases including *woe is me* and *methinks*, the former presumably having the force of 'woe is to me' and the latter 'to me there is a thinking'. Lowth also draws an analogy between *methinks* and the Greek phrase *emoi dokei*, which literally means 'it seems to me' but is often translated 'I think', and which includes the clearly marked dative pronoun *emoi*. He also indicates that these pronominal forms originate in Saxon datives and may be 'considered as still continuing such in the English, and including in their very form the force of the Prepositions *to* and *for*'.

Digressing somewhat from his analysis of Hindustani, Gilchrist (1796: 227 n.) engages with this very problem in his grammar. He begins by noting that Hindustani has several verbs that resemble the English *methinks,* and he is talking here about impersonal constructions such as *mujhe mālūm hotā*, literally 'it is known to me', which is usually translated 'I know'. He then comments respectfully on Lowth's analysis of *methinks*, but goes on to suggest a different way of conceptualising the form. The *me* in *methinks* is better viewed, he says, as an 'old nominative', and he presents a number of

---

[13] Percy (1997) also examines Lowth's defence of problematic forms on the grounds of 'poetic license'.

arguments for this view. First, an analysis of this kind would make *me* analogous to 'the French moi, &c.', which can refer to the subject of a verb. Second, it would account for the 'very common response in our language, *it is me, it was me, me*, and so on', where prescriptive grammarians had argued that the pronoun following the verb *to be* should be in the same case as that preceding it. Third, he says, Shakespeare uses it as a nominative: "'*Me* rather had my heart might feel your love'".[14] The three arguments presented here very closely parallel those presented by Lowth. Both writers draw an analogy with another language: Greek in Lowth's case and French in Gilchrist's. Both suggest that their analysis will help to explain other problematic forms or structures: Lowth's analysis will cover *woe is me*, while Gilchrist's can deal with *it is me*. And both refer to historical material: Anglo-Saxon to support the analysis of *me* and *thee* as datives; the language of Shakespeare to argue for *me* and *thee* being nominatives.

Of course, to the contemporary reader, Gilchrist's arguments are nowhere near as convincing as Lowth's. The point, however, is that, in his discussion of the problematic form *methinks*, we can see Gilchrist engaging with the methods of argumentation that Lowth himself used in 'resolving' difficult forms and structures. Processes of reanalysis supported by evidence drawn, first, from other languages, second, from other areas of the same language and third, from history, appear at a number of points when Gilchrist is trying to minimise the sense of strangeness surrounding a particular form or structure in Hindustani. When Lowth uses a historical argument in his account of English grammar, he presents well-attested evidence from Anglo-Saxon, citing George Hickes's *Thesaurus* of that language as a source.[15] In his own resolutions, Gilchrist sometimes attempts to do likewise, treating 'Hinduwee' as the Indian equivalent of Anglo-Saxon and supporting his argument by pointing to forms in Braj, which he sees as in some sense representing an ongoing manifestation of 'Hinduwee'. However, eighteenth-century thinkers were often prepared to push speculation about the history of language further than modern linguists find acceptable, and in this connection it is important to consider the origin of language debate, an important area of discussion in this period and one in which Gilchrist himself showed considerable interest.

---

[14] This is a reference to *King Richard the Second* (III.iii.192). In his *Dictionary*, Johnson gives this line as an example of the 'accusative' pronoun, *me*, being wrongly used as a 'nominative', so Gilchrist's intervention represents an attempt to 'resolve' the problem Johnson has identified. Abbot (1905: 152–3) notes that in Middle English the idea of preference is expressed, not by the phrase 'I had, or would rather (*i.e.* sooner)' but by '(To) me (it) were lever'. The word *lever* means 'more pleasant' and is comparable with the German *lieber*. He adds that these two idioms are confused in this example. Thus, it is Lowth's analysis that has been accepted.

[15] The full title of Hickes's text is *Linguarum Vett. Septentrionalium Thesaurus Grammatico-Criticus et Archaeologicus* and it dates from 1703–5. Lowth (1762: 132 n.) quotes a line from a poem reproduced in Hickes's *Thesaurus* as evidence that *him* was a dative in Anglo-Saxon: 'Wel is *him* that there mai be.'

The work that influenced Gilchrist most strongly in this field was John Horne Tooke's famous refutation of the theory of general grammar, *The Diversions of Purley* (1786). Horne Tooke's work fits into a larger debate over the way in which human language had originated, and this debate was closely connected with the emergent study of society. A typical thought experiment used in studying human institutions required the investigator to imagine human beings in some hypothetical state of nature before history began and to consider how such beings, relying only their natural faculties, could come to invent the political and cultural institutions that characterise modern society. Of course, before the narrative could unfold, the investigator needed to establish what human beings in the state of nature would actually have been like – what *are* our natural faculties and to what extent is human nature really the product of socialisation? In this context, Lia Formigari (1993: 2–4) points to the enormous interest that eighteenth-century thinkers took in wild children – children who had been abandoned in infancy, had grown up outside society and were presumably still in a pre-social state of nature. It was clear from the behaviour of these unfortunate children that they were not rational beings in the sense that fully socialised adults were. And this suggested that, in tracing the emergence of human institutions, it was necessary to see society and rationality as developing in parallel, social developments making advances in rationality possible and these in turn giving rise to an increasingly advanced mode of communal life. But at this point, the role of language became problematic. 'SPEECH', as Harris (1751: 1) puts it, 'is the joint Energie of our best and noblest Faculties [...] (that is to say, our *Reason* and our social *Affection*) being withal our peculiar Ornament and Distinction.' In the state of nature, however, our 'best and noblest faculties' were as yet embryonic and undeveloped. Language, therefore, must also have emerged over time, a third element advancing in parallel with reason and society. And the origin of language debate was primarily concerned with the way in which these parallel developments could be unravelled, a process that for eighteenth-century thinkers lay at the heart of sociological investigation.

The unravelling of language, reason and society often involved recasting the conventional material of general grammar into a narrative. Given that the various parts of speech and the different grammatical categories were felt to correspond to underlying logical and metaphysical categories, one way to produce an account of the emergence of language was to work out which of those categories were the simplest conceptually and to posit the corresponding categories as the oldest elements of language. Adam Smith, for example, provides an account of language emerging smoothly over time, one part of speech following another, with proper nouns coming first, then common nouns, then adjectives and so forth, up to abstract parts of speech like conjunctions. But in the work of Smith's contemporary and fellow Scot, James Burnet, Lord Monboddo, the idea that a 'regular and formed language' could emerge step by step from the 'jargon' of 'savages' is treated as wholly preposterous. Monboddo argued that there must have been a radical disjunction in the histories of all the 'languages of art', a point at which the original 'jargon' was abandoned or, at least, wholly reorganised along philosophical lines.[16]

As we shall see in Chapter 5, Gilchrist's treatment of the issue of analogy has much in common with Monboddo's. But when he engages in explicit discussion of the origin of language, he expresses more enthusiasm for the thought of Horne Tooke, the first volume of whose text, *The Diversions of Purley*, appeared in 1786. Gilchrist (1798b: xlv n.) describes the theory it presents as 'a grand discovery, in the pursuit of which, ages till now, have been spent in vain'. On the face of it this is surprising, because Horne Tooke's work constitutes an attack both on existing theories of general grammar – particularly that presented by James Harris – and on theories of the origin of language that rely on general grammar, Lord Monboddo's being a case in point. The conflict hinges on whether mental categories exist prior to language or not. For rationalists like Harris and Monboddo, language simply reflects categories of thought, both logical and ontological. But Horne Tooke takes a radically empiricist position, following Locke in characterising sensation as the basis of knowledge but going further and rejecting Locke's idea that a mental operation named 'reflection' can also be identified. He argues that the mind is merely the passive recipient of sensation, and he denies that there are any specifically mental operations at all. The processes that we describe as reasoning are, in fact, processes of language.

What then is the nature of these processes? Horne Tooke asserts that language consists entirely of the names of simple Ideas: 'A consideration of Ideas or of the Mind, or of Things (relative to the Parts of Speech) will lead us no further than to Nouns: i.e. the signs of those impressions or names of ideas' (Horne Tooke 1786: 70–71). He dismisses the idea that the other parts of speech – verbs, for example, or conjunctions – correspond to mental operations such as 'judgement' and 'reasoning'. These other parts of speech are merely the abbreviated forms of the names of Ideas, which, in turn, arise purely from sensation. Horne Tooke does admit that the verb is also necessary for communication: 'the Verb is QUOD *loquimur* [...]; the *Noun*, DE QUO' (Horne Tooke 1786: 71). This is potentially a problem: if the only function of language is to express simple Ideas, then why are there two parts of speech? This question is not addressed in *The Diversions of Purley*, and the existence of the verb has to be taken as an axiom of what follows. The important point is that all other parts of speech are

---

[16] Notoriously, Monboddo made use of an account of the North American language, Huron, published by the French Recollect missionary Gabriel Théodat-Sagard in 1632, as evidence for the nature of 'barbarous' languages. See Schreyer (1987; 1994; 1996) for discussion of this kind of argument from analogy.

abbreviations of nouns and verbs (Horne Tooke 1786: 67–9). When we construct a sentence that apparently incorporates words of different kinds we are merely listing, in abbreviated form, the names of a constellation of Ideas. Abbreviations make speech dispatchful, and without them the process of naming a set of Ideas would be unfeasibly slow. We should not imagine, however, that they are anything but the signs of simple Ideas with their origins in sensation. We might think, for example, that the use of a conjunction like *if* indicates that reasoning is taking place – that two propositions are being placed in a logical relationship. But this conclusion would be wrong. The word *if* is just the abbreviated imperative of the Anglo-Saxon verb *gifan* ('give') (Horne Tooke 1786: 67–9). Thus, a word which seemingly indicates that an abstract mental operation has taken place is in reality just a sign of the simple Idea of 'giving' and this, like all Ideas, has its origins in sensation. In this sense, our ability to reason rests entirely upon language – there are no mental operations, only linguistic ones.

Gilchrist does not seem to see any conflict inherent in citing both Harris and Horne Tooke as authorities. This may well indicate that he understood Horne Tooke's work to be presenting a less radical message than in fact it is. It would be perfectly possible to accept that reasoning depends on language to the extent that mental operations are always realised *through* language, while rejecting the stronger claim that there are no mental operations *beyond* the operations of language. And this less radical position would not constitute the damning attack on general grammar that Horne Tooke actually intended.[17] At any rate, what really caught Gilchrist's imagination in Horne Tooke's work was the idea that all language originally arose from primitive entities that were homogeneous in character. *The Diversions of Purley* contains a mass of etymologies in which modern English conjunctions, adverbs and prepositions are all derived from Anglo-Saxon nouns and verbs. The idea that a language might be broken into its most radical constituents in this way proved very exciting to Gilchrist and, as we shall see in Chapter 7, he attempted to apply the same principles of analysis to Hindustani and uncover the 'significant particles' from which the language was composed.

---

[17] There are eighteenth-century precedents for the kind of position outlined here. In his discussion of Wilkins's philosophical language, for example, Gilchrist (1798b: xviii n.) quotes the work of the Scottish philosopher Dugald Stewart, who asserts that 'errors in reasoning' often arise as a result of the use of words as an '*instrument of thought*'. Stewart's use of this expression does not indicate that he sees mental operations as reducible to the operations of language, but only that language is the vehicle through which mental operations such as abstraction are implemented and that, as such, it has considerable influence over our ability to reason. For this reason, he argues, some languages are better than others as vehicles of reasoning, and he briefly considers the possibility that a philosophical language might be invented, noting that Leibniz experimented with the idea and mentioning the new nomenclature of chemistry as evidence of the value of accurate naming. The quotation is from Stewart (1792–1827 I: 201–2).

In the meantime, it is worth making a brief comparison between Robert Lowth's handling of Old English data and John Horne Tooke's. The two approaches now look very different, not least because Lowth's arguments show the kind of caution we expect in contemporary historical work, while Horne Tooke's have the recklessness so characteristic of early modern etymology. But the two bodies of work probably seemed much more similar to Gilchrist and his contemporaries. Both writers resort to Anglo-Saxon to explain the philosophical status of forms in the modern language – Lowth 'resolves' the strange structure, *woe is me*, by suggesting that *me* is really an Anglo-Saxon dative; Horne Tooke argues that *if* is really an abbreviated form of the verb Anglo-Saxon verb *gifan*. There is a structural similarity to the two arguments and, what is more, a functional one as well, since both resort to history to explain the 'true' nature of language in the present, uncovering systematicity in places where it initially seems lacking. This, moreover, is the very point of Gilchrist's project – to show that a language previously thought to be wild, irregular and ungoverned by rules is perfectly orderly if one only pays enough attention. For all that Lowth and Horne Tooke look different to the modern reader, we should be aware that both are making arguments about the philosophical underpinnings of language and, as such, provide Gilchrist with very similar resources as he attempts to locate the philosophical basis on which the grammar of Hindustani rests.

3.4 CONCLUSION

The overall theme of this book is the relationship between the political and the technical dimensions of colonial language study as exemplified in the work of John Gilchrist. The first two chapters dealt with the sociopolitical contexts of Gilchrist's research and Chapter 1 explored the way in which other scholars have conceptualised the relationship between language and power in the colonial state. I suggested that previous accounts of the topic have often underplayed the extent to which language and communication were productive of an anxiety that, at some points in Gilchrist's work, borders on paranoia. This sense of danger arose from the difficulty of controlling one's own self-representation through the medium of a foreign language. To speak in a language other than one's own is to make oneself vulnerable, and commentators like Gilchrist saw this vulnerability as a space in which resistance and subversion might flourish. Gilchrist presented his grammatical work as an attempt to persuade his compatriots of the need to engage seriously with the forms and structures of Hindustani – to put aside the 'classical' languages and make a concerted attempt to master what he saw as the main 'vernacular' language of northern India. But the persistent belief that Hindustani was an irregular and chaotic 'jargon' – a belief that may, in itself, have been fuelled by colonial anxiety – stood in the way. An important function of Gilchrist's grammatical analyses was therefore to represent Hindustani to his readers as an orderly 'vernacular' rather than a barbarous 'jargon'. As we saw in Chapter 2, a number of specific contextual factors shaped this project, including Gilchrist's own lack of status as a scholar and the fact that the notion of Hindustani as 'jargon' had been propagated in the work of his commercial rival, George Hadley. But there were also difficulties arising from the structure of the language itself because, although Hindustani is an Indo-European language, it nevertheless differs sufficiently from the languages of western Europe for it to have seemed strange, and even troubling, to eighteenth-century westerners.

This chapter has provided an account of the intellectual climate in which Gilchrist conducted his defence of Hindustani. The discussion has emphasised the fact that the language study of the late eighteenth and early nineteenth centuries was not conceptualised as an empirical science, and that scholarly generalisations about language tended be laid down a priori within the disciplines of philosophy and rhetoric. The result was that, if a language resisted assimilation into the framework supplied by those disciplines, it might be condemned as an inadequate medium of communication. For a practical grammarian like Gilchrist, therefore, it was necessary to work with one eye on the 'science' of grammar, and develop an analysis of the language that fitted the patterns identified as essential to human language within areas such as general grammar or the debate over 'analogy' and 'anomaly'. To point to the way in which these forms of language study overshadowed the description of individual languages is not to say anything especially new. But commentators on this area frequently characterise fields such as general grammar in reductively political terms, the work of Olivia Smith and Janet Sorensen providing examples of this approach. I have argued here that none of the main areas of eighteenth-century language study can be characterised as inherently conservative or radical, if those terms are understood to mean privileging the classical languages and resisting the privilege of the classical languages respectively. They often *are* mobilised for conservative purposes, but it is simply not true to say that the universalist orientation of general grammar makes it inherently more conservative than the linguistic relativism that is often associated, rightly or wrongly, with Romantic thought. Operating within a universalist perspective, Gilchrist finds strategies that enable him to defend Hindustani against the charge that it is a 'jargon'.[18]

Gilchrist's engagement with contemporary debates over the nature of human language and languages also provided him with opportunities in

---

[18] Of course, his work on Hindustani must ultimately be seen as conservative in its close relationship with the maintenance of colonial power. However, it proceeds not by stigmatising Hindustani but by valorising it and, in this sense, has to resist conservative approaches to language, hence the need for precise definitions of the term.

terms of his own self-representation. In the last chapter we saw that, when Gilchrist first began his work on Hindustani, he had no scholarly credentials to speak of, his education having fitted him more to a practical career as a surgeon than to a literary career as a scholarly orientalist. Despite the fact that the debates outlined in this chapter functioned at a relatively technical level, it was nevertheless possible for Gilchrist to dramatise his participation in them in such a way that he invited the reader to form a particular picture of him as a scholar. The idea that grammatical scholarship can be conducted with showmanship may seem strange. But other kinds of technical enquiry are obviously susceptible to this sort of exploitation, and in this context it is helpful to remember the way in which natural science became a space for showmanship and performance over the course of the eighteenth century. Images of the period regularly explore the drama of experimental science, an excellent example being Joseph Wright's painting *An Experiment on a Bird in an Air Pump*, which is now in the National Gallery in London. The painting depicts an experiment in which a bird is imprisoned in a glass jar from which the air is being removed with a hand pump. The point of the procedure is that, as the jar is evacuated, the bird falls unconscious and eventually dies, thus demonstrating its dependence on air. The 'natural philosopher' who is demonstrating the experiment stands at the centre of the picture, pumping the air from the jar while a human drama is played out around him, the participants focused in a tight oval of artificial light. Two little girls cry openly at the suffering of their pet cockatoo; their father encourages them to look, anxious that they should not miss the instructive sight of their bird being suffocated; three young men are engrossed in the spectacle, one twisting his body uncomfortably in his desire to see what is happening; an older man in the foreground of the picture sits quietly, his hands resting on his cane – he will not look at the suffering bird but gazes at the table just in front of him and has even removed his spectacles, implying perhaps a desire not to witness the horrible events unfolding before him.

The 'philosopher' at the centre of Wright's picture is a showman as well as a scientist. He cuts a dramatic figure, his expressionless face framed by a cascading mane of hair and his gaze directed out of the picture and straight into the eyes of the viewer, demanding attention and involvement. He stands at the focal point of the image, controlling the spectacle and extorting every ounce of emotion from his audience before he finally releases the stopcock so that the bird can breathe. Thus, while the experiment is ostensibly intended to educate those who witness it in the biological needs of living creatures, it also constitutes a performance, the apparatus an exotic stage set and the action of the drama an archetypal struggle between life and death. If it seems an exaggeration to suggest that a grammarian could also be a showman, dramatising intellectual enquiry before an audience of readers, we should remember Gilchrist's image of himself at Faizabad, clothed 'in the dress of the natives' with 'a long black beard'. And we might also recall the narrative of his escape from death in the rainy season of 1785:

> The mere thought of closing my eyes forever among strangers, without a friend to witness the last sad office to the dead, animated me with the little vigour I had left, and hurried me by land across a district flooded with water, in the very height of the rains, to Bunarus. (Gilchrist 1798b: viii)

The picture that Gilchrist paints of himself here is scarcely less dramatic than the figure of the scientist in Joseph Wright's painting. He has cast himself in the role of hero, travelling in disguise, risking death for his scholarship, fighting his way across an exotic flooded landscape to find refuge in the holy city on the Ganges. But it is not only in his autobiographical narrative that Gilchrist takes on the role of showman. In the technical details of his grammatical work he is also able to dramatise the making of knowledge in a way that is reminiscent of Wright's long-haired natural philosopher. Thus, rather than merely alluding to the work of general grammarians or elocutionist rhetoricians as a way of justifying his analysis of a particular form or structure, he will often *reverse* the relation, claiming that his research into the grammar of Hindustani provides a way of justifying – or even modifying – the claims of the western scholars in question. In the preface of 1798, he discusses the applicability of John Horne Tooke's ideas to forms in Hindustani and, having presented derivations of a range of postpositions and conjunctions, concludes that much of the verbal morphology can also be derived from a couple of common verbs – *honā* ('be') and *jānā* ('go'). Inspired by this discovery, he redirects his gaze towards Europe and claims that the morphology of the Latin verb can be analysed in exactly the same way. If grammarians of Latin would only recognise the central role played by the verbs *esse* ('be') and *ire* ('go') in the formation of verbal morphology, it would be possible to 'reduce the Latin to one or two conjugations' and '*esse* and *ire* [would] take their place in the van, rather than in the rear, as they now do of Latin verbs' (Gilchrist 1798b: xlvi). Thus, he makes an observation about Hindustani and then uses that observation as the basis of an intervention in discussions about the analysis of a western language.

Arguments of this kind appear often in Gilchrist's writing – we shall find examples in his discussions of nominal and verbal morphology as well as in his work on etymology – and they are important partly because they contribute so strongly to the naturalisation of the language. The strategy of pointing out resemblances between languages itself reinforces this effect, raising the fundamental question of whether Hindustani can really be a 'jargon' if it resembles western languages in so many ways. But the effect is particularly striking when the focus of the comparison shifts and the reader is presented with the idea that the Latin verb can be illuminated through a comparison with Hindustani rather than Hindustani always being explained by means of comparisons with Latin. The structure of the argument forces readers, for a short time at least, to accept the naturalness of the Hindustani forms; otherwise they will not be able to follow the argument any further. They may ultimately reject the speculative point that Gilchrist is trying to make, but they have, for a moment, experienced Hindustani in a new and startling way. Thus, the process of reversing the expected direction of comparison serves to defamiliarise the western languages in a way that can be helpful to Gilchrist in his project of rendering the eastern language more familiar. Hindustani may look strange, but in fact Latin and English are also strange, and the two kinds of strangeness are actually very similar. Gilchrist himself draws attention to the unconventionality of this procedure and hints at its defamiliarising function. Following on from his discussion of the etymology of the Latin verb, Gilchrist acknowledges that his readers may find his argument unusual, and in making this point he uses a metaphor drawn from natural science: 'It will doubtless be deemed a curious inversion of opticks in philology, to examine English and Latin through a Hindoostanee medium' (Gilchrist 1798b: xlvi).

The choice of an optical image reinforces the idea that Gilchrist's texts are intended to transform readers' perceptions of the objects they discuss. In the century and a half since the foundation of the Royal Society in 1660, the development of more sophisticated optical instruments had had an enormous impact on scientists' understanding of the natural world, and to compare an investigative procedure with the use of a microscope or telescope is to underline its potential as a medium of research. Moreover, although Gilchrist acknowledges that what he has done may be seen as an 'inversion' – and we might think here of the experience of looking down the wrong end of a telescope or of seeing one's own eye reflected in a microscope – he emphasises that it has been productive and interesting, as if the jolt in perception has acted as a spur to further exploration in the way that experiences of altered vision have acted as catalysts in optical research.[19] And the very fact that Gilchrist uses an image drawn from natural science is also important. In the first section of this chapter I argued that Gilchrist's practice of looking for philosophical accounts of language that fit the data of Hindustani constituted a kind of unofficial empiricism – a movement in the direction of testing theory against data, despite the fact that this cut against the dominant paradigm of language study in the

[19] In the seventeenth century, for example, Christiaan Huygens, a supporter of the wave theory of light, noticed that, when light passes through a crystal of calcite, it produces two images. This led him to speculate that the orientation of the crystal must in some sense be related to the direction of the wave and, thus, the transforming effects of the calcite crystal led him to develop his theory of the nature of light itself (Lipson et al. 1995: 7).

period. The comparison of linguistic and optical research also hints at a conception of linguistic scholarship that was not acknowledged in the period when Gilchrist was writing but emerged soon afterwards. And, as I suggested earlier, the movement towards the new paradigm may at the moment be conceptualised too much in terms of the great thinkers of the comparativist movement and with insufficient reference to the experiences of practical grammarians like Gilchrist.

At any rate, as well as contributing to the naturalisation of the language, Gilchrist's 'inversions of opticks' can also be seen as having an impact upon his own self-representation. The very act of making such an argument – setting it down on paper and asserting its validity – can be seen as a performance of scholarship. Gilchrist could simply have presented an analysis of the Hindustani data and left it at that. Instead, he presents himself as a wide-ranging thinker who is not confined to the 'art' of grammar but is constantly intervening at the level of 'science'. James Harris, Robert Lowth, Thomas Sheridan, John Horne Tooke – Gilchrist presents these thinkers not as distant authorities whose wisdom justifies his own humble efforts but as his peers and sparring partners. He is constantly telling us how his researches 'confirm' their findings and cast light on their arguments in a range of different areas. Thus, even within his grammatical analyses, Gilchrist engages in a kind of showmanship, not simply setting out the results of his labours but drawing attention to himself in the process of research. And this mode of self-promotion is reinforced by the metaphors he uses. In the optical image quoted above, he presents himself as a scientist, surveying the heavens with his telescope or peering at insects through a microscope. Elsewhere, he implies that he is a lawyer, arguing in court on behalf of the language, an adventurer, rescuing Hindustani from a mauling by bears, or a traveller, journeying through the landscape of the language, opening up paths and leading the way.

There is a real sense of self-consciousness in Gilchrist's writing – a determination to draw attention to his achievements both in the way he structures his arguments and in the images through which he represents himself. Not all grammars read like this. Some are virtually seamless. I have already cited William Jones's famous description of Persian as a good example of a text that contains almost no indication of the processes of its own composition. But Gilchrist's works seem to textualise the very processes of his thought – to *dramatise* the making of knowledge in a very overt and performative way. This is no doubt connected with the marginal position that Gilchrist occupied when he first began his research. He was focusing on a language that many believed to be a 'jargon', and he had little social capital to draw on as he staked his claim to the status of a scholar. As such, his texts constitute acts of self-fashioning – in them and through them Gilchrist rendered himself visible as an expert in the eyes of the colonial establishment. It is unsurprising, then, that the texts gesture so frequently beyond the limits of the practical art of grammar, towards the marble halls where philosophers and rhetoricians, neglecting mundane particularities, debated the nature of human language as it essentially and necessarily was.

Each of the case studies in Part II examines a different aspect of Gilchrist's grammatical representation at a concrete level. Each provides a close reading of relevant portions of Gilchrist's grammatical works and, in the process, develops an account of the way in which he naturalised features of the language that might have seemed strange to western learners and foregrounded aspects of the language that fitted well into the patterns reified by philosophical and rhetorical thinkers. And each draws attention to the performative aspects of Gilchrist's publications – the dramatisation of research that is such a feature of his grammatical scholarship. Gilchrist's texts are fascinating documents. Despite their technicality, a strong sense of emotion often pervades them. And the feelings of triumph and frustration that emerge within them often seem to arise from the specific experience of struggling with technical problems, and doing so in the knowledge that the outcome of the struggle will seriously affect the way in which both language and author will be perceived. It is in these moments of struggle – or rather, in the textualisation of these moments of struggle – that the political dimensions of Gilchrist's project are played out. And to interpret these textualisations, we need to identify the way in which they are underpinned by a specific politics of representation. Terms such as 'classical', 'vernacular' and 'jargon' are simultaneously political and technical. Their use serves to insert a language into a hierarchical typology, indicating something about the cultural capital that accrues to it and the advantages of knowing it. But they also imply what it is like at a formal level, whether it has case endings, how it marks the tense of verbs and even what its phonological system might be like. Texts like Gilchrist's work with the complex semantics of these terms, reordering the reader's perceptions of the language with reference to both the political and technical meanings of the terms. The aim of the next four chapters is to show how that process works at a fine level of analysis and, in so doing, to point out the fact that the genre of the grammar can be as emotional, as performative and as disconcerting as any other mode of representation.

Part II

CASE STUDIES

4

NOUN CASE

4.1 INTRODUCTION

The category of noun case has an interesting place in the grammatical traditions of the western European 'vernaculars'. Originally developed as a way of analysing the rich nominal morphologies of Greek and Latin, the concept of case is less obviously applicable to languages like French and English, which express the semantic and syntactic roles of nouns not through changes in the morphology of the noun itself but through word order and prepositions. Early modern grammarians of the 'vernaculars' tended to cling to the category of case, partly because it provided a metalanguage for the discussion of syntax and partly, no doubt, just because it was familiar. To retain case in the analysis of languages like French and English required that they locate forms – or groups of forms – that could be seen as fulfilling similar functions to the case forms of Latin and Greek. Ian Michael (1970: 350–52), for example, points to a number of grammars in which the English cases are said to be marked through 'signs' positioned before the noun: '*[o]f* was the sign of the genitive, *to* of the dative, *by*, *with*, and *from* of the ablative.' By the late eighteenth century, however, it was commonplace to deny that English had cases and to see forms like *of*, *to* and *by* not as 'signs of cases' but as prepositions that stood in *place* of case endings.[1] What is more, neither general grammar nor the typological work that emerged from it suggested that case was a necessary feature of human languages. As we saw in Chapter 3, John Wilkins and James Harris, the two general grammarians of whom Gilchrist shows awareness, both characterise a Greek noun with a case ending as equivalent to an English noun constructed with a preposition. Furthermore, Wilkins asserts that his philosophical language will have no place for cases and will rely solely on prepositions, while Harris states that cases 'can be hardly said to fall within the limits of our Inquiry'. The typological essays of Gabriel Girard and William Smellie also cast doubt upon the necessity of case in that they characterise the case forms of 'transpositive' languages as functionally equivalent to the patterns of word order and the prepositional constructions of 'analogous' languages. Indeed, they imply that the latter are more natural than the former, if not always as expressive.

---

[1] See Vorlat (1975: 146–70) for a survey of approaches to case taken by English grammarians in the early modern period.

Thus, when Gilchrist began to analyse the structure of Hindustani in the early 1780s, he was under no intellectual obligation to use the category of case in his description. There were perfectly good precedents, both in practical grammars of the European 'vernaculars' and in the philosophical literature, for rejecting the category entirely and jettisoning the metalanguage associated with it. On the face of it, then, the issue looks very simple. Languages were widely understood to fall into two groups – those that had cases and those that relied on word order and prepositions to express the same roles and relations. For Gilchrist the problem was simply to decide which category Hindustani belonged to. In practice, however, the matter turned out not to be so simple. First, it proved very difficult to locate Hindustani within either of the mutually exclusive classes. In the face of the data, the dichotomy itself began to look simplistic, and when Gilchrist finally managed to resolve the technical difficulty of describing the properties of Hindustani nouns, he did so by cutting the Gordian knot and suggesting that there was in fact only one kind of language after all. Second, the abstract relations that were felt to underlie the formal structures of different languages were still too closely tied to particular western languages to accommodate some of the morphosyntactic properties of Hindustani. Despite the undoubted liberality of the typological view, with its power to release grammarians from the endless search for genitives, datives and ablatives, the categories of nominative and accusative remained much more deeply entrenched. Whether marked by case endings or by word order, the contrast between these two categories was seen as having a naturalness that made the ergative word order to be found in Hindustani seem very strange indeed.[2]

In the first part of this book, I argued that the resistance of some Asian languages to traditional western modes of analysis was problematic in the sense that it sometimes led to the stigmatisation of those languages and supported stereotypes of the chaotic and disordered colony. To the reader encountering Hindustani for the first time, the discussion of noun case in the grammar of 1796 certainly gives the impression of chaos and disorder. Gilchrist's use of the term 'case' is itself highly ambiguous, and his account of the Hindustani ergative is really very opaque. But in the more 'conciliating' publications that appeared subsequently, Gilchrist began to move towards a more coherent account of the formal and functional properties of Hindustani nouns, and as he did so, he quite explicitly drew attention to the way in which that movement served to normalise

---

[2] I have avoided using the terms subject and object here because, as Michael (1970: 481–5) shows and as will be evident from my discussion of James Harris later in this chapter, these terms were still very ambiguous in the later eighteenth century, the term 'subject' denoting sometimes what we would call the grammatical subject of a sentence and sometimes the semantic role of patient, which is often associated with what we would call the object of a transitive verb.

Hindustani and neutralise the accusations of strangeness to which it might otherwise be susceptible. As such, the example of noun case provides an excellent instance of the fusion of technical and political issues in the analysis of colonial languages. It beautifully illustrates the way in which the technical dimensions of grammar constituted a medium of representation through which writers like Gilchrist could construct the 'vernacular' languages of the colonies as more or less 'polished' and 'polite'. For this reason, the rest of this chapter will be devoted to a close look at the technicalities of Gilchrist's grammatical representation, focusing first on what Masica (1991: 231) has called the 'layering' of 'case-like elements' in Hindustani – the feature of the language that made it so difficult to place in relation to the typological dichotomy outlined above – and then on the issue of ergativity, which seemed so bizarre to early British commentators. In both cases, the solutions that Gilchrist finds to the mismatch between western expectations and Asian realities serve to minimise the sense of strangeness surrounding the language and to induce western readers to put aside their sense of Hindustani as a disordered 'jargon' ungoverned by rules or rational principles.

4.2 The 'layering' of 'case-like elements'

In discussing the place of Hindustani in the eighteenth-century typology of languages, I shall make extensive use of the word LAYERING, a term I have borrowed from Colin Masica's survey of the Indo-Aryan languages, which was first published in 1991. Masica (1991: 231) notes that in the modern Indo-Aryan languages it is possible to identify 'at least three layers of forms with case-like functions'. Old Indo-Aryan had rich system of inflectional morphology, and eight cases were marked in Classical Sanskrit. Indeed, this is one of the reasons that Europeans were so entranced by Sanskrit when they first encountered it. Here in South Asia was a language that displayed many of the features that they admired in Greek and Latin, including a rich morphology for the clear expression of all the conceptions of the human mind. When William Jones described Sanskrit as 'more *perfect* than the Greek' (my emphasis) in his famous 'philologer' speech of 1786, he was using a term traditionally employed in praise of the inflectional systems of the languages of learning. And the greater perfection of Sanskrit could be demonstrated on straightforwardly arithmetic grounds – a language with eight cases was in a higher state of perfection than a language with four or five. But in Middle Indo-Aryan this system began to disintegrate, with phonological changes leading to the erosion of case endings until eventually the roles of nouns were not marked with sufficient clarity. In the New Indo-Aryan languages, therefore, sets of 'secondary affixes' emerged in addition to the 'primary affixes' or residual inflections which remained from the original system. Unlike the primary affixes, these second-layer elements do not display declensional variation. They usually appear in combination with one of the first-layer inflections, and derive from words that were once independent nouns or verbs. Third-layer elements are also identifiable, and are typically mediated by a second-layer element. Their origins as independent lexical items are usually more obvious than those of the secondary affixes.[3]

In Hindustani, and in modern Hindi and Urdu, only one distinction is realised at the first level, that between the DIRECT and OBLIQUE forms.[4] In many sentences, both subject and object appear in the unmarked direct form, the oblique form appearing mainly when the noun is followed by a second-layer element.[5] A slight complication arises because the object of the verb sometimes appears in the oblique form marked with the second-layer element *ko*, the distinction between an unmarked object and an object marked with *ko* being one of definiteness.[6] In contemporary descriptions of Hindi and Urdu, second-layer elements are usually known as 'simple postpositions' and they always follow the oblique form.[7] Third-layer elements are mediated by an appropriate form of the simple postposition *kā*. They are usually known as 'compound postpositions', owing to their appearing in conjunction with *kā*, and they are far more numerous than the second-layer elements. For Gilchrist, the layering of these 'case-like elements' made it difficult to adjudicate on the issue of whether Hindustani did or did not have cases. The first-layer elements, being 'terminations' of the noun, are unambiguously case-like in a formal sense. But they do not fulfil anything like the range of semantic and syntactic functions which the classical cases do: the distinction between the direct and oblique forms does not correspond to the distinction between subject and object as the distinction between nominative and accusative does; nor does either of these forms express the kinds of relations marked by the classical genitive and dative. If anything, the oblique form is most like the Latin ablative, which, according to Harris (1751: 276–7), was invented by the Romans '*to associate with their Prepositions,* as they had deprived their *Genitive* and

---

[3] See Bloch (1965: 155–60), Masica (1991: 230–32) and Zograph (1982: 9–18) for some discussion of these forms and the diachronic processes responsible for their emergence. Schmidt (1999: 81–4) provides a very helpful summary of the Urdu compound prepositions.

[4] The oblique form can function as a vocative, however, and, when used in this way, certain forms with nasalized endings lose their nasalization. For this reason, the 'vocative' is sometimes cited as an additional third form.

[5] Nouns in the oblique form can also occur in adverbial expressions without any second-layer elements, and adverbial expressions of time frequently take this form.

[6] See Masica (1986) for a discussion of this issue.

[7] Zograph (1982: 35) lists all seven with suggested case descriptors: *ko* (accusative and dative), *se* (instrumental, sociative, and ablative), *mē* (locative, intensive), *par* (locative, superessive), *tak* (terminative), *ne* (agentive or ergative) and *kā, ke, kī* (adjectival). These are the forms that have survived into modern Hindi and Urdu. See Beg (1988: 216–20) for eighteenth-century variants.

Dative of that privilege'. Harris's little narrative is clearly inapplicable to Hindustani, since it does not have a genitive or dative and cannot therefore have 'deprived' those cases of any privileges. Moreover, Harris states that the ablative is 'certainly not necessary', and so it seems odd that it should be the one case that appears in Hindustani.

Given the failure of the direct and oblique forms to fulfil the semantic and syntactic roles expected of cases, one approach for a grammarian like Gilchrist would be to sweep them under the carpet and suggest that Hindustani, like English and French, is one of those languages where prepositions – or rather postpositions – fulfil the functions of cases.[8] The second- and third-layer elements clearly mark the kinds of roles and relations that the case endings do in Latin and Greek, so it would be perfectly possible to say either that these constitute 'signs of cases' in the way that some grammarians had of the English prepositions *of, to, by* and so on, or to reject the idea that Hindustani has case at all and say that, in the great typological dichotomy between 'analogous' and 'transpositive' languages, this is a language that falls into the former camp. This is very much the line that George Hadley takes in his grammar of 1772. There we are told that 'Moors' has a 'Postposition or Article governing the Case' and this entity is declined as follows:

Nom. —
Gen. Kau, *of.*
Dat. Ko, *to.*
Accus. —
Vocat. A<u>uou</u>! *O!*
　　　Sa, *with* or *from.*
Ablat. Ma, *or* maingh, *in.*
　　　Ka-wostah, *for.* (Hadley 1772: 3)

Here 'kau' (*kā*), 'ko' (*ko*), 'sa', (*se*) and 'ma' or 'maingh' (*mē*) are second-layer elements, 'auou' is an interjection and 'ka-wostah' (*ke vāste*) is a third-layer element. The idea that these forms constitute not a collection of postpositions but the case forms of a single postposition is a little odd, since prepositions, and hence presumably postpositions, were not generally seen as susceptible to declension in early modern grammar. In fact, this may be why Hadley supplies an alternative term for the 'postposition', namely the 'article'. The idea of an article that marks case was common in the French

---

[8] Hadley (1772: 3) implies that some people viewed the postpositions as themselves being case endings, an idea which is understandable given that they appear directly after nouns and fulfil some of the functions of case endings. As Hadley himself points out, however, if these forms were case endings, they 'would have been attached to an Adjective as well as a Substantive, and very likely would have altered in different words so as to have made a variety of declension; whereas there is but one regular method of declining a noun'. One cannot help feeling that this is a fairly sophisticated argument for a mere 'jargonist'!

and Italian grammatical traditions. In grammars of Italian, for example, the forms *il* ('the'), *del* ('of the'), *al* ('to the') and *dal* ('from the') were frequently described as the declined forms of a masculine article. Indeed, as Michael (1970: 356–7) notes, similar metalanguage is sometimes used in English grammars too, although it is far less convincing because there are no forms where there is any sense that the article has coalesced with a preposition. Fortunately for Hadley, there is no article in 'Moors' as such and so this difficulty does not arise. But the problem, of course, is that Hadley's account of the noun in 'Moors' leaves the direct and oblique forms completely unanalysed. He does not even smuggle them tacitly into the examples he gives, and so readers have no way of knowing that they need to produce the oblique form before all the forms of the 'article' so carefully set out in Hadley's matrix. The analysis *looks* coherent, but readers who follow it are likely to make a lot of mistakes when they are actually speaking the language. And this is the problem that Gilchrist struggles with in his own work. It is all very well developing a more liberal view of grammatical structure in which it is accepted that languages do not all have to be the same but can follow one of two different patterns. But what happens when one encounters a language that fits into a different pattern depending on how one looks at it?

In the grammar of 1796, Gilchrist does not manage to separate out the layers of case-marking in any very effective manner and ends up using the term in a highly ambiguous fashion. The category of case is discussed in chapter 2 of the text, 'Of The Noun', and particularly in the third section of the chapter, 'Of Declension'. The material presented in this section is organised into four rules, and appended to the final one is a table of postpositions which Gilchrist (1796: 58) describes as a 'scheme of general declension'. The first three rules are concerned with case in a strictly formal sense, focusing only on the way in which the form of the noun itself changes in order to express particular semantic and syntactic relations. Three cases are discussed – the 'nominative' (the form now labelled the direct), the 'oblique' or 'objective' (the form still known as the oblique), and the 'vocative' (the oblique form but without nasalization) (Gilchrist 1796: 55–6). In a footnote Gilchrist considers the possibility that there might be another case but rejects the idea: 'Though the inflected particle *ke*, and *izafut i* or *e* [...] resemble our genetive [*sic*] in *'s*, they can hardly be said to form a distinct case, since the first evidently belongs to the postpositions, and the last to the Persian language' (Gilchrist 1796: 55).[9] It is clear from this comment that, at

---

[9] The postposition, *kā* which inter alia expresses possession, has the distinctive property of changing its form according to the gender and number of the noun it precedes. Compared with some other features of Hindustani grammar, this seemed a relatively minor novelty to western observers, but it did attract some attention and will be discussed later in this chapter. The enclitic *izāfat* was borrowed from Persian, and is used in Hindustani and modern Urdu to link a noun and a qualifying word such as an adjective or another noun. When linking two nouns, *izāfat* 'shows a possessive relationship in which the first noun (or pronoun) belongs to the second' (Schmidt 1999: 246).

this point, Gilchrist is thinking of cases strictly as terminations or endings on the noun. The analysis focuses very much on the formal properties of various categories of nouns, using a group of terms that specify how many distinct forms each noun has – 'aptotes' for nouns that are invariable, 'diptotes' for nouns that have two forms, 'triptotes' for nouns that have three forms. Thus, for example,

> MASCULINES that terminate with *a, u, uh*, are [...] *Diptotes*, by these letters being inflected to *e, in the Singular oblique*, and nominative Plural; but Triptotes in this Number, changing the *e* above, to *o*, for the vocative, and *oṅ*, for the *objective case*. (Gilchrist 1796: 55)

This choice of terminology very much reinforces the idea of case as a formal rather than a semantic/syntactic category. The term 'case' is used strictly to describe the morphology of the noun, and forms that are functionally similar to cases in other languages – the particle, *kā*, for example – are refused the status of cases here on the grounds that a case must be realised by an ending on the noun.

However, in the fourth of the rules which constitute Gilchrist's discussion 'Of Declension', the term 'case' is employed quite differently. Here it is used of the whole range of semantic and syntactic roles that nouns can play and not the particular ones that are marked by endings on the noun. Thus, we are told:

> The GENERAL DECLENSION OF HINDOOSTANEE NOUNS, is founded as in our own language, on particles, that from their situation in this, have been very properly styled [...] postpositions [...] which will here point out, all the possible cases at once, without a servile adherence to the common forms of the Latin noun. (Gilchrist 1796: 57)

Here Gilchrist is clearly aligning Hindustani with western 'vernaculars' such as English and French in its reliance on adpositions rather than case endings for the expression of semantic and syntactic relations. But his insistence on calling all these relations 'cases' is a little unusual. English grammarians who want to retain the term tend to pick out a group of prepositions whose functions parallel those of the Latin cases and describe them as 'signs of cases'. Thus, *to* might be a sign of the dative case because a noun constructed with *to* can play a similar semantic role within a sentence to that played by a Latin noun in the dative case. But Gilchrist's position is more radical and resembles that of John Wilkins in his *Essay*. As we saw in Chapter 3, Wilkins asserts that 'the true notion of the *Genitive, Dative, Ablative* Case, is nothing else but that obliquity in the sence [*sic*] of a Substantive, which is caused and signified by some Preposition annexed to it' (Wilkins 1668: 352). This leads Wilkins to claim that there is no basis at all for marking some of these 'obliquities' with terminations and others with prepositions, and he goes on to reject the idea that case is a necessary feature of human language entirely. Gilchrist takes a very similar position but applies his terms differently, claiming that all the relations marked by postpositions are cases. He also states:

> [The learner] is or ought to be acquainted with the nature, properties, extent, and application of the prepositions, &. as possessive, passive, objective, vocative, causal, or locative signs, in his vernacular language; without being swayed in any language by these, and the rigid, often inapplicable, distinctions of genetive [*sic*], dative, accusative, and ablative. (Gilchrist 1796: 58)

Thus, Gilchrist takes a strongly anti-classical line, asserting the importance of the semantic and syntactic categories that underlie language in general rather than the particular distinctions marked on the Latin noun but choosing to redefine the traditional term 'case' to describe those underlying categories rather than simply abandoning it, as Wilkins does.

The picture presented in the grammar is interesting but confusing. The modern academic reader brings to the analysis a clear sense that cases are twofold entities in which the correlation between form and function is of primary importance. For this reason he or she will not find it so difficult to prise apart the two senses in which Gilchrist uses the term – in the first three rules Gilchrist is talking about entities that resemble the Latin cases formally and in the final rule he is talking about entities that resemble them in a functional sense. But for a young army officer in the late eighteenth or early nineteenth century, when the category of case was still very controversial, even supposing that he was reading material that dealt with such issues, it must have been very confusing to be told sternly that Hindustani has three cases and then immediately afterwards informed that it has a multitude of cases, all expressed by means of postpositions.

But by the time Gilchrist published *The British Indian Monitor*, the first volume of which appeared in 1806, he had settled on a much more effective treatment of these issues. The theory of noun declension that appears in this later text depends upon a distinction between 'inflexion' and 'case'. A noun is said to appear 'in the inflexion' if it is in what is now known as the oblique form, while cases are said to be realised through the combination of nouns and postpositions. In other words, the term 'case' is no longer used in the first of the senses discussed above, the term 'inflexion' being used instead and 'case' being employed only in the second sense discussed above. Thus, Gilchrist (1806–8 I: 67) tells us: 'By inflexion is meant that part of a noun or pronoun, which, with the aid of prepositions, or postpositions, forms what are called the various cases of nouns.' And he develops this idea in the following more detailed statement:

Nouns are declined, like those of both ancient and modern languages, on the twofold principle of inflexions and postpositions combined in one, which still exists among our pronouns, I, me; thou, thee; he, him [...] Particles termed, from their apparent preposterous situation, postpositions, perform the office of our prepositions, in the formation of the various cases of every noun, which must then appear, if declinable, in the inflexion, as our—of him, from thee; never—of he, from thou. (Gilchrist 1806–8 I: 140)

In setting out paradigms, Gilchrist (1806–8 I: 144–5) uses the traditional Latin case names and chooses one postposition to mark each, rather as Hadley had in his *Grammatical Remarks*. The resemblance to Hadley's text of course explains this apparently retrograde step – a scheme based closely on the Latin one appealed to less scholarly readers because it was familiar and, as such, easy to assimilate. Elsewhere, however, Gilchrist echoes the fighting talk of rule four of the grammar:

[T]he number and names of the various cases depend entirely on the nature of the postpositions, which the learner may subdivide into objective, dative, locative, social, instrumental, ablative, causal, communicative, &c. thereby forming as many cases as he pleases, in the true spirit of logical subdivision. (Gilchrist 1806–8: 140–41)

And so this is Gilchrist's developed theory of case: Hindustani has a certain formal resource, the 'inflexion', which in combination with postpositions forms 'cases' but is not itself one. These 'cases' are to be defined and categorised on the basis of the underlying semantic and syntactic relations that they express, and not on the basis of the way in which case works in any other particular language.

What is especially striking about this passage is Gilchrist's claim that the 'twofold principle of inflexion and postpositions' can be identified in both 'ancient and modern languages'. Far from being a strange and philosophically dubious entity, therefore, the oblique form is said to be the particular realisation in Hindustani of a phenomenon that is more or less universal. Gilchrist adds to the characterisation of this principle as a universal by stating that the 'inflexion' forms cases with the aid of either postpositions *or prepositions*, which makes it clear that the analysis is meant to apply to languages other than the particular one he is describing. In an earlier version of the explanation, which Gilchrist had sketched out in *The Anti-Jargonist*, he had also referred to his principle as 'the general doctrine of the difference between a case and an inflection' (Gilchrist 1800: lvii). The assertion of this 'general doctrine' cuts right across the typological distinctions described by Girard and Smellie, who had classified languages by considering how they marked the logical structure of the proposition at a formal level. Those that did so through prepositions and word order were described as 'analogous', while those that marked the relationships between words through terminations were labelled 'transpositive'. But here we are told that in both 'ancient and modern languages' it is normal to find the relations between words marked by prepositions, or rather adpositions, in combination with a termination, or inflection. Gilchrist does not state that all languages work in this way, but at the very least he is suggesting that an extensive third group of languages do.

This is typical of what I described in Chapter 3 as Gilchrist's showmanship. Rather than simply working out some coherent metalanguage for the description of Hindustani nouns and leaving it at that, he claims that the explanation he has produced applies to a wide range of other languages as well. He thus takes up a position at both the political and personal levels. Far from apologising for a feature of Hindustani that his readers may find problematic, he goes on the offensive and disrupts the received wisdom in the area of language typology, demanding that readers reconsider their views of other languages on the basis of what he has found out about Hindustani. If you find this language strange, he implies, then you are going to have to accept that all sorts of other languages are strange too, including English. By making claims to have uncovered a universal doctrine, Gilchrist also elevates himself beyond the level of the mere practitioner of the 'art' of grammar and makes claims to the status of a participant in 'science'. He is not simply reducing a particular language to rules but, as Smellie put it in his definition of the science of grammar, 'view[ing] language *in itself*' (my emphasis). Gilchrist's discussion of case constitutes an 'inversion of optics' of the kind discussed in Chapter 3. Instead of merely using ideas from western language study to help him with the description of Hindustani, Gilchrist uses the experience to look back at the west and challenge both its languages and its linguistics.

It is worth taking time to consider the models that underlie Gilchrist's approach and the influences that may have led him to move from the analysis in the grammar to the one developed in the *British Indian Monitor*. In the grammar, Gilchrist describes the oblique form as the 'oblique or objective case'. Now this terminology closely echoes the metalanguage of another grammar of an Indian vernacular, Nathaniel Halhed's *Grammar of the Bengal Language*, published in 1778. Gilchrist (1798: iv) refers very favourably to it in the preface to his dictionary and grammar, and it was often cited as one of the seminal works of early British scholarship in India. In his account of Bengali nouns, Halhed identifies a form 'made by the addition of the letter [...] a' and proposes that it be called 'the *Oblique case* in general, from its frequent use'. Now, this 'oblique case' is, as Halhed puts it, 'occasionally applied to five several cases':

To the nominative (redundantly) [...] To the passive or subjective case [...] It serves to convey the sense of the third, fifth and seventh of the Shanscrit cases: as [...] baana with an arrow; [...] gog*o*na from heaven: [...] maasa in the month: [...] k*olee*kaataay in Calcutta [...] It is added to the termination of the possessive case, to form the dative [...] It is also employed to distinguish the vocative, and may either be prefixed or subjoined [...] (Halhed 1778: 55–6)

Thus in both texts an 'oblique case' is involved in the formation of a whole array of other 'cases', and while the 'oblique case' is really just a formal resource, the 'cases' formed from it are defined more functionally. As the above quotation shows, Halhed identifies the cases at the functional level with reference to the large inventory of cases found in Sanskrit. Thus the 'oblique' case in Bengali is said to 'convey the sense' of a number of the Sanskrit cases. In contrast, Gilchrist's discussion of case at the functional level is more reminiscent of general grammar and, in particular, of Wilkins's *Essay* in its focus on the semantics of adpositions and in its preoccupation with 'logical subdivision'. In spite of this difference, however, it seems highly likely that Gilchrist's conception of the oblique form as an 'oblique case' which is involved in the formation of other 'cases' owes something to Halhed and his analysis of Bengali.

However, in the grammar, Gilchrist provides a second name for the oblique form, the 'objective case', and this is reminiscent of Robert Lowth's *Short Introduction to English Grammar*. Lowth (1762: 32–3) asserts that English pronouns have three cases:

[T]he Nominative; the Genitive, or Possessive; like Nouns; and moreover a Case, which follows the Verb Active, or the Preposition, expressing the Object of an Action, or of a Relation. It answers to the Oblique Cases in Latin; and may be properly enough called the Objective Case.

Lowth's 'objective case' is similar to Halhed's 'oblique case' in that both constitute forms that mark pronouns or nouns for a range of 'oblique', or non-nominative, roles. But while Halhed speaks vaguely about the 'oblique case' being 'applied' to other cases, Lowth provides a more concrete account of how his 'objective case' is involved in marking the sorts of roles played by the oblique cases in Latin. It does this by 'expressing the Object of an Action or a Relation'. What Lowth means is that the 'objective case' of a pronoun can form the object of a verb or, crucially, appear after a preposition. Thus, as well as Halhed, Gilchrist seems to draw on Lowth's conception of the 'objective case' as a form which is commonly constructed with prepositions.

By the time we reach the *Anti-Jargonist* and *The British Indian Monitor*, Gilchrist has dropped the term 'case' as a label for the oblique form, and it may be that it was through an exploration of the analogy between English pronouns and Hindustani nouns that he reached this point. As the paragraph above suggests, the use of the term 'objective case' suggests that this exploration had already begun when he was writing the grammar, in that 'objective case' is a term used by Lowth for the analysis of pronouns. By the time *The Anti-Jargonist* was published, Gilchrist was making the analogy quite explicit, listing the English pronouns and asserting:

> As we therefore cannot form the various cases of the above without the inflection and preposition united, neither can the Hindoostanees make their cases without observing the same rules, wherever the word is inflectible. (Gilchrist 1800: lvii)[10]

Now Gilchrist was certainly aware of two texts that analyse the phenomenon outlined by Lowth in his section on pronouns but do so without making use of the term 'case'. The two texts are John Wallis's *Grammatica linguae anglicanae*, which was published in 1653 and reached a fifth edition in 1765, and Thomas Ruddiman's *Rudiments of the Latin Tongue*, which was widely used in Scottish schools after its publication in 1714 and which Gilchrist cites on page 105 of his grammar.[11] In a section headed '*Pronominum status duplex*' ('the two states of pronouns'), Wallis states:

> [Pronouns] occur, both in singular and plural, in two different forms or states [*duplici fere forma seu statu*]; I call one of these *rect* and the other *oblique*. [...] The rect state is used when they appear in absolute position or before a verb, like the Latin rect case. Elsewhere the oblique state is used, that is, when they follow a verb, or a pre-position or another governing word. (Wallis 1972: 319–21)[12]

Thus, the oblique is described not as a 'case' (*casus*) but as a 'form' (*forma*) or 'state' (*status*). And the use of the term '*status*' reveals the origins of the

---

[10] The analysis of the oblique form as an 'inflexion' rather than a 'case' is hinted at in the account of personal and demonstrative pronouns presented in the grammar of 1796. Here Gilchrist (1796: 63) states: 'The first and second personals in this, as in other languages, are inflected irregularly; but like nouns, have their cases formed by the postpositions enumerated in the last chapter.' Similarly, in discussing the object forms of the personal pronouns (*mujhe, tujhe* and so on), he asserts that '*e* (and its plural *eñ*)' which appear at the ends of these forms are postpositions rather than 'inflections'. He defends this view on the grounds that 'every real inflection admits of some postposition or other after it; whereas mŏŏj,he, tŏŏj,he [...] never do' (Gilchrist 1796: 66–7). So, in the context of a discussion of pronouns we have inflection represented as a process distinct from the formation of cases and we have the idea that an inflection is a form which appears in construction with a postposition. It is probably no coincidence that the theory makes its first appearance in a discussion of pronouns, since grammatical accounts of the English pronominal system clearly had an important influence on Gilchrist's thinking in this area.

[11] See Duncan (1965: 85–96) for an account of Ruddiman's linguistic scholarship.

[12] All English versions of quotations from Wallis's *Grammaticae linguae anglicanae* are taken from J. A. Kemp's translation.

analysis in the Hebrew grammatical tradition, which employs the term *'status constructus'* to denote the form a noun must take in certain constructions where it is not head of the phrase.[13] Ruddiman's analysis is even more similar to Gilchrist's. In his 'Remarks on English Pronouns' he says:

> In the Nominative, or *Foregoing State* (as the English Grammarians call it) we use *I, Thou, He, She, We, Ye, They & Who*: But in the other Cases (which they name *The Following State*) we use *Me, Thee, Him, Her, Us, You, Them* and *Whom*. (Ruddiman 1714: 26)

Thus Ruddiman suggests that 'in the other Cases' a particular 'state' must be used, in much the same way that Gilchrist suggests that the various cases must be formed from an 'inflexion'.[14]

Gilchrist's terminology suggests that he used Halhed and Lowth as models when he developed the idea of an 'oblique' or 'objective case' that could be used in the formation of other cases and that was characterised by its appearance in construction with adpositions. His reading of Lowth may have led him to examine other accounts of English pronouns in which forms such as *me, him* or *us* were analysed using terms other than 'case' – 'state' or 'form', for example. And this strategy may have appealed to him in that it left the term 'case' free to talk about the way in which the semantic and syntactic roles of nouns were marked in a broader sense. But where does the term 'inflexion' come from? Why did Gilchrist settle on that term and not on 'state' or 'form'? The most likely explanation is that he went back to the text with which this discussion began, Halhed's grammar of Bengali, where we find the term 'inflexion' employed in discussions of the morphology of nouns. In his discussion of noun case in Sanskrit, for example, Halhed (1778: 52) tells us that each Sanskrit noun is 'capable of seven changes of inflexion, exclusive of the vocative', and in considering case in Bengali, he adds, 'The Inflexions of which a Bengal noun is capable are neither so copious nor so accurate; the terminations used for this purpose are four only, and consequently we can reckon but five cases at most' (Halhed 1778: 54). Thus, for Halhed, 'inflexion' is the process by which the citation form of a noun is altered formally in order to indicate that it is serving a particular function in a sentence. The terms 'inflexion' and 'case' are not systematically distinguished in Halhed's text, and as I indicated earlier, his 'oblique case' is formally and not functionally defined. Thus, Halhed's famous grammar of Bengali can be seen as supplying the materials for Gilchrist's final analysis but in a rather disordered form. The analysis of the English pronouns supplemented it by showing that the

---

[13] See Michael (1970: 513) on Wallis's use of the term *status*.

[14] Of course, by 'other Cases', Ruddiman may just mean 'other instances' rather than 'other grammatical cases'. But nevertheless, he does refer to the combination of a noun with a particle like *to* or *of* as a 'case' in the same way that Gilchrist does.

formal properties of pronouns, and hence nouns, could be described without resorting to the term 'case' at all.

Thus, in Gilchrist's account of the 'layering of case-like elements', we have a good example of the way in which he ransacks the existing grammatical literature in order to naturalise a feature of the language that initially seems difficult to explain. His account draws upon a range of different resources: Wilkins's idea that the theory of case is reducible to the theory of the preposition, Halhed's use of the terms 'oblique' and 'inflection' in reference to another Indo-Aryan language, Lowth's assertion that the 'objective case' of pronouns marks the 'object of a relation', and the rigorous refusal of the term 'case' in Wallis and Ruddiman's descriptions of English pronouns – a refusal that leads them to use a term from the Hebrew grammatical tradition to label forms such as *me*, *him* and *us*. Gilchrist does not copy any of these texts exactly but engages in the kind of unofficial empiricism discussed in the final section of Chapter 3, measuring the terms and concepts against the data of Hindustani and finally claiming to have developed a new theory in response to this experience. This new theory breaks apart the conventional typology of languages-with-case and languages-without-case, and is said to apply to a wide range of languages other than Hindustani. Gilchrist explicitly points out its applicability to the English pronominal system, and although he does not explicitly mention any other languages, it is true that in many languages prepositions have to be constructed with particular forms of nouns and pronouns.

I began this section by pointing out that the Hindustani oblique did not fit the picture of a classical 'case' since the one it most resembled was the Latin ablative, which Harris himself dismisses as 'certainly not necessary' and only present in Latin because the Romans had 'deprived' the genitive and dative of the 'privilege' of associating with prepositions. But, to look at it from Gilchrist's perspective, perhaps Harris is wrong and the ablative actually represents the universal 'inflexion' with which all – or many – languages mark the object of a relation. And maybe it is true that prepositions always demand special forms of nouns and pronouns, although in some languages all the nouns happen to be aptotes. Whether or not the reader finally agrees with Gilchrist, this kind of argumentation has a powerful naturalising effect on Hindustani, since it disrupts the easy sense of Latin as normal and Hindustani as strange, demanding that the reader set the forms of the languages side by side and ponder whether there is really any difference. And it allows Gilchrist to strike a pose as a philosophical thinker and not a mere grammarian. It is a strategy that he deploys again, furthermore, in describing how the idea of possession is expressed in Hindustani; and it will be useful to consider his treatment of this issue briefly before moving on to his account of ergativity.

4.3 THE POSSESSIVE ADJECTIVE

This issue hinges upon the fact that the Hindustani postposition *kā*, which is used to indicate possession, has a rather interesting formal feature – it must agree in gender and number with the noun that follows it. Thus, 'the boy's brother' could be translated *larke kā bhāī*, where *kā* is masculine singular to agree with *bhāī* 'brother'. Conversely, 'the boy's sister' would be translated *larke kī bahn*, where *kī* is feminine singular to agree with *bahn* 'sister'. Now, the idea that a preposition might be marked for number and gender sits ill with the traditional division of the parts of speech into two categories, variable and invariable. Prepositions belong firmly to the latter camp, and although Harris (1751: 35) for one questions the usefulness of the traditional distinction, he does so more on the grounds that the variations to which nouns and verbs are susceptible are not always necessary than with any sense that one might find a language in which prepositions are marked for number and gender. Some early grammarians of Hindustani remarked that *kā-kī-ke* (to present it in all its forms) was rather like an adjectival ending that could be used to convert nouns – even proper nouns – into adjectives. Thus, *larke kā bhāī* would be thought of as meaning something like 'the belonging-to-the-boy brother'. This explanation had the effect of naturalising the strange formal properties of *kā-kī-ke*, since adjectives in many familiar languages had to agree with the nouns on which they were dependent in number, gender and case.

One of Gilchrist's immediate successors, John Shakespear, took this line and states in his grammar of Hindustani:

> To the classical scholar this particle may, perhaps, best be explained by representing it as the termination of an adjective, liable to inflection for the purpose of agreeing with the substantive to which it has reference. (Shakespear 1826: 25)

But Gilchrist's approach to the issue is slightly different. Whereas Shakespear presents his analysis of the particle as a useful pedagogical device that will help the 'classical scholar', to whom a variable adposition may seem vexing, Gilchrist argues that *kā-kī-ke* is not merely best *explained* in this way but that it actually *is* in some real sense an adjectival ending. He refers to John Wallis's *Grammatica linguae anglicanae* and says, 'This genetive, like ours, so much resembles an adjective, that I cannot help thinking the learned Wallis had some reason for calling this form of the noun one' (Gilchrist 1796: 64 n.). The reference is to Wallis's chapter on adjectives, where he claims that there are two types of adjectives that are formed directly from substantives, the first of which is the 'possessive adjective' ('*adjectivum possessivum*'). He tells us that the 'possessive adjective' can be 'formed from any substantive, singular or plural, by the addition of *s* (or *es*, if required by the pronunciation)' (Wallis 1972: 304–5). Wallis does not explicitly discuss his motives for analysing *'s* as an adjectival ending, but the anonymous author of the *Bellum grammaticale*, a work published in 1712, provides an interesting contemporary explanation in the context of a discussion of three recent grammars of English. He criticises one of his targets, James Greenwood, for not following Wallis's analysis and remarks that, if that approach is adopted:

> [T]here is no need of endeavouring to thrust *one* Case into our Language, quite contrary to its *Genius*, which hates Cases, since the way Dr. *Wallis* has judiciously chose, answers the End as *well*, and agrees better with the Nature of our Tongue. (Anonymous 1712: 31)

Here we are in the realms of a politicised typology. English is not a pale shadow of the classical languages; it has a distinctive character – a genius – of its own; and it is an aspect of this genius that, unlike the classical languages, it does not make use of case endings. In fact, English 'hates' case endings, in the same way, presumably, that Englishmen hate tyranny. This said, the *'s* form is something of an embarrassment, since it is the only real candidate for a case ending in the grammar of English, and Wallis's insistence that it is an adjectival ending means that the English can assert the distinctiveness of their language without fear of contradiction.

This argument is clearly language-specific. In order to avoid saying that English has any cases at all, Wallis has made the one possible candidate into an adjectival termination. But Gilchrist treats the issue rather differently. He presents his own interpretation of *kā-kī-ke* in Hindustani as evidence for the validity of Wallis's account of *'s*. Thus he constructs Wallis's view of English and his own view of Hindustani as equivalent pieces of evidence for another of his universal theories. And this impression is reinforced in the *British Indian Monitor*:

> Ka, *of*, *'s*, has not only all the governing qualities of a postposition in the Hindoostanee, but is itself a declinable adjunct, that admirably proves the intimate connection between genitive and adjective forms in most languages. (Gilchrist 1806–8 I: 141)[15]

The claim is further supported with the observation that the Latin form *cujus* ('of whom', 'of which') is sometimes treated as the invariable genitive form of the relative pronoun and sometimes as an adjective that varies for gender, case and number. Once again, Gilchrist naturalises a feature of Hindustani that, on the face of it, might have seemed surprising to his readers. But instead of merely pleading that the variability of *kā-kī-ke* is normal, he once again proposes a universal theory and demands that readers put the data of Hindustani side by side with the data of English and

---

[15] This analysis is anticipated in Gilchrist (1802a: 23; 1802b: 9).

Latin and reconsider all of them in the light of the new theory. This strategy also contributes to the overall showmanship of his work, suggesting that he is more than a practitioner of the art of grammar and, while immersed in the forms of one particular language, always has his eye on the larger picture.

Gilchrist's remarks on the 'intimate connection' between 'genitive and adjective forms' look reasonable from the perspective of contemporary linguistics. Both entities occupy similar positions within the noun phrase; indeed, Michael Iserman (1996) argues that Wallis's classification of 's as an adjectival ending is one of a number of features of his grammar that suggest he was working with an embryonic conception of phrase structure. But I do not want to use this fact to lionize Gilchrist and suggest that he was ahead of his time. Whig history of that kind is neither interesting nor productive, and it almost always involves reading texts selectively – there are plenty of ways in which Gilchrist's work is extremely backward-looking, not least in its preoccupation with etymology in the style of John Horne Tooke. The important point is that, at a time when linguistic research was not conceptualised as an empirical discipline, Gilchrist's desire to naturalise the forms and structures of the Hindustani language, to minimise the sense of strangeness that surrounded them and show that the language was polite and not 'jargonic', led him into a kind of *unofficial* empiricism. His political objectives led him to test the conceptual frameworks of western grammar against the data of the Hindustani language, not on the basis that this was a scientific way to proceed – for us to interpret his work in that way would be wholly anachronistic – but with the aim of finding the framework that would cast Hindustani in the most reasonable light. All too often commentators castigate the grammarians of the past for allowing political considerations to interfere with scientific enquiry. It is ironic, therefore, that the political nature of Gilchrist's work sometimes makes it appear surprisingly modern in that it provides the motivation for him to test theory against data in a way that was not officially part of the protocol of language study during the period he was writing.[16]

4.4 ERGATIVE CASE-MARKING

The final part of this chapter will be concerned with a feature of Hindustani syntax that seemed particularly vexing to eighteenth- and early nineteenth-century grammarians. This issue was outlined briefly in the Introduction to

---

[16] In his grammars of Marathi and Punjabi, published in 1805 and 1812 respectively, William Carey also described nouns marked by the possessive postposition as adjectives. In the former he states: '[T]he genitive is properly an adjective' (Carey 1805: 15). In the latter he asserts that the possessive or genitive is 'properly an adjective, and varies its gender to agree with the substantive it governs' (Carey 1812: 20).

this book, since it provides such a compelling illustration of a feature of Hindustani that struck western learners as strange and baffling. But it will be appropriate here to return to the example presented earlier and develop a fuller account of why the Hindustani ergative caused such problems for Gilchrist and his contemporaries, given the attitudes to language study outlined in Part I of this book. The issue was illustrated earlier through a comparison of two sentences which can be translated as 'the boy came' and 'the boy wrote the book':

(1)   laṛkā   āyā
       boy. DIRECT   *come.*PERF.MASC.SING.
       'the boy came'

In this first sentence, the verb is intransitive and its subject, *laṛkā*, appears in the direct form. The verb also agrees with the subject in number and gender.

(2)   laṛke-ne   kitāb   likhī
       *boy.*OBLIQUE.AGENT   *book.*DIRECT   *write.*PERF.FEM.SING
       'the boy wrote a book'

But in this second sentence, the noun that appears to be the subject of the verb appears in the oblique form, *laṛke,* rather than in its direct form, *laṛkā,* and it is followed by the particle *ne.* What is more, the verb, *likhī,* has taken a feminine singular inflection to agree with what is apparently its object, *kitāb,* rather than its supposed subject, *laṛke-ne.*

The principle that these examples illustrate is that, when the aspect of the verb is perfect, the subjects of most transitive verbs appear not in the usual direct form but in the oblique form with the particle *ne,* and in this sense contrast with both (i) the subjects of verbs in sentences where the verb is not perfect and (ii) the subjects of intransitive verbs in sentences where the verb is perfect. To use contemporary terminology, the syntax of Hindustani sentences in the perfect aspect is ergative rather than accusative. As I suggested earlier, this kind of pattern is difficult for English-speaking learners to assimilate and, more problematically, seemed irrational to Gilchrist's contemporaries, owing to the way in which sentence structure was conceptualised within general grammar. In his discussion of case, for example, James Harris (1751: 279–80) naturalises the accusative sentence structure of languages such as Latin and English through a complex account of the relationship between metaphysical, logical and grammatical categories.

Despite its complexity, Harris's argument is alarmingly compressed. It begins with the metaphysical distinction between 'substances' and 'attributes', in other words things that exist in their own right and things that inhere in other things. Harris then states that the logical opposition between 'subject' and 'predicate' arises from this metaphysical contrast. The idea is that the logical subject is a substance – a thing that can be picked out as existing in its own right – while the logical predicate points to an attribute of that substance – something that inheres in it. Finally, Harris maps the grammatical contrast between 'substantive' and 'attributive' onto the two distinctions already introduced. A substantive – a noun, in contemporary terminology – indicates the substance that has been isolated as the logical subject. And an attributive – a sort of super-class that comprises adjectives, verbs and participles (Harris 1751: 87) – indicates an attribute that inheres in that substance and, as such, expresses the predicate of a logical proposition. Thus, a sentence like *the bird is flying* uses a substantive, (the word *bird*), to pick out a substance in nature (the actual bird itself), and make it the logical subject of a proposition (the bird conceptualised as something to which particular qualities may be attributed). Harris (1751: 280) goes on to say:

> [W]hen a Sentence is regular and orderly, *Nature's Substance*, the *Logician's Subject*, and the *Grammarian's Substantive* are all denoted by that Case, which we call the NOMINATIVE. For example, CÆSAR *pugnat* [Caesar is fighting], Æs *fingitur* [the bronze is being wrought], DOMUS *ædificatur* [the house is being built].

In other words, all sentences must include a substantive, the function of which is to pick out a substance in the world and characterise it as a subject of which something is to be predicated. This substantive must be in the nominative case; otherwise – and the normative language is important here – the sentence will not be 'regular' and 'orderly'. It may seem strange that Harris makes this use of the term 'nominative' in a discussion where he states explicitly that cases are not an essential element of human languages. This apparent anomaly is explained by the fact that 'subject', for him, is a logical and not a grammatical term. In order to indicate that a language should mark the logical subject consistently, he therefore makes use of the case name 'nominative'. However, he does not argue that the logical subject should be marked through a case ending, and accepts that languages like English use word order for that purpose and are quite 'regular' and 'orderly'.

Commenting on the three examples above, Harris notes that the way in which we understand the 'nominative' depends upon the nature of the verb:

> The Action implied in *pugnat*, shews its Nominative CÆSAR to be an Active efficient Cause; the Passion implied in *fingitur*, shews its Nominative ÆS to be a Passive Subject,[17] as does the Passion in *ædificatur* prove DOMUS to be an Effect.

---

[17] It is worth noting that, in this passage, the term 'subject' is used to refer not to the substance picked out for comment, as it was earlier, but to a kind of semantic role.

And later on in the discussion he returns to this issue, noting that 'when the *Attributive* in any Sentence is some *Verb denoting Action*, we may be assured the principal Substantive is some *active efficient* Cause' (Harris 1751: 282). But, because action requires not only an agent but also a 'subject' to work on and because it must produce some 'effect', in sentences where the verb denotes action and the 'nominative' is to be understood as an 'active efficient cause', a second substantive is required denoting the 'subject'[18] or 'effect' of the action. This second substantive will be in the 'accusative' case. Thus Harris (1751: 283) is able to provide a definition of the accusative: 'THE ACCUSATIVE *is that Case, which to an efficient Nominative and a Verb of Action subjoins either the Effect or the passive subject.*'

The naturalisation of accusative syntax in Harris's argument arises from the fact that he is working with an Aristotelian conception of the proposition that is itself closely tied to the structure of western languages. This does not represent lack of imagination on Harris's part. It is a result of the fact that Aristotelian syllogistic logic was what was available to him in the middle years of the eighteenth century. In this traditional type of logic, the proposition is understood as a twofold entity composed of a single subject and a predicate. This means that, if one sees sentences as embodying logical structure, then, to use Harris's own terminology, they have to have a 'principal substantive' – one noun in particular that corresponds to the logical subject. The problem is that the reason for isolating a single logical subject in a proposition is the occurrence in Greek and Latin sentences of a 'principal substantive' in the nominative case. Because the standard analysis of propositions derives from the structure of the sentence, to try to explain sentence structure in terms of the structure of propositions results in circularity. Of course ergative structures will look strange to anyone with a background in this kind of language analysis. If *larkene kitāb likhī* really expresses the same proposition as *the boy wrote the book*, then why is the logical subject of the proposition not expressed by the form that expresses the logical subject when the verb is transitive but not perfect or when it is intransitive and perfect?

It is commonplace to castigate the grammarians of the eighteenth century for their sense that language mirrored logical structure. But it is ironic that logic, the bogeyman of eighteenth-century language study, has provided immensely productive ways of thinking about language in more recent times. For example, modern predicate logic acknowledges that predicates may have multiple subjects or arguments, and this has led syntacticians to characterise verbs in terms of their argument structure, *scream* being described as requiring one argument, *hit* as requiring two, and so on. The verb is then seen as assigning semantic, or more properly thematic, roles to each of its arguments – 'agent', 'patient', 'goal', 'beneficiary' and so forth.

---

[18] Here again the term 'subject' is used to refer to a semantic role.

This way of looking at sentence structure has the interesting effect of removing the question of which is the 'principal substantive' from the picture. *All* the arguments are required and each is assigned a role by the verb. Different languages can mark these arguments in different ways. Some will mark the experiencer of a one-place verb in the same way as the agent of a two-place verb; others will mark the experiencer of a one-place verb in the same way as a patient of a two-place verb. The point is that the basic theory of argument structure and thematic roles, a theory strongly influenced by predicate logic, can accommodate both kinds of language without difficulty. It does not begin with any conception of which of the arguments is most important, and so the way in which the marking of arguments comes about can be seen as a variable feature of languages rather than something deriving from the nature of thought itself. Once again, it seems necessary to take issue with Janet Sorensen's contention that universalist approaches to language tend to involve a kind of conservatism that does not accompany linguistic relativism. The universalist account presented here actually minimises the difference between accusative and ergative languages, whereas, as Seely (1977: 196–7) shows, there are many examples of twentieth-century linguistic relativists who saw ergative syntax as reflecting a different, and usually inferior, mentality on the part of speakers.

As it happens, Harris's account of the nominative and accusative cases includes many of the ingredients found in the more contemporary account of syntactic structure outlined above. As we have seen, Harris acknowledges that a nominative substantive may have a variety of different semantic roles – 'active efficient cause', 'passive subject', 'effect' – and that nouns appearing in the accusative case may also take some of these roles – 'passive subject' or 'effect'. In other words, he not only understands but also has the metalanguage to explain that the nominative and accusative cases do not correspond to particular semantic roles in a straightforward one-to-one fashion. And he is also aware that the semantic role played by a substantive is, to use modern terminology, 'assigned' to it by the verb: 'We may remark [...] by the way, that *the Character of [the] Nominative* may be learnt from its *Attributive*'. So the nominative of a verb like *fights* will be an 'active efficient cause', because of the 'action' that is 'implied' in the verb and the nominative of a verb like *is built* will be an 'effect' because of the 'passion' that is similarly 'implied'. Thus we have quite a plausible eighteenth-century metalanguage for the discussion of thematic roles and the assignment of roles by the verb. But, because contemporary logic implied that all but one of a verb's arguments were inside the predicate and that the one that was not had the special status of 'subject', none of the other insights in Harris's text could be mobilised for the naturalisation of ergative syntax. The marking of what appeared to be the 'principal substantive' with an inflection and a postposition seemed odd, if not downright perverse, and Gilchrist had to find a way to tackle the problem given the resources then available to him.

In chapter 8 of his grammar, 'Of The Syntax', Gilchrist insists on the conventionality of Hindustani sentence patterns:

> In the Hindoostanee, the adjective precedes the noun; the subject and object, the verb; and the genetive, its own governing noun; the construction however differs very little from the general mode of other languages. (Gilchrist 1796: 197).

But one cannot help feeling that he is trying to soften the blow of the ergative by prefacing it with reassurances about how straightforward everything else is. He leads gently into the issue by remarking that the 'nominative' and 'accusative' are frequently used 'promiscuously' in the language, by which he clearly means that the direct form frequently appears in object position.[19] He sees the normal 'accusative' form as being the oblique in construction with the postposition *ko*, and so, when the direct form appears in object position, we are to understand that the nominative is being used instead. Clearly this 'promiscuous' use of the nominative is regrettable in a well-ordered language, but at the same time, it is as well that it takes place because Gilchrist relies on it for his 'resolution' of the ergative construction. In *The Anti-Jargonist* he states:

> In a language like the Hindoostanee, where the subject and object of a verb are so very liable to confusion from the *nom.* and *accus.* being used promiscuously, the particle *ne* was probably introduced to point out and clearly define on many occasions the one from the other. On this account it is perhaps almost always attached to the subject, and only before real transitive verbs. (Gilchrist 1800: lxvii n.)

Two years later, in *The Hindee Directory*, this idea has hardened into doctrine confidently expressed in the body of the text:

> As the nominative is much used for the accusative in short sentences, or where there would otherwise be two oblique cases, so is the oblique or inflection introduced for the nominative, followed by the expletive *ne*, before the transitive verbs in any *perfect* tense. (Gilchrist 1802b: 9)

Thus, for Gilchrist, the confusing use of what he sees as nominative forms appearing in object position has led speakers to draw attention to the real

---

[19] It has been suggested to me that the use of the term 'promiscuously' here is connected with colonial characterisations of Indian sexuality, and it is certainly possible that some humour is intended. However, according to the *Oxford English Dictionary*, the sexual connotations of the term have become more pronounced in recent years and it would be unwise to place too much interpretive weight on the term.

subject by putting an 'expletive' after it. What we have here is a resort to the notion of ambiguity in an attempt to explain a grammatical structure, one of the tactics that Robert Lowth uses in his 'resolutions' of problematic forms and structures. In his own discussion of syntax, Lowth explains that in English the nominative and accusative cases are 'determined' by word order:

> In English the Nominative Case denoting the Agent, usually goes before the Verb, or Attribution, and the Objective Case, denoting the Object, follows the Verb; and it is the order that determines the cases in Nouns: as 'Alexander conquered the Persians.' (Lowth 1762: 102)

He also notes, however, that 'the Nominative Case is sometimes placed after a Verb Neuter [i.e. an intransitive verb]: as, "Upon the right hand did stand the Queen:" "On a sudden appeared the King"' (Lowth 1762: 103). In these examples, his distributional criterion for the identification of the nominative is denied, but Lowth still wants to claim that the substantives *queen* and *king* are nominative because of the important connection between agent and nominative. He justifies sentences of this kind by stating that 'the Neuter Verb not admitting of an Objective Case after it, no ambiguity of case can arise from such a position of the Noun' (Lowth 1762: 103). Thus, if there is a danger of ambiguity, then the syntax must be more rigid; if the risk of ambiguity is more remote, then more flexibility is possible. To return to Gilchrist's resolution of the ergative, the use of an unmarked form in object position has brought the language to the point of ambiguity and so the 'expletive' *ne* has been introduced to keep the syntax clear. In accordance with this theory, Gilchrist sometimes refers to the oblique in subject position as an 'inflected nominative' (Gilchrist 1796: 215), or, more oddly, as an 'oblique nominative' (Gilchrist 1796: 222).[20] He implies that his explanation will account for the agreement that is found between a perfect verb and what he sees as its object, stating that such verbs 'for the same reason when *ko* is omitted agree with the gender of their objects entirely' (Gilchrist 1800: lxvii n.). It is not at all clear what he means by 'for the same reason', and it is possible that he has no real explanation for the phenomenon. He implies, however, that his failure to provide any clarification is due to limitations of space rather than lack of inspiration.

---

[20] His strategy here is similar to that found in a grammar produced in a very different theatre of colonial encounter, namely Danish contact with Greenland. A grammar of Greenlandic by Otto Fabricius appeared in Copenhagen in 1791 and a second edition was published in 1801. The work was entitled *Forsøg til en forbedret grønlandsk grammatica*, and it includes a discussion of an ergative construction. Fabricius (1801: 78–9) postulates the existence of two distinct forms – a 'nominativus transitivus' and a 'nominativus intransitivus'. Then he observes that the former has the same form as the genitive and the latter has the same form as the accusative. Thus, as in Gilchrist's grammar, the 'nominative' is characterised as having two different formal exponents, one of which is the same as the 'accusative'.

There is, he says, 'no room to follow up this hypothesis by examples', an assertion that may be true but that sounds like an excuse.

The term that Gilchrist uses to label the particle *ne* is particularly important. We saw earlier, that he describes it not as a postposition but as an 'expletive', a term denoting a particle that is inessential to the meaning of the sentence but that provides additional emphasis. Samuel Johnson states, for example:

> Other words there are, of which the sense is too subtle and evanescent to be fixed in a paraphrase; such are all those which are by the grammarians termed expletives, and, in dead languages, are suffered to pass for empty sounds, of no other use than to fill a verse, or to modulate a period, but which are easily perceived in living tongues to have power and emphasis, though it be sometimes such as no other form of expression can convey. (Johnson 1755 I: 1b2^r)[21]

As an 'expletive', therefore, *ne* serves to throw emphasis onto the word it follows, and, given Harris's sense that the nominative is the 'principal substantive' in a sentence, it seems reasonable that it should be emphasised with an expletive.

However, Gilchrist's immediate successors put forward alternative explanations of the troublesome ergative. In the first edition of his grammar of the language, John Shakespear, who was Professor of Hindustani at Addiscombe College between 1809 and 1829, follows Gilchrist in describing *ne* as an 'expletive' (Shakespear 1813: 54 n.). However, by the time the second edition was published in 1818, he had changed his mind. He discusses the issue at two separate points in this edition of the text, and states that 'the explanation of it more properly belongs to the Syntax' (Shakespear 1818: 52 n.). But since it is difficult to exemplify the perfect forms of the verb without introducing the ergative, and since the formal description of verbs clearly belongs in the accidence rather than the syntax, he also discusses the issue in a footnote to his material on the morphology of verbs.[22] In this section he

---

[21] Similarly Greenwood (1711: 167) states: 'An *Expletive* is a Word that is used to give an *Emphasis* or Force to the Expression, but is unnecessary either as to the *Construction* or *Sense* of the Discourse. Such are, *From, For, Now, The, Then, Well,* &c. As, From *whence come you?* for, whence come you, &c. *I go* for *to see,* i.e. I go to see.'

[22] This kind of hypertextual treatment of the ergative is quite common, chunks of explanation appearing in different parts of the grammar with cross-references linking them together. In her excellent grammar of contemporary Urdu, Schmidt (1999: xvii) says: 'If a person wishes to make a comprehensive review of the use of *nē* with perfective tense transitive verbs, he or she must consult all of the following sections: §211, §510, §629 and §809, because the *nē* construction involves a postposition, verb constructions, special forms of pronouns, and the notion of transitivity; and each of these is dealt with under its own heading. Cross references are provided to make the search easier.' In the same way that the conceptual framework of western grammar required rethinking if it was to deal with ergative structures convincingly, it requires an act of the imagination to fit the ergative into the generic framework of the grammar as a text.

attacks the idea that *ne* is an expletive. He does not mention Gilchrist by name but sets out an alternative explanation of the structure, asserting that, if his suggestion is adopted, '[t]he singularity in the use of [*ne*] here noticed, considered to be a mere expletive without meaning, will no longer exist' and that 'nothing contrary to the general rules of grammar will be found in sentences where [*ne*] occurs' (Shakespear 1818: 53–4 n.). Thus an important motive informing Shakespeare's analysis is the desire to show that Hindustani conforms to the underlying principles identified in general grammar, a goal which he clearly feels Gilchrist's talk of 'expletives' and 'inflected nominatives' has failed to achieve. His own explanation runs like this:

> It seems [...] highly probable that this [*ne*], like the same suffix which denotes the instrumental case in the cognate dialects of the Mahār-āttas, Sikhs, Braj, &c. deduced apparently from the [*ṇā*] or [*nā*] which is the sign of the like case in Sanskrit, is in fact a casual termination. (Shakespear 1818: 53 n.)

The suggestion is that the Hindustani particle *ne* is an instrumental case-marker, and, as such, should 'generally be translated by the English word "by" as pointing out the agent *by* whom anything has been done'. The verb itself is understood as 'being used in a passive form, like as is common in the Sanskrit as well as in the Mahārāttas, Panjābi, Braj, and other Indian dialects, with the same casual sign and under similar circumstances' (Shakespear 1818: 53 n.). This kind of explanation naturalises the ergative by reorganising it on the model of a sentence structure that is common in western languages and in which, to use Harris' contemporary terminology, the 'principal substantive' is the 'passive subject' or 'effect' of the action implied in the verb and the 'active efficient cause' is marked by an adposition.

It is interesting that Shakespear makes use of comparative evidence from other Indo-Aryan varieties here. Throughout the first two decades of the nineteenth century, more and more information became available about the language varieties of northern India. A number of grammars of Sanskrit were published in the first decade of the nineteenth century, one by William Carey in 1804 and another by Henry Colebrooke in 1805. Furthermore, Carey had published a grammar of Marathi in 1805 and one of Punjabi, Shakespear's 'dialect of the Sikhs', in 1812. The existence of an instrumental case ending, -*ina*, in Sanskrit suggested that *ne* might simply be a modern derivative of that ending. And in Carey's descriptions of Marathi and Punjabi, he quite explicitly describes particles cognate with Hindustani *ne* as instrumental case-markers and the 'preter tenses' of 'active and causal verbs' as passive structures. In the former text he states: 'It is highly probable that this tense is always expressed by the passive participle, governed by an agent in the third case [i.e. the 'instrumental' marked by *na* or *ne*]' (Carey 1805: 61). In the latter he asserts:

> The perfect tense is made by constructing the present tense of the auxiliary verb with a passive participle. The transitive verb is governed by the agent in the instrumental case, and the intransitive verb in the nominative. (Carey 1812: 41)

Trask (1979: 390) has shown that it was fairly common for ergatives to be seen as passives by early European commentators. However, what exactly writers like Shakespear meant when they made this claim is not entirely clear. Many, although certainly not all, contemporary scholars argue that the New Indo-Aryan ergatives derive from a passive structure in Sanskrit. However, this does not imply that they think the ergative structure still *is* a passive, as Shakespear implies it is. In the work of writers like Robert Lowth, historical evidence is often mobilised to 'resolve' forms and structures that seem problematic. In Chapter 3, for example, I discussed Lowth's analysis of *me* in *woe is me* as a dative. For Lowth, it does not seem to matter whether contemporary speakers feel that *me* has the force of 'to me' here. If the form derives from an Anglo-Saxon dative, then in some sense it *is* a dative, however native speakers perceive it. They may not be aware of the true nature of the form, but that is a failing in them – the language itself conforms to rational principles.

Gilchrist did not accept the alternative view of the ergative presented by Shakespear, but it is not clear whether this was because he felt that there was concrete evidence against that analysis or whether he was motivated by the kind of obstinacy that he often displayed in situations where he felt his authority was being questioned. At any rate, Gilchrist continued to teach his students that *ne* was an expletive, while at Haileybury and Addiscombe cadets were taught that the ergative was a passive and *ne* an instrumental case ending. In the 14th annual report of his lecture series in London, a document that forms part of the *Tuitionary Pioneer*, Gilchrist quotes a number of letters from former students, now living in India, one of which is concerned with the establishment of a board of examiners with a brief to test the language skills of all civilians – that is, members of the administrative rather than military sections of the East India Company – who had been in post for less than three months and anyone taking up such an appointment in the future. The letter is scathing about the performance of students educated in the Company's own college:

> The Hertford [Haileybury] youths find it a very different thing from their examination in England; many of them are hanging back, putting off the evil day; very few have passed, and there are not wanting examples of "*rejecting and remanding*." This will tend to shew the Honourable Court (as well as the Governor-General, on

the deficiency in Hindoostanee) that there is something *radically* wrong in their system of tuition, over and above its "muen ne, *by* me." (Gilchrist 1826: 14th report, 4)

Thus, the belief that *ne* is equivalent to 'by' in English, has become fetishised as a marker of all that is wrong with the teaching the Company is providing for its civilian recruits. And it is obviously a sore point:

> Apropos of that, every scholar I have mentioned this amusing discovery to, astonished at its absurdity, will hardly credit the fact; and one can with difficulty make a Moonshee comprehend what its author would wish to inculcate on this extraordinary expletive *ne*. (Gilchrist 1826: 14th report, 4)

This latter comment is interesting because it cuts against the view that the western scholar – the practitioner of the 'art' and 'science' of grammar – has a deeper understanding of the language than the native speaker. It implies that the author of the letter has attempted to talk with native language teachers about the idea of the ergative as a passive, and the fact that the teachers could not grasp the argument at all is presented as evidence that it is wrong: the 'learned natives' do not feel that the structure works in this way and so it obviously does not. As we have seen, the story of Gilchrist's relationships with 'learned natives' was rather chequered and there is something a little opportunist about his citing this information here. At the same time, however, the mapping of linguistic argument onto personal invective provides an excellent example of the way in which contextual factors sometimes forced Gilchrist into considering methods of enquiry and analysis unusual at the time.

The argument was still raging even after Gilchrist's death. In his grammar of Hindustani, Duncan Forbes, the great man's former assistant at the Oriental Institute, criticises those who 'have followed the learned doctor' in their use of the 'luminous explanation' that has 'stood for many years in one of the books hitherto read by beginners' (Forbes 1846: 105). The term 'expletive', he says, is 'as convenient in its way, as that of *the humours* in the jargon of quack doctors; it solves every difficulty, and forms a ready answer to all questions; it may mean any thing or nothing' (Forbes 1846: 105). In Forbes's view, to use the term 'expletive' is to admit that one has no explanation for a phenomenon, since expletives are simply words that cannot be explained, a fact that emerges even in Johnson's sympathetic account. The term is part of a deceptive discourse through which inferior grammarians attempt to establish their authority with those who know no better. And the terms in which Forbes expresses his point are particularly barbed. Roy Porter (1989; 1995) has explored the language used by quack doctors, and draws attention to the fact that it was frequently satirised in literature. Thus, the 'jargon of quacks' was a prototypical example of language employed with the sole intention of cajoling and deceiving. What is more, quack doctors were also known as 'empirics', a term that harks back to Plato's account of the distinction between an 'art' (*technē*) and a 'knack' (*empeiria*). Plato uses doctors (*iatroi*) as an example of people who practice an art and assistant doctors (*hupēretai tōn iatrōn*) as an example of people whose self-proclaimed skills rest not on a rational system of knowledge but on trial and error or experience. To associate the term 'expletive' with quackery is, therefore, to emphasise that it does not belong to the art of grammar but to a far less illustrious calling. The metaphor seems particularly harsh because Gilchrist himself was a surgeon, a practitioner of the less prestigious of the two branches of medicine. And he occasionally makes use of medical imagery in his own accounts of his linguistic work, at one point likening the process of uncovering the grammar of a living language to the dissection of a body (Gilchrist 1798b: xl). To refer to his terminology as 'jargon' is also bitterly ironic, given that Gilchrist was the self-appointed opponent of 'jargon' and the author of a book called *The Anti-Jargonist*. Thus, Forbes's attack undermines both Gilchrist's analysis of the ergative and his status as a practitioner of an 'art'. The resolution of the ergative was one of those points on which Gilchrist did not ultimately win the argument.

4.5 CONCLUSION

In his discussion of noun case, Gilchrist engages with a number of problems arising from the mismatch between the conceptualisation of language available in western thought and the data of the Hindustani language. Because language study was not conceived as an empirical science and tended to work with a priori principles derived from philosophy and rhetoric, mismatches of this kind threatened to suggest that the language was disordered and chaotic. And, because it was precisely this view of the language that Gilchrist needed to counter, it was important for him to find a way to 'resolve' the problematic forms and structures and, in so doing, naturalise the apparent strangeness of Hindustani for his western readers. One such problem arose from the 'layering of case-like elements' in Hindustani. Although, *pace* Sorensen, both general grammar and typological studies of language provided grounds for jettisoning the category of case in the analysis of 'vernacular' languages, they tended to construct the issue in terms of a dichotomy between languages-with-case and languages-without-case, the latter marking the semantic and syntactic roles associated with case in Latin and Greek by means of adpositions and word order. This was problematic because Hindustani can be seen as having formal case-marking to the extent that many nouns have different direct and oblique forms. However, these forms do not fulfil the range of functions that cases do in the European classical languages, and in order to look at how those functions are marked, it is necessary to look at the adpositions with which Hindustani nouns are constructed. Another problem arose from the existence of an ergative structure in Hindustani, a phenomenon that seemed inexplicable in the light of the principles set out by general grammar. This problem arose not from the wish to use logical categories in the exploration of natural language *per se*, but in the limitations of syllogistic, the type of logic available to mid-eighteenth-century thinkers. When predicate logic abstracted away from the structure of western languages, one of the effects of this movement was to make it better able to model the syntax of languages that were typologically different from it. The change obviated the need to specify just one entity as the 'logical subject' of the sentence.

In dealing with these problems Gilchrist drew on concepts and metalanguage from the western tradition to describe the relevant forms and structures in ways that would seem less problematic – less strange – to his readership. With regard to the 'layering of case-like elements', he drew on a number of different texts in order to produce an analysis that not only worked for Hindustani but also (to use his own metaphor) produced a 'reversal of opticks', providing readers with a lens through which to think again both about western languages and about language in general. Whether or not they ultimately accepted his claims about inflections and prepositions is, in a sense, irrelevant. The point is that he presented his readers with a powerful naturalisation of the nature of Hindustani – not a mere apologia but an aggressive argument for seeing all languages in the light of what he had found in India. And this kind of strategy can be viewed as an unofficial empiricism, in the sense that it involves using linguistic data to criticise philosophical accounts of language, despite the fact that contemporary understandings of language study did not officially regard linguistic theory as testable in this way. Turning to the ergative structure, Gilchrist attempted to save Hindustani from the charge of violating the principles of reasoning by analysing the particle *ne* as an 'expletive' used to throw emphasis onto the subject of a sentence when there was a risk that it might be confused with the object. But his immediate successors preferred to view the structure as a kind of passive and the particle *ne* as an instrumental case-marker. Bizarrely enough, this issue became fetishised as a tangible expression of the grievances that existed between Gilchrist and, as he saw them, his opponents. But even in this minefield of personal grudges, a conflict emerges between language history and the intuitions of speakers as means of understanding the nature of a language in the present.

The issues discussed in this chapter exemplify the intertwining of the political and the technical which is the central theme of this book. Gilchrist depicts the use of Indian languages as simultaneously essential and dangerous for servants of the Company. To exercise control, he argues, it is important to be able to use local languages, but to speak them badly is to run the risk of damaging the armature of colonial authority in ways that may ultimately be catastrophic. To speak a language well is to master the detail – to produce the oblique form whenever a noun is followed by a postposition and to use the construction with *ne* whenever a transitive verb appears in a perfect form. To induce his readers to engage with the language at this level of detail required Gilchrist to naturalise forms and structures that his readers perceived as bizarre and which, because they are difficult for English-speakers to acquire, might have led to a mapping of anxiety onto contempt – an explosive combination that many post colonial critics have seen as absolutely characteristic of colonial discourse. This process of naturalisation is achieved by producing a representation that seems to fit with the sense that westerners have about how languages should be, and this involves deploying metalanguage artfully so that the forms and structures of the language are seen to conform with patterns that are familiar. Lest anyone think that this argument presents Gilchrist's activities as politically benign, the point must again be emphasised that the learning of Indian languages is conceptualised as a way of tightening control over the colony and its people. Yes, Gilchrist argues that it will bring benefits to the ordinary people of India in the sense that it will allow the British to protect them from the depredations of their own unscrupulous leaders, but he also states that there is considerable Indian resistance to British rule and that it is necessary to speak Indian languages well in order to keep the population under surveillance and ensure their respectful acquiescence. While the fate of the colony may never have hinged upon the correct use of *ne* by junior servants of the Company, the fetishisation of detail that takes place in Gilchrist's work was certainly fuelled by a profound sense of anxiety about the stability of the empire in India.

5

THE VERBAL SYSTEM

5.1 INTRODUCTION

The last chapter examined features of Hindustani grammar that caused problems for Gilchrist as a result of the way they resisted analysis in terms of the concepts and metalanguage available within the western tradition. But not all areas of the grammar presented him with such problems. Some features of the language actually fitted western perceptions of what a language should be like more closely than varieties spoken closer to home. Hindustani verbs are a case in point. Throughout his published work, Gilchrist consistently singles the language's verbal system out for praise. And the feature of Hindustani verbs that captures his imagination and elicits his undiluted praise is their uniformity and regularity. He begins chapter 5 of his grammar, 'Of Verbs', with the following comment:

> We are now arrived at that part of the Hindoostanee, which of all others will prove the most agreeable and satisfactory; the whole of the verbs being reducible under one conjugation, whose changes of mood and tense [...] are as obvious and easy, as the personal inflections are simple and uniform. (Gilchrist 1796: 98–9)

In the preface to the dictionary, he repeats this point, stating that no other part of the grammar 'can afford so much to admire, and so little to censure' (Gilchrist 1798b: xliv–xlv). He also emphasises that the language has few irregular verbs. In the grammar he asserts that they are 'so few in number, as scarcely to merit a recital; which is a circumstance that has not probably a parallel in any ancient or modern language, and will be very acceptable to the reader' (Gilchrist 1796: 143).

Whereas the Hindustani ergative is often troublesome for English-speaking learners because it is difficult to assimilate and produce, the uniformity and regularity of the verbal system is attractive because it renders the language easier to learn and use. However, just as the ergative was problematic for Gilchrist on a deeper philosophical level, owing to its apparent violation of the principles of orderly sentence structure as set out within the theory of general grammar, so the uniformity and regularity of the verbal system fitted beautifully with philosophical accounts of what constituted rationality in language structure. In particular, it seemed to conform to the requirement that languages show as much analogy and as little anomaly as possible, analogy being rational and anomaly a regrettable breakdown in rationality. In other words, there should be a perfect one-to-one correspondence between form and function with all plurals, for example, or all preterites marked in exactly the same way. In Chapter 3 we saw that one of the features of John Wilkins's philosophical language was to be its perfectly analogous structure; Wilkins pushes this requirement to really quite a radical point, asserting that there will be no diversity of declension or conjugation in the grammar. In many languages, including Latin and Greek, the variable parts of speech fall into a number of different groups each of which marks grammatical categories relevant to that part of speech in a different way. In Latin, for example, there are five patterns of nominal morphology – the five declensions – and four patterns of verbal morphology – the four conjugations. As we have seen, the structures of Latin and Greek were often valorised as examples of how a well-organised language should be structured, and one might have thought that declensions and conjugations would therefore be seen as an acceptable aspect of any language in which they were encountered. But in the critique through which Wilkins emphasises Latin's inadequacy as a medium of scholarly communication, he castigates the language for its multiple declensions. 'They are', he says, 'unnecessary and inconvenient', while the 'four distinct ways of *conjugating* Verbs' result in an absurd proliferation of forms (Wilkins 1668: 444–6). His new philosophical language will not suffer from these failings; nor, according to Gilchrist, does Hindustani.

Thus, Gilchrist's statement that all Hindustani verbs are 'reducible under one conjugation' is more than mere reassurance that the language will be easy to learn. Read against Wilkins's assault on the 'classical' languages, it constitutes an assertion of the rationality of the 'vernacular'. And, of course, to be able to demonstrate that the language is analogous and rational will help Gilchrist in elevating Hindustani from the status of a 'jargon' to that of a polite and polished medium of exchange. However, despite the confidence with which Gilchrist makes this claim, it was not obvious to everyone in the late eighteenth century that it was true. Before the publication of Gilchrist's grammar and for many years afterwards too, a significant proportion of British learners routinely made use of Hadley's *Grammatical Remarks* in studying the language of 'Hindustan'. In the first three editions of this work Hindustani, or rather 'Moors', is said to have no fewer than five conjugations. To establish the analogous character of Hindustani grammar, therefore, Gilchrist needed to argue actively against this position at a technical level. His argument proved compelling: in the fourth edition of Hadley's text, only one conjugation is postulated. This change of heart, of course, elicited vociferous accusations of plagiarism from Gilchrist, and the image he uses in vilifying Hadley is interesting. He compares the grammar of Hindustani to a landscape and asserts that the verbal system is the most beautiful part of the 'philological champaign'. Hadley, meanwhile, is compared to an owl, 'who has long perched on the watch tower of Hindoostanee grammar [...] with hootings ominous and fatal enough, to have far encroached on the long secluded day' (Gilchrist 1798b: xlv). The point of the comparison is that the owl's 'nocturnal vision' has prevented it till now from seeing the beauty of the landscape. Thus Hadley's failure to grasp the simplicity of the verbal system is understood as a failure to appreciate its excellence, a failure which presumably explains why he insists on calling the language a 'jargon', when it is in fact the great 'national' speech of northern India.[1]

Even after their forms have been tidied up into conjugations and declensions, however, many languages still display traces of 'anomaly' – forms that simply do not fit into any of the larger morphological patterns and stand on their own as irregularities or, as Samuel Johnson has it, 'spots of barbarity'. As we saw in Chapter 3, Wilkins (1668: 449) saw Latin as riddled with anomaly and, in arguing his point, gestured rather gleefully to the large numbers of writers who had argued against analogy as a structuring principle of language on the basis of what they found in the classical tongues. Wilkins offers a 'brief view' of the anomalies found in Latin, stating that there are so many exceptions in the conjugations of verbs, particularly in the formation of preterites and supines, that is almost impossible to list them. Furthermore, he points out, there are some verbs that belong to none of the four conjugations, and these, of course, include some of the most common ones – *esse* ('be'), *velle* ('want'), *fieri* ('become') and *ire* ('go'). Now Hindustani certainly has some irregular verb forms, albeit very few, and Gilchrist clearly sees them as imperfections in the structure of what is otherwise a beautifully orderly system, blemishes that should, if possible, be explained away. Once again the western tradition provides resources for dealing with this problem. In discussions of analogy and anomaly it was quite conventional for writers to scrutinise anomalous forms and consider whether they really were unmotivated spots of irregularity or whether there was some explanation for their introduction into the language. The second part of this chapter will look in some detail at the arguments that James Burnet, Lord Monboddo, mobilises in his discussion of Latin and Greek, but it will be useful to mention one of them here by way of introduction.

In an attempt to defend the Greek language against charges of anomaly, Monboddo (1773–92 II: 507) states: 'We have, [...] in our common grammars, a long catalogue of irregular verbs; but these are nothing else but tenses regularly formed from themes that are obsolete.' Thus, when the perfect form of a verb seems to have an irregular relationship with the present form, that may be because the two forms are not really related at all and the perfect is derived regularly from another verb whose present form is

---

[1] For a more substantial discussion of this plagiarism dispute and the imagery that Gilchrist used in his attacks on Hadley see Steadman-Jones (2003).

now rarely in use. Gilchrist exploits exactly this kind argument in defence of four irregular verbs in Hindustani. The perfect forms of the verbs *karnā* ('do'), *marnā* ('die'), *denā* ('give') and *lenā* ('take') are all irregular. We would expect them to be *karā*, *marā*, *deyā* and *leyā*, and the fact that the forms *kiyā*, *muā*, *diyā* and *liyā* are in use clearly needs explanation. In all four cases, Gilchrist (1796: 143) claims that the problematic forms are not irregularly derived from contemporary infinitives but are regular forma- tions from old or disused infinitives, namely 'keena', 'moona', 'deena', and 'leena'. And the same explanation appears in *The Anti-Jargonist*:

> The ancient infinitives *keena, moona,* have probably left their regular preterites *kee,a, moo,a* as dying bequests to *kurna,* to do; *murna,* to die, and when proving too powerful mementos have almost buried in oblivion the regular tenses *kura, mura,* of these surviving legatees, who may thence be said to inherit rather superfluous than irregular preterites. (Gilchrist 1800: lxv)

Gilchrist goes on to say:

> [This explanation will] in a great measure rescue the language of Hindoostan from the reproach of a single irregular verb, in this philological attempt of ours to recover its disfigured body, from the clumsy paws of those bruins, who have preposterously endeavoured to lick its mangled carcase as a jargon, into some intelligible shape or form. (Gilchrist 1800: lxv)

This is an excellent example of Gilchrist's use of metaphor as a form of showmanship. He does not merely leave his explanations to speak for themselves but uses two extended metaphors to emphasise the redeeming effect that his work is supposed to have upon the Hindustani language. First, he uses a legal image to reinforce the idea that *kiyā, muā, diyā* and *liyā* have not been formed in contravention of the laws of language. On the contrary, the contemporary verbs, *karnā, marnā, denā* and *lenā*, have acquired these bequests through the legal process of inheritance, their original owners having died. By implication, Gilchrist himself is a kind of lawyer and the verbs – on trial for irregularity – are his clients. The second image alludes to the discussion of bears, or 'bruins', in the *Natural History* of the elder Pliny (8.54). There we are told that baby bears are born as unformed lumps of flesh, which the mother bears have quite literally to lick into shape with their tongues. The 'bruins' here are Gilchrist's predecessors, Hadley and Fergusson, whose grammatical work constitutes an attempt to lick the 'jargonic' variety of Hindustani spoken between westerners and their servants into some kind of shape. But what neither of them realise is that the language they are working on is a dead and mutilated corpse and with their 'clumsy paws' they are simply making matters worse. Gilchrist himself is presumably some kind of heroic adventurer who is trying to rescue the language from the bears. In this sense, the image is a little odd because Gilchrist obviously wants to consign the 'jargon' to oblivion and not rescue it. Nevertheless, through the two images, one legal and one from the classical bestiary, he underlines his sense of himself as a defender of Hindustani, rescuing it from the attentions of both critics and other grammarians, who simply cannot see its virtues.

Since morphological uniformity and regularity were both highly prized within the philosophical framework of eighteenth-century language study, the fact that the Hindustani verbal system exemplified both of these qualities in abundance provided Gilchrist with excellent opportunities to represent the language as both rational and beautiful. But, in doing this, it was necessary for him to dismantle the system of five conjugations that his rival George Hadley had been presenting to British readers for the last quarter century. And Gilchrist also felt it incumbent upon him to justify the few irregular verbs that exist in Hindustani by drawing upon strategies exemplified in the scholarly literature on analogy and anomaly. The first section of this chapter will deal with Hadley's system of conjugations at a technical level and examine how Gilchrist sought to destroy the image of complexity and chaos that it communicated to readers. Once again, we shall see him engaging with controversial aspects of linguistic scholarship – this time the theory of letters as developed by the elocutionist rhetoricians – in order to represent Hindustani in the most positive light. The second section will discuss the strategies Gilchrist used to defend the analogy of the language, focusing particularly on the relationships that were seen as existing between certain 'letters' or speech sounds, the rhetorical concept of 'harmony', and the use of disambiguation as a justification for apparently problematic forms and structures. Gilchrist was clearly very proud of his work on the Hindustani verbal system, and felt that through it he really had saved the language from the depredations of his predecessors. Once again, issues that may seem excessively technical – even trivial – to contemporary readers carried a heavy burden of significance in the context of eighteenth-century language study.

5.2 Conjugations – one or many?

To the English-speaking learner, the verbal system of eighteenth-century Hindustani, and indeed of modern Hindi and Urdu, looks strikingly uniform. However, there was, and is, some minor variation in the way different verbs form their perfects. The vast majority simply add the termination -$\bar{a}$ to the verbal root. In eighteenth-century texts, six verbs can be identified as having irregular perfect forms (Table 5.1).

Table 5.1 Hindustani verbs with irregular perfect forms

Infinitive	Perfect	Infinitive	Perfect
honā (be)	*hu(v)ā*	*marnā* (die)	*mu(v)ā*
karnā (do)	*kiyā*	*jānā* (go)	*gayā*
denā (give)	*diyā*	*lenā* (take)	*liyā*

In addition, verbs whose root ends in *ā* or *ī* display a semi-vocalic glide before this termination, while verbs where the root ends in *o* may display this feature.[2] Furthermore, *ī* is shortened to *i* before the glide (Beg 1988: 182–4). For several reasons, Hadley emphasises these differences more than a modern linguist would. First, in texts written before about 1750, when the verbal root ends in a vowel, a labio-dental semi-vowel, -*v*-, is inserted before the infinitive, imperfect and perfect terminations (Beg 1988: 180, 190). Although this -*v*- appears with roots ending in other vowels, Hadley seems only to associate it with those ending in *ā*, and, unlike contemporary scholars of the language, he assumes that it is an integral part of the verbal root.[3] Since the -*v*- does not appear in the perfect, this entails that the root itself changes in the formation of that form, which makes verbs of this kind appear very different from all others. This problem is reinforced by Hadley's system of transcription. Hindustani *āy* is phonetically very similar to the vowel in the English words *mine* and *thine*, and, like other eighteenth-century grammarians, Hadley associates this sound closely with the character <i>, so that he transcribes *gāyā* ('sang'), for example, as 'gi,ah', while rendering *gāvnā* ('sing') as 'gaouna'.[4] The result is that the perfect form looks entirely differently from the infinitive. Underpinning this problem is the fact that, in the mid-eighteenth century, it was not generally recognised that the sound in *mine* and *thine* was a dipthong. Samuel Johnson (1756 I: a2[r]), for example, says of the letter <i> that it 'has a long sound, as *fine*; and short, as *fin*', and it is clear that he does not see the sound in *fine* as diphthong because he adds that <i> 'forms a diphthong only with *e*'.[5] The

---

[2] See Masica (1991: 269–70) for a discussion of the origins of the glide in Hindustani perfect forms.

[3] In Hindustani the verbal root is used as a familiar imperative, and so Hadley and Gilchrist both refer to the form with the term 'imperative'. The term 'root' is used here instead because it is clearer for the contemporary reader and, in this context, presents no theoretical difficulties.

[4] Hadley (1772: 38–40) provides a brief account of his system of transcription but emphasises that his 'remarks' on this topic are just 'hints' and that the reader must supplement them with 'his own more accurate observations in the constant course of communication he must necessarily hold with the natives'.

[5] It might be objected that Johnson is using the term 'dipthong' to mean digraph, and that his insistence that <i> forms a dipthong only in conjunction with <e> therefore tells us nothing about his understanding of the sound represented by the character. This argument can be refuted by pointing to passages in which Johnson talks about diphthongs as 'uniting the *sounds* of two letters' (my emphasis), in his discussion of the vowel in *oil*, for example (Johnson 1756 I: a2[r]).

fact that Hadley understands the sound associated with <i> as a simple articulation means that he is unable to see that both *āy* and *āv* have the same articulatory starting point.

In order to express all these differences, Hadley makes use of the category of conjugation, as it is exemplified in Latin grammar. His method of distinguishing conjugations is modelled on school grammars, which often describe the four Latin conjugations in terms of the vowels that appear before the infinitive marker, *-re*: '*a* long' for the first, '*e* long' for the second, '*e* short' for the third, '*i* long' for the fourth (Anonymous 1758: 189). This type of classification works fairly well for Latin but produces considerable redundancy when applied to Hindustani. Hadley divides the verbs of the language into five groups according to whether their roots end in 'a' (*e*), 'ee' (*ī*), '[a]ou' (*āv*), 'o' (*o*) or 'a consonant'. And he gives the perfect forms for each as set out in Table 5.2

The result is a system in which verbs of the fourth and fifth conjugations form their perfects in exactly the same way. Moreover, in Hadley's system of transcription, 'e' and 'ee' are both transcriptions of *ī*, so verbs of the second conjugation do not apparently differ from those of the fourth and fifth either.[6] The forms 'dana' and 'de,ah' are Hadley's transcriptions of *denā* and *diyā*, and the only other verb that forms its perfect in this way is *lenā*. Thus, the second conjugation includes just two verbs.[7] The third conjugation comprises those awkward verbs in *-ānā*, the roots of which Hadley represents as undergoing some process of change in the perfect form. And he further adds to the sense of chaos and confusion with the casual remark, 'all of this is subject to exceptions' (Hadley 1772: 17).

For the reasons outlined earlier, this multi-conjugational scheme is unacceptable to Gilchrist, and he goes to considerable lengths to dismantle it. Although irregular verbs are also problematic, they can be mitigated through explanation. Gilchrist, therefore, reclassifies *denā* and *lenā* as irregular and thus eliminates the first conjugation at a stroke. However, with respect to the forms that display a semi-vocalic glide, he is faced with the same problems as Hadley. He solves the problem of the roots in *āv* by rejecting them as old-fashioned: 'the ancient infinitives *pa,ona, la,ona, ga,ona*, &c. have here been superseded by *pana, lana, gana*, according to the polite and modern articulation of such verbs.' And he adds that this will keep these verbs 'subservient to one common form', the

---

[6] The replacement of 'ee' with 'e' may hint at the shortening of *ī* to *i* before the glide and termination. this would also be appropriate in 'de,ah' (*diyā*). It is not surprising that Hadley does not mark the semi-vocalic glide itself, since English speakers would produce it automatically between *ī* and *ā*.

[7] However, both *denā* and *lenā* are very productive in the formation of compounds, and Hadley often lists such compounds in his vocabulary as independent items. A good example of such an entry is: '*To tell*. Khâydana. From Khâyna, *to speak* and Dana, *to give*' (Hadley 1772: 118).

Table 5.2 Hadley's five conjugations

	Root ends in	Example	Perfect ends in	Example
1	'a' (*e*)	'da-na' (*denā*)	'e,ah' (*ī[y]ā*)	'de,ah' (*dīyā*)
2	'ee' (*ī*)	'pee-na' (*pīnā*)	'e,ah' (*ī[y]ā*)	'pe,ah' (*pīyā*)
3	'[a]ou' (*āv*)	'l[a]ou-na' (*lāvnā*)	'i,ah' (*āyā*)	'li,ah' (*lāyā*)
4	'o' (*o*)	'do-na' (*donā*)	'o,ah' (*oā*)	'do,ah' (*doā*)
5	'a consonant'	'marr-na' (*marnā*)	'ah' (*ā*)	'marr,ah' (*marā*)

low-key metaphor of 'subservience' suggesting that he himself is something of a disciplinarian, exercising control over forms that are not
sufficiently 'polite' for the modern language (Gilchrist 1796: 99 n.).
Infinitives with -*v*- are indeed uncommon in texts written after about 1750
(Beg 1988: 179). Thus, Gilchrist's argument concerning 'modern articulation', which echoes the rhetorical principle that 'present' usage must form
the basis of any standard language, has its basis in the practice of
contemporary writers.[8]
      There is, however, another problem, and it arises from the way in which
Gilchrist spells the diphthong *āy*. In a footnote, Gilchrist remarks that the
perfect forms of verbs like 'ana' (*ānā*), 'pana' (*pānā*) and 'gana' (*gānā*) are
actually pronounced 'y,a', 'py,a' and 'g,ya'. He clearly associates the
sequence *āy* with the character 'y' in exactly the same way that Hadley
associated it with the character 'i'.[9] And, as in Hadley's analysis, this
association obscures the fact that the diphthong *āy* starts with the sound *ā*,
making it seem as though the formation of the perfect involves a change in
the root of the verb itself. For this reason, Gilchrist states that he neither
follows nor approves of the transcriptions with 'y', and he finds a solution
to the problem by basing his transcriptions of these problematic perfect
forms on written rather than spoken forms. In the Perso-Arabic script, the
sound sequence *ā-y-ā* is represented by the sequence of characters *alif-ye-
alif*. Gilchrist transliterates *alif-ye-alif* as 'a,e,a' and this is clearly more
acceptable to him than 'y,a' for the simple reason that it preserves the *ā* of
the root and allows him to say that the perfects of these verbs are formed by
adding 'e,a', a minor variant of the usual termination 'a'. Thus, he is able to
write a general rule for the formation of the Hindustani perfect:

---

[8] In his *Philosophy of Rhetoric*, for example, George Campbell (1776 I: 361) says: 'To me it is
[...] evident, either that the present use must be standard of the present language, or that the
language admits no standard whatsoever.' Gilchrist was certainly aware of Campbell's work
and quotes his comments on standard language in the preface to the dictionary and grammar
(Gilchrist 1798b: xxi n.).
[9] Again, the name of the letter 'y' includes the diphtong *āy*, reinforcing the association between
the written character and the sound.

> Every infinitive ends in *na* [...] *which* taken away, leaves the common
> contracted form of that mood, or the *imperative*; and this [...] with a
> [...] or e,a [...] (when the *imperative itself* terminates in *a*, or *o*,)
> [forms] the *perfect* tense and *participle*. (Gilchrist 1796: 99)

But, satisfyingly parsimonious as this is, it is clear that Gilchrist is a little
uneasy about it. His usual policy is to base his transcriptions on the
pronunciation of words rather than on their representation in the Perso-
Arabic script. As he puts it himself, we would not 'distract a foreigner' with
the written form 'colonel' if he only wanted to learn the '*oral denomination
of a gentleman holding such a rank in our service*' (Gilchrist 1796: 2).
Unless there is a perfect one-to-one correspondence between spoken and
written forms, placing too much emphasis on the written language can
actually make it more difficult to acquire correct pronunciation. Indeed,
with the exception of his first two publications, the dictionary and
grammar, Gilchrist tended to minimise the amount of Perso-Arabic script
that he presented to learners in his books, instead representing the forms of
the language through his own system of Roman transcription. And these
considerations lead him to develop an argument to justify his decision. The
'Moosulmans', he says, use the combination 'a,e' (*alif-ye*) to represent the
sound of '*i* in *riot*, *mile*, *nine*', since they have 'no letter that alone can
express this sound' (Gilchrist 1796: 21 n.). But is this a deficiency in their
writing system? Or is it in fact a virtue? Gilchrist frames his answer with one
of his characteristic 'reversals in opticks', stating that the use of 'a,e' to
represent the sound of 'i' confirms the observation judiciously made by
Thomas Sheridan that 'i and y are not simple vowels, as marked in our
alphabet' but diphthongs composed of the letters <a> and <e>. This is a
reference to Sheridan's elocutionist work, *A Rhetorical Grammar*, which
was first introduced in Chapter 3. Sheridan (1780: 4) states that the letter
<y> has two sounds, one of which is the same as the sound of <i> in
fight. This sound, he adds, is a diphthong. And later he gives some advice
on the best way to teach it to a foreigner:

> [Tell him to] open his mouth wide as if he were going to pronounce
> a^3, and meant to sound that vowel; but on the first effort of the voice
> for that purpose, to check its progress by a sudden motion of the
> under jaw towards the upper, stopping it in that situation in which
> the sound e^3 is formed, and then instantly cutting off all sound. thus
> as the sound of a^3 is not completed, nor the sound of e^3 continued,
> there results from the union of the two a third sound or diphthong
> which has no resemblance to either, and yet is a compound of both.

In his analysis of the 'layering of case-like elements' Gilchrist presents his
findings as confirming a 'general doctrine of the difference between a case
and an inflection'. In his discussion of the postposition *kā-kī-ke* he depicts

his work as supporting Wallis's decision to analyse the English *'s* as an adjectival ending. Now, in just the same way, his observation that in the Perso-Arabic script the sequence *alif-ye-alif* is used to represent the sound of the letters <i> and <y> is presented as evidence for the validity of Sheridan's assertions about the status of that sound as a diphthong. Gilchrist does not merely mobilise Sheridan's claim in defence of his decision to transcribe *āy* as 'a,e'. He reverses the direction in which the proof operates and claims that his researches have provided evidence for the claims made in a European text. Once again, he adopts a strategy that naturalises both the forms of the Hindustani verb and the Perso-Arabic spelling system by suggesting that, if English-speaking readers find them strange, then they will have to accept the strangeness of their own language too. And this form of argument also provides room for some showmanship, as Gilchrist steps out of the role of the mere practical grammarian and engages with linguistic issues more general than those raised by the Hindustani language itself. Once again, the politics of representation constitutes the engine that draws Gilchrist towards an unofficial empiricism in his linguistic work. His determination to show that the Hindustani verbal system really is the most beautiful part of this 'philological champaign', whatever his rival Hadley says about it, leads him to evaluate general claims about the articulatory nature of speech sounds. The telescope is turned back towards Europe and the metropolis receives scrutiny through the lens of the colony. But the reason for producing an argument of this kind at all is to support the picture of Hindustani as a polite and polished vernacular that requires careful study if it is to fulfil its political potential in the development of the empire in India.

5.3 EXPLAINING ANOMALIES

Having united the Hindustani verbs under one conjugation, Gilchrist was keen to mitigate the remaining irregularities through explanation. In the introduction to this chapter we saw him use an argument from obsolescence for this purpose, and reinforce it with two metaphors, one of which, the image of irregular forms as bequests, willed to extant verbs by dying ones, underlined the strongly normative character of the discussion. This kind of explanation is actually quite common in modern historical linguistics, but Gilchrist's use of it should not be seen as anticipating later techniques so much as rehearsing older ones. Unconcerned about whether there is any particular evidence for his claims, Gilchrist attempts to justify the few anomalous areas of the Hindustani verbal system with reference to ideas that derive their validity from their appearance in both ancient and contemporary authorities. This section will discuss three of those ideas: first, the notion that some 'letters' have a special relationship with one another, a relationship for which Gilchrist uses the term 'convertibility'; second, the idea that anomaly is justified when it helps to disambiguate forms that could potentially be confused; and third, the idea that anomaly is also justified if it helps to make the language more 'agreeable to the ear'. In each case, it will be necessary to examine precedents for the forms of argumentation employed by Gilchrist and, in particular, the way in which he constructs the relationship between his own findings and those of other thinkers.

5.3.1 *Convertibility*

In one of the now classic works of the history of linguistics, *The Study of Language in England, 1780–1860* (1967), Hans Aarsleff considers the question of why the new philology, the emergent comparative-historical method that began in Germany in the early nineteenth century, took so long to establish itself in England. The answer, he argues, is that, ever since the publication of John Horne Tooke's provocative work *The Diversions of Purley* (1786), English scholars had been obsessed with a kind of philosophically motivated and entirely speculative etymology that stood in the way of the careful consideration of forms required for the study of comparative grammar. Aarsleff's book paints an entertaining picture of the frenzied pursuit of etymology in late eighteenth- and early nineteenth-century England, a period and a place in which the most bizarre derivations were constructed on the flimsiest of evidence and in support of the most outrageous theories about the movement of populations and the relatedness of peoples. Gilchrist himself was very much part of this movement, and, as we shall see in Chapter 7, he expressed considerable enthusiasm for the work of John Horne Tooke. However, *The Diversions of Purley* represent the apotheosis of a much longer tradition of etymological speculation, and in the context of his work on the Hindustani verbal system, it will be important to look at some elements of Gilchrist's thinking that relate to this tradition in a wider sense.

The main reason that early modern etymology looks so absurd to contemporary readers is that it seems completely unsystematic. Just like the linguists of the later comparative-historical movement, practitioners of etymology were aware that forms in different languages – and within the lexicon of a single language – could be understood as having some kind of relationship with each other. And they would have agreed with the comparativists that, in order to uncover these relationships, it is often necessary to look at the ways in which the forms of words have changed over time. However, one of the important insights of the comparativists was that sound changes operated in specific languages at specific times to produce systematic changes across the lexicons of those languages. And, by the second half of the nineteenth century, the notion of 'sound laws' had become routinely used as a way of describing this kind of change. As Anna

Morpurgo Davies (1998: 171) puts it: 'From the 1850s, "sound laws" (the term *Lautgesetz* already occurs in Bopp) of the type "Indo-European *p* became Germanic *f*" or "Latin *s* became *r* between vowels" are in current use and the object of much discussion.' By contrast, the early modern etymologists worked at the level of individual words, content to point out similarities between particular items of vocabulary and often building grandiose historical theories on relatively few correspondences of this kind. They simply did not see language change as something that was ordered and systematic. Indeed, the opposition between *ratio* and *usus* discussed in Chapter 3 tended to lead scholars to view change as something that was *by definition* chaotic and disordered, the practice of ordinary people working to break down the proportionality that reason demands.

However, practitioners of etymology in the early modern period were not blind to the fact that some pairs of 'letters' seemed to have a particularly important relationship. What seems strange about their work to observers looking back from the other side of the nineteenth century is that they insisted on understanding these correspondences in universal rather than particular terms. So, whereas Grimm's Law characterises the relationship between sounds in different languages in terms of a change that affected a specific group of languages at a specific point in history, the early modern approach would be to suggest that there is a general correspondence between particular 'letters', which means that, if a pair of forms sound similar, the only difference being that one has <p> where the other has <f>, it is always legitimate to postulate a relationship, whichever two languages the forms are found in. And, in a sense, of course, contemporary linguists would agree that there *is* a general relationship between the sounds represented by the letters <p> and <f> to the extent that the two sounds are similar at an articulatory level, so that a change from one to the other has a kind of naturalness that makes it unsurprising when it occurs in the context of a particular language. Tables of correspondences for the use of etymologists constitute a kind of genre in the early modern period. In 1662, for instance, the Dutch humanist scholar G. J. Vossius published a work entitled *De literarum permutatione tractatus*, in which he lists a whole series of sound correspondences that etymologists need to be aware of with concrete illustrations of each. He tells us, for example, that <a> often changes to <e> ('*A mutatur in E*'), and illustrates this observation with the claim that the Latin form *dies* ('day') derives from the Phoenician '*Dia*' ('*Dies è punico Dia*') (Vossius 1662: 1A1ᵛ). The evidence Vossius presents for these relationships is broad. In some cases he claims that a word in one language is derived from a word in another; in others, the pairs represent dialectal variation in Greek; and sometimes one of the pair is formed from the other through an inflectional process.[10]

---

[10] See Rademaker (1981) for an account of the life and work of G. J. Vossius.

In the first chapter of his grammar, 'Of the Elements', by which he means the 'letters' of the Hindustani language, Gilchrist presents a table that fits exactly into this genre of etymological writing. He details all the sounds of the language, listing next to each the other sounds with which he thinks it is 'convertible'. We are told, for example, that <b> is convertible with <o>, <p>, <w> and <v>, while <l> is convertible with <n>, <r> and <s>. The term 'convertibility' seems to be borrowed from an etymological work entitled *The Way to Things by Words and to Words by Things*, which Gilchrist quotes directly in a text on the Persian verb that he published some five years after the grammar (Gilchrist 1801: xviii–xix). *The Way to Things by Words* was published in 1766 and was written by John Cleland, who is better known as the author of the libertine novel *Fanny Hill*.[11] In this text, Cleland (1766: ii–iii) claims to have uncovered many of the 'monosyllabic constitutives' of the 'universal elementary language of Europe, which he calls 'Celtic', and in explaining how he did it he states:

> My chief attention [...] was to discover and establish, on a satisfactory authority, those Celtic primitives precisely at their point of divergence into other languages, before the adventitious variations, by syllabic combination, by *convertibility of sound*, and other incident disguises, render it extremely difficult, if not impossible, to ascertain them. (my emphasis) (Cleland 1766: iii)

So, armed with a broad conception of the relationships that exist among 'letters' and a term for those relationships derived from the work of one of his own favourite etymologists, Gilchrist provides a barrage of evidence for the convertibility of particular pairs of letters. Some of his examples consist of pairs of words in Hindustani – in discussing the convertibility of <l> and <s>, for example, he cites the lexemes *nikāl* and *nikās*, which both mean 'outlet'.[12] But he makes use of a wide range of other material as well. In his account of the convertibility of <ch> and <k>, for example, he gives a pair from English and Scots (*church*, *kirk*), a pair from German and English (*milch*, *milk*) and a pair that are related by a derivational process (*duchess*, *duke*). He illustrates the relationship between 'd' and 't' with two pairs related by an inflectional process (*rend, rent* and *bend, bent*). And there is perhaps a foreshadowing of Gilchrist's later political radicalism in his comment that 'there is a kind of alliteration I cannot account for in *loyal, royal*; *lex, rex*; [...] *legal, regal*' (Gilchrist 1796: 25–30). Thus, his account of convertibility is typical of the work of early modern etymologists in the way it tries to identify relationships that apply universally and not

---

[11] The text was published anonymously and so Gilchrist was not aware that he was quoting from the work of a well-known pornographer.

[12] Actually, neither of these lexemes derives from the other. They are derived from two separate Old Indo-Aryan forms: *niṣkāla-* and *niṣkāsa-* respectively (McGregor 1993: 559–60).

just in one particular context. In this sense, then, Gilchrist manages to reach beyond the particularism of the 'art' of grammar, even in the context of a discussion of pronunciation, which one might have thought would remain resolutely language-specific. And the extraordinary display of etymological ingenuity presented in the chapter on the 'elements' also comes in useful, when Gilchrist turns his attention to the few spots of 'anomaly' that can be identified within the Hindustani verbal system. One important irregular form that learners have to acquire fairly early on in their study of the language is the perfect of the verb *jānā* ('go'), which is *gayā*. But, although this may seem problematic, the change is entirely predictable – and acceptable – because, as Gilchrist has already asserted, the 'letters' <j> and <g> stand in a relationship of convertibility (Gilchrist 1796: 102 n.).

5.3.2 *Disambiguation*

As we have seen, the concept of convertibility derives from a long tradition of etymological analysis. But the debate over analogy and anomaly itself supplied Gilchrist with resources for the explanation and justification of apparent irregularities. Already in book 9 of Varro's *De lingua latina* we find a series of arguments for the importance of analogy in language, and in this context Varro discusses an array of problematic forms, including, for example, the nouns *nemus* ('grove') and *lepus* ('hare'). Although these are alike in the nominative singular, they are not alike in the nominative plural, where they become *nemora* and *lepores*. Actually, much of Varro's discussion is concerned with sorting out the principles on which morphological patterns should be analysed, and his response to the problem of *nemus* and *lepus* is to point out that they are of different grammatical genders, *nemus* being neuter and *lepus* masculine. Thus, he does not provide an account of how the anomaly arose but simply asserts that the principle of regularity does not operate across distinctions of gender, a point that needs to be accepted if the patterns of Latin grammar are to be properly understood.

The types of explanation that Gilchrist employs are more akin to those used by classical grammarians to mediate between the rules of grammar (*regulae*) and the authority of literary texts (*auctoritas*). In discussions of language use, both grammarians and rhetoricians warn against the use of 'solecisms' – forms that are grammatically incorrect – and 'barbarisms' – local, foreign or unconventional forms. But in both Greek and Latin, word forms frequently appear in poetry that would be considered solecisms or barbarisms in prose. So must these forms always be condemned – even in the work of the most significant poets? To solve the problem of forms that violate the rules of grammar but appear in the work of authoritative writers, the concept of 'metaplasm' was adopted. This broad umbrella term covers a range of different ways in which words could be altered through the addition, omission, transposition or substitution of letters or syllables. Loss of material from the beginning of a word, for example, is known as *aphaeresis*; from the middle, *syncope*; and from the end, *apocope*.[13] The point of identifying metaplasm in its many forms as a figure (*figura*) was to distinguish the *ignorant* use of incorrect and unconventional forms from the *deliberate* alteration of conventional forms for artistic ends – to preserve the metre, for example, or to produce a particular kind of effect. As Donatus puts it, metaplasm is used '*metri ornatusve causa*' ('for the sake of metre or ornament') (Keil 1855–80 IV: 396).

Identifying metaplasm as a figure provided a way of acknowledging that, when poets use unconventional forms in order to achieve a metrical effect, they should not be castigated for their inability to use the Latin language properly. However, metaplasm came to have a second function, one that is already in use in the work of the late Latin grammarian Priscian. Considering the irregular Latin verb *fero* ('bear'), Priscian notes that some of its forms have undergone syncope – the loss of material from the middle of the form. Thus in the second person singular we find *fers* instead of *feris* and in the third person singular we have *fert* rather than *ferit*. This is the kind of example that the defenders of anomaly loved – surely the irregularity of *fero* is just another piece of evidence for the minor role that analogy plays in human language? But by describing these forms as examples of syncope, Priscian indicates that they have deliberately been rendered irregular for some specific communicative purpose, and he goes on to tell us what this purpose is. Forms such as *feris* and *ferit* have undergone metaplasm lest they be thought to derive from the verb *ferio* ('hit') (Keil 1855–80 I: 454). The irregular parts of *fero* should not be seen as violating the underlying principle of analogy because there is a reason (*causa*) for their taking these forms, and that reason is the avoidance of ambiguity. Thus, the explanatory range of metaplasm is extended from the decisions of individual writers to our collective practice as language users. Provided that there is some purpose to their adoption, there is no need to condemn irregular forms in terms of the triumph of ignorance over rationality.

It seems unlikely that Gilchrist would have read the late Latin grammarians – he rarely cites sources in languages other than English and does not seem to have had a particularly developed grasp of Latin. However, just as a writer like Cleland mediated Gilchrist's encounter with

---

[13] In the work of grammarians such as Donatus and Diomedes as many as 14 species of metaplasm are cited. Donatus' full list consists of *prosthesis, epenthesis, paragoge, aphaeresis, syncope, apocope, ectasis, systole, diaeresis, episynaliphe, synaliphe, echthlipsis, antithesis* and *metathesis*. Some of these terms are still used in historical linguistics, but it is important to note that, whereas today they simply denote a change in the form of word, no matter how the change came about, in the ancient world they denoted changes to the forms of words that came about as a result of the deliberate choices made by poets.

older etymological sources, so it is possible to identify eighteenth-century works published in English that transmitted ideas about metaplasm in a more accessible form. In 1758, for example, Thomas Nugent published a translation of a Latin grammar by Claude Lancelot, the grammarian who collaborated with Antoine Arnauld on the Port-Royal grammar. In this text, originally published in 1644, Lancelot rehearses the arguments found in the earlier sources, among them the one presented above: 'FERO, is irregular only as it drops the vowel after the R in some particular tenses, [...] which Priscian believes to have been designed to distinguish it from *ferio, feris, ferit*' (Lancelot 1758 II: 117). Ideas that originate in the late Latin grammarians were, therefore, circulating in the later eighteenth century in a far from inaccessible form, and so it is not surprising to find Gilchrist employing them in his discussion of the Hindustani verbal system.

In the last section we saw that the perfect form of the verb *jānā* is irregular. We would expect *jāyā*, but the actual form is *gayā*. Gilchrist justifies the change of consonant with reference to the concept of convertibility, but there remains another problem. The first vowel in the infinitive is long, whereas the first vowel in the perfect form is short. However, even this can be explained: 'the preterite of *gana*, to sing, being *ga,e,a*, sung; *gy,a*, or *ge,a* as some pronounce it, is at all events a convenient exception to a general rule, by thus distinguishing *gy,a*, gone, &c. from *ga,e,a*, sung' (Gilchrist 1796: 102 n.). And this is exactly the same argument that Priscian used to justify the forms *fers* and *fert*. The perfect of *jānā* ought to be *jāyā* or, given the convertibility of <j> and <g>, *gāyā*, However, *gāyā* is the perfect form of *gānā* and so, to avoid ambiguity, the irregular form *gayā* is preferable. Gilchrist's phrasing here is not particularly forceful. He presents the anomaly merely as 'a convenient exception to a general rule'. But in *The Oriental Linguist*, published just two years later, he confidently asserts that the avoidance of ambiguity was the reason why the irregular form was adopted. And, in this sense, it can be seen as a true metaplasm – a deviation from the norm deliberately made in order to achieve some specific communicative purpose.

5.3.3 *Euphony*

The concept of metaplasm is also deployed in a text that deals with one of the dominant intellectual issues of the later eighteenth century – the question of how language originated and developed to its present state. James Burnet, Lord Monboddo's six-volume work *Of the Origin and Progress of Language* was mentioned briefly in Chapter 3 as an example of a text that characterises language as contingent upon mental development rather than as the means by which mental development can take place – the position that John Horne Tooke adopts in *The Diversions of Purley*. Gilchrist was certainly aware of Monboddo's work, and would have found in it a developed example of the use of metaplasm as a means of defending a particularly favoured language against charges of anomaly. In Monboddo's case, however, the favoured language is classical Greek, the verbal system of which is, on the face of it, is much more irregular than that of Hindustani.

Monboddo's text is concerned with showing that a 'regular and formed language such as is used by every civilized nation' is a work of art, which has been consciously created by 'men of art' (Monboddo 1773–92 II: 5). He does not accept that such a language could have emerged through a smooth process of development from the 'jargons' of 'savages', arguing instead that there must have been a point of disjunction when the original 'jargon' was completely overhauled and reorganised according to philosophical principles. Like Adam Smith, Monboddo (1773–92: 300–490) suggests that the invention of language must have been motivated by the need of human beings to express their wants, and he argues that they would originally have done this by using gestures and inarticulate cries. As their wants increased, however, this method of communication would have become 'too confined'. At first they would have varied their vocal signals by uttering them at different pitches, but ultimately this would still not have provided enough signals to meet their needs, and the result would be the invention of articulated words. As it became necessary to express more and more ideas, new words would be invented. But they would be introduced on an ad hoc basis and would bear no resemblance to any existing words. So an action that took place in the present would be denoted by a completely different word from an action of the same kind that took place in the past. There would, in short, be no analogy. Eventually the 'jargon' would grow absurdly cumbersome, since there would be a huge number of words to learn and no rational principles organising them.[14] But by this stage, fortunately, reason and society would have developed far enough for a small group of philosophers to have the leisure to sit back, think through the problem and construct a new medium of communication on a philosophical basis.

These philosophers might well use the words of the old 'jargon' as raw material, but the new language would be substantially different from the former one, and, once created, it would be generally adopted, and the 'jargon' set aside. Thus there is an important break in Monboddo's narrative – a moment at which 'language' supersedes 'jargon' and *ratio* supersedes *usus*. In effect, he is suggesting that such existing languages as are 'regular and formed' are, like Wilkins's 'philosophical language', the

---

[14] Monboddo supports his deductions with evidence from existing languages. A number of 'barbarous' languages, he says, are still spoken in the world today, although grammars and dictionaries are only available for three: 'Huron', 'Galibi' and 'Caribee'. All three are said to confirm his conclusions (Monboddo 1773–92 I: 364).

products of conscious design. He discusses the nature of the philosophers' 'art' at some length and states:

> [T]here is one thing absolutely required in every art, that it should have some plan or system; by which I mean that it should propose some end to be attained, and proceed in a certain method, and according to certain rules, for the attainment of that end. (Monboddo 1773–92 II: 487–8)

And he emphasises the importance of systematicity in any activity claiming the status of art:

> [A] man would not be better than an empiric, who had collected the greatest number of facts and observations on any art, if he had not digested them into a system laying down principles and drawing from thence consequences to the practice, and so forming that [*hexis meta logou alēthous poiētikē*] ('efficient habit joined with sound and true reason').[15] (Monboddo 1773–92 II: 488 n.)

Thus Monboddo's narrative incorporates the typology of disciplines introduced in Chapter 3. Before the foundation of the languages of 'art', speech was an *empeiria* in the sense that there was no method or system underlying it and it was learned entirely through experience. But at some point the original 'jargon' was reformed according to the principles of art. For further discussion of the concept of an 'art', Monboddo refers us to another work by James Harris, the author of *Hermes*, namely his *Three Treatises*, which were first published in 1744 and the first of which is concerned with the definition of 'art'. From the references to classical sources that appear throughout the notes to the first treatise, it is clear that, for Harris, 'art' is a translation of the Greek term *technē* (Harris 1744: 251–83). He attempts to synthesise the ideas presented by these sources to produce a coherent account of what an 'art' is and, in making the point that an art must proceed '*according to a system of various and well-approved Precepts*', Harris (1744: 260) presents a number of definitions, including the one from Aristotle's *Nichomachean Ethics* that Monboddo cites in the quotation immediately above. When the philosophers step in, then, language moves from the status of *empeiria* to the status of *technē*, systematicity supplanting experience as its underlying principle.

Monboddo states that an art needs a goal – an end to which it is directed – and, in the case of language, the goal is to 'express the conceptions of the human mind'. In the attainment of this end, four requirements have to be met. It is necessary:

---

[15] The quotation comes from Aristotle's *Nichomachean Ethics* (vi.4). The translation is by the eighteenth-century author James Harris (1744: 260).

That all the conceptions of the mind should be distinctly expressed. 2do, That this should be done by as few words as possible. 3tio, That the connection of those words with one another should be some way marked. And, lastly, That the sound of the language should be agreeable to the ear, and of easy utterance. (Monboddo 1773–92 II, 488–9)

The first requirement is clearly connected with general grammar, the practice of working out the 'conceptions of the mind' that a grammar must instantiate. The second and third requirements demand the invention of a grammar in the sense of a means of marking the various grammatical categories proposed by general grammar at a formal level. Since it is the nature of an 'art' to bring its matter under the control of rules, this grammar should be as regular and rule-governed as is feasible. And this implies that it should embrace the principle of analogy as closely as possible, rejecting 'anomaly', which is unsystematic and 'jargonic'. The fourth requirement brings us to rhetorical issues such as typology and harmony, and Monboddo discusses at length the question of how a language should be organised in order to produce discourse that is aesthetically pleasing, using Dionysius of Halicarnassus as an authority throughout.[16] Thus, one of the characteristics of Monboddo's work is that it draws together the various areas of debate examined in Chapter 3 of this book to produce an account of the ascent from a 'jargon' to a language of 'art'.

When he comes to expatiate upon the virtues of Greek, Monboddo has to admit that the language contains many irregularities:

> For it is impossible but that some abuses must have crept into an art which is constantly practised by men who do not understand it; and that such abuses should grow into inveterate custom, so that even the men of learning would be obliged to submit to them. (Monboddo 1773–92 II: 506)

Thus, the failure of the language to meet the requirement of analogy is characterised initially in terms of the traditional opposition between *ratio*, the judgements of the philosophers, and *usus*, the practice of the ordinary

[16] Monboddo says that, in order to render a language 'agreeable to the ear', it is necessary to produce an analysis of 'elementary sounds', and that this analysis was performed to perfection by the inventors of Greek, who, in forming their language, 'did not employ only the soft and sweet-sounding letters, but also the strong and rough, in order to give strength and nerves to their language, as well as softness and beauty' (Monboddo 1773–92 II: 235). Next the letters have to be formed into syllables and 'it is to be observed, that all letters will not compound in this way with all' (ibid. 367). So, to use modern terminology, the language should place phonotactic restrictions on the combination of sounds. Similarly, when syllables are joined together into words, 'in order to make the sound of a language pleasant and flowing, the letter that concludes the preceding syllable should run easily into that which begins the next' (ibid. 373). Again, this is effectively a call for a normative phonotactics.

people. However, Monboddo also claims that 'there are fewer of [these abuses] than are commonly imagined', suggesting that many apparent anomalies can be explained with reference to metaplasm. He tells us, for example, that 'superficial grammarians' believe the regular infinitive of *tuptō* to be *tuptein* and the form *tuptemenai*, which also occurs, to be a 'poetic' – or, as he puts it in discussing another example, 'licentious' – usage. But, in fact, he argues, *tuptemenai* is 'truly the original infinitive, according to the analogy of the language'. The form *tuptenai* has been derived from it 'by syncope' and the form *tuptemen* 'by apocope'. From the latter, 'by leaving out the [*m*]', we have *tupteen*, from which the classical infinitive *tuptein* has been formed 'by contraction' (Monboddo 1773–92 II: 507). Thus, although *tuptein* is the most common of the forms, it is just one of a number that are regularly derived from what Monboddo sees as the original infinitive by a chain of minor changes. In this case, Monboddo simply labels these changes with the names of various species of metaplasm and makes no attempt to explain why each took place. Identifying them as metaplasm seems sufficient justification. But in other cases he does try to give reasons for alterations in the forms of words, often playing the requirement for analogy off against another one, the usual candidate being the requirement that the language should be 'agreeable to the ear'. An anomalous form may be justifiable if it contributes to the aesthetic qualities of the language.

Now this is very much a strategy that Gilchrist uses in the justification of irregularity in Hindustani. In discussing the verb *honā* ('be'), for example, he is forced to admit that the perfect has the irregular form 'hoo,a' (*huā*). In the grammar he seems unable to find any explanation for this irregularity, and he makes a conventional statement to the effect that the form 'hoo,a' is 'but a slight deviation in the substantive verb that in all countries appears to be very anomalous' (Gilchrist 1796: 102).[17] But in *The Anti-Jargonist* he suggests that the anomaly is 'reconcilable' because the regular formation would be 'a glaring cacophony, that necessarily glides into *hoo,a*' (Gilchrist 1800: lxiv). This seems something of an overstatement. The regular form would be *hoā*, and it is difficult to see why this is supposed to be so offensive. However, the important thing is that Gilchrist is playing off one of Monboddo's requirements against another. The anomaly can be justified because it helps to make the language more 'agreeable to the ear'. The term 'cacophony' harks back to the rhetorical tradition, deriving directly from the Greek *kakophōnia*, a term which, along with its cognates, appears in a range of rhetorical works. In his essay *On Literary Composition*, for example, Dionysius of Halicarnassus discusses the technique of disguising ugly words by mixing

---

[17] Halhed (1778: 103) makes the very same point: 'The verb substantive *to be* seems in all languages defective and irregular.'

them with harmonious ones ('*misgonta kakophōnois euphōna*').[18] And it is also a term that Monboddo himself uses in explaining particular features of Greek grammar that seem anomalous. For example, a large class of Greek nouns show a consonant in their oblique forms that does not appear in the citation form, and students of the language simply have to learn the oblique stem along with the citation form. In considering this point, Monboddo (1773–1792 II: 375) states: 'sometimes a letter is inserted between [*n*] and the succeeding letter, to prevent the cacophony, as in the word [*andres*] in place of [*aneres*] or [*anres*], the [*e*] being elided.' Once again, the modern reader may not feel that there is anything particularly cacophonous about the word *aneres*, but the important point is the way in which it is considered legitimate to present aesthetic considerations as a reason for violating the requirement that language be strictly analogous.

Gilchrist develops a similar argument in dealing with the polite imperatives of the verbs *denā* ('give') and *lenā* ('take'), which are the irregular formations 'dee,jee,e' (*dijīe*) and 'lee,jee,e' (*lijīe*). These forms are justifiable, he says, because '[t]he regular precative form of *dena, lena*' – and these he gives as 'de,ee,e' (*deīe*) and 'le,ee,e' (*leīe*) – 'would be very harsh' (Gilchrist 1796: 144 n.). He then directs us to a footnote in an earlier part of the text that deals with the pronunciation of the language: '*Ee* preceding *a* in the hurry of utterance, and to avoid the hiatus, often forms *ya*; *ee,ar*, or *yar* [...] friend, *ee,ad*, *yad* [...] remembrance' (Gilchrist 1796: 14 n.). This is helpful to him because it suggests that it was almost inevitable that 'de,ee,e' and 'le,ee,e' should become 'de,yee,e' and 'le,yee,e'. And, since <y> and <j> are convertible, it was quite natural that these forms should become 'dee,jee,e' and 'lee,jee,e'. The transformation of <ee> into <y>, Gilchrist suggests, is:

> [A] circumstance that may give some insight into our kindred vowel-consonants *y* & *w*, (on which so much has been observed by different grammarians) if we attend to *swan, sweet, swim, swop, swum*; thus, *soo,an, soo,eet, soo,im, soo,op, soo,um*, the hiatus here being as evident as in *ee ar* and equally well avoided by *swan*, &c. (Gilchrist 1796: 14 n.)

Thus, once again, he presents his findings in the field of Hindustani pronunciation as evidence for the ideas of various western thinkers, stating that he believes 'with Lowth, Johnson and Sheridan' that <y> and <w> are always vowels, 'forming a kind of diphthong with the one next to them, and no more consonants than *a*, *e*, *i*, *o*, *u*, in *genial, onion, neuter*,

---

[18] The term 'cacophony' is not always pejorative. In his work *On Style* (v.255), for example, Demetrius notes that it is appropriate in discourse dealing with certain kinds of subject matter. Like many things in rhetoric, it is all a question of appropriacy.

lieu, use, our'.[19] The telescope is again turned back on English and we are invited to view the European language through the lens of Hindustani.

When Gilchrist states that the transformation of <ee> into <y> helps to 'avoid the hiatus', he is using a term that, like 'cacophony', derives from the rhetorical tradition. Quintilian (*Institutio Oratoria* ix.iv.33), for example, in his discussion of '*iunctura*', the connection of words in discourse, turns his attention to '*vocalium concursus*' ('the clash of vowels'). This is generally undesirable, and especially so when the gap, or 'hiatus', occurs between two vowels that are pronounced '*cavo aut patulo maxime ore* ' ('with a hollow or open mouth'). And Monboddo (1773–92 II: 378) uses the term himself while discussing the factors that make some languages more harmonious than others. He notes that, in order that they should run into each other pleasingly in sentences, the Greeks 'ended all their words in vowels or liquids'. But he notes that, if two vowels appear together, one at the end and the other at the beginning of a word, this can produce a 'disagreeable hiatus'. For this reason, he suggests, the Greeks made provision for the letter *nu*, the Greek equivalent to <n>, to be added to verb forms such as *legousi* where it is desirable to break up a sequence of vowels. So, if disambiguation provides the motive for some instances of metaplasm, another can be found in the aesthetic considerations laid down in rhetorical accounts of style – issues such as the avoidance of 'cacophony' and 'hiatus'. In the original texts from which these concepts come, the assumption was that individual readers would use them to improve their speaking and writing. But here the same concepts are mobilised to assess the extent to which particular languages lend themselves to the construction of effective discourse.

5.4 CROSS-REFERENCING AND HYPERTEXT

In the last section I examined the way in which Gilchrist attempts to justify irregular verb forms and, in the process, 'rescue the language of Hindoostan from the reproach of a single irregular verb'. But observant readers may

---

[19] Lowth (1762: 4) states: '*Y* is in sound wholly the same with *i* [...] and it is always a vowel.' Furthermore, '*W* is either a vowel, or a diphthong: its proper sound is the same as the Italian *u*, the French *ou*, or the English *oo* [...].'

In the early editions of his English grammar, Samuel Johnson is noncommittal about the idea that <w> and <y> are vowels. In the first edition of the abridged version, for example, he simply states that they are 'thought by some' to be 'in all cases' vowels (Johnson 1756 I: a4[r]). In later editions, however, he is much more assertive: 'I am of the opinion that both *w* and *y* are always vowels, because they cannot after a vowel be used with the sound which is supposed to make them consonants' (Johnson 1773 I: a4[r]).

Sheridan (1780: 17), having explained the pronunciation of a number of English diphthongs, states: 'All the other diphthongs of our tongue are formed by the short sounds of o[3] and e[3] marked by the characters *w* and *y*, preceding all the other vowels and combining with them.' In the same context he also asserts that o[3] has the sound of <oo> in 'noose' and e[3] the sound of <ee> in 'beer'.

have noticed that most of the material discussed there appears in footnotes to the grammar and not in the main body of the text itself. This might lead some to ask whether the material on irregularity can really be so important, if it is always relegated to the foot of the page and not integrated into the main fabric of the work. Faced with this kind of question, I would argue that it is a mistake to see the material in the main body of the text as more highly foregrounded than the material in the footnotes. The very inclusion of notes constitutes a performance of scholarship. When the ideas in a work are straightforward, there is no need to annotate them, explain them, provide a commentary to justify them. In this sense, the provision of extensive notes has a kind of rhetorical function, assuring readers of the seriousness of the work before them. Moreover, the division of the page with a thick black line and the fact that, on some pages, more than half the paper is taken up with footnotes provides a striking visual reminder of the serious intent with which Gilchrist has set about his task.[20]

What is more, the notes in the grammar are heavily cross-referenced. On page 144, the main text includes a discussion of irregularities in the forms of *honā* ('be'), which is cross-referenced with page 102. There we find part of the paradigm of *honā* and are directed to a footnote that includes Gilchrist's explanation for the irregularity of the perfect form 'hoo,a'. Later, on page 144, there is an account of the irregular imperatives of *denā* and *lenā*. This leads us down to a footnote in which the forms are justified on grounds of euphony. The footnote in turn includes cross-references to notes on pages 14 and 22 in the chapter on the 'elements', and to page 108 further on in the chapter on verbs. The note on page 14 is concerned with the letter <y> and includes the discussion of whether Lowth, Johnson and Sheridan are right to see <y> and <w> as vowels. Unsurprisingly it includes a cross-reference to a similar note 'on the letter w', in which Gilchrist further agonises over the issue of whether these letters are consonants or vowels. That discussion ends with some relevant thoughts on the morphology of nouns, and whether it is better to choose spellings that are true to the etymology or ones that express the pronunciation. This in turn leads to a cross-reference with the chapter on nouns. The note on page 22 is very long, actually starting on page 21. It begins with a discussion of the sequence *āy*, which, as we have seen, Hadley and Gilchrist are inclined to represent with the letters <i> or <y>. By the end, however, we have returned to the subject of convertibility and whether the convertibility of <y> and <j> suggests that 'y' is a consonant or not. In the course of the discussion we are referred back to the note on page 14 and also to Sheridan's 'excellent prosodial grammar' along with 'Dr. Lowth's [grammar], page 15, note (1)'. The note on page 108 throws a spanner in the works by suggesting that the

---

[20] On p. 105, for example, the main text only occupies the top quarter of the paper and on p. 106 only the top third.

'respectful' imperative of *honā*, 'hoo,jee,e', which looks rather like the forms 'dee,jee,e' and 'lee,jee,e', is actually compounded from *honā* and *jānā*, and then sends us off to look at the imperative of *marnā* ('beat') and 'the note thereon'.

This dense web of cross-referencing effectively provides the reader with alternative pathways through the book. One can plough through the grammar, chapter by chapter, learning about each part of speech in the traditional order set out in the Greco-Roman tradition and occasionally glancing down at the material in the footnotes. Or one can read an alternative text that is held together by links in the form of cross-references and that deals not so much with things that the learner needs to know in order to communicate in Hindustani as with the issues that face grammarians as they attempt to engage with the real substance of a language – the vexing relationship between spoken and written forms, the competing claims of pronunciation and etymology, the knotty problem of how speech sounds should be described and, of course, the extent to which it is possible to find order in places where it does not initially seem to exist. In effect, the footnotes constitute the nodes of a hypertext, the cross-references acting as links that allow the reader to navigate along a range of possible pathways, each of which develops an argument intertwined with the main business of teaching Hindustani but distinct from it in its preoccupation with the experience of doing grammatical analysis. And it is in the footnotes that Gilchrist often presents his most personal response to the material, stating at one point:

> [A]s every body takes the liberty of finding fault with what they cannot perhaps amend, I reflect with pleasure that I have not only done my best to avoid errour, but have enabled future grammarians to shine, by pointing out here, whatever I myself am not altogether pleased with in my own labours. (Gilchrist 1796: 22 n.)

To suggest that the content of the footnotes is less important than the paradigms and lists in the main part of the text is to ignore the drama that is acted out below the long black rules. Not all grammarians draw attention to the processes through which their analyses are made, but Gilchrist's footnotes draw attention to the work he has done in a vivid and colourful fashion. They dramatise the process of research, providing us with pictures of the intrepid scholar at large as he grapples with difficult problems and reasons his way towards solutions. And they do not constitute isolated texts-within-a-text but, as a result of their interconnectedness, constitute a second text that is closely related to the first but that is concerned as much with the process of analysis as with its product. Thus, the fact that the discussion of irregularity takes place within the footnotes does not mean that it has been relegated to the periphery of the text. On the contrary, the footnotes constitute the space in which Gilchrist acts out the role of the original scholar most energetically and ostentatiously.

5.5 CONCLUSION

In the field of noun case, the encounter between Hindustani data and western ideas produced problems for the data. The forms and structures of the language began to look strange and problematic when viewed through the prism of both general grammar and typological classification. But the Hindustani verbal system, when examined in the light of prevailing ideas about analogy and anomaly, seemed remarkably 'philosophical'. Its uniformity and regularity came close to to the perfectly rational system that John Wilkins envisioned for his own philosophical language. And this provided enormous opportunities for Gilchrist in his project of demonstrating that Hindustani was a polite and polished 'vernacular' and not a barbarous 'jargon'. But in George Hadley's *Grammatical Remarks*, the text that had been the main source of information on Hindustani in the quarter-century before the appearance of Gilchrist's grammar, the verbal system is depicted very differently. According to Hadley, five conjugations were required in order to capture the morphology of the Hindustani verb, and even then the whole analysis was 'subject to exceptions'. In order for Gilchrist to convince his readers how much there was 'to admire' and how little 'to censure' in the language's verbal system, it was necessary for him to reorganise Hadley's five conjugations into one, and, ideally, demonstrate that any remaining anomalies were not the embarrassing products of corruption but were justifiable and motivated in terms familiar from contemporary language study.

Once again, the need to resolve these problems led Gilchrist to look in the western literature for methods of analysis and varieties of metalanguage that would allow him to produce a compelling representation of Hindustani. The most difficult problem facing him as he tried to 'reduce' the verbs to a single conjugation was the issue of verbs with roots ending in *ā*. The insertion of a glide between the root and the termination produced a form that was difficult to analyse, given the current state of articulatory phonetics when both Hadley and Gilchrist were writing. The close association of the sequence *āy* with the characters <i> and <y> tended to obscure the fact that *āy* was indeed a diphthong the first part of which was the same as the sound in roots such as *ā-*, *pā-* and *gā-*. Interestingly, Gilchrist represents his solution to this problem as having arisen from his knowledge of the Perso-Arabic spelling system. The fact that forms such as *āyā*, *pāyā* and *gāyā* were spelt with the sequence *alif-ye-alif* suggested to him that the sound he associated with the single character <y> might, in fact, be a diphthong. And he found confirmation of this idea in the work of the elocutionary rhetorician Thomas Sheridan. But rather than presenting the breakthrough as arising straightforwardly from a reading of Sheridan, he constructs it in terms of his own encounter with the Perso-Arabic script providing evidence for ideas first mooted in Sheridan's work, *A Rhetorical Grammar*. This strategy allows Gilchrist to present himself as an active contributor to the debate over the nature of speech sounds, and also to depict the written form of Hindustani as having an order and rationality that his readers might not suspect. Contemporary accounts of the South Asian writing systems are not always complimentary. But here, the script is seen in rather more positive terms as encoding information that has only recently emerged in the context of western language study.

In tackling the few irregular verbs that exist in Hindustani, Gilchrist uses a number of different strategies, all of them authorised by long use in western language study. He resorts to a notion of 'convertibility' – the relatedness of certain speech sounds, not in the context of particular sound changes affecting particular languages at particular times but in a general, even universal sense. Identifying relationships of this kind was commonplace within the etymological tradition, and provided Gilchrist with a way of naturalising the relationship between an infinitive form such as *jānā* and its irregular perfect form, *gayā*. The term 'naturalisation', appropriated from the discourse of ideological critique, is particularly appropriate here. The notion of convertibility implies that there is a natural relationship between certain pairs of sounds, and hence that the substitution of one for the other is also natural and not to be regarded as eroding the analogous nature of the grammatical system. Gilchrist also resorts to explanations that construct irregular forms as deliberate deviations from proportionality developed with the purpose of avoiding ambiguity or increasing the euphony of the language, as defined by the classical rhetoricians. These forms of explanation originate with the late Latin grammarians but were circulating in the eighteenth century both in Latin grammars, such as the one by Claude Lancelot, and in more philosophical texts, including Monboddo's monumental work, *On the Origin and Progress of Language*.

As he discussed the verbal system, Gilchrist engaged in more overt showmanship than in almost any other part of the grammar. He uses metaphors to construct himself as a lawyer, defending Hindustani against charges of irregularity, and as an adventurer, rescuing the mangled corpse of the language from a pair of bears that are absurdly trying to lick it into shape. He also generates vast quantities of footnotes, which, at a visual level, dominate the page and gesture towards the enormous volume of research that lies behind the rules and tables in the main body of the text. Through frequent cross-referencing, these textual fragments are linked together as a hypertext and provide alternative routes through the volume from the traditional structure of the Greco-Roman grammar, routes that prioritise the process of analysis over the definitive specification of forms and structures. Read together, the material on nominal and verbal morphology provides a vivid picture of Gilchrist grappling with the politics of representation and searching out technical solutions to problems generated by the project of assimilating the data of Hindustani into the framework of the western grammar. Is this language just a 'jargon'? And if it is, then is it really necessary to take it very seriously? How can an incomplete mastery of the language jeopardise colonial self-representation if there is in fact nothing to master – no rational principles underlying it and no regularity to its grammar? Gilchrist's answer to these questions is delivered at the technical level. Yes, Hindustani is ordered and rational – perhaps more so than the highly prized languages of the west.

6

DIALOGUES AND FAMILIAR PHRASES

6.1 INTRODUCTION

The last two chapters have examined the way in which Gilchrist tried to take control of the politics of representation through a close technical engagement with the forms and structures of Hindustani, naturalising aspects of the languages that seemed strange to westerners and foregrounding ones that fitted their perceptions of what a rational and well-ordered language should be like. However, the demands of his readership and the pressure they were able to place on him through the simple expedient of buying Hadley's books at times led Gilchrist away from technical grammar towards other types of pedagogical material, including collections of dialogues and phrases. It is clear that he was unhappy about this, and he argues that excessive reliance on dialogues and phrases results in a poor mastery of the language and perpetuates the use of 'jargon'. But, at the same time, Gilchrist was a natural entrepreneur and always saw his work not just in scholarly but also in commercial terms. He was, therefore, placed in something of a dilemma. Should he bow to commercial pressure and enjoy the financial rewards of giving the public what they wanted? Or should he resist the pressure to write dialogues and phrases, thus preserving the integrity of his project? What he tried to do, in fact, was to reconcile the two positions, including dialogues and phrases in his books but at the same time warning his readers about the importance of grammatical understanding. In attempting this reconciliation he became embroiled in a debate about the nature of language learning itself, and it is vital to understand that this was very much a live issue in the late eighteenth century, with advocates of 'reason' vying with advocates of 'practice' for the upper hand in both the intellectual and commercial spheres.

Practical grammar was essentially a pedagogical discipline. For William Smellie (1769–71 II: 728), the point of the art of grammar was 'to teach any language to those who are ignorant of it' by 'furnishing certain observations called rules, to which the methods of speaking used in [it] may be reduced'. Some participants in the debate over language learning emphasised the internalisation of grammatical rules over all else, and the status of grammar as an art is important here. Within the traditional typology of disciplines outlined in Chapter 3, an 'art' (*technē*) is superior to a 'knack' (*empeiria*) because it is founded on rational principles rather than on mere experience. To claim real mastery of an area of practical knowledge one must be able to articulate the principles underlying one's knowledge and not merely demonstrate some ad hoc skills picked up through practice. Furthermore, the distinction between an 'art' and a 'knack' has important sociopolitical reflexes. In a discussion of early modern gardening books, Rebecca Bushnell (2003: 123–4) has commented tellingly on the fact that publications purporting to provide comprehensive and systematic instruction in the practice of gardening were highly unlikely to have been read by the husbandmen who actually did the work, among whom rates of illiteracy were high. The workers themselves presumably acquired their knowledge of horticulture through constant experience, while the systematised knowledge of the book was for their employers. Similarly, in the field of language learning, participants who insist on the need to study grammatical rules often depict the alternative – learning based on practice – as the province of down-at-heel language masters running rather grubby businesses in rented rooms in London.

In late eighteenth-century London, there were certainly plenty of language teachers who made a living providing instruction in the modern, and sometimes the classical, languages of Europe. Among them was Louis Huguenin du Mitand, who described himself as a 'Teacher of Greek and Latin and of the Ten principal European living tongues' (Du Mitand 1788: i). Du Mitand fits the rather snobbish caricature of the commercial language master with a fashionable teaching method built on practice. In a textbook of French that he published in 1788 he asserts that, although he does not reject the study of grammar entirely, he does not believe that it is sufficient for the adequate mastery of a language:

> Nay practice is so very necessary that even the eminent professors of Greek and Latin, who have been for years in the habit of teaching those languages, could not express themselves readily in them on the common occurrences of life, merely for want of the practical part. (Du Mitand 1788: xi–xii)

In the same way, there are many people who can read French 'as well as Frenchmen themselves' but are unable to converse in it because they have never 'contracted the habit of speaking' (Du Mitand 1788: xi–xii) The idea that the production of spoken discourse is a 'habit' stands in stark contrast to the claim that real knowledge must be built upon systematic principles. And, far from advocating a system of study in which learners demonstrate their ability to articulate the basis of their knowledge by reciting grammatical rules and parsing sentences, Du Mitand proposes that they should spend the bulk of their time in the classroom experiencing the spoken language.

Most of his textbook is taken up with what he calls 'an authentic list of all the French verbs'. Aware, however, that a 'bare and dry list of them' would serve little purpose, since it would 'leave no impression upon the mind', he presents the verbs in short sentences, 'connected [...] with the substantives or other words they are most likely to be connected with in speech' (Du Mitand 1788: xiii). The verb *accepter*, for example, is exemplified in the sentence, '*Acceptez* mon offre', since 'when people do *accept* [...] they generally *accept offers*'. Thus, Du Mitand places considerable emphasis on the notion of collocation. The learner needs to establish a mental connection between the words *accepter* and *offre* because they frequently collocate in real discourse. And Du Mitand emphasises the role of the sense of hearing in building these connections, explaining that, when he uses his textbook in the classroom, he reads each of the sentences 'with a very loud and distinct voice'. Furthermore, 'to affect the learner's ear more forcibly', he makes 'a short stop at every sound':

> By that process, the sense of hearing soon becomes capable of dis-tinguishing sounds from one another, and as sounds so far act upon the soul, that words uttered excite certain ideas, the different notions, representative of those sounds, are at last durably engraved in the memory. (Du Mitand 1788: xxi)

Du Mitand does not ground his opinions in extensive philosophical discussion, but his comments have a flavour of the ideas developed by British empiricists (such as Locke and Hartley) or French sensationists (like Condillac and Bonnet). The claim that the spoken word can 'excite ideas' in the same way that sensation does clearly has its roots in the approaches associated with these philosophers. In *An Essay Concerning Human Understanding* (1790 III: 6), for example, Locke states:

> [T]here comes, by constant use, to be such a connexion between certain sounds and the ideas they stand for, that the names heard, almost as readily excite certain ideas as if the objects themselves, which are apt to produce them, did actually affect the senses. Which is manifestly so in all obvious sensible qualities, and in all substances that frequently and familiarly occur to us.

And, in the context of the debate over language learning, this characterisa-tion of language provides a radical critique of the idea that acquiring a language is essentially a mental activity involving the internalisation of rational principles, a critique that parallels the broader empiricist challenge to rationalism.

Of course, the two perspectives outlined here – learning through reason and learning through practice (or sensation) – are not mutually exclusive. Writers who advocate the rigorous study of grammar often suggest that learners seek out native speakers for practice, while writers like Du Mitand who emphasise the importance of practice often assume that learners will be studying grammar in parallel with their work in class. Nevertheless, the language masters of eighteenth-century London tended to identify themselves with one or other camp, the traditional grammarians or the modern advocates of practice. And the use of dialogues and phrases tended to be associated with the latter group. After all, materials of this kind do not provide much insight into how the grammar of a language works, their purpose being more to illustrate the way in which the language is used. As the last two chapters have suggested, Gilchrist's work is very much concerned with the relationship between language and reason. His representation of Hindustani served to demonstrate not only that the language could be 'reduced to rules' but also that those rules fitted western perceptions of what a rational and well-ordered language should be like. Furthermore, his own self-representation was built on his scholarly engagement with the Hindustani language and his ability to systematise its grammar. To give up on grammatical analysis and start writing dialogues was effectively to put both projects aside. The dialogue – a genre associated not with reason but with practice – was hardly an effective medium through which to conduct a rational defence of Hindustani. And, what is more, by putting aside grammatical scholarship and turning out popular materials, Gilchrist might have jeopardised his own status and relegated himself to the level of the London language masters, desperate for a new gimmick to lure in the punters.

In examining these issues, it will be useful first to look at the dialogues and familiar phrases that Hadley was providing for his readers. After all, it was the very fact that his rival was supplying material of this kind that pushed Gilchrist into offering dialogues and phrases for the first time in *The Oriental Linguist*. Furthermore, Hadley's dialogues have a demonstrable relationship with those provided by the teachers of French and Italian who plied their trade in eighteenth-century London, a fact that is important for an understanding of how Gilchrist and his contemporaries viewed them. Having decided to give in to commercial pressure, Gilchrist drew on the work of one of the London language masters, Lewis Chambaud, and included a long quotation from one of his books in the introduction to *The Oriental Linguist*. It is easy to see that, if Gilchrist had refused to have anything to do with the demands of the popular readership and continued to turn out dense and difficult grammatical material akin to his earliest publications, he would simply have lost readers to Hadley. That being the case, Chambaud was useful to him because he had the virtue of having authentic experience in the market for popular language teaching while being virulently opposed to dialogues. By quoting Chambaud, Gilchrist was able to condemn the use of dialogues, while simultaneously sounding as if he understood the needs of ordinary learners. And Chambaud's work also suggested a way of using dialogues that did not rely entirely on rote learning and practice but could be seen as promoting a rational engagement with the language.

The final section of this chapter will consider events that took place in the 1820s, long after Gilchrist had returned from India. Attempting to make a living by teaching Hindustani in London, Gilchrist came into conflict with yet another French language master, Nicholas Gouin Dufief. Like the conflict with Hadley, Gilchrist's feud with Dufief was to some extent a commercial rivalry dressed up as an intellectual disagreement. Dufief had trodden on Gilchrist's toes in part because he had ventured beyond the teaching of French and had staked a claim to the market in colonial language teaching, an area that Gilchrist saw as by rights exclusively his. It will therefore be useful to consider the ways in which those two aspects of Gilchrist's work – the scholarly and the commercial – remained intertwined and, if anything, became more closely entangled as time went by. However, there was also a political side to Gilchrist's quarrel with Dufief, and the chapter will end by considering the ways in which Gilchrist's emergent persona as a radical is connected with his views both on language study and as an advocate of British colonialism in India.

6.2 HADLEY'S DIALOGUES

Dialogues and familiar phrases first became available to learners of Hindustani when the third edition of Hadley's *Grammatical Remarks* was published in 1784.[1] Hadley presents the material under three different headings. First there is a collection of 'familiar phrases' or useful expressions in Hindustani with literal English translations, organised under 12 functional headings: 'to consult', for example, or 'to assent and dissent' (Hadley 1784: 106–9). Under the former heading, Hadley includes items such as 'I what shall do? Hum keah kurringa? Your advice what? Tumaurau muslhut keah?' (Hadley 1784: 108–9). He explains the bizarre nature of the English sentences by noting that they are arranged 'as near as possible in the order of the Hindostannic [...] by which if attended to, the Syntax and idiom of the language may be easier learned' (Hadley 1784: 105). So, although Hadley's grammar does not include a section on syntax, these phrases will remedy that deficiency by providing the learner with the means to make inferences about the way in which Hindustani sentences are structured. Next, Hadley provides a group of 'familiar dialogues', which differ from the 'familiar phrases' in that they are not simply lists of exponents but, to some extent, represent exchanges, generally between masters and servants. This being the case, it is not surprising that many of the 'dialogues' are little more than lists of imperatives. Some of them are very much rooted in the Indian context. The financial running of a colonial

---

[1] In the first edition of his grammar, Hadley had written: 'Should [this work] prove acceptable, a complete translation of the Vocabulary (Moors and English) will be given, with some dialogues' (Hadley 1772: xvi).

household was often placed in the hands of a servant called the *sirkar*, and the dialogue 'Of account' represents a response to the anxieties about loss of control that this arrangement sometimes provoked in the British (Hadley 1784: 126–9). The last four 'familiar dialogues' are specifically for the use of women. 'To rise in the morning' (Hadley 1784: 138–9) is similar to the earlier dialogue, 'To rise in the morning and ride out' (pp. 122–5), but depicts a woman talking to her maid rather than a man talking to his servant.[2] Finally, Hadley includes a set of 'military dialogues', which depict the activities of a British officer on active service. Read as a group, they form a narrative sequence constructed around an actual historical event, the battle of 'Moonipur'. Troops are moved into a trouble spot, spies are sent out on reconnaissance, a surprise attack is made, and the victory is even celebrated with a song (Hadley 1784: 157–71). The sequence almost has the character of a theatrical text, as if Hadley had dramatised his own experience in a series of short scenes.

Hadley's models for the familiar dialogues and phrases were works used in the study of modern European languages. Texts of this kind represent some of the earliest printed material to appear in Britain, and Caxton himself produced a book of bilingual dialogues in the late fifteenth century. The sixteenth and seventeenth centuries represent the heyday of the genre, and many of the texts in use in the eighteenth century were simply new editions of works that had appeared in that original period of creativity. Radtke (1994) provides an excellent survey of the French and Italian dialogues in circulation in the seventeenth and eighteenth centuries, and argues that by the end of this period, the constant reissuing of much older material meant that the speech exemplified in books of dialogues and phrases was becoming increasingly dated.[3] An example of a work that enjoyed this kind of longevity was *The Complete French Master* by Abel Boyer, originally published in 1694. Boyer came from a Huguenot family and was born at Castres in the south of France in 1677. He left France after the Edict of Nantes was revoked in 1685 and Protestantism effectively

---

[2] Pal and Dehejia (1986: 23) note that the last quarter of the eighteenth century saw an influx of British women to Calcutta, many of them allegedly in search of husbands. These women were unkindly nicknamed the girls of the 'Fishing Fleet' and those who returned home unmarried were known as 'Returned Empties'.

In the 4th edition of Hadley's grammar, published in 1796, a note is attached to the dialogues for the use of women. In this note Hadley defends the reputation of British women in India pointing out that there is no real difference between travelling to Calcutta in search of a husband and frequenting a fashionable resort such as Bath for the same purpose.

On 6 March 1772 one George Hadley, a passenger on the *Ponsbourne* travelling from Bengal, married a fellow passenger, Elizabeth Carolina Thompson, on the island of St Helena (British Library Oriental and India Office Collections N/6/1/f.3). Since George Hadley the grammarian retired from the Company's service in 1771 and returned to England, it is likely that he is the same person as George Hadley husband of Elizabeth. It is possible, therefore, that Hadley's note in fact represents a defence of his own wife's reputation.

[3] See also Howatt (1984: 5–11) on the earliest printed dialogues.

became illegal. After a brief stay in Holland, he came to Britain and engaged in a variety of literary pursuits. As Cormier (2003: 22) says:

> When he died in the London suburb of Chelsea on November 16, 1729, Abel Boyer left a rich literary legacy. In addition to his *Royal Dictionary*, he had published a grammar and various translations, not to mention a body of correspondence in French and English. His numerous historical works included a life of William III, a life of Queen Anne, and historical records [...] which still serve as a reference for historians of the period.

The Complete French Master was one of the most popular French textbooks of the eighteenth century and in 1783, the year before Hadley's dialogues were published, it reached its 25th edition. There is some evidence that Boyer's name was particularly associated with the use of dialogues in language learning. In 1792, for example, Robert Jones published a collection of Persian dialogues at the Company's Press in Calcutta under the title, *A New Persian and English Work, after the Method of Boyer and Others.*

Hadley's familiar phrases are closely comparable with Boyer's. Hadley has 12 categories of phrases, while Boyer (1783: 209–36) has 22. However, all but one of Hadley's categories are included under the same or a similar heading in Boyer's list (Table 6.1).

Table 6.1

Hadley		Boyer	
1.	To call and to ask	1.	To ask something
2.	To assent and dissent	4.	To affirm, deny, consent, &c.
3.	To consult	5.	To consult or consider
4.	To speak and to tell	8.	Of speaking, saying, doing, &c.
5.	To understand and remember	10.	Of understanding or apprehending
6.	To hear	9.	Of hearing, hearkening, &c.
7.	To go and come	7.	Of going, coming, stirring, &c.
8.	Of the weather	19.	Of the weather
9.	Of news	–	Of news (among the dialogues)
10.	Of the hour	20.	Of the hour
11.	Of age, life, and death	14.	Of the age, life, death &c.
12.	To eat and drink	6.	Of eating and drinking

The material presented under each heading is also comparable. For example, in Boyer's category 'To affirm, deny, consent, &c.' we find exponents such as: '*Il est vrai*. It is true. *Il n'est que trop vray*. It is too true. [...] *Je crois qu'oüy*. I believe yes. *Je crois que non*. I believe not.' Under the equivalent heading, 'To affirm and deny', Hadley gives us: 'That true is it?

Ooah sutch hy? True it is. Sutch hy. A lye it is. Joot hy.' Boyer also has a range of 'familiar dialogues' and some of these are directly comparable with Hadley's: 'To speak to a Groom', for example (Boyer 1783: 308). An important difference between the two texts lies in the social range of the phrases they present. Boyer's cover a wide range of contexts – interactions with servants but also conversation with social equals and superiors. Hadley's, by contrast, are very much intended for use with sepoys and servants. I have argued elsewhere (Steadman-Jones 2005: 203–4) that books of dialogues from the early modern period can be understood as having a moral function as well as a linguistic one. In the context of the early capitalist economy, where informal credit networks built on trust were essential to the expansion of commerce, the cultivation of a sound moral reputation was an important aspect of the merchant's livelihood. A significant proportion of the market for dialogues and phrases was made up of merchants engaged in trade with continental Europe, and the material in these texts provided them not merely with the linguistic knowledge needed for survival in France or Italy but with models of the kind of polite communication on which their public reputations might depend. That being the case, to produce dialogues in a non-European language sometimes fulfilled the rhetorical function of representing the language's speakers within a framework of civility and sociability.[4] But in Hadley's text the main mode of self-representation modelled in the dialogues is that of assertive command, and instead of creating the conditions for readers' impressions of Indians to expand, the genre itself contracts to fit the limited contexts of the kitchen and the barracks.

In 1796 the fourth edition of Hadley's grammar appeared complete with four new dialogues: 'Of a Suckhee', which takes place at the self-immolation of a Hindu widow (Hadley 1796: 2B1^r–2B4^r), 'Of Mahometan superstition and ghosts', in which a Muslim servant expresses concern that his saddlebag may be made of pigskin (Hadley 1796: 2B^v–2C1^v), and two exchanges in which we learn about the local fauna (Hadley 1796: 2C1^v–2D2^v). Although they are purportedly pedagogical materials, these dialogues in fact bring an air of exoticism to Hadley's text, and also construct the author as someone with a first-hand knowledge of the country. As Nussbaum (1995: 169) notes, novels and plays set in India became increasingly common in late eighteenth-century England, and a familiar trope in such texts was the fate of the *satī* – the widow who either voluntarily or under compulsion mounted her husband's funeral pyre and was burnt alive. The experience of the *satī* was often used as a means of representing Hindus, or at least Brahmins, as blind slaves of tradition, quite prepared to commit unspeakable acts of cruelty in the name of religion.

---

[4] I have argued this in the case of Roger William's text, *A Key Into the Language of America*, which was first published in 1643 and contains dialogues in the language of the Narragansett Indians of Rhode Island (Steadman-Jones 2005).

And a British character was often cast in the role of hero, saving the widow from the oppressive demands of her compatriots and, in the process, metonymically figuring the benefits of British rule.[5] Hadley's dialogue 'Of a Suckhee' trades on the interest that such works had aroused, but the Hindu widow in Hadley's text does not express any reluctance to die and the British officer does not intervene to save her. On the contrary, there is a resigned quality to the dialogue and it is best understood perhaps in terms of another trope common in British representations of India – the notion of the country as ultimately beyond western comprehension.

As this brief discussion has suggested, most of Hadley's dialogues and phrases had their origins in resources used in the study of modern European languages, and were clearly designed to meet a demand from readers who were used to that kind of material. In John Gilchrist, however, they found a critical reader. In Chapter 2 we saw that, in the preface to *The Oriental Linguist*, Gilchrist (1798a: i) admits that he has been forced to render his work more 'conciliating' because of 'pecuniary embarrassments' brought about by the sale of Hadley's 'insignificant catch-penny production'. In the same passage he announces his reluctant decision to include dialogues in the texts, and it is clear that this is one of the features of Hadley's work that has rendered it popular:

> People who arrive in this country seem to hold the acquisition of the current speech in so secondary a light, as to be bent on acquiring the language of Hindostan at once, by the dronish medium of dialogues alone; I have therefore accommodated them with a few here, though against my own judgement. (Gilchrist 1798a: iv)

He goes on to warn the reader that the best progress will be made by 'those scholars who meddle least with hum-drum collections of ready-made dialogues'. They will become 'working bees in the hive of oriental learning', while the others will 'never surpass the rank of drones at best' (Gilchrist 1798a: iv–v). In this Mandevillean image, the importance of language learning to the collective is again prioritised over the benefits to the individual. New arrivals in India are expected to play an active role in colonial society, and those who fall short of Gilchrist's expectations are condemned as drones. As we saw in Chapter 1, he depicts the actions of individuals as having a major impact on the sustainability of the British empire in India, and this latest image from the Gilchrist bestiary reinforces that sense of shared responsibility. But what exactly is the problem with dialogues? In what sense are they a 'dronish medium'? And why is the

---

[5] In 1791, for example, Mariana Starke's play *The Widow of Malabar* was published in Dublin. The work was an adaptation of a French play entitled *La Veuve du Malabar* and was currently in performance at the Theatre-Royal, Covent Garden (Starke 1791: 5). At the end of the play a young Hindu widow, Indamora, is saved from having to immolate herself by a British officer, Raymond.

provision of dialogues an 'accommodation' and not something Gilchrist is willing to do as a matter of course?

6.3 GILCHRIST AND THE LONDON LANGUAGE MASTERS

Unfortunately it is difficult to ascertain how exactly eighteenth-century learners used dialogues in their studies, but Gilchrist expresses his hostility to material of that kind in terms of his fears about what learners would do with it. His expressions of disquiet echo a number of texts depicting the conditions under which French and other modern languages were studied in contemporary England. British newspapers of the eighteenth century are filled with advertisements in which private tutors offer to prepare adult learners for naval, military and commercial careers by providing instruction in a wide range of practical subjects. Some of them offer a curriculum specifically directed at candidates for the service of the East India Company, with lessons in skills such as navigation and even the rudiments of Persian. Amongst all the vocational subjects – mensuration, merchants' accounts and so on – the academies and private masters also offered teaching in French, similarly as a response to the aspirations and ambitions of their clients. An interesting account of such classes comes from Louis Du Mitand, who was mentioned in the introduction to this chapter. Du Mitand ran a school in Great Suffolk Street, Southwark, in the 1780s. In the preface to his textbook he discusses the importance of French as a medium of communication and observes:

> The ardour to learn it has established schools, solely appropriated to that end, in every quarter of Europe, and particularly in England [...]. In effect, what cheesemonger or shoemaker is there within the bills of mortality, whose back-parlour or front-garret is not let to a day-school, where French is boldly taught by such as can scarcely read it[...]? (Du Mitand 1788: vii)

The native speaker's contempt for his underqualified rivals clearly informs the tone of these comments. However, Du Mitand is not much more complimentary about their students, and goes on to depict them as idle layabouts who only want to learn French for social advancement, do not have the application to move beyond the definite article and expect to acquire the language without effort. It is beyond them, he complains, even to attend classes regularly:

> The master's door groans under a porter's massy fist, who having enforced ready admission, flings in the following half-card half-billet—'There is to be a *bruising-match* today at *Hockley-in-the-hole* on the event of which I have a cool thousand depending; I hope

therefore you will excuse me. 12 o'clock. SQUIRE SAPSCULL. (Du Mitand 1788: ix)

According to Francis Grose's *Classical Dictionary of the Vulgar Tongue*, a 'sapscull' is a 'simple fellow'. And in Henry Carey's play *The Honest Yorkshireman*, first published in 1736, Squire Sapscull is an unsophisticated young man from the East Riding of Yorkshire who first appears with his servant, Blunder, new to London and staring about him while he attempts to find 'Grozveneer Square'. Du Mitand's vividly sketched scene evokes a world in which the most unlikely people are learning French, whether or not they are really interested and whether or not they have any aptitude for it, simply because it is the conventional thing to do. This is a world in which knowledge is a commodity and students expect to be able to purchase it without applying themselves in any way.

In the preface to *The Oriental Linguist*, Gilchrist quotes at length from the work of another private language teacher, Lewis Chambaud, whose grammar of French was first published in 1750 and was reprinted throughout the second half of the eighteenth century.[6] Like Du Mitand, Chambaud links declining standards to the commercial demands of the private master's clients, but unlike Du Mitand, he also characterises the use of dialogues and phrases as symptoms of this decline. Chambaud is really talking about classes for children here, but Gilchrist suggests that his comments are equally applicable to adults:

> The generality of people, being incapable to reflect duly upon the nature of a language, and the faculties of the human mind, have hardly put their children to the study of the French language, than they expect them to be able to speak it, before they had learnt how to speak: and in case they don't, never fail to tax the master either with incapacity or neglect of his business. (Gilchrist 1798a: v; cf. Chambaud 1797: xvi)

Thus, like Du Mitand, Chambaud suggests that clients want results without application; the result, we are told, is that, instead of starting from first principles, the teachers make their pupils learn dialogues and phrases by heart and 'beat common sentences into them pretty near after the same manner as parrots are instructed'. In other words, the children are made to practise the language before they have learnt how it works and, as a result, 'acquire the knack of talking a gibberish, which nobody can make anything of'. Their parents, however, knowing no better, 'think them great proficients in the French tongue' (Gilchrist 1798a: v; cf. Chambaud 1797: xvi).

---

[6] See Cohen (2003) for an account of French teaching in eighteenth-century England and, in particular, a discussion of the work of Lewis Chambaud.

Chambaud goes on to 'set before the Reader a specimen of that barbarous language wherein School-boys are trained up, under the specious pretence of speaking French'. The specimen consists of a long list of mistakes that schoolboys commonly make, and these errors are constructed as the inevitable result of teaching French through practice.[7] Chambaud further attacks the idea that languages are best learnt through experience by pointing out that many French refugees who have lived in Britain for a long time still cannot speak English, despite being exposed to the language almost constantly (Chambaud 1797: xxi). Students, he says, should instead learn the 'art' of speaking, which implies the use of the reason in the acquisition of grammatical principles, and to this end his grammar begins with a 'succinct, but clear and exact analysis of the analogy and foundations of languages' and then sets out 'the true and perfect notions of the parts of Speech and other Grammatical terms used in the work'. These definitions 'will be found grounded in the nature of things, and formed after the most exact rules of Logic' (Chambaud 1797: vi). Thus, at the same time as acquiring French, the students will be introduced to the principles of general grammar, and in the process will learn 'the art of speaking, the reason of the words they utter, the œconomy of all languages' (Chambaud 1797: vi).

Chambaud's preface is a powerful example of assertive self-representation, serving both to establish the authority of its author and to guarantee the effectiveness of the text that it precedes. It draws attention to the rationality of the author's methods of teaching and alludes to the typology of disciplines in which a 'knack' (*empeiria*) is considered inferior to an 'art' (*technē*), the two types of knowledge being connected here with two genres of pedagogical literature. Through the constant experience of chanting dialogues, pupils merely acquire a 'knack of speaking', whereas by internalising the rational principles set out in a grammar, they arrive at the 'art'. What is more, Chambaud's analysis uses definitions 'founded in the nature of things' and 'established through the most exact rules of logic'. General grammar always had a pedagogical function, the idea being that, if learners could understand why languages are as they are, they would find it easier to acquire them; and Chambaud's allusion to this idea reinforces his prioritisation of reason over practice.[8] What is more,

---

[7] For example, when they mean 'He has been at school these four years', they often say, 'Il a été a l'école ces quatre années', instead of 'Il y a quatre années qu'il va à l'école'. Similarly, when they want to say 'Call for bread', they will say, 'Appelez pour du pain', instead of 'Demandez du pain' (Chambaud 1797: xviii).

[8] See Aarsleff (1967: 16; 1982: 105, 166). Lowth (1762: xiii) suggests that, if children were introduced to general grammar through the medium of their own language, they would find it much easier when they came to learn Latin, 'and would hardly be engaged so many years, as they now are, in that most irksome and difficult part of literature, with so much labour of the memory, and with so little assistance of the understanding'.

the issue of reason against practice is linked to the trope of increasing commercialisation. Teachers who use dialogues do so not because they really believe in their effectiveness but because they are browbeaten inadequates who cannot establish their authority over their own students. The implication is that Chambaud himself is made of sterner stuff, and is able to persuade his clients to accept what is truly good for them rather than what they want.

There are a number of suppressed premises in Chambaud's argument. He assumes that teachers who employ methods founded in practice are doing so because they are afraid that their demanding clients will take their business elsewhere if progress is slow. Ironically, this dismissive attitude to the commerciality of education provides Chambaud with an effective way of attacking his competitors, allowing him to present himself as one of the very few language masters who still have any integrity. Furthermore, Chambaud assumes that most students are learning dialogues as an *alternative* to studying grammar, a claim that may well be unfair. In the early editions of Boyer's *Complete French Master*, the familiar phrases were presented under the heading 'The niceties of the French tongue', a title that strongly suggests they were intended to exemplify the subtleties of polite usage and illustrate the use of the language in different social contexts. Indeed, in his own book of dialogues taken from the plays of Molière, Chambaud states that he has chosen extracts that 'comprehend the Idiom of the Conversation of Courtiers, Commoners, Merchants, Tradesmen, and almost all the States and Professions in Life'. By using this material, he says, the learner can acquire 'a new stock of Expressions and Phrases, which will enable him to act his part in Conversation' (Chambaud 1761: iii). He thus implies that his own dialogues are unlike those of his rivals in that they are intended to supplement the study of grammar by helping the learner to navigate more confidently the socially dangerous waters of French conversation. And the theatrical image is important here: to converse is to take on a role, and what better way to learn how to do this than by studying the plays of one France's most illustrious playwrights? Thus, when he is criticising his rivals, the provision of dialogues is a cowardly concession to the unrealistic expectations of clients. But when he is promoting his extracts from Molière, they constitute an important resource for the study of polite conversation.

To a large extent Gilchrist's hostility to dialogues was a matter of prestige. He wanted to be seen as an orientalist scholar of the calibre of Jones or Halhed and not as the kind of language master who operated out of a shoemaker's 'back parlour'. But, when Gilchrist decided that he would have to publish dialogues for commercial reasons, he found in Chambaud's books a useful framework of self-representation. Chambaud had the virtue of being both a well-known popular language teacher and a proponent of rigorous grammatical study. By quoting his views on dialogues, therefore, Gilchrist was able to gesture towards the more popular market and show his readers that he was sympathetic to the needs of ordinary learners, while at the same time presenting himself as firmly committed to careful, traditional scholarship. To put it another way, Chambaud supplied a handily populist argument for an uncompromisingly elitist approach. He also provided a new way for Gilchrist to present his disdain for Hadley. As one reads Chambaud's comments about language masters who are more concerned with keeping their clients happy than with pursuing effective methods of teaching, it is clear that Gilchrist means us to make the connection with his rival's cynical 'catchpenny production'. And, in the same way that pandering to the ill-informed demands of clients leads to their children speaking dreadful French, Hadley's provision of populist trash will result in dismal standards of Hindustani among the British. After all, they have already attempted to learn Hindustani without reference to grammar and the result was the 'mangled carcase' that Hadley describes. Indeed, the terms in which Chambaud describes the French of schoolboys who have been taught by rote – 'barbarous language' and 'gibberish' – are the very ones used by Gilchrist of Hadley's 'jargon'.

Having shown that his resistance to dialogues has nothing to do with snobbery and everything to do with effective pedagogy, Gilchrist nevertheless goes ahead and publishes a set of dialogues. Like Chambaud, he justifies his actions by emphasising that learners should not attempt to learn them by heart. But, in suggesting what they *should* do with them, he turns not to the dialogues from Molière as a model but to another of Chambaud's pedagogical works. In his attack on methods founded in practice, Chambaud concedes that some kinds of practice are important, but that useful practice must be carefully distinguished from learning by rote. Beginners, he says, cannot practise what they have not already learnt, and so they must start by acquiring both vocabulary and rules. Vocabulary can be memorised but rules must be learnt through 'judgment and reflection':

> The right placing and using of words in speech require a constant and steady application of the mind, and cannot be acquired but by much meditation upon the language, either by one's self or with a teacher; by frequent construing and turning the language into our Mother-tongue, and vicissim our Mother-tongue into that language, and comparing all along the Genius and Idiom of the two languages. (Gilchrist 1798a: vi; cf. Chambaud 1797: xvii)

Once all this foundational material is in place, it then becomes appropriate to start practising, and to assist with this process, Chambaud published a book of exercises, the first edition of which appeared, like his grammar, in 1750. Gilchrist (1798a: v) describes these exercises as 'so judiciously contrived' that he would be 'happy to see something of the same kind in Hindoostanee'. The exercises are graded and provide practice in grammatical rules through translation. Thus, grammar is still the organising principle of the work rather than functional contexts. In each, an English text is set out for the student to translate and relevant French vocabulary is presented in citation form. Effectively Chambaud has provided Gilchrist with a non-empiricist account of practice – one that conceptualises pedagogical exercises in terms of the strengthening of the mental faculties rather than in terms of the cultivation of associations between words and ideas through a process of repetition.

Gilchrist suggests that the dialogues included in *The Oriental Linguist* be used as exercises in the very same anti-empiricist sense. The learner can work on them with a native teacher or 'moonshee', and 'vary them at pleasure' with his assistance (Gilchrist 1798a: iv). It is not entirely clear what Gilchrist means by 'vary them at pleasure', but the idea may be that the learner can recast sentences from the first person to the third or from the present tense to the past, and so on. Thus the material will serve to structure the encounter between the European student and the Indian teacher, a relationship that Gilchrist maintains is fraught with difficulty, as this quotation from the preface to the grammar and dictionary indicates:

> As Moonshees commonly possess at best, but a smattering of any grammar, the scholar will do well to consider himself in the philosophical department of it, more than a match for his language master, who ought notwithstanding this to meet with due deference in the practical and idiomatical side of the question. (Gilchrist 1798b: xlvi)

Thus, Gilchrist characterises native teachers as incapable of offering the guidance that learners need as they engage in the 'constant and steady application of the mind' that is essential in acquiring grammatical knowledge. But he suggests that the dialogues can provide a way of focusing the problematic encounter and ensuring that it is productive. And this, in turn, allows him to include dialogues in his book with a clear conscience. Surely no one will try to learn them by heart after all his strict warnings?

Having made the initial concession in *The Oriental Linguist*, Gilchrist went on in 1804 to publish a volume consisting entirely of a collection of dialogues. The work was very successful commercially and a third edition was published in 1820. But even then, Gilchrist continued to warn his readers about the dangers of dialogues as a method of study, and the text is littered with notes admonishing the reader not to rely too heavily on this material. In one case, for example, Gilchrist includes a sentence that exemplifies the ergative construction:

What did he say when you told	Jub toom ne mere p,hir ane tuk
him to remain untill [*sic*]	oos se kuha ki ruho tub oos ne kya
I returned?	kuha? (Gilchrist 1804a: 6)

In a footnote he states that the sentence 'translated literally' must be rendered: 'When you _____ my again coming till, him to said, that stay! then he _____ said?' The inclusion of blanks reflects Gilchrist's feeling that the 'expletive' *ne* is largely untranslatable and, in a late example of the interlinked footnotes that are so characteristic of the grammar, the reader is referred to another note for an explanation of the significance of that particle. The purpose of including this literal translation and drawing attention to the problems associated with the particle *ne* is to convince the reader of the need to study grammatical principles:

> [T]he slightest attention to any of the dialogues, in which the transposition of words from our order of construction [...] must convince the learner how very little a simple dialogist has to expect, from so clumsy a method as he prefers, for acquiring the vernacular speech of India. (Gilchrist 1804a: 6)[9]

There are two important points to make about this strategy. First, it constitutes a reversal of Gilchrist's usual technique of *naturalising* Hindustani grammar. In the last two chapters we saw him artfully deploying grammatical metalanguage to make the forms and structure of Hindustani fit the familiar patterns approved within the various components of western language study. But here we see him deliberately disrupting any sense of familiarity by producing a translation that is utterly unlike any sentence that an English speaker might utter, and even incorporating blanks to mark places where there is so little resemblance between the languages that translation is wholly impossible. The point, of course, is that when learners have agreed to engage with the grammar of Hindustani, they need to be persuaded that it all lies within their grasp. But, while they are still refusing to learn about grammar, they need to be shown what a minefield the language is until it is properly understood. The second important point is that this practice of literal translation exactly parallels what Hadley does in his own familiar dialogues, the difference lying in what the practice is supposed to signify. For Hadley, literal translation is intended to help learners to master syntax – they are supposed to examine the English carefully in order to work out how the Hindustani original is organised. For Gilchrist, by contrast, it is supposed to show them how little they can expect to learn

---

[9] The discontinuity in the syntax of this passage – the relative clause contains no verb – is there in Gilchrist's original text and is not a misquotation.

from dialogues. In fact, one could believe that Gilchrist was intentionally parodying Hadley's practice, implicitly saying, 'This method works for sentences as simple as "That true is it?" "Ooah sutch hy?", but how will it cope with this...?'

Later on in the same text, Gilchrist returns to the troublesome particle *ne* and suggests that a failure to grasp its functions is a particular mark of 'jargonists':

> This expletive *ne* is the grand stumbling block of Jargonists, and the scarecrow of raw scholars. The former constantly confound it with the negative *nu*, and the latter know not with what to assimilate this *ne*, in any other known language. (Gilchrist 1804a: 12 n.)

It is particularly interesting that Gilchrist depicts the desperate attempts of the 'raw scholars' to 'assimilate' the particle to some feature in a language that they know. Assimilations of this kind form the basis of Gilchrist's own attempts to naturalise the grammar of Hindustani, and this comment suggests that the strategy was appropriate for his audience. But a few pages later Gilchrist warns his readers against assimilating Hindustani *ne* to a Latin particle with the same form:

> [F]or the latter neither inflects nouns, nor is its use restricted to any species or tense of verbs; though perhaps more applicable to inter-rogative sentences, than any other, but which does not apply to the Hindoostanee *ne*, in the smallest degree. (Gilchrist 1804a: 19 n.)

Given that Gilchrist has seen fit to warn his readers about this possible source of error, it seems likely that he had come across British learners who actually made this kind of mistake. At any rate, by filling the footnotes of his dialogues with these ubiquitous warnings about the need to understand the functions of *ne* properly, Gilchrist is able to meet the demands of his readers while simultaneously holding to his position that only the study of grammar leads to effective mastery of a language. His readers receive the kind of material they found so attractive in Hadley's work, but are also presented with constant reminders of Gilchrist's seriousness and scholar-ship. And again, it is in what Gérard Genette has called the 'paratext' – the supposedly marginal or supplementary parts of the work – that a central element of Gilchrist's message is communicated.

6.4 THE LATER DEBATE

In his later works, Gilchrist continued to characterise reason as the basis of effective language learning, and, as we shall see in the next chapter, he went on to develop a method of language study that was intended to subordinate memory entirely to the exercise of the intellectual faculties. In the *The*

Oriental Green Bag!!!, the polemical work that he published in 1820 to defend his reputation against attacks from his opponent William Smyth, he described this new method as 'a plain, practical, rational highway to oriental literature'. Furthermore, he also drew a contrast between his own approach to language learning and that advocated by a French teacher who was then attracting a great deal of attention in England, Nicholas Gouin Dufief, an émigré who had fought on the royalist side during the French Revolution. Dufief claimed to have identified a method of language learning that was entirely 'natural', and the title of his textbook is *Nature Displayed in Her Mode of Teaching Language to Man*. The naturalness of the method was supposedly demonstrated by the story of its discovery. Forced to 'abandon France', Dufief had travelled first to the West Indies and then to Philadelphia, where he realised that he needed to learn English. He was intending to follow conventional methods of language learning and his preparations were, as he puts it, 'in the beaten track' – he bought a range of English texts, both poetry and history, along with 'two Grammars, written for French learners; Boyer's Dictionary, in quarto; and Sheridan's, for pronunciation'. However, his studies were disrupted by an outbreak of yellow fever in Philadelphia. Taking refuge in Princeton, New Jersey, he found on arrival that, 'in the consternation of [...] flight', he had left both his grammars in Philadelphia. And, unable to find any replacements, he says that he decided to teach himself 'through the medium of the books in my possession':

> By a method essentially the same as the one here detailed, NATURE and NECESSITY enabled me to obtain my object. In four months, entirely unassisted, I acquired a tolerable knowledge of the English language, and, by the aid of Sheridan's Dictionary, even pronounced without inaccuracy. (Dufief 1818 I: iv–v)

This story dramatises Dufief's claims in a very effective fashion. The method he discovered in Princeton was not in any sense artificial because the trappings of 'art', the grammars he had purchased, were far away in quarantined Philadelphia. And if it was not 'art' that taught him English, then it must have been nature. The lesson he learnt from this was that direct exposure to language is the natural way to learn, and not the study of grammar. Moreover, the contents of his book reflect this philosophy.

First, the learner is presented with 'three vocabularies of familiar phrases' – the first comprises numbers, basic adjectives and 'an adequate collection of abstract nouns'; the second covers 'those important words which are known in Grammar by the denomination of ARTICLES, PRONOUNS, PREPOSITIONS, ADVERBS, CONJUNCTIONS, and INTERJECTIONS'; and the third includes 'the names of objects which occur most frequently in conversation'. All these words are embedded in phrases, and this 'renders the fundamental words more striking, – in the same manner as a frame renders the picture which is contains more conspicuous'. Of course, there is nothing new about the idea of presenting vocabulary in the context of 'familiar phrases'. This is exactly what Du Mitand had been doing back in the 1780s. And Dufief's argument for the practice is very similar to Du Mitand's. There are, he says, 'certain nouns which naturally awaken to the memory certain *verbs*'. The word 'kitchen', for example, naturally evokes the ideas of '*to cook*' and '*to roast*'. Thus, to present these words together is to exploit the collocations into which they naturally enter. After the 'three vocabularies', we find two lists of verbs, which, again, are all embedded in sentences (Dufief 1818 I: viii–ix). These are followed by '[t]wo collections of peculiar phrases'. The first includes a 'formulary of conversation' and consists of material that, far from being 'peculiar', conforms to what is normally found under the heading of 'familiar phrases' – a range of useful French expressions organised under 12 functional headings. The categories Dufief uses are reminiscent of Boyer's and include 'For Asking Questions, Affirming, Denying &c.' and 'Of the Time of Day' (Dufief 1818 I: 1h4^r). The second collection offers 'a vast number of proverbial, idiomatical, and figurative modes of expression', which are allegedly drawn from more than 500 plays. Dufief gives his reasons for borrowing material from theatrical texts:

> As plays, and especially comedies, are designed to portray us as we are, or as we appear in the various walks and scenes of life, it must be obvious to every one that these are the proper sources for the discovery of such turns and idioms as are peculiar to the people whose manner they are meant to pourtray. (Dufief 1818 I: x)

This explanation has clear parallels with Chambaud's discussion of his dialogues from the plays of Molière. Dramatists are characterised as expert observers of linguistic usage and nuance, so, by studying appropriate extracts from their work, learners can better appreciate how to use language as they present themselves in their various social roles.

The preface to *Nature Displayed* includes a long discussion of Dufief's approach to teaching, but in essence his method is to work systematically through the various collections of phrases, reading them aloud to the class and making the students repeat them back in unison along with an English version. The teacher then picks out individual words from the phrase and these are also repeated along with English translations. So the lesson will sound something like this: 'Master—*Prêtez-moi un de vos livres*; Class—Lend me one of your books, *Prêtez-moi un de vos livres*; M.—*Un, masculin*; Cl.—One, *un, masculin* [...]' (Dufief 1818 I: xxxvii). The students are taken through the phrases over and over again, repeating them aloud, breaking them up into their constituent words, and identifying a few rudimentary grammatical features such as the genders of nouns. The second volume of *Nature Displayed* includes an array of more traditional grammatical material, but students are not exposed to any particular part of the grammar until, through repetition and drill, they have already assimilated a range of phrases that exemplify that principle.

Dufief's method is built upon learning through practice. Students do not start with grammatical principles and then move on to practise them; they begin by internalising a vast array of sentences, and only when this material is firmly ingrained in their memories are they presented with explicitly formulated rules. The second part of *Nature Displayed* is concerned with justifying this method, and to those who object that he has completely abandoned the study of grammar, he replies that grammar must not be confounded with language itself. Like Du Mitand, he points out that one can learn the grammar of a language thoroughly and yet still be incapable of speaking it. Grammatical rules are, after all, observations upon language, and so to learn them before one has encountered the language itself is to learn 'observations upon nothing,—a description without a subject (Dufief 1818 I: lxix). The purpose of language, he says, is to express human wants and, when we learn our mother tongue, it is our wants that motivate us to speak, long before we know what grammar is:

> The transition from the knowledge of phrases to the knowledge of a language, is almost magical. The scholar who surrenders himself to this system will soon be surprised at his own facility. How dark, tedious, and fruitless, when compared with this, by which we have been taught our native tongue [...] are the methods which grammars prescribe,—the tender mother will more readily comprehend, than the cold grammarian! (Dufief 1818 I: lxviii–lxix)

I suggested earlier that Du Mitand's comments on language learning suggest the influence of either British empiricist or French sensationist thought. But whereas the earlier writer's intellectual debts are only implied by the terminology he uses, Dufief quite explicitly acknowledges the influence of Condillac and supports his argument with quotations from the philosopher's work. First, he points to a passage in which Condillac denies that the study of grammar is sufficient for the acquisition of a language: '[M]erely to understand the rules of the art of speaking, and to commit them to memory, does not constitute a perfect knowledge of those rules: we must also be in the habit of applying them' (Dufief 1818 I: lxx). The metalanguage deployed here will by now be very familiar. The use of the term 'art' implies an approach to language that is built upon systematised rules. However, this is not sufficient for successful language learning, which necessarily involves 'habit', a term that is also used by Du Mitand and that is anchored in the sensationist account of repeated experience as the basis of knowledge. Dufief supplies another quotation from Condillac to reinforce and develop this point: 'The recollection of a language is not [...] solely in the habits of the brain: it is, besides, in the habits of the organs of hearing, of speech, and of sight' (Dufief 1818 I: lxxxv). This assertion reinforces the importance of sensation in no uncertain terms. When a word excites an idea in the mind, it not a purely mental event. To hear the sound of a word or to see it represented on the page is to experience a sensation – a sensation that stands in proxy for another one but a sensation nevertheless. And it is because the eyes, ears and vocal organs are all involved in contracting the habit of speaking that repetition is at the heart of Dufief's pedagogical method. Dufief also discusses the 'vices of expression' to which writers like Chambaud see rote learning as giving rise. In fact, he says, mistakes like these arise from placing too much and not too little emphasis on grammar. Rules, after all, cannot be prescribed for idioms, and the only way to learn them is through experience.

It is not entirely surprising that Gilchrist was critical of the method outlined by Dufief in *Nature Displayed*. It represents an extreme example of the approach to language learning that Gilchrist had already attacked in the paratexts surrounding his own collections of dialogues. Indeed, Dufief's collections of phrases are very similar to those of Boyer or Du Mitand. What is more, a large part of the preface is devoted to exploring the use of the system for mass teaching. Since the core of the method is simple repetition, vast numbers of people could all be taught at once, thousands of them converging on public spaces around London to chant their way through Dufief's book under the direction of a single teacher. This vision of classes as huge public events is clearly very far from Chambaud's ideal of solitary 'meditation' upon the language and, for that matter, Gilchrist's image of the western learner working on his dialogues and 'varying them at pleasure' with the quiet assistance of his 'moonshee'. By contrasting his work with Dufief's, Gilchrist once again gestures towards his own self-representation as a rational grammarian. His approach to learning does not depend upon mindless repetition unstructured by rational explanation. What is more, the key to wiping out 'jargon' is not yet more imitative learning, but a reasoned and rule-governed understanding of the 'vernacular' languages of India.[10]

There is clearly a commercial dimension to this debate. In yet another section of the preface to *Nature Displayed*, Dufief asserts that his method has an important role to play in colonialism, and it is clear that this claim played at least as an important role in fuelling Gilchrist's sense of hostility as the nature of Dufief's method or the philosophy that lay behind it. Dufief (1818 I: cxvi) remarks that 'the want of a common medium of communication prevents the amalgamation into one common people of

---

[10] Eventually Gilchrist turns the matter over to the reader with the words: '*de gustibus non disputandum* [there is no arguing about matters of taste], and everyone has a right to prefer a regal turnpike to a common passage, should he find it the nearest or best of the two for his journey's end' (Gilchrist 1820: 69).

those who speak various languages, and yet live beneath the same ruler'. But since the system outlined in *Nature Displayed* is ideal for mass teaching, this problem could easily be overcome. Moreover, the use of a rapid printing process such as stereotyping, which was then coming into more widespread use, would allow the multitudes passing through the system to be supplied with cheap copies of Dufief's textbook, a little profit presumably accruing on each one. The system could be used in a wide range of different contexts. The eastward and southward expansion of Russia had brought a wide range of non-Russian-speaking peoples under the control of the Czar and, using Dufief's system, all of them could learn Russian in a matter of months. What is more:

> [B]y the same means, the English language might accompany the extension of the English government, and be rendered universal, in the same short time, throughout the chequered population of its realm, from the millions who people the banks of the Ganges, to the Candians, the Hottentots, the Negroes at Sierra Leone, the Maltese, the Charibs, the Canadians, the Irish, the Scotch, the Welsh, and the Greeks of the Seven Islands. (Dufief 1818 I: cxvi)

Clearly there is much in this proposal to fire the anger of a man who had spent much of his life attempting to induce the Servants of the East India Company to learn Hindustani properly, and Gilchrist (1820: 69) suggests sarcastically that the 'liberal minded foreigner' is perhaps unaware 'of my having already, in great measure anticipated him in the most unexceptionable parts of his own practice'. As usual, commercial considerations are in the air here, although there is clearly some political content to the confrontation as well. The idea that Dufief's system might be used to consolidate monarchical power seems to have offended Gilchrist's republican sympathies, and he makes much of Dufief's royalist allegiances. He refers to his own method of study as 'the *radical way* to the art and practice of thinking, not only upon *words* and *deeds*, but every object under the sun', contrasting it with Dufief's system, which is a '*royal road*' (Gilchrist 1820: 68). As we shall see in the next chapter, Gilchrist's own system is 'radical' in the sense that it involves analysing words into their roots, or, to use the Latin term, *radices*, a process that was supposed to harness the power of the reason and downplay the role of memory in the acquisition of a language. However, Gilchrist is also alluding to his own reputation as a political radical and contrasting it with his rival's conservative politics, a slightly dangerous game, given that the point of *The Oriental Green Bag!!!* was to refute Smyth's charges that he was unfit to teach the younger servants of the Company. A strong suggestion emerges from Gilchrist's satire that the cultivation of the reason is a political matter. His own method of language study, he indicates, will educate young Britons to take a rational and independent approach, not just to language, but to life in general, whereas Dufief's method is intended for colonised peoples themselves and, far from working to 'stimulate the mind', 'surfeits the memory' and reduces its users to a vast chanting mass. There is here a confluence of radical politics and colonial ideology that may appear strange to contemporary readers. But, as we saw in Chapter 1, late eighteenth-century texts often express the idea that the British empire in India has liberated the people of India from centuries of oppressive government. The radical gaze that focuses so sternly on the social and political institutions of Britain settles, when directed towards India, not on the institutions of the colonial state itself but on the structures of power that immediately preceded it and that coexist with it, still inviting intervention, improvement and reform.

6.5 CONCLUSION

The function of a dialogue is to present a snapshot of a language in use, and not to provide an account of how that language actually works. Thus, when Gilchrist adopted the dialogue as a pedagogical medium, he was turning to a genre that yielded few opportunities for an analytical investigation of language structure. And this was, in some ways, a problem for him. Through a detailed engagement with the morphologies of Hindustani nouns and verbs, he had made important progress towards his goals of naturalising the language for his western readers and establishing his reputation as a serious and insightful scholar. But now he found himself developing materials that provided no such opportunities for the representation of either language or self, a situation forced on him, he claims, by commercial pressures. The inclusion of 'dialogues and familiar phrases' in the third edition of Hadley's *Grammatical Remarks* had allegedly affected the sales of Gilchrist's own works in a fairly serious way, and the resulting 'pecuniary embarrassments' had led him to prepare a set of dialogues for his new book, *The Oriental Linguist*. But, despite his decision to bow to popular pressure, Gilchrist remained resistant to the dialogue as a medium of education and continued to emphasise the importance of grammatical analysis as the key to mastering a foreign language properly. Learners, he says, would do best to knuckle down to the study of grammar – an arena in which he himself was firmly in control – and resist the temptation to 'meddle with 'ready-made dialogues'.

The frustrations connected with the non-analytical nature of the dialogue were no doubt reinforced by the association of the genre with the London language masters, who made a living by teaching the modern languages of Europe and were always looking out for a 'new' method that would impress potential clients. Gilchrist aspired to the status of a serious orientalist scholar, not to that of a commercial language teacher running classes for reluctant students in the 'front-garret' of a Southwark shoemaker. His irritable condemnation of pedagogical dialogues must also be read as an attempt to assert his credentials as a practitioner of the 'art' of grammar, and to deny any connection with the dubious world of the popular teachers of French and Italian. Language masters like Louis Du Mitand often supported their use of dialogues with reference to an empiricist or sensationist view of epistemology. The dialogue was said to provide a means of inculcating the 'habit' of speaking through a process of constant practice. And this idea coheres well with the notion, found in Locke and Condillac, that, through constant association, the sound of particular words comes to 'excite' ideas in the mind in the same way that the perception of physical objects would. To a teacher whose priority was to attract as many students as possible, this philosophical justification no doubt provided useful support for a method that many learners seem to have found more enjoyable than the study of grammar. But, seen from the perspective of the traditional disciplinary typology, a focus on practice constituted a retreat from the realm of 'art' (*technē*) into a space where unsystematic habituation could offer students nothing more than the acquisition of a 'knack' (*empeiria*) ungrounded in a knowledge of rules.

Faced with the difficult task of providing the punters with what they wanted while simultaneously expressing hostility towards methods of language learning built on habituation, Gilchrist sought inspiration in the work of Lewis Chambaud, who was himself a teacher of French in eighteenth-century London. Chambaud articulated a critique of the pedagogical dialogue from *within* the popular marketplace, and thus helped Gilchrist to assure his readers that he understood the contemporary debate, even though he held to a fairly traditional line. At the same time, Chambaud provided Gilchrist with a non-empiricist model of 'practice' – one that focused on the exercise of the intellectual faculties rather than on the use of repetition as a means of forging associations between words and ideas. This allowed Gilchrist to point his readers towards a way of using dialogues that was consistent with his overall emphasis on the systematic study of grammatical rules. Learners were to work through the dialogues, 'varying them at pleasure', and in this manner developing a rational grasp of the way in which the language functioned. If used like this, the materials would also serve to structure what Gilchrist saw as the highly problematic encounter between the western learner and the native teacher or 'moon-shee', whose lack of awareness of grammar – by which Gilchrist, of course, meant western grammar – threatened to become a serious obstacle to learners' acquiring a systematic understanding of the language. The inclusion in the footnotes of endless warnings over the ineffectiveness of dialogues also provided a means by which Gilchrist could give his readers what they wanted while emphasising his status as a practitioner of rational grammar.

In 1820, long after he had returned home from India, Gilchrist was still embroiled in debates over the use of dialogues in language learning. This time his venom was directed towards the work of Nicholas Gouin Dufief, who justified his system of language learning with reference to Condillac's sensationist epistemology. In depicting this wholly 'natural' system as the solution to all the problems of communication presented by the expansion of the European powers, from the Russian annexation of Georgia to the British occupation of the Ionian islands, Dufief threatened Gilchrist's sense of himself as the central contemporary figure in colonial language learning. Gilchrist's hostility to Dufief was no doubt underpinned by a strong sense of commercial rivalry. But his invective also has a political flavour, focusing on the émigré's royalist allegiances and constructing Gilchrist's own teaching – 'radical' in both the etymological and political senses – as a training in 'the art and practice of thinking', applicable not only to language but to 'every object under the sun'. Both Gilchrist's espousal of 'vernacular' language and his insistence that education should train the critical intellect have a clear connection with the domestic radical agenda. Within the British context, the promotion of the 'vernacular' could cohere relatively straightforwardly with disparagement of the elitist pretensions of classicism. And calls for the development of the critical intellect sat easily with opposition to the use of education – and under-education – to produce conformity and quietism. But in the colonial context both aspects of Gilchrist's thought become more problematic – at least for the modern reader. In Gilchrist's work, colonialism itself is understood as the liberatory force. The study of Hindustani, the 'vernacular' speech of northern India, is presented as a means of eroding the power of corrupt Indian elites, especially in areas such as the administration of justice, where their control over communication between the British and the 'masses' might allow them to exploit the latter without the knowledge of the former. And the purpose of the critical education that Gilchrist advocates seems to be the delivery of a more effective and meritocratic colonial administration rather than any self-reflexive critique of colonialism itself.

The debate over dialogues thus has important consequences for the argument of this book, not because of the functions that dialogues actually served but because of the what they could *not* do and what they *obscured*. For Gilchrist, the use of dialogues distracted attention from the important business of understanding how Hindustani functioned at a structural level. And, as always, the importance of this kind of understanding lay in the now familiar themes of resisting 'jargon' and making claims to scholarship. But in the debate over dialogues, another issue opened up in the later stages of the controversy – the question of the politics of education. And this question is intimately connected with the other two. For Gilchrist, colonialism was liberatory in the way that it disempowered an Indian elite that he saw as corrupt and predatory and also in the sense that it provided him specifically with a means of transcending his personal circumstances. As he saw it, both depended upon a close critical engagement with the reality of life in the colony, an attention to the details of what was happening and an ability to make his compatriots understand what he had seen. But dialogues had the potential to stifle that critical engagement, providing a ready-made vision of the colony rather than one arrived at through the exercise of the individual intellect. No wonder, then, that Gilchrist saw the popularity of dialogues as a threat to the overall effectiveness of his work, and no wonder, too, that he went to some lengths to develop the 'radical' approach to language study that is discussed in the fourth and final case study of this book.

7

ETYMOLOGY

7.1 INTRODUCTION

In late eighteenth-century Britain, etymological speculation became something of an intellectual craze and the fashion was fuelled by the publication of volume I of *The Diversions of Purley*, in which John Horne Tooke mobilised a barrage of etymological evidence in support of a philosophical attack on general grammar. The appearance of Horne Tooke's work in 1786 confirmed the sense that all kinds of vital information lay hidden in the structure of language itself and could be uncovered through a process of historical investigation. By tracing the origins of words back into history, it was thought that a range of intellectual problems could be tackled and solved – the nature of the human mind, the movement of populations in ancient times and the underlying character of peoples and nations. John Gilchrist was very much of his time in his fascination with this pursuit, and etymological analysis is a constant feature of his published work. The aim of this chapter is to examine the role that this kind of material plays in his representations of Hindustani, an issue that brings together many of the themes explored in earlier chapters, while also raising new ones.

At one level, etymology constituted a means of locating order in material that seemed disordered and of finding motivation behind phenomena that, on the face of it, seemed arbitrary. Ordinary grammatical analysis supplied the metalanguage for a descriptive account of the morphology of verbs:

> Every infinitive ends in *na* [...] *which* taken away, leaves the common contracted form of that mood, or the imperative; and *this* assuming *ta* [...] forms the *present* tense and *participle*; with *a* [...] or *e,a* [...] (when the imperative itself terminates in *a* or *o*,) the *perfect* tense and participle; with *oonga* [...] the future [...]. (Gilchrist 1796: 99)

But etymological analysis offered something more – a means of explaining *why* the endings '*ta*', '*a*' and '*oonga*' should correlate with the categories of present, perfect, and future. According to Gilchrist, these suffixes derive from independent verbs with the respective meanings 'remain', 'come' and 'go'. Thus, following Horne Tooke, he sees more abstract elements of the language – its tense markers – as deriving from more concrete elements, namely verbs of rest and motion. In Chapters 4 and 5 we saw how much importance Gilchrist placed on systematising phenomena that his readers might see as disordered, and the kind of explanation outlined here provided a means of pushing systematisation to a new level. It allowed Gilchrist to move beyond the claim that the Hindustani verbal system was unusually regular and uniform, and to suggest that the particular forms through which the tenses were marked reflected a conceptualisation of reality in which temporal categories were connected with spatial ones through a process of metaphorical extension. In this way he was able to characterise the forms of the language as reflecting an underlying conceptual order. Thus, the use of etymological analysis opened up endless possibilities in terms of explanation and systematisation, processes that were central to Gilchrist's project of defending Hindustani against the charge that it was a 'jargon'.

The discovery of new layers of orderliness in Hindustani also provided a way of resisting pedagogical methods built on habituation. As we saw in Chapter 6, Gilchrist opposed the use of dialogues in language learning because, for various reasons, he wanted to prioritise the role of the rational faculties. Presumably, however, there are limits to the role of reason in language acquisition. No matter how much one argues that effective language learning requires an intellectual understanding of the principles on which the language is structured, surely the fact that the present, perfect and future tenses are marked by the endings '*ta*', '*a*' and '*oonga*' is something that just has to be learned and preferably anchored in the mind through a lengthy process of repetition? Etymological analysis provided Gilchrist with a way of resisting this charge, in the sense that it characterised the correlation between particular forms and functions as having a rational basis that could be grasped by the intellect. True, it would still be necessary to learn the three verbs that supposedly gave rise to the tense markers. But at least the need for rote learning would be confined to the lexicon, while the grammar itself was preserved as the province of reason. Thus, the field of etymology was relevant not only to issues of language structure but also to questions of language acquisition, and, as we shall see, etymological analysis supplied Gilchrist with the inspiration for a method of language learning built as far as possible on the exercise of the rational faculties. In fact, this dimension of etymological analysis became increasingly prominent in his work, as his confidence in the historical reliability of the method apparently faded.

But etymology also raised new questions that have only been touched upon briefly in the previous chapters. To the modern observer it seems obvious that to investigate the histories of Modern Indo-Aryan languages one needs to engage with the rich evidence for Old Indo-Aryan embodied in the corpus of Sanskrit literature. In the late eighteenth century, the relationship between the modern Indian 'vernaculars' and the 'classical' language of the Hindu scriptures was more controversial than it is today. Indeed, there was a significant body of opinion that saw Sanskrit not as the parent of the northern 'vernaculars' but as an entirely artificial language created by high-caste Hindus as a way of preserving the secrets upon which their hegemony was built. Despite this, however, Gilchrist himself admitted that, in identifying the 'significant particles' of which Hindustani was composed – items such as '*ta*', '*a*' and '*oonga*' – it would be worthwhile to compare these particles with similar forms in Sanskrit, hinting that, if such a comparison were undertaken, some very interesting conclusions might be reached. The problem was that he did not have the expertise to undertake this kind of work. Whereas John Horne Tooke was able to mobilise a range of evidence from Anglo-Saxon to support his etymological analyses of modern English conjunctions and prepositions, Gilchrist was unable to read Sanskrit and simply could not engage with the kind of evidence necessary for the comparative work he had suggested.

The irony is, of course, that India possesses well-developed indigenous traditions of linguistic analysis that would have supplied powerful fuel for Gilchrist's etymological imagination, if only he could have engaged with them. At a time when western grammarians were operating with a stock of relatively unsophisticated morphological concepts, the Sanskrit tradition, *vyākaraṇa*, exemplified an intricate method both of analysing grammatical forms into their morphological components and of describing morpho-phonological processes. Furthermore, the study of the Vedic texts had also given rise to a form of hermeneutics known as *nirukta* or *nirvacana*, which focused on morphologically simple items, including proper names, and sought to explain their significance by means of etymology. When western scholars explored these traditions in the nineteenth century, they tended to understand them as providing diachronic accounts of how the morphology and lexis of Sanskrit had emerged over time. And, while modern commentators usually emphasise that this was a misinterpretation and that both traditions were concerned with producing synchronic – or, more accurately, timeless – accounts of Sanskrit, it is nevertheless the case that both disciplines dealt with a range of technical and philosophical problems applicable to the kind of etymological enquiry that Gilchrist was interested in pursuing. In the Arabic tradition too, forms were routinely analysed into base and supplemental elements, the latter being organised into alphabe-tical inventories similar to Gilchrist's catalogues of particles, a practice that found its way into the Indo-Persian lexicographical tradition and is exemplified in a range of texts that were circulating in late eighteenth-century Bengal. Thus, the very issues that Gilchrist examines in his etymological analyses are pre-empted in a range of material developed within the intellectual life of South Asia.

It is idle to speculate on what might have happened had Gilchrist known more about this material. What we can say, however, is that during his lifetime, western scholars became more and more of aware of the traditions of linguistic analysis that had arisen from the study of the Vedas and the Qur'ān. And, as European scholars began to engage with these traditions,

Gilchrist's speculative pronouncements on the history of Hindustani must have begun to look less and less well founded. Early in his career, Gilchrist attempted to minimise the significance of indigenous linguistic scholarship and particularly of the study of Sanskrit. He was, after all, an advocate of 'vernacular' learning, and was building a career on the idea that the study of the 'classical' languages was of dubious value to the colonial state in comparison with a thorough knowledge of the languages of modern India. However, language history is one area where the opposition between 'classical' and 'vernacular' scholarship becomes highly problematic. As parallels emerged, for example, between Gilchrist's 'significant particles' and the items identified in Pāṇini's *dhātu-pāṭha* or list of Sanskrit roots, it became less tenable to talk about the former without reference to the latter. And these problems may well explain why, in *The British Indian Monitor*, the two volumes of which were published in 1806 and 1808, Gilchrist does not present his etymological analysis in historical terms but purely as a pedagogical strategy. Viewed in the light of rhetorical accounts of argumentation, the use of etymology in this work can be understood as an attempt to construct a purely rational method of language study. Thus, the enthusiastic speculation that characterised Gilchrist's earlier work now subsides, and etymology is promoted not as a way of understanding history but as a means of restructuring the encounter with the living language.

The first part of this chapter will examine the presentation of etymological material in *The British Indian Monitor*, which in some ways constitutes Gilchrist's most radical venture into the field. As we shall see, the discussion of 'significant particles' dominates that text, cutting right across the conventional structure of the western grammar and replacing it with something that, at least superficially, seems more akin to the process-oriented analyses of the Sanskrit and Arabic traditions. The second part of the chapter will move on to consider the origins of this approach in the footnotes of Gilchrist's earlier works, where the etymological analysis clearly constitutes a tribute to the heroic figure of John Horne Tooke and fulfils an avowedly historical function. In this way, the first two sections will identify a particular interpretive problem – the question of why, as Gilchrist's treatment of etymology comes to occupy a more and more prominent place in his writing, it is simultaneously drained of historical content. The third section will deal with this question by examining the parallels that emerged in the early nineteenth century between the western forms of etymology employed by Gilchrist and the analytical procedures found in *vyākaraṇa*, *nirukta* and Indo-Persian lexicography. The important point is that, as these parallels became more obvious to western observers, it became increasingly difficult to speculate about the histories of modern Indian languages without engaging directly with 'classical' material, something that Gilchrist was not equipped to do. Thus, Gilchrist's retreat from historical enquiry will be characterised in terms of a conflict between his commitment to the 'vernacular' and the opportunities presented by 'classical' learning. Despite his wish to focus attention on Hindustani at the expense of Sanskrit and Persian, his interest in the fashionable field of etymology led Gilchrist back into an engagement with those languages which, because of his lack of expertise, was not sustainable.

Thus, in order to preserve the 'vernacular' as a hermetically sealed space in which his expertise could not be disputed, Gilchrist was forced to take the emphasis off historical enquiry. And, with this in mind, the final part of the chapter will return to *The British Indian Monitor* and examine the way in which Gilchrist converts etymological analysis from a tool of historical enquiry into a medium of pedagogy. As we shall see, the discussion of 'significant particles' presented in this text characterises the material in a way that distinguishes it sharply from superficially similar texts found in the Sanskrit and Arabic traditions. Rather than constituting a *synthetic* account of the language – an explanation of how the forms and structures of Hindustani can be built up from its smallest elements – Gilchrist's list of particles is supposedly intended to support the learner in an *analytical* engagement with authentic texts. By pushing the learner towards this kind of analytical approach, Gilchrist suggests that the use of reason in language learning can be maximised and the use of memory, with all its associations of habituation and practice, downgraded. And, in a sense, this rational engagement is intended to replicate Gilchrist's own experience of learning the grammar of Hindustani, directing the reader along the route that the grammarian himself followed when he first travelled to Faizabad and began the long process of preparing his dictionary and grammar. Gilchrist's own journey did not begin with neat tables of nominal and verbal forms – clear, straightforward and accessible – but with a direct engagement with texts and speakers. Through etymological analysis, he suggests, the learner can experience the language in the same way that he did, finding the grammar through an encounter with the living language and in this way experiencing the truth of Gilchrist's claims about its rationality, sophistication and complexity.

7.2 ETYMOLOGY IN *THE BRITISH INDIAN MONITOR*

Etymological analysis occupies such a prominent position within *The British Indian Monitor* that it actually cuts across the conventional organisation of the grammatical text. Gilchrist's earlier works all conform broadly to the traditional structure of the western grammar. They begin with the 'elements' of the language – the 'letters' from which its words are formed; they then proceed to the accidence, or inflectional morphology, dealing first with the variable parts of speech – nouns, pronouns, adjectives and verbs – and only then, if at all, considering the invariable ones – conjunctions, postpositions, adverbs and interjections; a section on syntax may follow; and in the grammar of 1796 Gilchrist also includes a discussion of prosody. But in *The British Indian Monitor*, a work in two volumes published in Edinburgh a few years after Gilchrist had returned from India, this traditional structure is significantly disrupted. The work begins conventionally enough with an account of the 'elements' of the language, but after this it follows a highly distinctive course. A long section headed 'Hindoostanee significant particles' is presented with sections on 'prepositives', 'adjunctives' and 'intermediates'. These are followed by material concerning the four invariable parts of speech. And then, at last, on page 139 we come to schemes of declension and conjugation. But even here we are presented, not with the usual nominal and verbal paradigms, but with collections of 'terminations' unattached to any root or stem. These are followed by a passage of Hindustani for the reader to analyse. And only then do we come to a conventional account of the accidence, which is almost the same as those found in earlier texts such as *The Stranger's East Indian Guide* and *The Hindee Directory*. Thus, the grammatical analysis is presented in a highly unusual order and makes use of some very distinctive metalanguage. What, then, is the nature of the material presented in this strange and unorthodox text?

The section headed 'Significant particles' consists of a long list of letters and syllables, the sequence of individual letters structuring the list, vowels appearing before consonants, and each individual letter being followed by a series of syllables in which that letter appears. Thus, after the letter <s>, the reader encounters the syllables 'su', 'sa', 'se' and so forth (Gilchrist 1806–08 I: 87–8). Next to each item in the list we are provided with an explanation of its 'significance', and the information presented here is distinctly heterogeneous. Gilchrist says of the letter <e>, for example:

> *e* may be met with as a vocative sign, e sahib! *O sir!* a singular postposition among the pronouns, oos-e, *to him, him*; and as the singular affix of the 2d and 3d persons of the aorist or subjunctive, mar-e, *if thou* or *he beat*, &c.; nor must we forget its use already noticed, as a genitive sign, lolee e fuluk, the *courtezan of the sky*, viz. Venus, or the star so called. (Gilchrist 1806–8 I: 69)

Thus the letter <e> is said to be the exponent of a range of different grammatical functions: it can mark two cases of nouns – the vocative and genitive; it is a verbal inflection marking the second and third persons of the aorist subjunctive; and it is a postposition marking the object forms of some pronouns. In the traditional western grammar, information concerning inflectional morphology is organised according to semantic and syntactic criteria. And, for this reason, the material presented here would be dispersed throughout the accidence, the relevant comments appearing in the sections on nouns, pronouns, and verbs. Here, however, it is organised according to formal criteria, grammatical functions that are marked by the same letter or syllable appearing together. Furthermore, the list includes information about derivational as well as inflectional morphology. Gilchrist states, for example, that '[t]he affix un resembles our *ly*, ittifaq-un, *accidental-ly*, quṣd-<u>un</u>, *purpose-ly*' (Gilchrist 1806–8 I: 82). Again, in a grammar organised along traditional western lines, information of this kind would appear separately, perhaps in a section headed 'Derivation and composition'. But here it appears in the same list as the inflectional information mentioned above, slotted into the list under the letter <n>.

Even more disconcertingly, Gilchrist's list of particles also includes material unconnected with either species of morphology. So, for example:

> p,hu seems a radical, denoting the blowing with the breath, and the blooming of a flower, or the expansion of anything; p,hookna; *to blow, breathe*; p,hool, *a flower*, p,hul, *a fruit*; p,hoolna, *to swell*; p,hulna, *to bear fruit*; p,hun, *a snake's hood or crest*; p,hen, *foam, froth*; p,hootna, *to burst*; p,huṭna, *to crack*; p,hoolka, *light*; p,haha, *a flake* [...]. (Gilchrist 1806–8 I: 79)

Thus, the syllable 'p,hu' is characterised as a 'radical' – a kind of root – which has a broad semantic content and from which a wide range of lexical items have been derived. Material of this kind occasionally appears in western grammars. For example, the 'Brightland Grammar' of 1711[1] presents a discussion of derivation which includes the observation that '(*Sn*) is an ending that generally implies the Nose, or something belonging to it', and, amongst the words said to be formed with this 'ending', we find '*[s]nout*', '*sneeze*', '*snore*' and '*snot*' (Gildon 1711: 127). However, this kind of material is not a regular part of the conventional western grammar, and its inclusion in Gilchrist's list constitutes a further sign of the text's strange and distinctive properties.

Thus, in *The British Indian Monitor*, Gilchrist does not merely reorder the traditional categories of the western grammar but cuts right across them, reorganising material from different parts of his earlier works into a single list and even incorporating material from beyond the conventional boundaries of the grammatical text. The list is organised according to formal rather than semantic or syntactic criteria, and this principle is applied with considerable rigour. For example, Gilchrist (1806–8 I: 89) says of the letters <z> and <zh> that 'unless as a contraction of uz, *from* &c., in the Persian, [they] have no significant power'. The letters are included because they constitute forms that must be accounted for, but they have no particular significance, a fact that is duly recorded in the list. This radical account of the 'significant particles' of Hindustani has an interesting

---

[1] The authorship of this grammar was long disputed, but it is now generally agreed to be by Charles Gildon.

relationship with the etymologies to be found in Gilchrist's earlier works. In some ways it is very different from the speculative footnotes to be found in *The Oriental Linguist* or the preface to the dictionary and grammar. In those earlier works etymological enquiry is presented very much within the framework of the debate over the origin of language, the clear message being that to engage in this kind of analysis is to examine the ways in which both language in general and the Hindustani language in particular have developed over time. But this diachronic perspective on etymology is largely absent from *The British Indian Monitor*, a fact that marks the later text out as a new departure for Gilchrist. However, the earlier texts also convey a second message about etymology – that it holds the key to a fuller systematisation of the language – and this is the idea that seems to inform the analysis described in this section. It will therefore be important to examine the treatment of etymology in Gilchrist's earlier work, drawing attention to the fact that historical speculation and the use of etymology as a means of finding order in apparent disorder go hand in hand throughout these works. This will set the scene for a discussion of Gilchrist's motives in abandoning historical interpretations of etymology, and also for an account of the pedagogical functions of the list of 'significant particles' presented in the pages of *The British Indian Monitor*.

7.3 ETYMOLOGY AND THE ORIGIN OF LANGUAGE

Gilchrist's first extended discussions of etymology appear in *The Oriental Linguist* and in the preface to the dictionary and grammar, both of which appeared in 1798. Although these two sources are more or less contemporary and contain similar material, they are slightly different in the way they construct Gilchrist's relationship with other thinkers, and in particular with John Horne Tooke. In a footnote from the introduction to the dictionary and grammar, Gilchrist attributes his interest in etymology to a formative encounter with Horne Tooke's *Diversions of Purley*, and describes the theory presented in that work as 'a grand discovery, in the pursuit of which, ages till now have been spent in vain'. He adds:

> [Horne Tooke's] sentiments are in my opinion completely confirmed by such of the Oriental tongues as I know, and from which I shall give in the order our author observes, as far as the coincidences are obvious, the most incontestable proofs in favour of his system, which he formed by an intuition that is highly honourable to his genius, and well deserves the name of a grand discovery [...]. (Gilchrist 1798b: xlv n.)

He then sets out an array of etymologies in imitation of those presented in *The Diversions of Purley*, the purpose of the material being to demonstrate that the postpositions, adverbs and conjunctions of Hindustani are all derived from terms expressing more concrete ideas. Gilchrist notes, for example, that the conjunction *jo* means 'if', and he suggests two possible derivations: it may come from the imperative of *jānā* ('go') or from that of *jānnā* ('know'). The postpositions *līe* and *par*, meaning 'for' and 'on', are said to originate in the imperatives of *lenā* ('take') and *parnā* ('fall'). Similarly, the sequence *dhar* in words such as *idhar* ('hither'), *udhar* ('thither') and *jidhar* ('thither') is identified with the imperative of *dharnā* ('place'). Gilchrist also discusses the postposition *kā*, which he glosses 'of', and the syllable *rā*, which appears in possessive adjectives like *merā* ('my') or *terā* ('your'), linking them with the verbs *karnā* ('do') and *rahnā* ('stay') and referring to them as 'significant letters and syllables'. This terminology clearly prefigures that of *The British Indian Monitor* and suggests that, despite the lack of historical discussion in that later text, the analysis that it presents has antecedents in Horne Tooke's account of the origin of language. Hindustani can be resolved into items below the level of the word because the complex forms of contemporary languages originally developed from more concrete entities expressing ideas originating in ordinary experience.[2]

But in a note in *The Oriental Linguist* Gilchrist presents a rather different version of his theory, and in so doing establishes a little distance between his own work and that of Horne Tooke. Drawing attention to the imperatives of some common verbs – 'a' from *ānā* ('come'), 'ja' from *jānā* ('go'), 'ho' from *honā* ('be'), 'kur' from *karnā* ('do') and 'rah' from *rahnā* ('stay') – he says of them: 'They are probably the first regular significant words, that man articulated, and on them I have reason to believe the whole system of *verbs* and *grammar* was originally founded' (Gilchrist 1798a: xvi n.). He provides some concrete evidence for this claim, evidence relating to both verbal and nominal morphology. Thus, he makes the connection noted earlier between the perfect and future endings -*ā* and -*gā*, and the imperatives *ā* ('come') and *jā* ('go').[3] And he links the syllable *rā*, as found in the possessive adjective *merā*, with the imperative of *rahnā* ('stay'), suggesting that we will not find this derivation surprising 'when we recollect that possession consists in a thing remaining with one [...]' (Gilchrist 1798a: xvi n.) But, whereas the function of the equivalent material in the preface to the dictionary and grammar is to provide confirmation of the truth of

---

[2] In Ch. 3 I noted that, although Horne Tooke develops his etymological analyses in the context of an attack on general grammar, Gilchrist seems unconcerned with this aspect of the work and happily cites a range of general grammarians in the very same text in which his eulogy of Horne Tooke appears. The 'grand discovery' that Gilchrist finds expressed in *The Diversions of Purley,* and that these examples are supposed to prove, seems not to be that general grammar is unfounded but that all language, including the most conceptually abstract parts of speech, originate in nouns and verbs.

[3] The change in the consonant of the future ending is explained by the concept of 'convertibility' discussed in Ch. 5.

Horne Tooke's theory, here it is meant to illustrate Gilchrist's own claim that, in the earliest stages of human language, the only linguistic entity in existence was the imperative form of the verb. In addition to the etymological evidence he provides for this claim, he tries to show that it is plausible that the imperatives should be the first entity to appear in the state of nature:

> [T]his form must exist in great perfection among all animals, endowed with vocal powers, who in the most untutored states of *society* will clearly perceive the force of *come, go, stand, run,* &c. though they may never acquire reason sufficient, to figure and comprehend, to come, going, to stand, running, &c. in their abstract infinitive or verbal capacity. (Gilchrist 1798a: xvi n.)

This brief meditation on the origin of language clearly fits into the framework of the larger debate as outlined in Chapter 3 above. If language, reason and society are intimately connected, then a plausible account of human progress must show how all three developed in parallel from very modest beginnings. For Gilchrist, it is likely that imperatives emerged right at the beginning of this process, since they would have met the communicative needs of beings in an 'untutored' state of society and would have been readily graspable even when the power of reasoning was fairly limited. He reinforces his point with some criticism of other linguistic thinkers:

> Grammarians have [...] erred most egregiously in assigning any other *root*, but the *imp[erative] sing[ular]* to a verb, *which* will I dare say yet be found the *matrix* or *ovum* of the verbs in every language, and moreover, that *come*, and *go*, will appear the primum mobile of the whole. (Gilchrist 1798a: xvi n.)

With this claim, Gilchrist asserts that he is not merely following other thinkers but is developing an original claim about the way in which language originated. As it happens, Gilchrist's choice of the imperative as the first part of language to be invented is relatively unusual. Horne Tooke himself derives the prepositions and conjunctions of English from both nouns and verbs in Anglo-Saxon. However, he never actually *argues* for the verb as a primitive, the philosophical part of his work developing the argument that apparently complex forms of reasoning depend entirely upon simple ideas formed through sensation and labelled by nouns. Adam Smith argues for proper names as the first elements of speech. Lord Monboddo suggests that the first utterances were labels for unanalysed experiences. The verb plays a more important role in Herder's account of the origin of language, but even there it is not the use of the verb as a means of directing the behaviour of others that is at the centre of the theory. Thus, Gilchrist's claim to have made an original observation has a kind of plausibility, even if it seems trivial to modern readers.

In both texts, Gilchrist uses his discussion of etymology as a medium of self-representation. In the preface to the dictionary and grammar, he follows the (by now) familiar procedure of presenting his own research as confirming or corroborating an idea developed by a western authority. In *The Oriental Linguist* he goes further and draws attention to his speculation as an original contribution to the origin of language debate. One might wonder how effective these strategies would be in the final years of the eighteenth century, and it is true that the status of etymology as a method of enquiry had been challenged in 1786, when William Jones delivered his third anniversary discourse, 'On the Hindoos', and used the opportunity to attack the use of etymological speculation in historical research: 'it is a medium of proof so very fallacious, that, where it elucidates one fact, it obscures a thousand, and more frequently borders on the ridiculous, than leads to any solid conclusion' (Jones 1993: 25). His main criticism was that there was no reliable method by which purely internal evidence could be used to show that an etymology was correct, and that many etymologies known to be sound as a result of external evidence could never have been proved without that evidence.[4] But despite Jones's comments, etymological speculation continued to appear in the pages of *Asiatic Researches*, much of it flowing from the pen of Francis Wilford, who had arrived in India in 1781 and had been encouraged in his scholarly pursuits by no less a figure than Warren Hastings. Wilford published frequently until his death in 1822, and made extensive use of etymology in developing theories in the field of ancient history. What is more, his ideas were taken seriously: Kejariwal (1988: 68) notes that three meetings of the Asiatic Society were spent on just one of Wilford's etymological papers. Thus, Jones's comments should not be taken to imply a total rejection of etymological enquiry on the part of the whole British community. Gilchrist's use of this field as a space for the overt performance of scholarship was not as ill-judged as Jones's comments might lead us to believe.

In both these early texts Gilchrist links the practice of etymology to the grammarian's task of uncovering the systematicity of a particular language, and he does this with reference to the grammar of Latin. In *The Oriental Linguist* he remarks that Latin forms such as *amavi* ('I have loved') and *amabo* ('I shall love') are clearly derived from the imperative of the verb

---

[4] 'We know *a posteriori*, that both *fitz* and *hijo*, by the nature of two several dialects, are derived from *filius*; that *uncle* comes from *avus*, and *stranger* from *extra*; that *jour* is deducible, through the Italian, from *dies*; and *rossignol* from *luscinia*, or the *singer in groves*; that *sciuro, ecureuil*, and *squirrel* are compounded of two Greek words descriptive of the animal [...]'. However, none of these could have been 'demonstrated *a priori*' (Jones 1993: 25). In a sense, comparative philology can be seen as a working through of these evidential problems – an investigation of what might *constitute* internal evidence for the relatedness of forms.

'love', *ama*, in combination with parts of the verb 'be', *fui* ('I was') and *ibo* ('I shall go'), respectively. Thus *amavi* can be analysed as *ama-fui* ('love!-I was') and *amabo* as *ama-ibo* ('love!- I shall go'). And the same point is made in the preface to the dictionary and grammar:

> Had our grammarians originally considered the *imp[erative] sin-g[ular]* of the Latin verbs properly, they would have taught their readers to begin the conjugations with *esse* ['be'], and *ire* ['go'], instead of preposterously ending them with those fundamental verbs, from which the slightest inspection will prove that *esse* ['be'] like *hona* ['be'], is subservient to the active voice, while *ire* ['go'], is [...] conspicuous in the *r* of the passive [...]. (Gilchrist 1798b: xlvi n.)

It is absurd, he states, that the verbs *esse* ('be') and *ire* ('go') are placed after the regular verbs in grammars of Latin. Learners should be introduced to them at the very beginning of their studies, since the forms of all other verbs are derived from them. What is more, 'a good etymologist', working with 'the rules to which letters are subject' – by which he presumably means the principles of 'convertibility' set out in the early sections of his grammar – could 'reduce the Latin to one or two conjugations'. This statement clearly relates closely to Gilchrist's strenuous efforts to discredit Hadley's five-conjugation analysis of the Hindustani verbal system. It is the duty of the grammarian to bring out the systematicity of a language as far as possible and grammarians of Latin have been remiss in this respect, insisting that that the language has four conjugations, when in fact it could be shown to have just one. At this point we should recall John Wilkins's critique of Latin, in which he complains about the fact that there are 'four distinct ways of *conjugating* verbs' (Wilkins 1668: 446). To collapse the conjugations into one would be to defend the language against criticisms of this kind, just as Gilchrist's analysis of the Hindustani verbal system constitutes a defence of the language against the charge of irregularity levelled at it by Hadley. There is a beautiful irony in the fact that Gilchrist's call for a revaluation of the Latin system is inspired by his experiences of analysing Hindustani and this is, in fact, the issue that elicits from him the metaphor of the 'inversion of opticks', which I have cited at a number of points in the preceding discussion. The claim he is making is that the grammar of Hindustani is so orderly and transparent that it provides clues as to how languages that seem less orderly might be subjected to a more economical analysis. Hindustani in effect becomes the microscope through which the grammar of Latin can be examined and its real structure revealed.

In 1801, moreover, Gilchrist published his only work devoted entirely to the grammar of Persian, *A New Theory and Prospectus of the Persian Verbs*, in the preface to which he criticises two of the leading figures in British orientalism, William Jones and Francis Gladwin, another contemporary expert on the language, on the grounds that they should have made more effort to reduce the number of conjugations in their descriptions (Gilchrist 1801: iii–iv). As it happens, Jones states quite clearly at the start of his discussion of verbs that 'properly' there is only one conjugation in Persian. However, later in his analysis he distributes what he calls 'irregular'[5] verbs into 13 classes according to how they form their present stems (or 'imperatives', to use his own term), and this is presumably what Gilchrist is talking about. Gladwin similarly (1795: 47) states: 'Persian grammarians arrange the verbs under eleven classes', and sets out the classes one by one. Gilchrist's own work is intended to reduce the number of verb classes to two, but the self-proclaimed improvements in his analysis are largely cosmetic, and one suspects that it would have been considerably more difficult to grasp the morphology of Persian verbs from his text than from either Jones's or Gladwin's. Nevertheless, the work is interesting because the reanalysis of Persian verbs into two classes is intertwined with an argument to the effect that certain elements of Persian inflectional morphology should really be seen as independent verbs. And this leads Gilchrist to assert yet again that the terminations of the Latin verb are all in fact parts of *esse*, *ire* and, in a new departure, *volo* ('want'), any discrepancies being explicable by the Romans' desire for euphony:

> These [i.e. the various forms of *amo* ('love')] it is granted are metamorphosed so far, probably in order to please a Latin ear, to which *ama fui essem* might be perhaps intolerable, and would of course insensibly glide among the Romans into *amavissem*. (Gilchrist 1801: 16)

Furthermore, having once again expressed his debt to Horne Tooke, Gilchrist (1801: ii) refers to two new sources of inspiration that he drew upon as he undertook his reanalysis of the Persian verbs. The first of these he describes as 'an anonymous work [...] on Celtic derivatives', an allusion that clearly refers to John Cleland's slim volume, *The Way to Things by Words and to Words by Things*.[6] In this text, Cleland (1766: ii–iii) claims to have uncovered many of the 'monosyllabic constitutives' of the 'universal elementary language of Europe', which he calls 'Celtic'. Gilchrist goes so far as to suggest that Horne Tooke himself might have 'had a peep' at this work, although he is careful to insist that, by putting forward this speculation, he does not mean 'to detract in the smallest degree from [Horne Tooke's] well earned fame'. The second of Gilchrist's sources, 'Dr. Vincent's hypothesis of the Greek verb', is rather more interesting. William

---

[5] Jones sees verbs whose infinitives end in *-idan* as regular and treats all others as irregular. This distinction is often not made in more modern Persian grammars. Boyle (1966: 31), for example, states that '[t]he rules for obtaining the present stem vary according to the class of verbs' and includes verbs in *-idan* as the first of these classes, simply noting that they are 'by far the commonest type of verbs'.

[6] Cleland is better known as the author of the libertine novel *Fanny Hill*.

Vincent was the headmaster of Westminster School, and in 1794 and 1795 he published two works arguing that the morphology of both the Greek verb and those of other languages were originally constructed from primitive particles, which he calls 'bases'. His arguments are typical of those found in earlier accounts of the origin of language, and are built both on a priori assumptions about how language must have been when human society and reason were in earlier states of development[7] and on analogical evidence from the speech of children and 'savages'.[8] Like Gilchrist's, Vincent's etymological analysis is intended to minimise the anomalies of the Greek verbal system. 'Individuals there are in Greek,' he admits, 'and anomalies there are in all languages, which are not reducible to one analogy. But if the principles of reduction are not intimated, and the common anomalies accounted for, I am much deceived in my expectations' (Vincent 1795: 81).

After his brief excursion into the analysis of Persian Gilchrist returned to Hindustani, and in 1802 he published *The Hindee Directory*, a work in which he moved his etymological analyses out of the footnotes into the main body of the text. The etymological material presented in this work appears after the conventional grammatical material and not before, as it does in *The British Indian Monitor*. It is also described as a 'retrospective', suggesting that the reader might use it to consolidate grammatical knowledge acquired by more traditional means. Gilchrist repeats his assertion that the future marker, *gā*, and the perfect marker, *ā*, are derived from the imperatives of *jānā* ('go') and *ānā* ('come'), and notes that 'the connection between the sign of the future and the verb 'to go' is 'evident in more tongues than one' (Gilchrist 1802b). He also discusses the present participle, which is formed by adding *tā* to the root of the verb. He notes

---

[7] Vincent (1795: 6) argues that the first idea to be formed in the human mind was 'existence': 'if the first man at the moment of consciousness, had the power of expression, the first sentiment of his mind would be, WHAT AM I? On these grounds I assume EXISTENCE as the primary idea.' He goes on to suggest that the expression of this idea 'should be as simple as nature can produce', and observes that 'the sound expressed by the vowel E' is the 'simplest of articulate sounds, and as such the most suitable to express the primary idea'. In 1795, one Thomas Gunter Browne published a philological work entitled *Hermes Unmasked*, in which he mocks Vincent on the grounds that it is absurd to suggest that such an abstract idea as 'existence' would be the first notion to present itself to the human mind.

[8] Vincent (1795: 19) argues that, in earlier states of language, there can have been no pronouns and no distinction between the first, second and third persons. As evidence for this claim he notes that 'as a child says of himself *John will go to bed*; so men, before language assumed its form, ever spoke of themselves in the third person.' And he adds that the same is true in the 'language of New Holland', Australia. In 1792 Bennelong, an Indigenous Australian from Port Jackson in the area of modern Sydney, was brought to London, where he became the focus of considerable attention. Vincent tells us that he 'desired a question to be proposed' to Bennelong, 'which he ought to have answered in the first person'. The question, he tells us, was '*Do you eat fish?*' and the answer 'in his own language' was '*Baneelong eats fish*'. Vincent admits that this experiment is not absolutely conclusive, but states that 'this was the result of several other questions proposed', a circumstance that makes him 'suspect they have no pronoun'.

that the letter <t> also appears in many of the second person pronouns, and that this is true of 'many languages' (Gilchrist 1802b: 24–5). He suggests that there is a conceptual link between the idea of the second person and the idea of present time, the former denoting physical and the latter temporal presence. He suggests that this view is supported by Arabic grammatical terminology, noting that 'the 2d person [is] often called *hazir* present, instead of *moòkhatub*, addressed' (Gilchrist 1802b: 25). And, finally, he speculates about origins of this 'significant letter':

> Could we yet discover a verb like tu-*na*, ta-*na*, ut-*un* to *be, stand, remain, stay*, the whole theory of Hindoostanee verbs might soon be completed, because it would require little metaphysical acumen to reconcile *coming, advancing*, with *perfection, standing* with *presence*, and *going* with *futurity*. (Gilchrist 1802b: 25)

This echoes claims made the year before in the book on the Persian verb, where Gilchrist (1801: xvi) similarly asserts that through etymological analysis it is possible to 'descry, through the sable mantle of time, the glimmering traces [...] of an original nomenclature, that once shone with meridian splendour among the sons of men'.

In the texts written between 1796 and 1802, therefore, Gilchrist both treats etymology as a tool of historical enquiry and, more particularly, attempts to show that the verbal morphology of modern languages derives from independent lexical items through a process of metaphorical extension in which terms denoting particular ideas are gradually extended to other, metaphysically similar ideas. At the same time, he asserts that analysis of this kind can help the grammarian to order the forms of individual languages, reducing the number of conjugations needed for the analysis of their verbal systems and pointing out the conceptual links that order the language at an underlying level. As usual, he uses these alleged discoveries as opportunities to draw attention to his own inventiveness as a scholar and to normalise the structure of Hindustani by showing how similar it is to that of other languages, including Latin, Greek and Persian. His pleasure in etymological speculation is evident throughout this period of his work, and in the introduction to his book on the Persian verb he writes of his 'relish' for it. Given that etymological discussion fitted so neatly into his explanatory project and given also the pleasure that it evidently brought him, it therefore seems strange that the etymological material in *The British Indian Monitor* should be presented in such an ahistorical fashion. The role of etymology as a tool of historical research underpinned its usefulness as a means of bringing order to the grammar. The reason that it would be desirable to find evidence for a verb with a form such as *tanā* and a meaning such as 'stand' is that it would support an argument to the effect that historically all the terminations of the Hindustani verb originated as verbs of motion or rest, and hence that the present state of the verbal system had a conceptual order not evident from the verbal forms alone. But despite the prominence given to 'significant particles' in *The British Indian Monitor*, arguments of this kind are conspicuously absent. What happened in the interim that caused Gilchrist to draw back from historical speculation?

7.4 SOUTH ASIAN TRADITIONS OF LANGUAGE ANALYSIS

It is always difficult to explain why something did *not* happen, but the change in Gilchrist's approach seems entirely reasonable when one considers that in the first decade of the nineteenth century British scholars were becoming more aware of India's indigenous traditions of language study. A number of these traditions dealt with the analysis of language below the level of the word. And while the purpose of these forms of analysis was different from that of western etymological research, the accounts of word formation presented within them impinged on the kind of work that Gilchrist was attempting to develop within the framework of the origin of language debate. It is not that Gilchrist's ideas were discredited overnight by this material. The point is more that it raised the stakes in terms of the kind of expertise that was required if one was to discuss the history of Indian languages in an informed and authoritative way. Since Gilchrist did not know Sanskrit and had a far less convincing grasp of Persian than he did of Hindustani, it is not entirely surprising that he should have withdrawn from historical discussion at the point he did. Two bodies of thought are particularly important in this respect – the Sanskrit grammatical tradition and the Indo-Persian tradition of lexicography. In dealing with each, it will be important first to consider the nature of the tradition itself and then to discuss the reception of texts from that tradition by early nineteenth-century westerners. In both cases, a perceived resemblance between the indigenous tradition and the practice of western etymology meant that elements of the former seemed to raise questions about the latter, questions that Gilchrist himself was not in a position to answer.

The Sanskrit language itself posed a problem for Gilchrist. If one accepts that Hindustani is related to Sanskrit in the same way that French and Italian are related to Latin, then surely any enquiry into the origins and development of Hindustani should make reference to Sanskrit data. Yet Gilchrist's claims about the history of Hindustani were built entirely on an etymological response to the forms of the modern language, and did not involve any consideration of material from the parent language. In *The Diversions of Purley*, the text that provided Gilchrist with the motivation to develop an etymological account of Hindustani, Horne Tooke looks for the origins of English conjunctions and prepositions in Anglo-Saxon nouns and verbs. Indeed, much of the argument is built on the fact that many

Anglo-Saxon conjunctions and prepositions resemble nouns and verbs more closely than their modern English equivalents do. Thus, the origins of *if* seem much clearer if one notes that the Anglo-Saxon equivalent is *gif*, which resembles the verb *gifan* ('give'). Given that Gilchrist attributed his interest in etymology to the example of Horne Tooke, one might have expected that he would make use of Sanskrit data in much the same way that Horne Tooke had engaged with the forms of Anglo-Saxon. And the problem was all the more pressing for Gilchrist because of one of the achievements of the Sanskrit grammatical tradition itself, namely the success of the Sanskrit grammarians in analysing both the nominal and verbal forms of the language into roots and suffixes. Within the tradition, the root – or *dhatū* – is an abstract, meaning-bearing entity that forms the basis of morphologically complex forms. The root is abstract in the sense that, as a result of morphophonological processes minutely described in the body of the grammar, it does not necessarily appear in its citation form within the attested forms of the language. Thus the roots of traditional Sanskrit grammar bear an uncanny resemblance to Gilchrist's 'significant particles'. Both are meaning-bearing entities that never appear in their raw form in attested states of the language, but are postulated as a way of understanding the forms that actually do occur. When Gilchrist talks about the desirability of finding a verb such as *tanā* in order to explain the form of the Hindustani present participle, one might have expected him to search for such an entity among the roots of traditional Sanskrit grammar. But this he never does.

Lest it seem that this discussion is asserting too close an identification between the project of the Sanskrit grammarians and that of the early nineteenth-century etymologists, it will be helpful to look more closely at the role of the root in traditional accounts of Sanskrit. The following discussion is indebted to that of Scharfe (1977), whose account of Sanskrit grammatical enquiry remains one of the clearest descriptive accounts of the tradition and provides a useful framework for understanding the functions of the particular kinds of material that developed within it. The Sanskrit grammatical tradition, *vyākaraṇa*, is one of the six 'limbs of the Veda', the disciplines originally developed for the interpretation of ancient Hindu sources, and the most important text in the tradition is Pāṇini's *Aṣṭādhyāyī*, the date of which is uncertain but which may have been composed in the fifth or sixth centuries BCE. Today it is generally accepted that the focus of the Paninian grammar was the provision of a synchronic description of the forms and structures of the Sanskrit language, and that the purpose of the material contained within it was to build a bridge between the 'desire of the speaker' for expression and the actual forms and structures through which that expression was realised (Scharfe 1977: 98). In considering Pāṇini's account of Sanskrit it is also important to understand that it constitutes a *synthetic* account of the language – an ordered body of rules by which the forms and structures attested in the Vedic texts can be built up from the underlying roots of the language. The main body of the grammar consists of just under 4,000 concisely expressed rules, the ordering of which suggests that descriptive economy was one of the principles guiding the composition of the work. The roots are the raw material on which these operate, and they are appended to the grammar in a list known as the *dhāthu-pātha*.

The main body of the work begins with a group of preliminary rules for the interpretation of what follows, after which the reader encounters a set of concepts that mediate between the intentions of the speaker and the attested forms and structures of the language. These concepts, the six *kāraka*-s, constitute semantic entities very loosely analogous to the thematic roles postulated by contemporary syntacticians. Grammarians contemporary with Gilchrist often blurred the distinction between the *kāraka* terms and the names of cases, tending to see *kartr*, the name of the third *kāraka* ('agent'), for example, as an equivalent for the western term 'nominative' and *karman*, the name of the sixth *kāraka* ('object' or 'deed'), as an equivalent for the term 'accusative'. But within the Sanskrit tradition the *kāraka*-s can be expressed through a variety of different case endings, the role of 'agent' being variously marked by the nominative case (in an active sentence) the instrumental case (in a passive sentence), and even the genitive case (in a phrase such as 'the boy's singing'). What is more, the *kāraka*-s play a role in the explanation both of verbal morphology and of phenomena such as compounding, and as such have functions ranging far beyond the marking of case on nouns. After the presentation of the *kāraka*-s, Pānini goes on to give an account of the suffixes that may be added to roots to define their roles in sentences. The roots listed in the *dhāthu-pātha* are treated as the basic input for both nominal and verbal inflectional processes, the choice of particular suffixes depending, as Scharfe (1977: 96) puts it, 'on the direction of growth: verbal or nominal'. The order in which the suffixes are introduced is related to their proximity to the root in the actual forms of the language, another feature that illustrates the synthetic nature of the description. Having presented the underlying semantic categories that are to be expressed and the formal entities that are available to express them, Pānini finally gives what Scharfe (1977: 97) calls 'the order to start the whole process of word and sentence formation'. And as the forms and structures of the language are at last called into existence – or, risking anachronism, generated – the mapping of suffixes onto *kāraka* roles forms a central part of the mechanism.

Pānini's grammar constitutes an extraordinary technical achievement, and the other two central texts of the tradition, the commentaries of Kātyāyana and Patañjali, both of whom were working in the second century BCE, are essentially concerned with refining the analysis presented in the *Astādhyāyī* and examining technical and philosophical problems raised by the kinds of analysis that Pāṇini had developed. The refinements include changes in particular rules, the insertion of additional ones and the omission of ones that seem redundant, while the meta-discussions include serious consideration of the conceptual foundations on which grammatical analysis is built. Patañjali, for example, examines the justification for isolating particular forms as roots or affixes, building on Kātyāyana's account of agreement (*anvaya*) and difference (*vyatireka*) as the twin bases of grammatical analysis. Scharfe (1977: 148) summarises the argument as follows:

> [T]he word *vrkṣas* 'tree' suggests a certain physical object with roots, branches, fruit and leaves; the word *vrkṣau* 'two trees' suggests likewise roots, branches, etc., but in two specimens. We conclude that the constant meaning 'tree' is carried by the element *vrkṣa-*, the notions 'one' and 'two' by the sounds /s/ and /au/ respectively.

But Patañjali also demonstrates the limits of this kind of analysis by pointing out that, although considerations of agreement and difference might lead the grammarian to search for a relationship among words such as *kupā* ('well'), *supā* ('sauce') and *yupā* ('sacrifical post'), which agree to the extent that they all include the sequence *-upā* but differ in their initial consonants, this would involve making the implausible claim that the objects denoted by these words must share some essential qualities, a commonality denoted by the sequence *-upā* (Scharfe 1977: 148). It is hard to avoid feeling that the western etymologists of the late eighteenth and early nineteenth centuries could have learnt a lot from this kind of discussion, if only they had known about it.

It is perhaps natural that, on encountering a new and complex body of thought, one tends to read one's own concerns into the material, and this was certainly what happened when eighteenth-century westerners turned their attention to *vyākaraṇa*. The first really influential account of the tradition by a westerner was that of the Jesuit missionary Jean François Pons, which was first published in 1743. Pons (1743: 224) comments approvingly on the success the Sanskrit grammarians had had in reducing 'the richest language in a world to a number of primitive elements', and characterises their work as a mechanism by which a 'simple scholar' can derive 'several thousand words which are truly *Samskret*' merely from the application of a body of rules to a 'root or primitive element'. In this respect, his account of the tradition is not so different from that of modern scholars. But Pons also sees the tradition as an intervention in the form of the language itself, an intervention akin to those dreamed of by the philosophers of seventeenth- and eighteenth-century Europe. As far as he is concerned, the Sanskrit grammarians had not only provided a description of the language but had exercised a kind of control over it, rendering it, in the process, all but 'perfect'. As a result of Pons's remarks, many European scholars came to see Sanskrit as the archetype of a regular, rule-governed language, disciplined into perfection through the efforts of its grammarians (Rocher 1995: 188). Thus, early modern commentators, preoccupied with the supposedly flawed state of natural languages and the need to improve them, found hope in the achievements of grammarians such as Pāṇini, Kātyāyana and Patañjali.

What is more, the account of how the complex forms and structures of the classical language could be formed from roots and affixes was often interpreted as a diachronic account of how the language of the Vedas had in fact emerged from the 'primitive' elements first uttered by man in the state of nature. Thus, for some commentators, the roots catalogued in the *dhāthu-pāṭha* were not abstract entities postulated as part of a synchronic description but the first signs coined by speakers before the complex edifice of grammar described in the rest of the text had first come into existence. This view can be found in one of the texts that Gilchrist himself describes as having influenced his own work on etymology, *The Way to Things by Words and to Words by Things*, which John Cleland had published anonymously in 1766. Although this text is mainly concerned with uncovering the 'monosyllabic constitutives' of 'Celtic', the 'universal elementary language of Europe', it also includes a short essay described as 'a succinct account of the SANSCORT, OR Learned Language of the BRAMINS'. In this section of the text, which is heavily plagiarised from Pons, Cleland (1766: 88) states that his 'Vocabulary of the Celtic radicals' has been constructed on the 'analytic and synthetic plan of the Bramins' *Sanscort*'. Thus, the work of the Sanskrit grammarians is characterised as an enquiry into the historical formation of Sanskrit from a limited number of 'radical' elements, and as such becomes the inspiration for a similar account of 'Celtic'. In one of the texts that inspired Gilchrist's etymological enquiries, therefore, the roots of Sanskrit are assimilated into the debate over the origin of language and presented as the primitive entities from which the complex forms of developed languages emerged.

European commentators interpreted other areas of Indian scholarship from a similar diachronic perspective, a case in point being the Sanskrit tradition of etymological hermeneutics or *nirvacana*. Another of the 'six limbs of the Veda', *nirvacana* analysis was concerned with unpacking the meanings of terms found in the sacred texts not through grammatical analysis, as *vyākaraṇa* did, but through the etymological analysis of individual lexical items, including proper names. The key text in the *nirvacana* tradition is Yāska's *Nirukta,* and Kahrs (1998: 26) points to an example from this text that usefully illustrates the nature of the procedures it explores. In the *Nirukta* (2.18) we are presented with the etymology: *'uṣāh kasmāt, ucchatiti satyāh'*, which Khars glosses as 'Why [is Uṣas called] Uṣas? [Because the name is] of her who really exists so that one says "she dawns/shines".' Thus, the name of the goddess, Uṣas ('Dawn'), is explained through its formal resemblance to the root √*ucch* ('dawn', 'shine'). Throughout his discussion of the *nirvacana* tradition, Kahrs emphasises that this kind of etymology was postulated not as a diachronic account of how the relevant terms had come into existence historically but as a synchronic account of the meanings implicit in terms: 'The main intention behind a *nirvacana* analysis is to explain the *tattva*, the "that-ness" or "essence" of things by stating explicitly the semantic content of the words that denote them' (Kahrs 1998: 25). He characterises the model of meaning underlying such explanations as one of substitution, a term like Uṣas being a place-holder, the place of which can be taken by a substitute. Thus, the relationship between Uṣas and √*ucch* is not one of diachronic derivation but one of synchronic substitutability. Indeed, the same model is applied to the analysis of morphophonological processes in the Sanskrit grammatical tradition. As Scharfe (1977: 109) puts it, /b/ does not 'become' /p/ as a result of an inflectional process – /p/ is seen as being 'substituted' for /b/. For the purposes of this book, *nirvacana* is less relevant than *vyākaraṇa*, since it took longer for western scholars to engage with it, a scholarly edition of Yāska's text only becoming available in 1852 (Kahrs 1998: 24). But, as with the grammatical tradition, early European commentators interpreted *nirvacana* as providing a historical account of the origins of particular terms akin to the derivations that were postulated first within eighteenth-century etymology and subsequently in nineteenth-century comparativism. As such, the reception of this second tradition of linguistic analysis also demonstrates the way in which western observers have tended to understand Indian scholarship in terms of their own interests and preoccupations.

Gilchrist was well aware that what he refers to as the Sanskrit '*d,hats*', if understood as the 'primitive' particles from which the language had been formed, were of relevance to his account of the origins of Hindustani. But he circumvented this problem by insisting that the origins of Hindustani should be sought in 'Hinduwee', the 'ancient' language that he associated with varieties such as Braj, rather than in Sanskrit, which he characterises as a wholly artificial language, invented by the Brahmans as a way of guarding the knowledge that was so crucial to their status within the Hindu social hierarchy. Thus, rather than seeing Sanskrit as the variety from which both 'Hinduwee' and Hindustani had emerged, he depicts 'Hinduwee' as the parent language from which both Sanskrit and Hindustani were derived, the former through a conscious process of reinvention and the latter by a more normal process of historical change. This account of the origins of Sanskrit interprets the work of the Sanskrit grammarians as a process not of description but of invention, and is closely connected with Gilchrist's view of the British regime as a progressive force, liberating ordinary Indians from the tyranny of indigenous elites:

Various devices were of course used to prevent the laity from detecting their own wayward lambs tongues [i.e. 'Hinduwee'] when devoured amidst the sonorous inarticulate bellowings of Bruhminical wolves, in sheeps cloathing, by whom the iniquitous division, of the Hindoo fold [i.e. the caste system], was first effected. An event, that must excite the wonder and indignation of every manly soul, though its period and history should continue for ever, shrouded by the dark mantle of time and still blacker artifices of a villanous [sic] priesthood. (Gilchrist 1798b: xxiv)

Looking at the matter from this perspective, Gilchrist can happily claim that the Sanskrit '*d,hats*' are identical with the 'significant particles' he has uncovered through the analysis of Hindustani but, at the same time, represent the latter as the more authentic material and the former as the less interesting derivative. For example, in discussing the relationship between Hindustani and its supposed parent, 'Hinduwee', he states:

> The imperative singular of verbs will be one clue perhaps, for this investigation, being the simplest least mutable part of all languages, and which I once hazarded a conjecture to a Sunskrit scholar, could be no other than the *D,hats* or verbal *roots* noticed by Halhed in the preface to his Grammar; a conjecture that turned out, on enquiry, to be well founded. (Gilchrist 1798b: xxiv)

Thus, it is the imperatives of 'Hinduwee' and Hindustani that are likely to be the most revealing objects of enquiry for anyone interested in the history of the language, the inventors of Sanskrit merely having exploited these imperatives as the basis for their arcane grammatical art. In the introduction to *A New Theory and Prospectus of the Persian Verbs*, Gilchrist goes further again and suggests that, at some later date, he may himself investigate the nature of the Sanskrit '*d,hats*'. He states that he is aware that his speculations 'encroach on' the Sanskrit roots and adds:

> I may yet, from this conviction, extend my researches into the radical department of that wonderful language, should any able literary pioneer previously condescend to clear away the pedantic rubbish, which ages have accumulated in the very vestibule of this divine tongue. (Gilchrist 1801: xv)

This depiction of the Sanskrit tradition is clearly highly pejorative – the achievements of Pāṇini, Kātyāyana and Patañjali are dismissed as 'pedantic rubbish' that needs clearing away by a European before any really useful work can be done. And when this task is accomplished, Gilchrist implies, his own conjectures will be shown to be sound:

> When some of the scholars who have already gained so much credit for Sunskrit lore shall liberally pave the way for the progress of

others, by publishing a rudiments, introduction or grammar of that ancient, but artificial language, the public may be enabled to decide how far my present conjectures are well founded. (Gilchrist 1801: xv)

The reference to scholars who have 'already gained so much credit for Sunskrit lore' but have not yet managed to publish a grammar of the language seems tinged with the 'vernacular' grammarian's hostility to the advocates of classicism. The implication is clearly that Gilchrist has contributed more than his fair share to the historical study of Indian languages and that it is time that the proponents of classical learning did the same. It is as if the Brahmans who conceal the secrets of their language and the British scholars who vaunt their own knowledge without making it available to others are both denying him the glory that will be his when the truth is finally revealed.

Unfortunately for Gilchrist, the truth was revealed all too soon after this statement was published, and the fact that he rapidly dropped the subject of the relationship between the '*d,hats*' and the 'significant particles' of Hindustani suggests that he did not like what he saw. In 1804 and 1805 two grammars of Sanskrit appeared in English, one by William Carey, the first text of its kind, and the second by Henry Thomas Colebrooke. Such was the demand for this material that a second edition of Carey's grammar appeared in 1806. Both grammars are informed by the Indian classical tradition. Although, as noted earlier, they do not accurately reproduce its ideas, one way in which they demonstrate its influence is in the inclusion of lists of Sanskrit roots on the model of Pāṇini's *dhāthu-pāṭha*.[9] It is true that some of these roots resemble 'significant particles' identified by Gilchrist in one or other of his works. As noted in the first section of this chapter, Gilchrist includes the particle 'p,hu' in the inventory that forms the first section of *The British Indian Monitor*. He characterises this particle as a formative element in a range of words, both nouns and verbs, asserting that in each case it retains its core semantic content and expresses the idea of 'blowing', 'blooming' or 'expanding'. Meanwhile, Carey (1804 appendix: 84), lists an item that in Gilchrist's system of transcription would be written 'p,hul'. And this form, so similar to Gilchrist's, is also glossed as 'expand'. But examples such as this are few and far between. The startling revelation predicted by Gilchrist did not take place, and it is easy to see why the grandiose assertions that he had made in earlier works now disappeared from view. Moreover, the promise of Sanskrit as an object of historical enquiry was becoming more and more established as time passed, Friedrich Schlegel's ground-breaking call for a comparative grammar, *Über die Sprache und Weisheit der Indier*, appearing just two years after the publication of the second edition of

---

[9] See Law (1993: 240–44) for a discussion of the ways in which material from the Pāṇinian tradition is transformed by writers such as Carey and Colebrooke.

Carey's grammar. Gilchrist had attempted to build a wall around his own research and maintain his authority over everything contained within it. Given his interest in etymology, this required that he assert the possibility of studying the origins of Hindustani without a knowledge of Sanskrit. For a time he managed to do this through the twin strategies of denying that Sanskrit was the parent of Hindustani and claiming that, once information about Sanskrit was more widely available, the '*d,hats*' of the language would soon be revealed as identical with the 'significant particles' of Hindustani. But developments in the study of Sanskrit made these claims untenable, the water broke through the wall and Gilchrist's patch of private property was in the process overwhelmed.

Similar threats to his authority arose from another tradition of language study – the Indo-Persian lexicographical tradition. The compilation of dictionaries has a long history in several of the major languages of the Islamic world. Indeed, scholars contemporary with Gilchrist often pointed to the great dictionaries of Arabic, foremost among them the *Qāmūs* of the fourteenth-century lexicographer al-Firuzabadi, as a way of illustrating the legendary copiousness of the language. During the Mughal period, a range of Persian dictionaries were produced within India itself, and for the purposes of this discussion it will helpful to focus on two – the *Farhang-i-Jahāngirī*, compiled by the Iranian scholar Mir Injū Shirāzī, under the patronage of the emperors Akbar and Jahāngir, and the *Farhang-i-Rashīdī*, the work of the Sindhi scholar 'Abd ur-Rashīd, completed during the reign of Shah Jahān.[10] The former appeared in 1608 and was, as Jeremiás (1993: 64–5) notes, the first Indo-Persian dictionary to include a grammatical preface, a feature that also appears in the *Farhang-i-Rashīdī*, which to a large extent constitutes a critical response to the material collected by scholars such as Injū. The material presented in the grammatical prefaces to both texts, and in similar works by both Turkish and Indian writers, is strongly influenced by the Arabic grammatical tradition, which, like the Sanskrit tradition, is strongly process-oriented. In the Arabic tradition, it is conventional to analyse words into base and supplemental elements, the latter being organised into alphabetical inventories. In Persian dictionaries, these supplemental elements may be sorted into sub-groups, but the basic principle for the presentation of grammatical material is nevertheless through an alphabetical list of forms, with suffixes appearing under the final letter and prefixes under their first. Several grammatical functions may be ascribed to the same letter. Thus, the letter <t> – or rather the Perso-Arabic letter corresponding to it – may be said to have two functions: it is a second person singular personal suffix and it is a third person singular copula

---

[10] See Blochmann (1868: 12–15) and Hadi (1995: 259–60) on the *Farhang-i-Jahāngirī* and Blochman (1868: 20–24) and Hadi (1995: 25) on the *Farhang-i-Rashīdī*.

(Windfuhr 1979: 11).[11]   The alphabetical list of 'significant particles' in *The British Indian Monitor* seems closely modelled on inventories of this kind, although it differs in its inclusion of forms such as 'phu', which are more akin to the material found in Sanskrit lists of roots.

Both the dictionaries under discussion here were well known to British scholars in late eighteenth-century Bengal, and were used as source material in some of the dictionaries and vocabularies they produced. What is more, in 1802 an anonymous letter appeared in the section of *The Asiatic Annual Register* devoted to 'miscellaneous tracts'. The author draws attention to the fact that, '[a]mong his other desiderata', Sir William Jones had taken 'special notice' of the need for a translation of 'that noble production', the '*Ferheenge Jehangeeri*'. He then asserts that he himself is 'equal to this task' and will 'gladly undertake it, provided there be sufficient encouragement' (Anonymous 1802: 133). He gives several reasons for his feeling that such a translation is now overdue, and one of them is connected with the study of Persian grammar:

> [T]he introduction to this work would afford as such a grammar and syntax of the Persian tongue, as the institution of the College, and the turn the young men have lately taken to study this language radically, render absolutely necessary and which Sir William Jones's Grammar (a jewel in its way) cannot well, in our improved state of this sort of literature now-a-days, supply. (Anonymous 1802: 133)

This letter was published just one year after Gilchrist's book on the Persian verb, and the comment concerning the new methods of study adopted by the young men at Fort William College is clearly a reference to that text. The implication is that Gilchrist's work attempts to achieve a similar analysis to that found in the *Farhang-i-Jahāngīrī* but, at the same time, is no match for it. The author includes some extracts translated from the Persian that have obviously been chosen in order to illustrate the derivative nature of Gilchrist's work. For example, he quotes a passage from the ninth section of the *Farhang* 'which shows that the [*an*] and not [*tan*] or [*dan*] is considered by Persian grammarians as the sign of the [...] infinitive' (Anonymous 1802: 139). This is transparently a response to the observation with which Gilchrist opens his work:

---

[11] In fact, as Windfuhr (1979: 11) notes, these two grammatical functions have different exponents, the first being the morpheme *at* and the second the morpheme *ast*. However, the formal principles on which the material is organised result in both being said to belong to the letter < t >. Jeremiás (1993: 54) notes that phenomena such as this arise from the fact that the structure of syllables in Persian is different from that in Arabic, so that the analysis in terms of letters, which is borrowed from the Arabic tradition, serves to conceal the morphology of the Persian word.

> It is evident enough, that the particles *dun* and *tun* are vulgarly but erroneously called the infinitive signs, whereas it is most probably that *un*, as in the old Hinduwee (and *na* in the modern speech) occurs in the same manner also in the Persian tongue. (Gilchrist 1801: 1)

In the preface to the same work, Gilchrist actually acknowledges similarities between his account of the Persian verb and that found in the grammatical sections of the *Farhang*. He notes that the text is based on a shorter work prepared for the use of his students, and states that he submitted the text 'in its original state for correction and criticism to a Gentleman of considerable abilities, who also possesses much knowledge of the Persian tongue'. This gentleman's reaction to the work was not positive: 'He supposed some ignorant Moonshee must have stolen the little which was right from the Furhungi Juhangeeree, and had palmed it on me without examination, as a new Theory of his own.' Undeterred, however, Gilchrist asserts that this opinion must have arisen from the sketchy nature of the work, and that the more developed account presented within the present text will obviate any further criticism (Gilchrist 1801: i). One wonders whether the anonymous author of the letter in the *Register* was in fact the same gentleman who had been so critical of the original manuscript. If so, his patience had clearly been tested by Gilchrist's insistence on going ahead with publication, since the letter conceals a still more insulting reference to Gilchrist and his work. One of the grammatical examples presented in the text is translated as 'he [...] bestowed on me a professorship'. But the term that the author has rendered as 'professorship' is actually an abstract derivative of the Persian word for an 'ass' (Anonymous 1802: 135). Gilchrist had taken up his professorship at Fort William College the previous year, and it is not difficult to infer the anonymous author's view of his appointment.

As in his accounts of the Sanskrit '*d,hats*', Gilchrist's excursion into the description of Persian, and in particular his wish to apply etymological analysis to the grammar of the language, led him into dangerous territory. In discussing Sanskrit, he made arrogant claims that started to unravel when information about the language and its grammatical tradition became more widely available in English. In his account of Persian, the problem lay in the derivative nature of the analysis that he had so triumphantly presented as a solution to problems that even William Jones and Francis Gladwin had so far failed to solve. In late eighteenth- and early nineteenth-century Bengal there were few Britons who knew as much about Hindustani as Gilchrist, and Wellesley acknowledged this fact when he offered him the professorship at Fort William College. But etymology has expansionist tendencies. By definition it involves examining the relationships that exist among different languages or among different states of the same language. And, in Gilchrist's case, it drew him from Hindustani – the territory that he had indisputably occupied – into the discussion of Sanskrit and Persian – areas on which his hold was much more tenuous. His failure to engage convincingly with the material of the indigenous traditions, and the arrogance of his claims on subjects of which he had little knowledge, make his use of etymology as a tool of historical enquiry seem hollow and ill-judged. He did not discuss his withdrawal from historical speculation on Indian languages in any public forum, but the intellectual developments described in this section make it clear that his position was becoming more and more untenable and his ideas on the subject increasingly indefensible.

7.5 ETYMOLOGY AS A PEDAGOGICAL TOOL

Despite the collapse of Gilchrist's historical enquiries, *The British Indian Monitor*, as we saw earlier, includes the most radical presentation of etymological material to be found in any of his published works. But if the primary purpose of this material was not to illustrate the origins and development of the Hindustani language, what was the point of including it? It is clear from Gilchrist's own comments that the 'significant particles' presented in this later text were intended to fulfil a pedagogical function. He introduces the inventory by stating that he will leave it 'entirely to the learner's opinion whether he shall try to acquire the Hindoostanee in this new way, or prefer the old beaten path of regular declension, conjugation &c.' (Gilchrist 1806–8 I: 63). Thus, although he gives the reader permission to ignore the etymological material and turn straight to the more traditional grammatical exposition in the later part of the book, he also indicates that the 'significant particles' are not intended as a supplement to that exposition but as an alternative that can, in some way, replace it. What is more, in the introduction to the book Gilchrist presents pen portraits of two kinds of learner, and although he does not explicitly state that the two kinds of material are intended to meet the needs of these two different groups, it is certainly possible to read the pedagogical materials in those terms.

The first group of learners consists of mature gentlemen who are already 'versed in the principles of general grammar' and for whom a 'practical' approach to language learning is the most appropriate course. Since gentlemen of this kind already know the universal principles underlying the formation of human languages, all that remains is for them to acquire the 'particular modifications' through which the universal categories are instantiated in the language they are studying. They can do this by exposing themselves to the forms of the language through both reading and conversation. Then, as they encounter particular forms, they will be able to hang them onto the conceptual framework that they have already internalised as a result of learning other languages. Younger people who do not have this kind of grasp of general grammar will need to learn the organisational principles of language in general at the same time that they learn the 'particular modifications' of the language they are studying, and this effectively means that they will need to use a traditional grammar. At this point we might recall Chambaud's description of the mangled French spoken by over-ambitious schoolboys whose parents insist that they learn the language through 'practice' rather than through grammatical study. The purpose of Chambaud's description is to illustrate what happens when inexperienced learners engage in conversation without studying the rules of the language, and Gilchrist's allusion to it appears in the preface to *The Oriental Linguist*, where he set out to warn his readers about the danger inherent in studying Hindustani through dialogues.

Clearly the younger students described in the preface to *The British Indian Monitor* will need to turn directly to the traditional material that begins on page 139 of the text. But mature gentlemen, armed with a knowledge of general grammar, might wish to begin instead on page 127, where a passage of Hindustani is set out for their perusal. If they analyse passages like this carefully, they will encounter all the particular 'modifications' of the language and will be able to fit them into the general framework that they internalised when they studied other languages. And the list of 'significant particles' will help them as they do so. If they see a word ending with the letter < e >, for example, they can turn to the section of the inventory dealing with that letter, and there they will be presented with the four choices set out in the first section of this chapter. Realising that the word in question is a verb, they will conclude that the letter < e > must, in this context, be the 'singular affix' of the 'aorist subjunctive', and insert the letter at the appropriate place in their mental grammar. The beauty of this method, as far as Gilchrist is concerned, is that it subordinates the exercise of the memory to the exercise of the intellect. Even the acquisition of vocabulary enters the domain of reason because of the inclusion of 'roots' like 'p,hu' in the list of 'significant particles'. On encountering any word that contains this particular sequence of sounds, the reader will be invited to consider which English word expressing the concept of expansion would be most appropriate in the given context. Thus, the list of 'significant particles' allows the reader to engage in a mode of learning whereby the role of the memory is minimised and the rational analysis of texts forms the primary method of enquiry:

> A sedulous examination of this analysis will do more to pave the way
> for analysing [...] any other piece of Hindoostanee, than a thousand
> mere rules acquired by rote, with which a poor school-boy's memory
> is generally overloaded, like an ass's back, while his mind is allowed

to remain as empty of thought, its proper food, as a heron's belly is of meat [...]. (Gilchrist 1806–08 I: 137).

In the context of the conflict over dialogues, Gilchrist railed against pedagogy that placed too much emphasis on memory and habituation on the grounds that it was likely to result in 'jargonism'. His contention was that, to speak a language well, one needs to grasp the principles on which it is formed, and this requires the exercise of the intellect. To a large extent this distinction between language learning as the mastery of rules and language learning as habituation maps onto the traditional contrast between an 'art' and a 'knack' acquired purely through experience, a contrast that derives from the classical typology of knowledge. Given the greater prestige of knowledge derived from the exercise of pure reason, we can see that the emphasis Gilchrist places on the role of the intellect in language learning constitutes a bid to construct himself once again as the practitioner of an 'art' and not as someone who merely trains recalcitrant children in an imitative skill.

In *The British Indian Monitor*, Gilchrist pushes things a step further by arguing that even the mastery of grammatical rules places too much emphasis on memory and habituation, and that the learner should develop an understanding of general grammar through the rational study of his (or, perhaps, her) own language and then engage with the forms of other languages by employing this general framework of knowledge in the analysis of texts. This second contrast has a close relationship with a distinction that was widely discussed in the discipline of logic and which is explored in some detail by Joseph Priestley. Priestley (1777: 42) notes that in logic there are two 'methods' of argumentation – ANALYSIS and SYNTHESIS. The synthetic method begins with general truths and then explores their implications in particular instances, whereas the analytic method begins with particular observations and leads the listener from these to more general truths. The two types of material presented in *The British Indian Monitor* communicate knowledge of Hindustani through these two different methods. The traditional grammatical material teaches the general principles of the language, and once these have been mastered the student can explore the way in which these principles are instantiated in particular sentences. This corresponds to the method of 'synthesis' in the sense that it guides the student slowly from the general to the particular. The etymological material encourages the learner to engage directly with 'particular observations' in the form of texts and to recreate the general principles of the language through a process of analysis. This corresponds to the method of 'analysis' in the sense that the student begins with the particular – actual examples of writing in the language – and moves from those to a grasp of general principles, prompted where necessary by the list of 'significant particles'.

In *The Hindee Moral Preceptor*, a pedagogical text published in 1803, Gilchrist makes an explicit distinction between methods of language learning that move from the general to the particular and methods that move from the particular to the general. There he states that one can learn a language by 'commencing rigidly with its first principles and ascending gradually to the practice of speaking, reading, and writing it with certainty, ease and propriety', or one can move in the opposite direction, descending 'while reading short amusing lessons or stories' until one reaches 'the first rudiments' of the language. And, in a comment that further reinforces the interpretation of *The British Indian Monitor* presented above, he states that the two methods are suited to different groups of learners:

> [The former is] adapted to the capacity, energy and leisure of very young men, who have not yet perhaps acquired that extensive and accurate idea of general Grammar, in its application to every tongue, which would qualify other people, at more advanced periods of life, and surrounded with other avocations, to profit by the second System of Study. (Gilchrist 1803a: vii)

In this allocation of pedagogies to learners, Gilchrist is also echoing Priestley's account of the relative merits of the two communicative methods, where he argues that synthesis is quicker and less painful for the learner, while analysis is more tedious but 'perhaps more sure':

> In the [synthetic] method it is generally more convenient to explain a system of science to others. For, in general, those truths which were the result of our own inquiry, may be made as intelligible to others as those by which we arrived at the knowledge of them; and it is easier to show how one general principle comprehends the particulars comprised under it, than to trace all those particulars to one that comprehends them all. (Priestley 1777: 42–3)

For all these reasons, it is 'absolutely necessary' to use the synthetic method when knowledge is to be communicated to schoolchildren, whose inexperience and lack of general knowledge demands a clear and straightforward mode of exposition. However, the advantage of the analytic method is that it replicates the procedure through which knowledge was first created:

> In fact, almost every branch of science (except some parts of pure mathematics, capable of the strictest demonstration) hath been delivered at first by an investigation of it in this method of analysis; and it hath not been till after some time that the patrons of it have digested it into a synthetic or systematic form. (Priestley 1777: 44)

It is important to be careful about terminology here. Priestley's point is that much of our knowledge is arrived at through a process of induction, and the communicative method known as 'analysis' parallels the line of inductive reasoning. When Gilchrist was writing, the 'science' of grammar did not arrive at general principles through an inductive approach to linguistic data. But in *The British Indian Monitor* he is writing not about the 'science' of grammar but about the 'art' – the process of working out how the forms of a particular language are patterned – and this involves scrutinising the data of the language and moving from those particulars to the general rules that underlie them. Again, Priestley's account of the analytic method includes advice about who will benefit most from it, namely 'persons who have gone through their preliminary studies and who have leisure for *new speculations*' (Priestley 1777: 44). Thus, Gilchrist's comments about the appropriateness of analysis as a method of language learning for gentlemen already 'versed in the principles of general grammar' parallel Priestley's more general comments about the use of analysis as a method of communicating knowledge. Having said all this, however, even in the case of younger learners, Gilchrist would prefer to avoid rote learning as much as possible, arguing that it is inefficient and provides a poor training for life in the wider world:

> [W]hence from our public seminaries we have spouting automatons in abundance, who seldom evince great mental energy or conception, till they learn the positive necessity through life of thinking and acting for themselves, rather as intelligent, efficient beings, than sheer passive machines or vehicles of useful knowledge. (Gilchrist 1806–08 I: 137)

Thus, if the synthetic method degenerates into the rote learning of rules, then the cause of education is far from well served. And through comments such as these Gilchrist pushes the philosophy of 'anti-jargonism' into a yet more extreme position. Assimilating rules is better than picking up unanalysed scraps of language from dialogues, but simply learning rules by heart is still not enough to ensure a full understanding of the language. Such a pedagogy is likely to result in nothing more than the production of 'spouting automatons' who are unable to show independence at the level of either thought or action.

One further aspect of Priestley's discussion deserves comment, and this is his observation that the analytic method leads learners to knowledge along the route taken by the original creators of that knowledge. This implies that learners who follow Gilchrist's method of analysis will find themselves treading the same path that he himself followed when he travelled to Faizabad in the early 1780s and began to work on his dictionary and grammar of Hindustani. In the preface of 1798, Gilchrist makes the rather exaggerated claim that no dictionaries or grammatical descriptions of the language existed before he began his work so that he himself had to follow the path of analysis, engaging with Hindustani texts and trying to work out the grammatical rules that underlay their construction. If they work with authentic texts right from the start and through this engagement build their own mental grammars of Hindustani, learners can experience what Gilchrist himself experienced, albeit in the privacy of their studies. One result of this experience will be to communicate to learners the nature of Gilchrist's achievement. And another will be to create in them a certain attitude to the language. Priestley (1777: 43) states that the analytic method is particularly appropriate for the communication of 'sentiments not generally admitted', that is, particularly controversial topics, because it begins with 'no principles or positions but what are common, and universally allowed' and leads readers 'insensibly, and without shocking their prejudices, to the right conclusion'. This is significant because in 1806 there were still those who continued to promote the use of 'jargon' and hence, even then, Gilchrist's 'sentiments' about Hindustani were not 'admitted' by everyone.

In 1801 a Russian writer named Herasim Lebedeff had published a new work entitled *A Grammar of the Pure and Mixed East Indian Dialects*, of which Bhatia (1987: 90) is critical on the grounds that it shows 'massive interference from Bengali and Sanskrit' and, as such, is very localised in the picture of Hindustani that it presents. What is more, in 1801 and 1804, the fifth and sixth editions of Hadley's *Compendious Grammar* were published with a number of new features, including a half-hearted gesture towards the acknowledgement of Indian scripts. Gilchrist (1806–8 I: xi) rails against these competitors in the introduction to *The British Indian Monitor*, and is particularly scathing about Hadley, stating that his work is now much more 'pernicious to learners' than 'at any period of his reign'. And if one thinks about Priestley's characterisation of analysis as the method more suited to communicating what is not 'generally admitted', Gilchrist's advocacy of an analytic method of language learning makes complete sense. It would be relatively easy for the advocates of 'jargonism' to claim that the rules of Gilchrist's grammar were over-elaborate, pedantic or fastidious, but it would harder to dismiss an authentic text that was known and accepted by native speakers themselves. By starting with such a text and encouraging learners to use it as a means of developing their own mental grammars of the language, Gilchrist had created a means of coaxing his readers 'insensibly' towards an acceptance of Hindustani as fully rule-governed language. The whole point of his new method is that it pushes readers to find out for themselves the ways in which Hindustani marks the categories that underlie all languages and are well known to anyone who is familiar with general grammar. This kind of process, as Priestley's comments suggest, will lead readers 'insensibly' and 'without shocking their prejudices' to a correct understanding of the nature of the language itself. And to promote this kind of understanding was the goal of all Gilchrist's philological work. The aims of the material presented in *The British Indian*

Monitor are no different from those of Gilchrist's other publications. But by leading readers to an acceptance of the elegant and ordered nature of the language through their own engagement with real Hindustani data, this new text aims to produce a conviction in the reader beyond that which can be achieved through mere authoritarian assertion.

Thus, although the organisation of *The British Indian Monitor* is unusual, it can be understood in terms of the communicative goals that inform all Gilchrist's earlier work. The list of 'significant particles' supports a pedagogy that emphasises the role of the intellect and minimises the role of memory in a fashion that is familiar from Gilchrist's earlier comments on the dangers of using dialogues as a method of language learning. By following this path, the reader will also replicate Gilchrist's own journey of discovery, albeit in a more controlled fashion. Thus, the promotion of an analytical engagement with Hindustani texts can also be seen as dramatising Gilchrist's achievements in the same way that the explicit discussion of problems of analysis in the footnotes of the grammar did. Finally, by encouraging readers to learn Hindustani through an analytic rather than a synthetic method, Gilchrist was using the method that was seen by contemporary commentators as surer and more persuasive. This is significant because, in the first decade of the nineteenth century, Gilchrist was still trying to convince ordinary readers that the vision of Hindustani presented by writers such as Lebedeff and Hadley was a gross distortion of the truth. By presenting a text and giving his readers just enough information to analyse it, he was effectively pushing them to see for themselves the truth of his assertions about the regular and orderly nature of the language he had devoted his adult life to describing.

7.6 CONCLUSION

The pursuit of etymology opened up both problems and possibilities for Gilchrist. Inspired by the work of John Horne Tooke, he saw etymological analysis as the key to unlocking the history of human languages, and in his earlier publications he explicitly presents his etymological speculation as a contribution to the contemporary debate on the origin of language. The problem with this work was that it led Gilchrist out of the area in which he was an acknowledged expert and into territory where his authority was far more questionable. In particular, it induced him to make pronouncements on the nature of both Sanskrit and Persian grammar, fields in which he was unable to demonstrate a convincing knowledge of the material. Indigenous traditions of analysis had produced highly sophisticated accounts of both languages, and although Gilchrist was inclined to dismiss the work of South Asian scholars as mere 'pedantry', the weight of opinion in the British community was against him. Other British scholars were engaging actively with primary material from both the Sanskrit and Persian traditions, and in the light of their work Gilchrist's claims about both the Sanskrit '*d,hats*' and the structure of the Persian verb looked increasingly hollow and unconvincing. Although he gives no explicit reasons for his decision to downgrade the status of historical speculation in *The British Indian Monitor*, it is difficult to see how he could have continued with it, given the appearance of accessible materials on the grammar of Sanskrit in the early years of the nineteenth century and the criticism that his foray into Persian grammar had elicited in the pages of *The Asiatic Annual Register*.

But etymology provided Gilchrist with possibilities other than the opportunity to present himself as an active participant in the debate over the origin of language. By correlating Hindustani conjunctions, postpositions and verbal morphology with the roots of common verbs, a technique obviously inspired by Horne Tooke's practice in the first volume of *The Diversions of Purley*, Gilchrist attempted to show that Hindustani grammar was underpinned by a conceptual order that was not immediately evident to the casual observer. Thus, by deriving the temporal markers from verbs of rest and motion, Gilchrist was able to claim that forms which seemed on the face of it arbitrary and unmotivated in fact provided evidence that the conceptualisation of time embodied in the structure of Hindustani had been derived through a process of metaphorical extension from a more basic conceptualisation of space. Since one of the fundamental goals of his project was to show that a language long thought to be disordered and irregular was in fact highly orderly and rule-governed, this method of finding order where none was immediately apparent constituted a powerful explanatory strategy. At a number of points, Gilchrist criticises other grammarians' accounts of verbal morphology on the grounds that they are not as economical as they could have been had full use been made of techniques of etymological analysis. But even when the emphasis is placed on economy of description and not on diachronic enquiry, historical issues continue to interfere with the project. The claim that the morphology of the Hindustani verb derives from verbs of rest and motion is, in the end, an assertion about the history of the language, even if its rhetorical function is to show how orderly the language is in the present.

Even when Gilchrist withdrew from historical speculation, however, he continued to present his readers with etymological material, representing the list of 'significant particles' in *The British Indian Monitor* as a means of supporting an analytical engagement with the forms of the language rather than as a means of understanding its history. Oddly, this makes the material presented in that text more like the inventories found in traditional accounts of Sanskrit and the prefaces of Indo-Persian dictionaries than any of the etymological material set out in Gilchrist's earlier works. As with the list of roots in Pāṇini's *Aṣṭādhyāyī* and the inventory of affixes in Injū's *Farhang-i-Jahāngīrī*, there is no suggestion that the list of 'significant particles' in *The British Indian Monitor* is anything other than a synchronic description. But here the provision of etymological material still seems designed to meet goals that Gilchrist had set for himself in his earlier work. It constitutes a means of allowing the reader to replicate Gilchrist's own experience of analysing the structure of the language, and thus dramatises his achievements as a grammarian in much the same manner that his discussion of the adjectival nature of possessive forms or his discussion of speech sounds and their representation in writing had in earlier texts. Futhermore, it provides a means both of emphasising the use of the intellect in language learning and of leading the reader 'insensibly' towards an appreciation of the rule-governed nature of the language, objectives closely tied to Gilchrist's ongoing campaign against 'jargonism'. Thus, even after he had retreated from his grandiose assertions about the historical breakthroughs to be expected from the etymological analysis of Hindustani, Gilchrist clung to etymology because of the sheer pleasure that was to be had from the independent analysis of linguistic forms. In *The British Indian Monitor*, the impulse to take the forms of a language apart and analyse them into their component parts loses its status as a mode of historical enquiry and finally becomes a good in itself – a means of reliving the achievements of his youth, of promoting active enquiry, and of once again attacking the claims of his rivals who saw the forms of the Hindustani language as disordered and irregular in contrast with the languages of the west.

CONCLUSION

John Gilchrist's grammatical descriptions of Hindustani constitute a sustained attempt to transform readers' perceptions of the language. And this property of the work is underlined through an extended metaphor that appears in the preface of 1798. In the context of a passage dealing with the process of language learning itself, Gilchrist depicts the student's progress through the grammar in terms of a physical journey through the landscape, and, casting himself in the role of guide, he invites the reader to accompany him as he goes: 'Come courteous reader! Give me your hand, and let me beseech you to note the premises as we march along with a penetrating eye, and proportional mental reflection' (Gilchrist 1798b: xliv). He provides a detailed narrative of the journey, comparing each part of the grammar to a different kind of terrain, and the result is a description bearing a close resemblance to the picturesque guidebooks of the period, texts produced with the intention of helping travellers to interpret the landscapes that they passed through according to the aesthetic principles laid down by contemporary theorists. As in those texts, the focus is not so much on *what* is to be seen as on the traveller's *response* to the natural scene. And so, just like the metaphor of the 'inversion of opticks', which occurs in an earlier passage of the same text, this much more extended metaphor focuses attention on the very act of looking and particularly on the pleasures and rewards that it can bring.

The journey begins with the 'elements', the section of the grammar that deals with speech sounds and their representation in writing. This Gilchrist compares to a 'porch' composed of 'curious rock work', and he encourages the learner to note the 'varying hues, changes, or metamorphoses, to which its materials are subject'. The nature of these metamorphoses is unclear from the text. Are we to imagine an edifice of stone glittering with quartz or mica? Or is the point rather that the basic substance of the rock can take on innumerable forms as it is eroded by the weather? Whichever interpretation we choose, the image of the variegated rock face evokes the 'convertibility' of the Hindustani 'letters'. For Gilchrist, the basic material of the Hindustani language is subject to constant transformation, so that apparently dissimilar letters, $<j>$ and $<g>$, for example, are really the same entity seen from different angles or in different lights. We might also recall the way in which the orthography of Hindustani led Gilchrist to change his perception of some of the English speech sounds, most notably the sound which he represents with the letter < y > and which he decided, on the basis of its spelling in the Perso-Arabic script, must be a diphthong. The mastery of the 'letters' also opens up the possibility of research in the field of etymology, and Gilchrist expresses this idea by describing the landscape unfolding before the reader in a succession of beautiful vistas. The rocky porch 'points hereafter to alluring prospects, that lose themselves in all directions, amidst the venerable shades of Indian speech, or more usefully emerge in the meandering streams of the modern current tongues'. This passage was written in the years when Gilchrist was still an enthusiastic proponent of historical etymology, and the description of the 'alluring prospects' opened up by this kind of research aptly captures the sense of excitement and discovery that accompanied speculative etymology for many eighteenth-century thinkers.

Moving on to the variable parts of speech, Gilchrist depicts the verbal system as 'teem[ing] with beauties' and states that '[n]o other part of this philological champaign can afford so much to admire, and so little to censure' (Gilchrist 1798b: xliv–xlv). The somewhat archaic term 'champaign' evokes an expanse of open country – flat, fertile land like the plains of northern India where Gilchrist himself had conducted so much of his research – and again the focus is on the emotional state that the landscape will produce in the traveller who encounters it. The reader is to make a 'long halt' here and take 'special care to string all the indispensable tenses in regular rosaries or garlands, at [his] finger ends'. As we saw in Chapter 5, Gilchrist's admiration for the Hindustani verbal system derives from its uniformity and regularity, qualities which ensure that the study of the verbs is not an arduous chore but a delightful pastime akin to gathering flowers in a meadow. But all is not well, even in this idyllic tract of country. A malevolent owl sits 'perched on the watchtower of Hindoostanee grammar, with an effrontery suited to the darkness of night', and this owl is Hadley, Gilchrist's competitor and rival. In the fabular tradition that originates with Aesop, the owl is a symbol of foolishness, unable to appreciate the beauty of the day because of the limitations of its own nocturnal vision. Once again, then, we have an image centred upon the nature of perception – Hadley's insistence that Hindustani verbs needed to be divided into five conjugations is evidence of his inability to *see* the beautiful simplicity of the language's verbal morphology. And the implication is that readers should reject his work and turn to Gilchrist, whose work will enable them to see the beauty of Hindustani grammar.[1]

After a period of recreation in the flowery meadows of the verbal system, Gilchrist tells his readers that they should proceed to the 'unbounded

---

[1] See Steadman-Jones (2003) for a fuller analysis of the metaphor of the owl on the watchtower.

wilderness, or *soondurbun* of Hindoostanee derivation, and composition'. The term '*soondurbun*' refers specifically to the 'tract of intersecting creeks and channels, swampy islands, and jungles, which constitutes that part of the Ganges Delta nearest the sea' (Yule & Burnell 1985: 869). Ships approaching Calcutta from the ocean would have to pass through this region, and passengers frequently disembarked there and picnicked, despite the fact that, as one eighteenth-century visitor remarks, 'tygers' were often to be seen 'issuing from [the] delicious shades' (Archer 1980: 19). Gilchrist states that the 'inquisitive student' should not move on without fully investigating 'these mazy wilds, whence light will rush upon him, at every turn, and point out an unerring clue for the innumerable labyrinths of that copious variegated language' (Gilchrist 1798b: xlv–xlvi). As with the 'alluring prospects' visible from the 'rocky porch' of the elements, this image figures a particular aspect of Hindustani – in this case, the derivational morphology – as a kind of visual tourism. The morphology of the language is a lush tract of jungle, enclosed and labyrinthine in the best picturesque tradition, but it is not impenetrable and, as one passes through it, the flashes of light filtering through the trees will open it up for contemplation and enjoyment. Again, it is significant that Gilchrist's description dwells not on the dangerous nature of the '*soondurbun*' but on its beauties. Indeed, the way in which he names this tract of territory itself has positive connotations. The etymology of '*soondurbun*' is still disputed, but Gilchrist's spelling of the term indicates that he sees it as a compound of *sandar* ('beautiful') and *ban* ('forest'). Thus, the very name gestures towards the alluring nature of the place.

In each of these three passages, Gilchrist focuses on aspects of the terrain that are in some sense beautiful or pleasurable, and it is in this sense that his text resembles a picturesque guidebook. In the late eighteenth century the emergent theory of the picturesque was motivating the production of a wide range of travel literature. Between 1780 and 1800, for example, William Gilpin published five 'tours' or descriptive guides, each of which deals with a different region of Britain and presents a critical discussion of the landscapes and scenery to be found there. And in the 1780s and 1790s British painters had begun to travel to India and interpret its landscapes according to the principles of the picturesque. William Hodges, who had travelled with Captain Cook on his second expedition to the Pacific and was in India between 1780 and 1783, went so far as to falsify perspective so that his landscapes would more closely fit the schema imposed by the classical landscape tradition (Stuebe 1979: 45). Thomas and William Daniell, who travelled in India between 1786 and 1793, adhered to more rigidly topographical principles and sought out views that could in themselves be described as 'picturesque', invoking the term (which occurs repeatedly in their journals) to describe the ruined city of Rajmahal, the riverside buildings at Patna, the banks of the Ganges at Kara and the ghats at

Hardwar, to name just a few examples (Mahajan 1983: 20–26). The images that the Daniells produced as a result of their travels could easily be used to illustrate Gilchrist's narrative – their aquatints of rock-cut temples present a visual expression of Gilchrist's 'rocky porch'; their depictions of the Gangetic plain present just the kind of idyllic landscapes that Gilchrist associates with the verbal system; and their images of the '*soondurbun*' depict clearings opening up in the dense foliage to let the light rush in, just as Gilchrist describes (Archer 1980: 18–19, 37–98, 190–218).

What is significant about Gilchrist's turn to the picturesque is its epistemological implications. In his foundational work, *On the River Wye*, William Gilpin (1782: 1–2) summarises the guiding principles of the genre he was developing:

> The following little work proposes a new object of pursuit; that of not barely examining the face of a country; but of examining it by the rules of picturesque beauty: that of not merely describing but of adapting the description of natural scenery to the principles of artificial landscape.

Thus, the picturesque travel writer does not simply present a description of a particular tract of land but assesses the extent to which it conforms to principles of artistic composition as they had developed within the classical tradition of landscape painting. And this process of interpreting the landscape for the reader has obvious parallels with Gilchrist's practice of assessing the extent to which Hindustani conforms to the normative principles set out in disciplines such as philosophy and rhetoric. It is important to remember that, in the eighteenth and early nineteenth centuries, these principles were not derived from an empirical investigation of linguistic data but had been laid down a priori before the practical grammarian even approached the forms and structures of a particular language. Just as a landscape might be dismissed if it did not conform to aesthetic qualities required by the theory of the picturesque, a language might also be dismissed if it did not instantiate the qualities laid down by philosophers and rhetoricians. Thus, the image of the picturesque journey aptly evokes the evaluative nature of language study in the later eighteenth century, and is in harmony with the interpretation of Gilchrist's work presented in this book. Like Gilpin in the Wye Valley, Gilchrist sought not merely to describe the object of his enquiries but to show that it conformed to a framework of normative principles that existed a priori. In both cases, those principles described a kind of ideal, in Gilpin's case for a landscape and in Gilchrist's for a language – an ideal against which actual landscapes and languages could be measured.

But the evaluation of landscapes and languages was not a purely intellectual activity. In both cases, the process of analysis could be dramatised in such a way that it would affect the reader's *feelings* about the object of discussion. Gilpin (1782: 2) states that the purpose of a picturesque guidebook is to describe natural scenery according to the principles of artificial landscape and thus '[open] the sources of those pleasures, which are derived from the comparison'. In his *Three Essays*, published in 1792, while Gilchrist was working on his grammar, Gilpin (1792: 47) elaborates on the pleasures of picturesque tourism, stating, for example, that the experience of searching for beauty, 'the expectation of new scenes continually opening, and arising to view', is an important source of pleasure for the 'picturesque traveller'. In the same way, Gilchrist's picturesque narrative constructs his texts as the means by which readers will experience the pleasures to be had from the study of Hindustani, the verbal system being the most prominent example. This sense of pleasure is notably absent from Hadley's grammar, where the verbal system is described as complex, difficult and shot through with irregularities. Thus, the idea that the order and uniformity of the language can bring pleasure to the learner is an important element of Gilchrist's 'anti-jargonism', his ongoing attempt to mediate between language and reader in such a way that the virtues of the language are truly understood. Furthermore, the sense of pleasurable anticipation evoked in Gilpin's account of 'new scenes continually opening, and arising to view' is directly paralleled in Gilchrist's descriptions of 'alluring prospects, that lose themselves in all directions, amidst the venerable shades of Indian speech' and in his account of the 'mazy wilds' of the '*soondurbun*', where 'light will rush upon [the traveller], at every turn, and point out an unerring clue for the innumerable labyrinths of that copious variegated language'. The very fact that the view reveals itself slowly and cannot be seized immediately is a part of the pleasure to be had from the study of grammar.

Another point of contact between Gilpin's work and Gilchrist's lies in the possibility that both landscapes and languages which initially seem unpromising can be unlocked through the application of an appropriate body of theory. According to Gilpin (1792: 54–5), landscapes that do not at first appear to be picturesque can be productive of negative feelings. When confronted by 'some large tract of barren country', for example, we are 'apt [...] to express our discontent in hasty exaggerated phrases'. But, if we know what to look for, 'even scenes the most barren of beauty' can 'furnish amusement'. Thus, 'that tract of barren country, through which the great military road passes from Newcastle to Carlisle' is not picturesque in any conventional sense:

> But even here [...] [t]he interchangeable patches of heath, and green-sward make an agreeable variety. Often too on these vast tracts of intersecting grounds we see beautiful lights, softening off along the sides of hills [...]. Even a winding road itself is an object of beauty; while the richness of the heath on each side, with the little hillocs,

and crumbling earth may give an excellent lesson for a foreground. (Gilpin 1792: 55–56)

By applying notions such as 'agreeable variety' or 'the appropriate composition of the foreground', the traveller can find new ways of enjoying the landscape. And, in the same way, Gilchrist attempts to transform the reader's response to aspects of Hindustani grammar through the application of theory. In the narrative of the journey, for example, he describes the Hindustani adverbs as a 'barren waste', a phrase that evokes Gilpin's description of the tract of country between Newcastle and Carlisle (Gilchrist 1798b: xlv). He notes, however, that the adverbs will at least present the reader with 'the pleasing opportunity of admiring *en passant* [...] the penetration and genius of a real scholar'. The adverbs are barren in the sense that they do not exhibit interesting grammatical properties in the same way that the inflecting parts of speech do. But the idea that there is nothing here to stimulate the mind is challenged by the theory of John Horne Tooke, which proposes that each is derived from some primitive noun or verb. This notion provides the reader with a new way of engaging with them and, more than that, of appreciating their conceptual organisation – the fact that they are metaphorically derived from an underlying conceptualisation of space. Thus, the use of speculative etymology renders the contemplation of the adverbs pleasurable in much the same way that the principle of 'agreeable variety' renders the journey from Newcastle to Carlisle entertaining for the picturesque traveller. Just as the travel writer can use aesthetic theory to depict unpromising tracts of country as a source of pleasure and delight, the practical grammarian can use elements of linguistic theory to change the reader's feelings about a language.

And the connection between Gilchrist's narrative and Gilpin's is also evident in the political dimensions of the work. In the introduction to their influential collected volume on the politics of the picturesque, Stephen Copley and Peter Garside (1994) comment on the various ways in which scholars have understood the picturesque as an ideological as well as an aesthetic formation, the most important here being the way in which picturesque texts and images *appropriate* landscapes, effacing potential signs of conflict and dissent. By focusing on the tourist's aesthetic response to the natural environment, picturesque narratives effectively conceal the fact that land is often a focus of economic and political conflict. As Copley (1994: 42–61) demonstrates, for example, Gilpin himself chose to erase industrial sites from his picturesque narratives as a way of negotiating the moral ambiguities of tourism as a cultural practice. In so doing, he drew back from the uncomfortable prospect of drawing privileged tourists with the leisure and means to travel into too close an engagement with the economic exploitation on which their privilege was built. And in colonial contexts, this kind of appropriation was of particular significance:

In the case of the Scottish Highlands, for instance, the combination of political repression, economic exploitation, and aesthetic sentimentalisation of the Scottish landscape in the early nineteenth century clearly renders the Picturesque 'invention' of the region a hegemonic cultural manifestation of the English colonising presence. (Copley & Garside 1994: 6–7)

As we saw in Chapter 1, the study of South Asian languages in the earlier phases of British colonialism has usually been seen as a form of appropriation. Linguistic varieties that were the property of Indians themselves were transformed into tools for the government of the empire. And Gilchrist's use of a picturesque travel narrative as a metaphor for the study of Hindustani grammar aptly evokes this aspect of colonial linguistic scholarship. There are no people in the landscapes Gilchrist describes – no existing inhabitants to complicate the traveller's relationship with the prospects unfolding before him. The traveller/reader is entirely free to take possession of the landscape/language, which is laid out as an object of consumption to be judged, explored and enjoyed.

Thus, the image of the journey confirms the account of Gilchrist's work that has been developed in the earlier chapters of this book. The central argument of this study is that Gilchrist's descriptions of Hindustani are neither purely technical nor reductively political. The technical difficulties he experienced in assimilating the forms and structures of Hindustani into the framework of the western grammar were – to him and his readers – *real* problems. It is easy to look back into history and sneer at the grammarians of earlier periods on the grounds that they forced the languages they were describing into the structures of Greco-Roman grammar. But linguists in the twenty-first century still approach new data with a certain set of assumptions about how language in general works, and a range of conceptual tools developed in advance of their present research. The principal difference between grammarians like Gilchrist and contemporary practitioners of linguistics is the way in which they understand the relationship between data and theory. Contemporary linguists usually understand their work in terms of the epistemology developed by natural scientists for the study of the material world. If there is a lack of fit between data and theory, then it is the theory that is challenged and not the data. But grammarians of the later eighteenth century faced the prospect that, if they could not assimilate new forms and structures into the patterns reified within philosophical and aesthetic discussions of language, the very object of enquiry – the language itself – would be dismissed as irrational, irregular and disordered. And this was the point at which technical problems became political. The sense that newly encountered languages – or, at least, languages that had only recently been viewed through the lens of western grammar – were inferior to European ones was congruent with the pejorative views of colonised cultures that were developed more broadly within the parameters of colonial discourse. However, we should be careful about castigating individual grammarians for their failure to engage sympathetically with the diversity of human language. The problem was more deeply embedded and, as this discussion suggests, lay in the epistemology of language study as it was generally understood in the period.

Gilchrist's work constitutes an attempt to reorder his readers' perceptions of the Hindustani language within this epistemological framework. Whenever the language resisted assimilation into familiar patterns, he searched the contemporary literature for other authoritative ways of interpreting the data he had collected. Conversely, when Hindustani lent itself to analysis within the western framework, he foregrounded the relevant features of the language and drew attention to their beauty and faultlessness. It is important to note that his attempt to defend the structure of Hindustani did not rest on the assertion that all languages were equally effective as vehicles of reason and communication – the strategy that Sorensen (2000: 179) identifies with a 'Romantic' understanding of language. Gilchrist accepted that some languages and varieties were better than others, and his reference to the 'vileness' of English 'butchered by Negroes in the West Indies' is a case in point. His point is that Hindustani is an ordered, rational language and should not be viewed as a corrupt and irregular 'jargon', as Hadley and his ilk had suggested. His defence of Hindustani did not constitute a benign and liberal attempt to assert the worthiness of all peoples and all languages. We should be in no doubt that it was undertaken as a way of shoring up the authority of the colonial state. It was necessary for the servants of the Company to learn Indian languages if they were to undertake their legal, administrative and military responsibilities effectively. And the need to recognise the sophistication of Hindustani arose from the risks inherent in speaking a language badly. To use a simplified version of the language with servants might just about be acceptable but, as Bayly (1996: 289) so eloquently puts it, 'incorrect usage would debase [the Servants of the Company] in the eyes of Indian notables'.

Thus, when Gilchrist struggled to redeem the Hindustani language from the stigmatisation it had received at the hands of writers such as Hadley, he did so in order to render the language available for appropriation. I suggested in the Introduction to this book that the 'jargonisation' of Hindustani – the use of a simplified version of the language and the insistence that no other variety existed – was the product both of technical problems in grasping the structure of more sophisticated varieties and of anxiety about the risks inherent in speaking a foreign language. The former problem arose from the lack of fit between data and theory and the latter from the normal sense of danger that arises from the use of a language other than one's own – the feeling that one is at a disadvantage, vulnerable to humiliation and ridicule. To insist that the problem lay in the language and not in the colonial agent's own grasp of it can be understood as a strategy of self-preservation through which feelings of anxiety and vulnerability were projected onto the colonised other and not attributed to the colonising self. Gilchrist's valorisation of Hindustani served to dismantle this complex machinery of frustration, anger and fear by normalising the structure of the language and, in particular, anticipating and minimising the problems that English-speaking learners were likely to experience with it. In the process, the language was rendered a less threatening object of engagement and thus became available for appropriation as an instrument of government, the technical and political dimensions of language study mapping onto each other in a subtle but powerful fashion.

Of course Gilchrist's political argument was underpinned by personal ambition. In arguing for the importance of Hindustani as a medium of administration, he was effectively marketing his own texts, which he hoped would bring him advantages at a material level. Furthermore, his anti-classicism can be understood in the light of this fact. The emphasis placed on the classical languages of India in the elite circles of the Company reinforced the downgrading of 'vernaculars' such as Hindustani, and Gilchrist's insistence that the object of his own enquiries was more important politically than Persian to a certain extent represents an attempt to push the 'vernaculars' up the agenda and create a demand for his own work. At the same time, the 'classical' languages – both eastern and western – were seen as paradigmatic examples of how languages should be. Gilchrist's repeated attempts to show that contemporary analyses of Latin should be responsive to etymological work on 'vernaculars', and his insistence that Sanskrit was a wholly artificial language that could tell scholars little about the history of the modern Indian languages, both constitute attempts to elevate the status of 'vernacular' languages in relation to 'classical' ones. But even if the engine of Gilchrist's work was personal ambition, the arguments he presented for the study of Hindustani were political ones. Thus, we are not confronted with a choice between interpreting his work as a political or a commercial project. Both impulses are present in his writing, intertwined and inseparable.

Gilchrist's work normalised the Hindustani language for western readers and retraced the line of argument developed centuries earlier by grammarians of the European 'vernaculars', an argument to the effect that modern languages could be just as ordered and regular as 'classical' ones. His metaphors of vision – the 'reversal of opticks' and the picturesque journey – underline the way in which his texts attempted to transform his readers' perceptions of the language, and in so doing they draw attention to the interpenetration of the technical and the political in his work. Solving technical problems – eleminating the sense that Hindustani data did not fit the patterns reified within western theory – served to valorise the language for readers and thus render it available for political appropriation. Just as Gilpin's narratives worked to influence perceptions of natural scenery and, in so doing, foregrounded the privileged traveller's engagement with the world at the expense of a focus on political or economic conflict, Gilchrist's descriptions of Hindustani also worked on his readers' perceptions, wearing away the belief that the language was essentially a 'jargon' unworthy of serious attention. To engage with Hindustani, he suggests, need not be a source of conflict and anxiety. Indeed, it can be a pleasure, the written grammar providing a space for a detailed engagement with the language, a space unpopulated by native speakers, whose judgements might give rise to the kinds of anxiety that are palpable in contemporary accounts of 'jargon'.

Gilchrist's practice of searching for models of analysis that would normalise the structure of Hindustani for his readers has a flavour of empiricism about it. When he asserts that the sound represented by the letter < y > is a diphthong, for example, he does so on the grounds that it explains the Hindustani data better than an account in which the sound is understood as a simple articulation. This does not mean that Gilchrist should be seen as a hero in a narrative of scientific progress. The most cursory engagement with his texts indicates that they are firmly located in the dominant paradigm of his day, one in which generalisations about language derive a priori from philosophy and rhetoric rather than from the detailed scrutiny of data. However, it is interesting to note that the political pressure to take colonial languages seriously created, for Gilchrist at least, an environment in which theory could be examined critically. And this grass-roots experience of linguistic diversity led him to create a text in which a phenomenon such as ergativity was not simply ignored or stigmatised but laid open for discussion in a reasoned and critical fashion. The metaphor of the journey provides an uncannily appropriate image for this ambivalent approach to the relationship between data and theory. It is noticeable that, during the nineteenth century, the emergence of a more empirical approach to human language is accompanied by a series of images in which language is compared to natural objects such as animals, plants or geological formations.[2] Throughout this period, languages are seen less and less as products of human ingenuity comparable with buildings or musical compositions and more and more as natural phenomena beyond the scope of human intention. By comparing a language to a landscape, Gilchrist's text looks forward to this new way of thinking, eliminating human actors from the picture and focusing on the language as a natural phenomenon. But, by evoking the practice of picturesque viewing, Gilchrist simultaneously remains in touch with the evaluative approach to language that was

---

[2] Morpurgo Davies (1998: 86–94, 190–91) discusses the influence of both organicism and geology in nineteenth-century linguistics.

such a dominant part of the scholarship of his day. The language is a natural object but it is also open to critical scrutiny, just as the scenes in Gilpin's narratives are natural vistas available for examination with reference to the 'principles of artificial landscape'.

In summary, Gilchrist's linguistic works, even when they are at their most technical, are *representations* of languages, and the process of representation – depicting a person, place or practice in a particular light – is inherently political. To understand the ways in which Gilchrist's contemporaries might have read his representations requires us to consider the connotations of the metalanguage out of which they are constructed. In the twenty-first century, the study of grammar no longer has a central place in western culture. That is not to say that grammars are not still published in their thousands. Nor is it to say that the contemporary approaches to grammar developed within the academy are not important. But in the eighteenth and nineteenth centuries the study of grammar formed a central part of even a basic education, and the majority of readers would have been sensitive to issues of linguistic representation in a way that only a rather specialised readership is today. The metaphor of the journey serves as a salutary reminder of this fact. As we examine the grammatical texts that emerged from the cultural and colonial encounters of the eighteenth and nineteenth centuries, we should imagine the grammarian as a guide, leading his (in some cases, her) readers through terrain very different from that of the metropolitan centre. As they pass through the landscape, the grammarian deploys a range of arguments to modify their response to what they see, to change their feelings about the strange sights that confront them and to overcome their initial alienation. This is not to say that the grammarian's role is necessarily beneficent, although in some cases it might be. The altered experience of the language/landscape often forms the first step in a politically motivated process of appropriation. The point is rather that grammatical texts played a more complex role in cultural encounters and display a more complex dynamic than is often acknowledged, and this study serves to demonstrate how that role and that dynamic can be explored and understood.

BIBLIOGRAPHY

THE WORKS OF JOHN GILCHRIST

1787–90. *A Dictionary, English and Hindoostanee, in which the words are Marked with their Distinguishing Initials, as Hinduwee, Arabic, and Persian*, 2 vols., 2nd edn. 1810, 3rd edn. 1825, Calcutta: Stuart & Cooper (vol. 1); Cooper & Upjohn (vol. 2).

1796. *A Grammar of the Hindoostanee Language; or, Part Third of Volume First, of a System of Hindoostanee Philology*, Calcutta: Chronicle Press.
(Gilchrist gave this text the subtitle, *Part Third of Volume First, of a System of Hindoostanee Philology*, in order to indicate that the two volumes of the dictionary and the single volume of the grammar are to be considered as a single comprehensive work.)

1798a. *The Oriental Linguist, An Easy and Familiar Introduction to the Popular Language of Hindoostan*, 2nd edn. 1802, Calcutta: Ferris & Greenway.

1798b. *Preface* [to *A Dictionary, English and Hindoostanee*; *A Grammar of the Hindoostanee Language*; & *The Oriental Linguist*], Calcutta: Mirror Press.
(This item is listed independently because, although it is often bound into copies of the dictionary, it alludes to all three of Gilchrist's earlier works and, as such, is better considered as a new publication, reviewing and justifying the works immediately preceding it.)

1800. *The Anti-Jargonist; or, A Short Introduction to the Hindoostanee Language, (vulgarly but erroneously called the Moors,) comprising the Rudiments of that Tongue, with an Extensive Vocabulary, English and Hindoostanee and Hindoostanee and English, accompanied with some Plain and Useful Dialogues, Translations, Poems, Tales, &c. with the View of illustrating the Whole on Practical Principles, Being partly an Abridgement of The Oriental Linguist, but greatly Altered and Improved, embellished with the Hindoostanee Horal Diagram*, Calcutta: Ferris.

1801. *A New Theory and Prospectus of the Persian Verbs, with their Hindoostanee Synonimes in Persian and English*, Calcutta: Hollingery.

1802a. *The Stranger's East Indian Guide to the Hindoostanee; or Grand Popular Language of India (Improperly Called Moors)*, 2nd edn. 1808, 3rd edn. 1820, Calcutta: Hindoostanee Press.

1802b. *The Hindee Directory; or, Student's Introductor to the Hindoostanee Language*, Calcutta: Government Press and Ferris.

1802c. *The Hindee Story-Teller; or, Entertaining Expositor of the Roman, Persian, and Nagree characters in their Application to the Hindoostanee Language, as a Written and Literary Vehicle*, 2nd edn. 1806, Calcutta: Hindoostanee Press.

1803a. *The Hindee Moral Preceptor: and Persian Scholar's Shortest Road to the Hindoostanee Language; or Vice Versa*, 2nd edn. 1821, Calcutta: Hindoostanee Press.

1803b. *The Oriental fabulist; or, Polyglot Translations of Æsop's and Other Ancient Fables from the English Language into Hindoostanee, Persian, Arabic, Brij Bhakha, Bongla, and Sunskrit, in the Roman Character by Various Hands, under the Direction of John Gilchrist, for the Use of the College of Fort William*, Calcutta: Hurkaru.

1804a. *A Collection of Dialogues on the most Familiar and Useful Subjects. Calculated to Facilitate the Colloquial Intercourse of Europeans lately Arrived in Hindoostan with the Natives*, 2nd edn. 1809, 3rd edn. 1820, 4th edn. 1826, Calcutta: Hindoostanee Press.

1804b. *The Hindee-Roman Orthoepigraphical Ultimatum; or, A Systematic View of Oriental and Occidental Visible Sounds on Fixed and Practical Principles for the Languages of the East, Exemplified in the Popular Story of Sakoontula Natuk,* 2nd edn. 1820, Calcutta: Hindoostanee Press.

1806–08. *The British Indian Monitor; or, the Anti-Jargonist, Stranger's Guide, Oriental Linguist, and Various Other Works, compressed into a Series of Portable Volumes on the Hindoostanee language, improperly called Moors; with Considerable Information respecting Eastern Tongues, Manners, Customs, etc.,* 2 vols., Edinburgh: Manners & Miller, Constable, and Black & Parry.

1815. *Parliamentary Reform, on Constitutional Principles; or, British Loyalty against Continental Royalty, the Whole Host of Sacerdotal Inquisitors in Europe, and Every Iniquitous Judge, Corrupt Ruler, Venal Corporation, Rotten Borough, Slavish Editor, or Jacobitical Toad-Eater within the British Empire,* Glasgow: W. Lang.

1820. *The Oriental Green Bag!!! or, A Complete Sketch of Edwards Alter in the Royal Exchequer, containing a Full Account of the Battle with the Books between a Belle and Dragon, by a Radical Admirer of the Great Sir William Jones's Civil, Religious, and Political Creed,* London: the author.

1821. *A Succinct Narrative of Dr. Gilchrist's Services from 1782 to 1821,* London: n.p. (This work was published anonymously but is almost certainly by Gilchrist himself.)

1825. *The General East India guide and Vade Mecum, for the Public Functionary, Government Officer, Private Agent, Trader or Foreign Sojourner, in British India, and the Adjacent Parts of Asia, being a Digest of the Work of the late Capt. Williamson by J. B. Gilchrist with Improvements and Additions,* London: Kingsbury, Parbury & Allen.

1826. *The Orienti-Occidental Tuitionary Pioneer to Literary Pursuits, by the King's and Company's Officers of all Ranks, Capacities, and Departments, either as Probationers at Scholastic Establishments, during the Early Periods of Life, their Outward Voyage to the East, or while actually Serving in British India; A Complete Regular Series of Fourteen Reports earnestly Recommending also the General Introduction, and Efficient Culture immediately, of Practical Orientalism, simultaneously with Useful Occident Learning at all the Colleges, Respectable Institutions, Schools, or Academies, in the United Kingdom; A Brief Prospectus of the Art of Thinking made Easy and Attractive to Children, by the Early and Familiar Union of Theory with Colloquial Practice, on Commensurate Premises, in some Appropriate Examples, Lists, &c., besides a Comprehensive Panglossal Diorama for a Universal Language and Character; A Perfectly New Theory of Latin Verbs,* London: n.p. (Elements of this work, including the 14 reports on the activities of the Oriental Institution, had been published previously and are collected in this volume to give an overview of Gilchrist's work in the 1810s and 1820s.)

1833a. *A Practical Appeal to the Public, through a Series of Letters, in Defence of the New System of Physic by the Illustrious Hahnemann, Letter the First,* London: Parbury & Allen.

1833b. *A Bold Epistolary Rhapsody, addressed to the Proprietors of East-India Stock in Particular and to every Individual of the Welch, Irish, Scottish, and English Nations in General, as Members of that British Constituency which has been too long Misrepresented in the House of Commons,* London: Ridgeway.

1977. *Poems of Dr. Gilchrist,* edited by Ebadat Brelvi, Lahore: University Oriental College. (Some of the poems in this collection were published in periodicals in the early 1780s.)

LEGAL DOCUMENTS

Appendix to the Case of the Respondents: a compendium of printed material relating to the dispute over John Gilchrist's will, held among the papers of the Gilchrist Trust.

UNPUBLISHED SOURCES

Unpublished sources from the following archives are cited:

The Public Record Office, Kew
The British Library Oriental and India Office Collections
The Records of George Heriot's School, Edinburgh

CLASSICAL AUTHORS

When reference is made to a classical author, the name of the author is given along with the title of the work and the relevant book and section numbers. References are to the following editions.

ANONYMOUS, *Rhetorica ad Herennium*. Caplan, H. (ed.), 1955. *Rhetorica ad Herennium*, Cambridge, MA, and London: Harvard University Press.
ARISTOTLE, *Nicomachean Ethics*. Bywater, I. (ed.), 1894. *Aristotelis ethica Nicomachea*, Oxford: Clarendon Press.
DEMETRIUS, *On Style*. Halliwell, S., Hamilton Fyfe, W., Russell, D., Innes, D.C. and Rhys Roberts, W. (eds.), 1995. *Aristotle, Poetics; Longinus, On the Sublime; Demetrius, On Style*, Cambridge, MA: Harvard University Press; London: Heinemann, 309–525.
DIONYSIUS, *On Literary Composition*. Usher, S. (ed.), 1974–85. *Dionysius of Halicarnassus: The Critical Essays*, 2 vols., Cambridge, MA: Harvard University Press; London: Heinemann, 1–243.
PLATO, *Gorgias*. Burnet, J. (ed.), 1900–1907. *Platonis opera*, 5 vols., Oxford: Clarendon Press, vol. 3 447–527.
PLATO, *Laws*. Burnet, J. (ed.), 1900–1907. *Platonis opera*, 5 vols., Oxford: Clarendon Press, vol. 5 624–969.
PLINY THE ELDER, *Natural History*. Rackham, H. (ed.), 1967. Pliny, *Natural History*, 2 vols., Cambridge, MA, and London: Harvard University Press.
QUINTILIAN, *Institutio oratoria*. Winterbottom, M. (ed.), 1970. *M. Fabi Quintiliani institutionis oratoriae libri duodecim*, 2 vols., Oxford: Clarendon Press.
VARRO, *On the Latin Language*. Kent, Roland G. (ed.), 1951. *Varro, On the Latin Language*, 2 vols., Cambridge, MA, & London: Harvard University Press.

ALL OTHER AUTHORS

AARSLEFF, HANS, 1967. *The Study of Language in England, 1780–1860*, Princeton: University Press.
AARSLEFF, HANS, 1982. *From Locke to Saussure: Essays on the Study of Language and Intellectual History*, London: Athlone Press.
ABBOTT, E. A., 1905. *A Shakespearian Grammar: An Attempt to Illustrate some of the Differences between Elizabethan and Modern English*, 3rd edn., London: Macmillan.
ABERCROMBIE, DAVID, 1948. 'Forgotten phoneticians', *Transactions of the Philological Society*, 1–34.
ANONYMOUS, 1712. *Bellum grammaticale; or, The Grammatical Battel Royel. In Reflections on the Three English Grammars, Publish'd in about a Year Last Past*, London: J. & M. Jerund.
ANONYMOUS, 1725. *A New Canting Dictionary: Comprehending all the Terms Antient and Modern, Used in the Several Tribes of Gypsies, Beggars, Shoplifters, Highwaymen, Foot-Pads, and all other Clans of Cheats and Villains*, London: Booksellers of London & Westminster.

ANONYMOUS, 1758. *An Introduction to the Latin Tongue, for the Use of Youth*, Eton: Pote.

ANONYMOUS, 1802. 'Extract of the Ferheenge Jehangeeri', *Asiatic Annual Register: Correspondence with the Editor on Literary and Miscellaneous Subjects*, 133–9.

ANONYMOUS, 1835. 'Biographical account of John Hadley, Esq., V.P.R.S., the inventor of the quadrant and of his brothers George and Henry', *Nautical Magazine* 4, 12–22, 137–46, 529–38, 650–57.

ANQUETIL-DUPERRON, A.-H., 1771. *Zend-Avesta, ouvrage de Zoroastre, contenant les idées théologiques, physiques & morales de ce législateur, les cerémonies du culte religieux qu'il a établi, & plusieurs traits importans relatifs à l'ancienne histoire des Perses*, 3 vols., Paris: Tilliard.

ARCHER, MILDRED, 1980. *Early Views of India: The Picturesque Journeys of Thomas and William Daniell 1786–1794*, London: Thames & Hudson.

ARNOT, SANDFORD & FORBES, DUNCAN, 1828. *An Essay on the Origin and Structure of the Hindoostanee Tongue, or General Language of British India, with an Account of the Principal Elementary Works on the Subject*, London: Oriental Institution.

ASHER, R. E. & HENDERSON, E. (eds.), 1981. *Towards a History of Phonetics*, Edinburgh: Edinburgh University Press.

BAYLY, C. A., 1990. *The Raj: India and the British 1600–1947*, London: National Portrait Gallery.

BAYLY, C. A., 1996. *Empire and Information: Intelligence Gathering and Social Communication in India 1780-1870*, Cambridge: Cambridge University Press.

BEG, M. K. A., 1988. *Urdu Grammar: History and Structure*, New Delhi: Bahri Publications.

BENZIE, W., 1994. 'Thomas Sheridan 1719–1788', in M. G. Moran (ed.), *Eighteenth-Century British and American Rhetorics and Rhetoricians: Critical Studies and Sources*, Westport, CT: Greenwood Press, 187–206.

BHABHA, HOMI K., 1994. *The Location of Culture*, London: Routledge.

BHATIA, TEJ K., 1987. *A History of the Hindi Grammatical Tradition: Hindi–Hindustani Grammar, Grammarians, History and Problems*, Leiden: Brill.

BLAIR, HUGH, 1783. *Lectures on Rhetoric and Belles Lettres*, 2 vols., London: Strahan & Cadell; Edinburgh: Creech.

BLOCH, JULES, 1965. *Indo-Aryan from the Vedas to Modern Times*, English edn., revised by the author and trans. A. Master, Paris: Adrien-Maisonneuve.

BLOCHMANN, HENRY F., 1868. 'Contributions to Persian lexicography', *Journal of the Asiatic Society of Bengal* 37, 1–72.

BOYER, ABEL. 1783. *The Complete French Master, for Ladies and Gentlemen*, 25th edn., London: Ballard et al.

BOYLE, JOHN A., 1966. *Grammar of Modern Persian*, Wiesbaden: Harrassowitz.

BROWNE, THOMAS G., 1795. *Hermes Unmasked; or, The Art of Speech Founded on the Association of Words and Ideas*, London: T. Payne.

BURKE, EDMUND, 1981. *The Writings and Speeches of Edmund Burke*, vol. 5: *India: Madras and Bengal 1774–1785*, ed. P. J. Marshall, Oxford: Clarendon Press.

BURKE, PETER & PORTER, ROY (eds.), 1995. *Languages and Jargons: Contributions to a Social History of Language*, Cambridge: Polity Press.

BUSHNELL, REBECCA, 2003. 'The gardener and the book', in Natasha Glaisyer & Sara Pennell (eds.), *Didactic Literature in England 1500–1800*, Aldershot & Burlington, VT: Ashgate, 118–136.

CAMPBELL, GEORGE, 1776. *The Philosophy of Rhetoric*, 2 vols., London: Strahan & Cadell; Edinburgh: Creech.

CANNON, GARLAND, 1990. *The Life and Mind of Oriental Jones: Sir William Jones, the Father of Modern Linguistics*, Cambridge: University Press.

CAREY, HENRY, 1736. *The Honest Yorkshireman*, London: L. Gilliver & J. Clarke.

CAREY, WILLIAM, 1804. *A Grammar of the Sungskrit Language*, Serampore: Mission Press.

CAREY, WILLIAM, 1805. *A Grammar of the Mahratta Language*, Serampore: Mission Press.

CAREY, WILLIAM, 1812. *A Grammar of the Punjabee Language*, Serampore: Mission Press.

CARTWRIGHT, F. D. (ed.), 1826. *The Life and Correspondence of Major John Cartwright*, 2 vols., London: Colburn.

CHAMBAUD, LOUIS, 1750. *Thèmes françois & anglois; or, French and English Exercises*, London: Millar.

CHAMBAUD, LOUIS, 1761. *Dialogues French and English, upon the most Entertaining and Humorous Subjects. Extracted out of the Comedies of Molière, and containing the Idiom of the Conversation of Courtiers, Citizens, Merchants, Tradesmen, and almost all States and Professions in Life*, 2nd edn., London: Keith.

CHAMBAUD, LOUIS, 1797. *A Grammar of the French Tongue: With a Preface containing an Essay on the Proper Method for Teaching and Learning That Language*, 12th edn., London: Longman et al.

CHAMBERS, ROBERT (ed.), 1875. *A Biographical Dictionary of Eminent Scotsmen*, new edn., rev. T. Thomson, 3 vols., London: Blackie.

CHATTERJI, SUNITI K., 1972–79. *Select Papers: Angla-Nibandha-Chayana*, 2 vols., New Delhi: New Age.

CIFOLETTI, GUIDO, 1989. *La lingua franca mediterranea*, Padua: Unipress.

CLELAND, JOHN, 1766. *The Way to Things by Words and to Words by Things: Being a Sketch of an Attempt at the Retrieval of the Antient Celtic or, a Primitive Language of Europe*, London: Davis & Reymers.

COHEN, MICHÈLE, 2003. 'French conversation or "glittering gibberish"? Learning French in eighteenth-century England', in Natasha Glaisyer & Sara Pennell (eds.), *Didactic Literature in England 1500–1800*, Aldershot & Burlington, VT: Ashgate, 99–117.

COHN, BERNARD S., 1985. 'The command of language and the language of command', in Ranajit Guha (ed.), *Subaltern Studies IV: Writings on South Asian History and Society*, Delhi: Oxford University Press, 276–329.

COHN, BERNARD S., 1996. *Colonialism and Its Forms of Knowledge: The British in India*, Princeton: Princeton University Press.

COLEBROOKE, HENRY T., 1805. *A Grammar of the Sanscrit Language*, Calcutta: Honourable Company's Press.

COPLEY, STEPHEN, 1994. 'William Gilpin and the black lead mine', in Stephen Copley & Peter Garside (eds.), *The Politics of the Picturesque: Literature, Landscape and Aesthetics since 1770*, Cambridge: Cambridge University Press, 42–61.

COPLEY, STEPHEN & GARSIDE, PETER (eds.), 1994. *The Politics of the Picturesque: Literature, Landscape and Aesthetics since 1770*, Cambridge: Cambridge University Press.

CORMIER, MONIQUE C., 2003. 'From the *Dictionnaire de L'Académie Françoise, dedié au Roy* (1694) to the *Royal Dictionary* (1699) of Abel Boyer: tracing inspiration', *International Journal of Lexicography* 16, 19–41.

CRAWFORD, DIROM G., 1930. *Roll of the Indian Medical Service*, London: Thacker.

DAS, SISIR K., 1978. *Sahibs and Munshis: An Account of the College of Fort William*, New Delhi: Orion.

DAVY, WILLIAM, 1783. *Institutes Political and Military, Written Originally in the Mogul Language by the Great Timour, Improperly Called Tamerlane*, Oxford: Clarendon Press.

DEFOE, DANIEL, 1719. *The Life and Strange and Surprising Adventures of Robinson Crusoe, of York*, London: W. Taylor.

DHARKER, C. D. (ed.), 1946. *Lord Macaulay's Legislative Minutes*, Madras: Oxford University Press.

DIDEROT, DENIS & D'ALEMBERT, JEAN LE R. (eds.), 1751–76. *Encyclopédie; ou, Dictionnaire raisonné des sciences, des arts et des métiers, par une societé de gens de lettres*, 35 vols., Paris: Briasson et al.

DIXON, ROBERT M. W., 1991. *Ergativity*, Cambridge: Cambridge University Press.

DOBRÉE, BONAMY, 1963. *Alexander Pope*, London: Oxford University Press.

DODSLEY, ROBERT, 1761. *Select Fables of Esop and Other Fabulists*, London: R. & J. Dodsley.

DREYFUS, HUBERT L. & RABINOW, PAUL, 1982. *Michel Foucault: Beyond Structuralism and Hermeneutics*, 2nd edn., Chicago: Chicago University Press.

DUFIEF, NICHOLAS G., 1818. *Nature Displayed in her Mode of Teaching Language to Man*, 2 vols., London: the author.

DU MITAND, LOUIS, 1788. *A New Method of Learning French in a Practical and Easy Way*, London: the author.

DUNCAN, DOUGLAS, 1965. *Thomas Ruddiman: A Study in Scottish Scholarship of the Early Eighteenth Century*, Edinburgh: Oliver & Boyd.

FABRICIUS, OTTO, 1801. *Forsøg til en forbedret grønlandsk grammatica*, 2nd edn., Copenhagen: Sehnsart.

FARUQI, SHAMSUR R., 2001. *Early Urdu Literary Culture and History*, New Delhi: Oxford University Press.

FERGUSSON, JOHN, 1773. *A Dictionary of the Hindostan Language, to which is prefixed a Grammar of the Hindostan Language*, London: the author.

FERREIRA-BUCKLEY, LINDA, 1994. 'Hugh Blair (1717–1800)', in M. G. Moran (ed.), *Eighteenth-Century British and American Rhetorics and Rhetoricians: Critical Studies and Sources*, Westport, CT: Greenwood Press, 21–35.

FIRTH, J. R., 1946. 'The English school of phonetics', *Transactions of the Philological Society*, 92–132.

FLOOD, GAVIN, 1996. *An Introduction to Hinduism*, Cambridge: Cambridge University Press.

FORBES, DUNCAN, 1846. *A Grammar of the Hindustani Language in the Oriental and Roman Character, with numerous Copper-plate Illustrations of the Persian and Devanāgarī systems of Alphabetic Writing*, London: Allen.

FORMIGARI, LIA, 1993. *Signs, Science and Politics: Philosophies of Language in Europe 1700–1830*, Amsterdam: Benjamins.

FOUCAULT, MICHEL, 1980. *Power/Knowledge: Selected Interviews and Other Writings 1972–1977*, trans. and ed. Colin Gordon, Brighton: Harvester Press.

FOUCAULT, MICHEL, 1990. *The History of Sexuality*, vol. 1: *An Introduction*, trans. Robert Hurley, Harmondsworth: Penguin.

FOUCAULT, MICHEL, 1991. *Discipline and Punish: The Birth of the Prison*, trans. Alan Sheridan, Harmondsworth: Penguin.

GENETTE, GÉRARD, 1997. *Paratexts: Thresholds of Interpretation*, trans. Jane E. Lewin, Cambridge: Cambridge University Press.

GIBB, H. A. R., KRAMERS, J. H., LÉVI-PROVENÇAL, E., SCHACHT, J., LEWIS, B. & PELLAT, CH. (eds.), 1960–97. *The Encyclopaedia of Islam*, new edn., 10 vols., Leiden: Brill.

GILDON, CHARLES, 1711. *A Grammar of the English Tongue, with Notes, Giving the Grounds and Reason of Grammar in General*, London: Brightland.

GILPIN, WILLIAM, 1782. *Observations on the River Wye, and Several Parts of South Wales, &c. relative chiefly to Picturesque Beauty; made in the Summer of the Year 1770*, London: Blamire.

GILPIN, WILLIAM, 1792. *Three Essays: On Picturesque Beauty; On Picturesque Travel; and on Sketching Landscape: To which is added a Poem, on Landscape Painting*, London: Blamire.

GIRARD, GABRIEL, 1747. *Les Vrais Principes de la langue françoise; ou, La parole réduite en méthode, conformément aux lois de l'usage*, 2 vols., Paris: Le Breton.

GLADWIN, FRANCIS, 1795. *The Persian Moonshee*, Calcutta: Chronicle Press.

GREENWOOD, JAMES, 1711. *An Essay towards a Practical English Grammar describing the Genius and Nature of the English Tongue giving likewise a Rational and Plain Account of Grammar in General, with a Familiar Explanation of its Terms*, London: Keeble et al.

GROSE, FRANCIS, 1785. *A Classical Dictionary of the Common Tongue*, London: S. Hooper.

GUHA, RANAJIT (ed.), 1985. *Subaltern Studies IV: Writings on South Asian History and Society*, Delhi: Oxford University Press.

HADI, NABI, 1995. *Dictionary of Indo-Persian Literature*, New Delhi: Indira Gandhi Centre for the Arts.

HADLEY, GEORGE, 1772. *Grammatical Remarks on the Practical and Vulgar Dialect of the Indostan Language commonly called Moors*, 2nd edn. 1774, 3rd edn. 1784, London: Cadell.

HADLEY, GEORGE, 1776. *Introductory Grammatical Remarks on the Persian Language, with a Vocabulary English and Persian, the Spelling Regulated by the Persian Character*, Bath: T. Cadell.

HADLEY, GEORGE, 1796. *A Compendious Grammar of the Current Corrupt Dialect of the Jargon of Hindostan (commonly called Moors)*, 4th edn. of Hadley (1772), 5th edn. 1801, 6th edn. 1804, 7th edn. 1809, London: Sewell.

HALHED, NATHANIEL B., 1778. *A Grammar of the Bengal Language*, Hoogly: n.p.

HARRIS, JAMES, 1744. *Three Treatises: The First Concerning Art. The Second Concerning Music, Painting and Poetry. The Third Concerning Happiness*, London: Nourse & Vaillant.

HARRIS, JAMES, 1751. *Hermes; or, A Philosophical Inquiry Concerning Universal Grammar*, London: Nourse & Vaillant.

HASNAIN, S. IMTIAZ & RAJYASHREE, K. S., 2004. 'Hindustani as an anxiety between Hindi–Urdu commitment', *Yearbook of South Asian Languages and Linguistics*, 247–65.

HIBBERT, CHRISTOPHER, 1984. *The Dragon Wakes: China and the West, 1793–1911*, London: Penguin.

HICKES, GEORGE, 1703–1705. *Linguarum Vett. Septentrionalium Thesaurus Grammatico-Criticus et Archaeologicus*, Oxford: Sheldonian.

HORNE TOOKE, JOHN, 1786. *Epea Pteroenta; or The Diversions of Purley*, vol. 1, London: Jonson.

HOWATT, ANTHONY P. R., 1984. *A History of English Language Teaching*, Oxford: Oxford University Press.

HÜLLEN, WERNER, 1996. 'Some Yardsticks of Evaluation 1600–1800 (English and German)', in Vivien Law & Werner Hüllen (eds.), *Linguists and Their Diversions: A Festschrift for R. H. Robins on His 75th Birthday*, Münster: Nodus, 275–306.

ISERMAN, MICHAEL, 1996. 'John Wallis on adjectives: the discovery of phrase structure in the *Grammatica Linguae Anglicanae* (1653)', *Historiographia Linguistica* 23, 47–72.

JEREMIÁS, ÉVA M., 1993. 'Tradition and innovation in the native grammatical literature of Persian', *Histoire Épistémologie Language* 15, 51–68.

JOHNSON, SAMUEL, 1747. *The Plan of a Dictionary of the English Language*, London: J. & P. Knapton et al.

JOHNSON, SAMUEL, 1755. *A Dictionary of the English Language*, 2 vols., London: J. & P. Knapton et al.

JOHNSON, SAMUEL, 1756. *A Dictionary of the English Language: in which the Words are Deduced from the Originals, Explained in their Different Meanings, and Authorized by the Names of the Writers in whose Works they are Found. Abstracted from the Folio Edition by the Author*, 2 vols., 5th edn. 1773, London: J. Knapton, C. Hitch & L. Hawes, A. Millar, R. & J. Dodsley; & M. & T. Longman.

JONES, ROBERT, 1792. *A New Persian and English Work, after the Method of Boyer and Others*, Calcutta: Honourable Company's Press.

JONES, WILLIAM, 1771. *A Grammar of the Persian Language*, London: W. & J. Richardson.

JONES, WILLIAM, 1772. *Poems consisting chiefly of Translations from the Asiatick Languages. To which are added Two Essays, I. On the Poetry of the Eastern Nations. II. On the Arts, commonly called Imitative*, Oxford: Clarendon Press.

JONES, WILLIAM, 1773. *The History of the Life of Nader Shah, King of Persia: Extracted from an Eastern Manuscipt, which was translated into French by Order of His Majesty the King of Denmark*, London: Cadell.

JONES, WILLIAM, 1784. 'Dissertation on the Orthography of Asiatick Words in Roman Letters', *Asiatick Researches* 1, 1–56.

Jones, William, 1993. *Discourses Delivered at the Asiatick Society 1785-1792*, ed. R. Harris, London: Routledge.

Kafker, Frank A., 1994. 'William Smellie's edition of the *Encyclopaedia Britannica*', in Frank A. Kafker (ed.), *Notable Encyclopaedias of the Late Eighteenth Century: Eleven Successors of the Encyclopédie*, Oxford: Voltaire Foundation, 145–82.

Kahrs, Eivind, 1998. *Indian Semantic Analysis: The Nirvacana Tradition*, Cambridge: Cambridge University Press.

Keil, Heinrich (ed.), 1855–80. *Grammatici latini*, 8 vols., Leipzig: Teubner.

Kejariwal, O. P., 1988. *The Asiatic Society of Bengal and the Discovery of India's Past*, Delhi: Oxford University Press.

Kidwai, Sadiq-ur-Rahman, 1972. *Gilchrist and the 'Language of Hindoostan'*, New Delhi: Rachna Prakashan.

King, Christopher R., 1994. *One Language, Two Scripts: The Hindi Movement in Nineteenth-Century North India*, Oxford & Bombay: Oxford University Press.

Kirkpatrick, William, 1785. *A Vocabulary, Persian, Arabic, and English, Containing such Words as have been Adopted from the Two Former Languages and Incorporated into the Hindvi*, London: J. Cooper.

Kopf, David, 1969. *British Orientalism and the Bengal Renaissance*, Berkeley: University of California Press.

Lancelot, Claude, 1758. *A New Method of Learning with Facility the Latin Tongue*, 2 vols., trans. Thomas Nugent, London: Nourse.

Lancelot, Claude & Arnauld, Antoine, 1660. *Grammaire générale et raisonnée, contenant les fondemens de l'art de parler*, Paris: Le Petit.

Law, Vivien, 1993. 'Processes of assimilation: European grammars of Sanskrit in the early decades of the nineteenth century', in D. Droixhe and Ch. Grell (eds.), *La linguistique entre mythe et histoire*, Münster: Nodus, 237–61.

Lebedeff, Herasim S., 1801. *A Grammar of the Pure and Mixed East Indian Dialects*, London: the author.

Lelyveld, David, 1993. 'Colonial knowledge and the fate of Hindustani', *Comparative Studies in Society and History* 35, 665–82.

Lipson, S. G., Lipson, H. & Tannhauser, D. S., 1995. *Optical Physics*, 3rd edn., Cambridge: Cambridge University Press.

Locke, John, 1790. *Essay Concerning Human Understanding*, London: T. Basset.

Lowth, Robert, 1762. *A Short Introduction to English Grammar*, London: Millar & R. & J. Dodsley.

McGregor, Ronald S., 1972. *Outline of Hindi Grammar*, Oxford: Clarendon Press.

McGregor, Ronald S., 1992. *Urdu Study Materials*, Delhi: Oxford University Press.

McGregor, Ronald S., 1993. *The Oxford Hindi–English Dictionary*, Oxford: Oxford University Press.

MacKenzie, John M., 1995. *Orientalism: History, Theory and the Arts*, Manchester: Manchester University Press.

Mahajan, Jagmohan, 1983. *Picturesque India: Sketches and Travels of Thomas and William Daniell*, Delhi: Lustre.

Majeed, Javed, 1995. '"The jargon of Indostan": an exploration of jargon in Urdu and East India Company English', in Peter Burke & Roy Porter (eds.), *Languages and Jargons: Contributions to a Social History of Language*, Cambridge: Polity Press, 182–285.

Masica, Colin P., 1986. 'Definiteness-marking in South Asian Languages', in B. Krishnamurti (ed.), *South Asian Languages: Structure, Convergence and Diglossia*, Delhi: Motilal Banarsidass, 123–46.

Masica, Colin P., 1991. *The Indo-Aryan Languages*, Cambridge: Cambridge University Press.

Michael, Ian, 1970. *English Grammatical Categories and the Tradition to 1800*, Cambridge: Cambridge University Press.

MIYAWAKI, MASATAKA, 2002. *James Harris's Theory of Universal Grammar: A Synthesis of the Aristotelian and Platonic Conceptions of Language*, Münster: Nodus.

MONBODDO, LORD (JAMES BURNET), 1773–92. *Of the Origin and Progress of Language*, 6 vols., Edinburgh: Balfour; London: Cadell.

MONBODDO, LORD (JAMES BURNET), 1779–99. *Antient Metaphysics*, 6 vols., Edinburgh: Balfour; London: Cadell.

MORPURGO DAVIES, ANNA, 1998. *History of Linguistics*, vol: 4: *Nineteenth-Century Linguistics*, London and New York: Longman.

MORSE, HOSEA B., 1926–29. *The Chronicles of the East India Company trading to China 1635–1834*, 5 vols., Oxford: Clarendon Press.

NARAIN, VISHNU, A. 1959. *Jonathan Duncan and Varanasi*, Calcutta: Mukhopadhay.

NICHOLS, J. & NICHOLS, J. B. (eds.), 1817–58. *Illustrations of the Literary History of the Eighteenth Century*, 8 vols., London: the authors.

NUSSBAUM, FELICITY, 1995. *Torrid Zones: Maternity, Sexuality and Empire in Eighteenth-Century English Narratives*, Baltimore: Johns Hopkins University Press.

PAL, PRATAPADITYA & DEHEJIA, VIDYA, 1986. *From Merchants to Emperors: British Artists and India 1757–1930*, Ithaca, NY: Cornell University Press.

PERCY, CAROL E., 1997. 'Paradigms lost: Bishop Lowth and the "poetic dialect" in his English grammar', *Neophilologus* 81, 129–44.

POCOCKE, EDMUND, 1661. *Lamiato'l Ajam: Carmen Tograi, poetae arabis doctissimi; unà cum versione latina, & notis praxin illius exhibentibus*, Oxford: Davis.

PONS, JEAN-FRANÇOIS, 1743. 'Lettres du Père Pons, Missionnaire de la Compagnie de Jésus, au P. Du Halde de la même Compagnie', in Jean-Baptiste Du Halde (ed.), *Lettres édifiantes et curieuses, écrites des missions etrangeres, par quelques Missionnaires de la Compagnie de Jésus*, vol. 26, Paris: Le Mercier & Bordelet, 218–345.

PORTER, ROY, 1989. *Health for Sale: Quackery in England 1660–1850*, Manchester: University Press.

PORTER, ROY, 1995. '"Perplex't with Tough Names": the uses of medical jargon', in Peter Burke & Roy Porter (eds.), *Languages and Jargons: Contributions to a Social History of Language*, Cambridge: Polity Press, 42–63.

PRIESTLEY, JOSEPH, 1777. *A Course of Lectures on Oratory and Criticism*, London: Johnson.

PROBYN, CLIVE T., 1991. *The Sociable Humanist: The Life and Works of James Harris 1709–1780, Provincial and Metropolitan Culture in Eighteenth-Century England*, Oxford: Clarendon Press.

QAYYUM, MUHAMMAD A., 1982. *A Critical Study of the Early Bengali Grammars: Halhed to Haughton*, Dhaka: Asiatic Society of Bangladesh.

RADEMAKER, C. S. M., 1981. *Life and Work of Gerardus Joannes Vossius 1577–1649*, Assen: Van Gorcum.

RADTKE, EDGAR, 1994. *Gesprochenes Französisch und Sprachgeschichte: Zur Rekonstruktion der Gesprächskonstitution in Dialogen französischer Sprachlehrbücher des 17. Jahrhunderts unter besonderer Berücksichtigung der italienischen Adaptionen*, Tübingen: Niemeyer.

RAI, AMRIT, 1984. *A House Divided: The Origin and Development of Hindi/Hindavi*, Delhi: Oxford University Press.

RALEY, RITA, 2000. 'A teleology of letters; or, From a "common source" to a common language', in Daniel J. O'Quinn (ed.), *The Containment and Re-Deployment of English India*, College Park: University of Maryland, [unpaginated], http://www.rc.umd.edu/praxis/containment/raley/raley.html.

RICHARDSON, JOHN, 1777. *A Dissertation on the Languages, Literature, and Manners of the Eastern Nations (Originally Prefixed to a Dictionary Persian, Arabic and English)*, Oxford: Clarendon Press.

ROBINS, ROBERT H., 1987. 'The life and work of Sir William Jones', *Transactions of the Philological Society*, 1–23.

ROBINS, ROBERT H., 1997. *A Short History of Linguistics*, 3rd edn., London: Longman.

ROCHER, ROSANNE, 1983. *Orientalism, Poetry and the Millennium: The Checkered Life of Nathaniel Brassy Halhed*, Delhi: Motilal Banarsidass.

ROCHER, ROSANNE, 1995. 'Discovery of Sanskrit by Europeans', in E. F. K. Koerner & R. E. Asher (eds.), *Concise History of the Language Sciences from the Sumerians to the Cognitivists*, Oxford: Pergamon, 188–91.

ROSNER, LISA, 1991. *Medical Education in the Age of Improvement: Edinburgh Students and Apprentices 1760–1826*, Edinburgh: Edinburgh University Press.

RUDDIMAN, THOMAS, 1714. *Rudiments of the Latin Tongue; or, A Plain and Easy Introduction to Latin Grammar*, Edinburgh: Freebairn.

SAID, EDWARD W., 1995. *Orientalism: Western Conceptions of the Orient*, 2nd edn., with a new afterword, London: Penguin.

SALE, GEORGE, 1734. *The Koran, commonly called The Alcoran of Mohammed, Translated into English immediately from the Original Arabic; with Explanatory Notes, taken from the most approved Commentators. To which is prefixed a Preliminary Discourse*, London: Wilcox.

SALMON, VIVIAN, 1979. *The Study of Language in Seventeenth-Century England*, Amsterdam: Benjamins.

SCHARFE, HARTMUT, 1977. *A History of Indian Literature*, Vol. 5: *Scientific and Technical Literature*, pt. 2, fasc. 2: *Grammatical Literature*, Wiesbaden: Harrassowitz.

SCHLEGEL, FRIEDRICH, 1808. *Über die Sprache und Weisheit der Indier: Ein Betrag zur Begründung der Alterthumskunde*, Heidelberg: Mohr & Zimmer.

SCHMIDT, RUTH L., 1999. *Urdu: An Essential Grammar*, London & New York: Routledge.

SCHREYER, RÜDIGER, 1987. 'Linguistics meets Caliban or the uses of savagery in 18th century theoretical history of language', in Hans Aarsleff, Louis G. Kelly & Hans-Jürgen Niederehe (eds.), *Papers in the History of Linguistics, Proceedings of the Third International Conference on the History of the Language Sciences (ICHoLS III)*, Amsterdam: Benjamins, 301–14.

SCHREYER, RÜDIGER, 1994. 'Deaf-mutes, feral children and savages: of analogical evidence in 18th century theoretical history of language', in G. Blaicher & B. Glaser (eds.), *Anglistentag 1993 Eichstätt, Proceedings*, XV, Tübingen: Niemeyer, 70–86.

SCHREYER, RÜDIGER, 1996. 'Take your pen and write. Learning Huron: a documented historical sketch', in Even Hovdhaugen (ed.), *... and the Word was God: Missionary Linguistics and Missionary Grammar*, Münster: Nodus, 77–121.

SEELY, JONATHAN, 1977. 'An ergative historiography', *Historiographia Linguistica* 4, 191–206.

SHACKLE, CHRISTOPHER & SNELL, RUPERT (eds.), 1990. *Hindi and Urdu since 1800: A Common Reader*, London: School of Oriental and African Studies, University of London.

SHAKESPEAR, JOHN, 1813. *A Grammar of the Hindustani Language*, 2nd edn. 1818, 3rd edn. 1826, London: the author.

SHAW, GRAHAM W., 1981. *Printing in Calcutta to 1800: A Description and Checklist of Printing in Latin Eighteenth-Century Calcutta*, London: Bibliographical Society.

SHAW, WILLIAM, 1778. *An Analysis of the Galic [sic] language*, London: Strahan, Donaldson & Elliot.

SHERIDAN, THOMAS, 1780. *A General Dictionary of the English Language. One Main Object, of which, is, to Establish a Plain and Permanent Standard of Pronunciation. To which is Prefixed a Rhetorical Grammar*, London: J. Dodsley, C. Dilly & J. Wilkie.

SHUTTLEWORTH, UGHTRED J. K., 1930. *Gilchrist Educational Trust: Pioneering Work in Education*, Cambridge: Cambridge University Press.

SIDDIQI, M. ATIQUE, 1963. *Origins of Modern Hindustani Literature: Source Material, Gilchrist Letters*, Aligarh: Naya Kitab Ghar.

SMELLIE, WILLIAM, 1769–71. *Encyclopaedia Britannica; or, A Dictionary of Arts and Sciences Compiled upon a New Plan*, 3 vols., Edinburgh: Bell & MacFarquhar.

SMITH, ADAM, 1774. *The Theory of Moral Sentiments; or, An Essay towards an Analysis of the Principles by which Men naturally judge concerning the Conduct and Character, first of their*

Neighbours and afterwards of themselves. To which is added, A Dissertation on the Origin of Languages, 4th edn., London: Strahan et al.

SMITH, OLIVIA, 1984. *The Politics of Language 1791–1819*, Oxford: Clarendon Press.

SMYTH, WILLIAM C., 1824. *The Hindoostanee Interpreter, containing the Rudiments of Hindoostanee Grammar, an Extensive Vocabulary, English and Hindoostanee and a useful Collection of Dialogues*, London: Richardson.

SORENSEN, JANET, 2000. *The Grammar of Empire in Eighteenth-Century British Writing*, Cambridge: Cambridge University Press.

STARKE, MARIANA, 1791. *The Widow of Malabar: A Tragedy in Three Acts as it is performed at the Theatre-Royal, Covent Garden*, Dublin: Wogan, Byrne, Moore et al.

STEADMAN-JONES, RICHARD, 2003. 'Lone travellers: the construction of originality and plagiarism in colonial grammars of the late eighteenth and early nineteenth centuries', in Paulina Kewes (ed.), *Plagiarism in Early Modern England*, Basingstoke: Palgrave Macmillan, 201–14.

STEADMAN-JONES, RICHARD, 2005. 'Questions of genre in seventeenth-century descriptions of Native American languages', in Nicola McLelland & Andrew R. Linn (eds.), *Flores Grammaticae: Essays in Memory of Vivien Law*, Münster: Nodus, 197–209.

STEVEN, W., 1859. *History of George Heriot's Hospital with a Memoir of the Founder*, Edinburgh: Bell & Bradfute; London: Simpkin & Marshall.

STEWART, DUGALD, 1792–1827. *Elements of the Philosophy of the Human Mind*, 3 vols., London: Strahan & Cadell; Edinburgh: Creech.

STUEBE, ISABEL C., 1979. *The Life and Work of William Hodges*, New York: Garland.

SUBBIONDO, JOSEPH, 1992. *John Wilkins and 17th-century British Linguistics*, Amsterdam: Benjamins.

SWIFT, JONATHAN, 1735. *The works of J.S., D.D., D.S.P.D.*, 4 vols., Dublin: Faulkner.

TRASK, ROBERT L., 1979. 'On the origins of ergativity', in Frans Planck (ed.), *Ergativity: Towards a Theory of Grammatical Relations*, London: Academic Press, 385–404.

TRAUTMANN, THOMAS R., 1997. *Aryans and British India*, Berkeley: University of California Press.

ULMAN, H. LEWIS, 1994. *Things, Thoughts, Words, and Actions: The Problem of Language in Late Eighteenth-Century British Rhetorical Theory*, Carbondale: Southern Illinois University Press.

VAN DER WAL, MARIJKE J., 1995. 'Early language typology: attitudes towards languages in the 16th and 17th centuries', in Klaus D. Dutz & Kjell-Ake Forsgren (eds.), *History and Rationality*, Münster: Nodus, 93–106.

VINCENT, WILLIAM, 1794. *The Origination of the Greek Verb: An Hypothesis*, London: G. & C. Ginger.

VINCENT, WILLIAM, 1795. *The Greek Verb Analysed: An Hypothesis. In which the Source and Structure of the Greek Language, and of Language in General, is Considered*, London: [n. p.].

VORLAT, EMMA, 1975. *The Development of English Grammatical Theory 1586-1737 with Special Reference to the Theory of Parts of Speech*, Leuven: University Press.

VOSSIUS, GERARDUS J., 1662. *Etymologicon linguae latinae. Praefigitur ejusdem de literarum permutatione tractatus*, Amsterdam: Elzevir.

WALLIS, JOHN, 1972. *Grammar of the English Language: With an Introductory Grammatico-Physical Treatise on Speech (or on the Formation of all Speech-Sounds)*, ed. and trans. J. A. Kemp, London: Longman.

WASHBROOK, DAVID, 1991. '"To each a language of his own": language, culture and society in colonial India', in Penny Corfield (ed.), *Language, History and Class*, Oxford: Blackwell, 179–203.

WEBSTER, NOAH, 1789. *Dissertations on the English Language: With Notes Historical and Critical*, Boston, MA: the author.

WILKINS, CHARLES (ed.), 1785. *The Bhăgvăt-Gēētā or, Dialogues of Krĕĕshnă and Ărjŏŏn; in Eighteen Lectures; with Notes*, London: Nourse.

WILKINS, JOHN, 1668. *Essay towards a Real Character and a Philosophical Language*, London: Gellibrand & Martyn.

WINDFUHR, GERNOT L., 1979. *Persian Grammar: History and State of its Study*, The Hague: Mouton.

WOODWARD, ERNEST L., 1962. *The Age of Reform 1815–1870*, 2nd edn., Oxford: Clarendon Press.

YOUNG, GEORGE M., 1935. *Speeches of Lord Macaulay with his Minute on Indian Education*, Oxford: University Press.

YULE, HENRY & BURNELL, ARTHUR C., 1985. *Hobson-Jobson: A Glossary of Colloquial Anglo-Indian Words and Phrases, and of Kindred Terms, Etymological, Historical, Geographical and Discursive*, new edn., ed. W. Crooke, London: Routledge & Kegan Paul.

ZAIDI, ALI J., 1993. *A History of Urdu Literature*, New Delhi: Sahitya Akademi.

ZOGRAPH, GEORGIĬ A., 1982. *Languages of South Asia: A Guide*, London: Routledge & Kegan Paul.

INDEX